Hendon Football Cl
The first 100 years

David Ballheimer and Peter Lush

London League Publications Ltd

Hendon Football Club
The first 100 years

© Copyright David Ballheimer and Peter Lush. Foreword © Rod Haider. Introduction © David Bedford

The moral right of David Ballheimer and Peter Lush to be identified as the authors has been asserted.

Cover design © Stephen McCarthy

Front cover photo: Rod Haider with the Amateur Cup in 1972 (Photo: *Hendon Times*). Back: Hampstead Town FC 1921–22 (Courtesy Hendon FC). Photo on title page: Hendon versus AFC Hornchurch, September 2007 at Claremont Road (Photo: Peter Lush)

A CIP catalogue record for this book is available from the British Library.

Published in October 2008 by:
London League Publications Ltd, P.O. Box 10441, London E14 8WR

ISBN: 978–1903659–42–7

Cover design by: Stephen McCarthy Graphic Design
                   46, Clarence Road, London N15 5BB

Layout: Peter Lush

Printed & bound by: CPI Antony Rowe
                      Eastbourne, Great Britain

This book is dedicated to the memory of Bill Fisher,
who as a player, coach and manager gave
a lifetime's service to Hendon Football Club.

Foreword

Hendon Football Club, its officials, loyal supporters and players – past and present – owe a great debt of gratitude to the diligent research work David Ballheimer and Peter Lush have put in to complete this chronicled history of the club, the teams and players over its first 100 years. In a few decades' time, football fans will not know about the halcyon days of amateur football, when players with decent jobs chose not to sign as professionals and to play in a good standard of football for top non-league clubs that were well supported.

Players also had the opportunity to play amateur international football against sides around the world and for Great Britain in the Olympics. Now the vast amounts of money paid to professional footballers means we will not recapture the former glory days of the Amateur Cup when the Final at Wembley was so well supported and shown live on television.

Hendon was one of the top sides from the 1950s onwards with many good players and teams that my parents and I watched and subsequently I played both for and against. My time at Hendon was the most successful period of my playing career and I have many fond memories of the people at the club – players, staff and supporters.

My family spent their early years growing up at the club – my children probably not watching me play. This was a time when players' social lives revolved around their football club and there was always good humoured banter between players, supporters and opposing teams and their supporters.

Following the commencement of the open era of football many non-league teams have found it financially difficult to continue and have had to make the decision to close down, amalgamate with other teams or ground share. Hendon Football Club today is in this position.

I am honoured and privileged to be one of the profiled players featured in this book which helps provide information and different players' perspectives of Hendon Football Club that will be of interest to football fans.

Rod Haider
August 2008

Rod Haider was one of the club's most distinguished players. He captained the team in the Amateur Cup Final at Wembley in 1972. He also holds the record for England amateur caps, 65, of which 55 were in his Hendon days, and played for the Great Britain Olympic team. He was given a testimonial by Hendon in 1977–78.

Introduction

I was born in 1949 in Queen Mary's Hospital, at the top of East Heath Road in Hampstead, less than 100 yards from Christ Church, where our club was founded in 1908. My youth was spent on the Pennine Drive estate and my earliest memories are of thousands of people walking up Claremont Road to the football ground on Saturdays.

One such memory was in 1960, when after Hendon had defeated Kingstonian in the Amateur Cup at Wembley, my Dad took me to the ground to meet the team returning to the ground with the trophy. The locals gave the team a great welcome back.

I was first taken to a game by my next door neighbour when I was about 10. I can't remember the game but after that I was there most weeks, for first team games from half-time as entry was free, and reserve games from the start. Details are vague but I was a real supporter, running on the pitch before the game and kissing the centre spot, abusing (without swear words) the opposing fans, swapping ends at half time and the associated banter ... No change there then.

These were the days of Laurie Topp, Miles Spector and, a little later, John Swannell and Rod Haider. Miles Spector subsequently joined Wingate. I had a massive scrapbook with autographs, bootlaces (John's) and every bit of memorabilia of the time. It is a shame it has been lost, along with so many other memories.

I remember us winning a London Senior Cup semi-final tie against Kingstonian before beating Enfield 1–0 at Wealdstone. There were the away trips by coach to places such as Maidstone, Fareham and other far away towns. I remember the first game under floodlights against Wolverhampton Wanderers, in September 1962 and the magic that the ground seemed to have under lights. I remember the Supporters' Association clubhouse, with a bar billiards table, at the back of the car park next to the wall.

In 1964 I started running and I had less time for games because of training and races, but, with much of my running being around Clitterhouse Park, I was never far away. Around this time I was a regular darts player and occasional light and bitter drinker in the clubhouse. In 1972, before the Olympics, the club had a whip round to help raise funds for me to go to altitude training. The sum of £250 was raised, which was a lot of money then, and I was away training when we won the Amateur Cup again that year, maintaining my record of never seeing Hendon play at Wembley.

I went just occasionally during the 1980s and 1990s, but still maintained contact although I had become a Spurs season ticket holder. Then I met Ivor Arbiter, who had just become the club's owner and he talked me in to being more regular again. For this, I owe him thanks. At Spurs when you call the referee a b*****d he never hears; at Hendon not only does he hear you, but also he can see you saying it. At Spurs, no one notices if you don't turn up or renew a season ticket. At Hendon you have to justify to others why you miss a game.

In this our centenary year, I hope the ghosts of the past are pleased with our attempts to keep the club alive. What a great year for the Supporters Trust to take over the running of our famous club. We are the famous... the famous Hendon!

David Bedford

David Bedford is one of Great Britain's most distinguished post-war long distance runners. He is a former 10,000 metres world record holder and world cross country champion. He is currently race director of the London Marathon. He has a key role in the Hendon FC Supporters Trust.

Playing at Claremont Road

Many supporters have played at Claremont Road in the end of season match against the players. But Ian Lush recalls playing on the famous pitch in front of 1,000 people: "One of the more unusual charity matches to take place at Claremont Road was in November 1991, when a team representing the *Jewish Chronicle* (JC) newspaper played one from Cannon Cinemas. Over 1,000 people attended the game, and they witnessed an exciting battle between two determined teams, although somewhat lacking in refinement. The Cannon Cinemas team were regulars in charity matches, while the JC XI had been specially assembled for this match. I was playing for the JC through a link with their advertising department – and after all I am Jewish. It was quite scary – I hadn't played football for 10 years, and never in front of a crowd or a proper stadium. And it clearly mattered to the Cannon team.

Fortunately our goalkeeper was a non-league veteran, who had represented Great Britain in the Maccabi Games (the Jewish Olympics). He single-handedly kept the score to a respectable 2–0 to Cannon at half-time.

This turned out to be a game of two halves, with some experienced Sunday league players used as subs by the JC after the break who had very tenuous connections to the newspaper. Gradually the tide turned as the mainly older (and heavier!) Cannon players tired, and the JC pulled a goal back on the hour mark. More substitutions occurred, and I finally retired on 83 minutes, exhausted, to be replaced by the JC's then editor, Ned Temko, an American journalist who had never seen 'soccer' before, let alone played. A sustained spell of JC pressure followed a corner on 89 minutes, the ball broke to Temko, and more by luck than judgement he forced it home from two yards. Wild celebrations took place with the whole JC bench leaping to its feet, showing our collective inexperience as we banged our heads on the roof of the dugout. The game ended 2–2, much to the disgust of the Cannon team, and plenty of money was raised for good causes.

Ian Lush

Ian Lush supported Hendon from around 1973 to 1978, when he went to university in York. After a career in music, both playing professionally and as managing director of the London Mozart Players, he is now chief executive of the Architectural Heritage Fund. He goes to the occasional Hendon game, and is a member of the Supporters Trust, but has had a season ticket at Chelsea for many years.

About the authors

David Ballheimer

Disillusioned with professional football, David Ballheimer fell in love with Hendon FC in 1972. His first big Hendon match was the 1972 Amateur Cup final at Wembley and, three dozen years later, he has spent more time and certainly more money than a sane human being should on a pastime. David has come to the conclusion that being pessimistic is the best way for a football fan: when the worst happens it is nothing less than was expected; when there is glory it can be celebrated even more.

A book editor, journalist, Hendon FC press officer, occasional author and total sports junkie, especially football, cricket, rugby league, baseball and American football, David loves numbers and is quite pleased that he has reached his personal half-century in the same year that his beloved Football Club reached 100. He thinks it is entirely appropriate that he has lived in only two areas in his life: Golders Green and Hendon; while he passes through Hampstead to work and, on his way home, he walks by Christ Church.

Peter Lush

Peter Lush grew up in Cricklewood, and went to King Alfred's School in Hampstead, who curiously also played football in green. He started supporting West Ham United in 1964, as they won the FA Cup, he liked the name, and no one else in his class supported them. However, he attended his first football match in May 1966 at Claremont Road, Hendon versus Clapton, aged 11, and followed Hendon home and away until 1973, when he started playing football on Saturdays. He was one of the 34 supporters who went to Italy in 1972, and has great memories of the Newcastle trip in 1974. One of his delights in working on this book has been to interview some of the players who were his childhood heroes, and to be able to include their experiences in these pages.

After 1974, he went to college, got involved in other things and moved away from Cricklewood. He went to a match in 1987, and again in 1999. But meeting David Ballheimer through rugby league led to the idea of this book, and more − if erratic − matches at Claremont Road, and away games, especially in east London, where he lives.

With Dave Farrar, he set up London League Publications Ltd in 1995, mainly to publish books on rugby league. When not writing about sport, he is the director of a small training charity in King's Cross, and does freelance work in the voluntary and social housing sectors.

Photographs and illustrations

We would like to thank the *Hendon Times* for providing photographs for this book. These photos are credited (HT) or *Hendon Times*.

We would also like to thank Arsenal Football Club and Wembley National Stadium Limited for permission to use programme covers from matches at Highbury and Wembley Stadium respectively. Photographs by Peter Lush are credited (PL). The photographs and other illustrations in this book are from Hendon Football Club or private collections unless otherwise credited. No copyright has been intentionally breached. Please contact London League Publications Ltd if you believe there has been a breach of copyright. We could not find good individual photos of Junior Lewis, Simon Clarke or Mark Burgess, although Simon is in a team photo.

Hendon memories

My first memory of Claremont Road was in the mid-1960s, a reserve game against Tooting & Mitcham United. We won 1–0, but the player who stood out most was Tooting's, short, balding, portly centre-forward, who – I believe – dived to win a penalty (car park end), but put the spot-kick wide of the keeper's left post.

Even my first professional match subsequently had a Hendon link. It was Chelsea versus Arsenal on Boxing Day 1966, and the Blues won 2–1 after Terry Neill scored a penalty for the Gunners. I asked him about the game almost 40 years later and his memory of it was astonishingly vivid.

I went to two Amateur Cup ties a couple of years later, but didn't see another Hendon match until late January 1972, when Hendon beat QPR 3–0 in a friendly. My father took me to Wembley that April and though I clearly remember the 2–0 defeat of Enfield, I didn't understand its significance. As for the following season, although I went a number of times – tatty programmes tell the tale – I cannot remember a single detail of any games.

The 1973–74 season is a different matter. I recall the night we beat Barnet 3–0 to reach the first round – I heard the pop when Roger Connell broke his ankle after completing a hat-trick. Ten days after the Leytonstone win in round one of the FA Cup, I contracted tonsillitis and had to miss the trips to both Merthyr Tydfil and Newcastle, but I was first in the queue at Vicarage Road to buy a ticket for the replay.

Most of my favourite Hendon memories have been of matches away from Claremont Road, but there are three exceptions. First, the day we beat Reading in the FA Cup on 22 November 1975; second, the victory over Burton Albion in the 1987 GMAC Cup; and, third, the almost miraculous victory against Tonbridge Angels in August 2007. I also remember with enormous fondness my 30-yard run and 20-yard piledriver past Ken Payne in the Supporters match in May 1981; I've never struck a shot as perfectly and I turned away in triumph even before the net bulged.

My all-time favourite match was the 1997 FA Cup replay at Leyton Orient. Tuesday 25 November 1997 will, I hope, live in my memory for the rest of my life. To all the players and management staff, thanks. Close behind this was 29 April 1986, the 4–1 win at Slough Town to preserve our Premier Division status when, six weeks earlier, all seemed lost.

After much thought, I have decided not list my favourite players or managers – because so many deserve mention, not least the current management trio of Gary McCann, Freddie Hyatt and Bontcho Guentchev, in their playing days, the latter two were artists whose canvases were football pitches.

But I cannot finish this piece without recalling two people without whom this book could never have been completed: First, Ivor Arbiter, who took over the club when it almost disappeared in the summer of 1994 and was chairman until his death in 2005. Second, Graham Etchell, the club's secretary in our centenary year, and the man whose steady hand on the tiller has kept the club afloat in the stormiest of waters.

I dedicate my work on this book to you, Graham.

David Ballheimer

Reflections on supporting Hendon

One of my great regrets in life is that I am not a couple of years older. This may seem an odd statement from someone who became 54 while this book was at the printers. However, I started watching Hendon in 1966, aged 11, and therefore just missed the great years of 1963 to 1965. By a horrible coincidence, my other team, West Ham United, also had their best years from 1963 to 1965, so I missed out both in north west and east London. I also missed being able to participate in the best bits of the '60s'.

Despite this, I have many fond memories of supporting Hendon. I watched the team at home in 1966–67, as I was not allowed to go to away games as my mother said I was too young, (aged 12!) and then home and away, hardly missing a match, until 1972. I then started playing football on Saturdays, but still went to midweek matches, Italy and to the Newcastle United away match. I missed the replay as I was playing football at college on the Wednesday afternoon. After then I watched West Ham, feeling that I had seen Hendon win everything they possibly could.

Going to away matches took me to parts of London that I barely knew existed, and started a fascination with visiting new sports grounds that lives with me today. Now, the Hendon matches I like most are visits to grounds I have not been to before, which last season included Folkestone, Harlow and East Thurrock United.

Even more fascinating were trips 'up north' for Amateur Cup matches. We arrived in Newcastle after an overnight coach trip first thing on a Saturday morning, before going to North Shields. I went to Evenwood twice, after the first match was abandoned because of fog. The locals spoke with such thick Durham accents as to be incomprehensible to us Londoners.

By now I was involved in football at school, and in 1972, as a sixth former, had arranged a trip to the Amateur Cup Final to give some of the younger students a chance to go to a match at Wembley. Little did I know that Hendon would be playing. But that glorious goal from Peter Deadman against Wycombe at Brentford, when we were hopelessly outnumbered by their supporters, meant that I enjoyed the match against Enfield while counting heads to make sure I had not lost anyone!

This led to the Italy trip. At home I was not in a strong position to argue for this, as I had done badly in my 'A' levels, and was having to retake them, maybe due to too much football, but my parents relented and the supporters embarked on a coach journey that seemed to go on for ever. However, it was an unforgettable experience.

But maybe the most valuable experience of my time watching Hendon was the people I met at the club. They were from all sorts of backgrounds, with different jobs and occupations, and I learnt much from talking to them about football, work and life.

I used to stand at matches with Ken Thorn, Chris Rogers and Mike Cox. They were all older than me and were very patient at times with my questions. I valued their company enormously. It was slightly surreal to meet Chris again, after a gap of almost 30 years, when we started work on this book. And I was pleased to learn that Mike still follows the team.

Sadly, Ken Thorn died a few years ago. I would like to dedicate my work on this book to his memory.

Peter Lush

Contents

The club committee – we're not sure when this photo was taken, probably in the late 1950s, but felt it deserved to go in the book anyway!
(Courtesy Hendon FC)

Acknowledgements

This book has been a team effort. However, the initial work up to 1974 was done by Peter Lush and that from 1974 to the present day by David Ballheimer, although there was much discussion and collaboration. Hendon FC club secretary Graham Etchell provided enormous help and assistance, and the first chapter and appendix on the original Hendon FC is based on his work for the match programme, and drew on research by Mike Bondy.

Chris Rogers also gave invaluable support, especially with statistics and records, and this part of the book owes much to his record keeping over the years. He also helped with information and proofreading.

Peter Beal from the *Hendon Times* scoured his archives to find photos for us, and offered important support. Bob Perkins provided copies of old programmes. John Swannell kindly lent us many old photos from his collection.

We would like to thank Rod Haider for writing the foreword and David Bedford for writing the introduction.

We would like to thank everyone who agreed to be interviewed, lent us material or helped with information. Ian Lush read the draft and provided helpful comments.

Thanks to the staff of Barnet local history centre, especially Yasmine Webb, and the staff at the British Library National Newspaper Library at Colindale.

Thanks also to Steve McCarthy for designing the cover, and the staff of Antony Rowe for printing the book.

About this book

Even in 336 pages there are some limitations to this book, and areas we would have liked to have covered more. We felt that our first priority was to provide a basic history of the club. This was supplemented by interviews with past players and, to a limited extent, memories from supporters and club officials.

We were limited by space in both these areas. There are many fine players who gave long service to the club who are not profiled in this book. We originally set a target of one player per decade, but that proved too small. But from every era, there are players we would like to have researched more. In some cases, the information is lost in the mists of time.

This is even more apparent with supporters and club officials. We originally hoped to include a chapter on the Supporters Association, who have given invaluable support to the club over the years, and supporters' memories and experiences. Sadly this was not possible, and we know that there are many stories and memories still to be recorded– we participated in some of them!

The main research for this book was done from local newspapers, match programmes and handbooks. The club has very limited records, as do the Middlesex FA and London FA.

And finally, we have done our best to avoid mistakes, but some are inevitable. We take full responsibility for any errors, and would welcome correspondence that throws new light on the fascinating history of Hendon Football Club.

David Ballheimer and Peter Lush

Bibliography

The Athenian Football League 1912–1939 and *1945–1966* by Mike Wilson
Association Football (Volume 1) edited by A.H. Fabian and Geoffrey Green
The History of the Football Association by Geoffrey Green
Various *FA Yearbooks*
Non League Retrospect Volume 8 number 1
The League Tables of the London League by Bob Perkins
Hendon, Child's Hill, Golders Green and Mill Hill by Stewart Gillies and Pamela Taylor

Prelude

At Wembley Stadium on 23 April 1960, with just three minutes left, the FA officials were starting to tie the red and white ribbons of Kingstonian FC onto the Amateur Cup. The Isthmian League side were leading their Athenian League opponents, Hendon, 1–0 in the Final, and looked certain to take the Cup back to Surrey.

But in one of the most dramatic finishes ever to a Wembley Cup Final, veteran Laurie Topp equalised for Hendon. And with a minute left, Terry Howard got the winner for the green and whites, and took the Cup to Claremont Road for the first time in the club's history. Even then, there was time for Kingstonian to hit the post.

Now 100 years old, Hendon FC has a distinguished history, with many triumphs in cup and league competitions. Some of the greatest amateur players in English football played for the club, and in the 'open' era since 1974, it has kept non league football alive in this corner of north-west London. And it all started at a church in Hampstead in 1908.

1. 1908 to 1918: Early days

In the beginning

Hendon Football Club was founded in 1908, as Christ Church Hampstead FC. However, the club secretary, Walter Styles, at the 1925 AGM, said that he had been dealing with the club's correspondence for 18 years, which would put the founding date at 1907. He also said that the club played for several seasons as Christ Church Hampstead, records of league tables show only one. Remarkably, Charles Farrer, Walter Styles and the treasurer Arthur Crawley had all been involved in the club as officers from its inception. Curiously, the 1925 AGM report also says that the club was founded 20 years ago (i.e. in 1905). However, playing records from this time are few and far between, and the Christ Church Hampstead club clearly does appear in the league tables in 1908. It is always possible that friendly games were played before then.

What seems to be beyond dispute is that it was set up as part of the activities of the church, which is part of the Church of England and which was built in 1851 to 1852, and still stands in Hampstead. It is north east of Hampstead village, near the Heath and is in the eighteen century development of New End. Its distinctive spire stands out. There is a primary school linked to the church.

Hampstead was clearly a thriving football area. Hampstead Heathens were members of the Football Association in 1871, although they seem to have vanished from the scene by the first decade of the 20th century. At the turn of the century, West Hampstead were playing in the Middlesex League, and competed in various leagues until the First World War.

In 1908, Hampstead Tenants played in the Middlesex Senior Cup, Hampstead Druids played in the Amateur Football Association (AFA) Cup, and a Hampstead team played in the Southern Amateur League, finishing sixth in Section B. The Southern Amateur League was affiliated to the AFA. This probably explains why Christ Church Hampstead adopted the name Hampstead Town. The Hampstead club disappeared from the football scene in 1922, allowing Hampstead Town to become the simpler Hampstead. Since then, a new Hampstead club has been formed and plays in junior football today.

In 1908 there was also a Hampstead League of 16 clubs, split into two divisions. It is interesting to speculate why a club based around a church in the centre of Hampstead competed in the Finchley & District League, particularly at a time when transport was far more difficult than now. Even today, the journey from Hampstead to Finchley is not an easy one.

Amateur football

The amateur football setup in 1908 was divided following the breakaway of some clubs to form the AFA in 1907. Space does not allow for a detailed analysis of what became known as 'The Schism', but it is fair to say that it reflected tensions between the professional and sections of the amateur parts of the game. Matters came to a head over an organisational issue: the role of professional clubs in the County Football Associations. The Surrey and Middlesex FAs, largely made up of Old Boys clubs, were opposed to professional clubs having to join the County FAs. In 1906, an Amateur Football Defence Federation was founded, and in 1907, around 10 per cent of the FA's 8,000 clubs split away.

Tension between amateurs and professionals was not uncommon in class-ridden British sport at this time. These events occurred only 12 years after the split in rugby football, cricket still had 'gentlemen' and 'players', and in golf and tennis, professionalism was frowned upon. By 1912, the AFA reconciled its differences with the FA, although the issues of 'amateurism' and 'broken time' payments (i.e. payments for missing work) were important in football in international relations for many years to come, in particular in the FA's relationship with FIFA.

The FA Amateur Cup was founded in 1893–94 season, when it was clear that professional teams were going to dominate the FA Cup. Old Carthusians were the first winners, beating Casuals in the Final. Many of the old boys teams did not enter the competition after the AFA split, and within 10 years of the new competition's launch, the winners started to come from clubs that would be involved in amateur football until the game went 'open' in 1974.

In 1905, the Isthmian League was founded. It was initially limited to six clubs, and attracted some of the strongest amateur clubs in the south east. By the First World War, it could claim to be the strongest amateur league in the south east. In 1908, the Spartan League was founded and in 1912, the Athenian League was formed. Some of the clubs joined because they preferred to play other amateur clubs, rather than the reserve sides of professional sides in the London League. This was a fluid time in football, with some clubs experimenting with professionalism, and others choosing the amateur game. Some leagues had amateur club's first teams competing with reserve teams of semi-professional or professional clubs.

Christ Church Hampstead

Christ Church Hampstead's first season for which records exist was 1908–09. Records are scarce from that time, and the first match recorded is a Middlesex County FA Junior cup tie played at home on Saturday 26 September 1908 against St Gabriel's. The football season probably only started in mid-September, so this was clearly one of the first matches. Christ Church Hampstead lost 4–0, but things improved in the Third Division of the Finchley & District League. The Finchley & District League was founded in 1898 and in 1909 had 35 clubs in membership with 760 players, who had played a total of 246 games.

One of the first league results that season was on 21 November 1908, a 0–0 draw at home to Caledonian Old Boys. The League table on 4 December showed Christ Church in second place and the only unbeaten side in the division. The table at 28 November showed the team in second place.

Christ Church Hampstead (PL)

	P	W	D	L	F	A	Pts
Old Grovians	7	5	0	2	19	13	10
Christ Church Hampstead	4	3	1	0	11	4	7
Prior Athletic	6	3	1	2	12	10	7
Tollington	5	3	0	2	12	7	6
St Johns Friern Barnet	5	3	0	2	10	10	6
East Finchley Institute	4	2	1	1	8	4	5
Caledonian Old Boys	5	2	1	2	7	5	5
Johnsons Athletic	5	2	0	3	6	8	4
Pakeman Old Boys	3	0	0	3	2	10	0
Ashley United	6	0	0	6	7	23	0

The club was successful during the rest of the season and finished the season as league champions. In January, East Finchley Institute was beaten 6–0, and the team scored six again in a friendly against Hendon Crescent in March. The club won the Finchley & District League Third Division by just two points.

	P	W	D	L	F	A	Pts
Christ Church Hampstead	16	12	1	3	55	15	25
Caledonian Old Boys	16	11	1	4	38	16	23
Tollington	16	10	0	6	38	26	20
Old Grovians	16	9	1	6	40	28	19
Priory Athletic	16	7	2	7	24	27	16
Johnsons Athletic	16	6	2	8	22	28	14
East Finchley Institute	16	4	2	10	18	36	10
Pakeman Old Boys	16	3	3	10	11	47	9
St Johns Friern Barnet	16	4	0	12	19	42	8

After winning the Third Division title, the club began the next season with a new name, Hampstead Town, and some fresh opposition having been promoted to Division Two. An increase in playing membership also meant that the reserve side played in the Fourth Division of the same League. The first team got off to a great start, and at the turn of the year were unbeaten and sitting proudly at the top of the division:

	P	W	D	L	F	A	Pts
Hampstead Town	9	7	2	0	26	4	16
Totteridge	8	5	2	1	15	5	12
East Barnet	6	3	1	2	15	14	7

Unfortunately during January and February, two clubs Bramleigh and North Islington both had to drop out of Division Two and their records were removed from the league table. This was a blow to Hampstead who had played them both twice and collected the maximum eight points plus a useful 14-0 goal difference. Close rivals Totteridge meanwhile dropped just four points and two goals from those fixtures then gained even further ground by claiming a valuable 3-1 win at Hampstead. On 26 March 1910 the league table showed that there was absolutely nothing separating the two top sides: they even shared identical goal records and a goal average of 3.888. There was just one game left to play.

	P	W	D	L	F	A	Pts
Hampstead Town	11	8	2	1	35	9	18
Totteridge	11	8	2	1	35	9	18
Edgware Athletic	11	5	2	4	30	20	12

On Saturday 9 April 1910, the last day of the season, the league was finally decided. On paper at least, Hampstead Town had by far the easier match, a trip to Caledonian Old Boys who were struggling to get any sort of side together in the last few weeks of the season. Totteridge were also away, but they faced a tougher task at Edgware Athletic who were unbeaten in the league at home, having dropped just one point in a 1-1 draw against Hampstead Town. Things couldn't have worked out better for Hampstead. They took advantage of weak opponents by rattling up an impressive 12-0 win against Caledonian Old Boys that considerably helped their goal average. Totteridge had to better that. In the event the margin of Hampstead's victory did not matter, a draw would have been enough as Edgware were tough opponents for Totteridge, beating them 1-0 in a tight encounter. The outcome of these two games meant that Hampstead Town were champions by two points. It was promotion for the second year running and the 1910-11 season would see them playing in Division One.

This season saw another fresh challenge for the ambitious Hampstead Town Football Club. They had gained higher status by their promotion to Division One of the Finchley & District League and were now one of the strongest junior clubs in North West London. The prestigious National Athletic Ground at Kensal Rise was rented to stage their home matches and fixtures were arranged to cover the majority of Saturdays throughout the season. There are reports that the club played at this site before 1910, but probably on one of the pitches by the stadium, not on the main pitch.

Research done by the club shows that the ground had been laid out in 1890, and could be reached by two long walkways: one from College Road (house number 80 currently stands at the old entrance) and the other from directly behind the side of the Kensal Rise station. The scale of the Ground is shown by the fact that 34 houses now sit across the width of the athletics stadium and the site is now bordered by Chamberlayne Road, Leigh Gardens, College Road and Liddell Gardens.

Plans of the original site at Kensal Rise, dated from 1894 to 1896, show that the immediate area around the National Stadium was largely undeveloped. The stadium is shown sitting within very large grounds. Purves Road just beyond its south boundary and Ashburnham Road just beyond that are developed, but only on one side of the road. Immediately to the stadium's west are allotments. The Athletic Stadium seemed to have banking around the perimeter of the track while a pavilion was by the north straight.

At the start of the First World War, plans show that the area had changed dramatically. Not only did new streets and housing appear, but many of the new houses had been built on what was previously the stadium's outer grounds. The outer area was now covered by Clifford Gardens. This had been created immediately behind the stadium and has housing on both sides. Behind the pavilion now stands Liddell Gardens. Four new roads cover the allotments. The ground was still there in 1920, but had apparently gone in 1921, presumably in preparation for the building of Whitmore Gardens, which was occupied by 1926.

The team

The side was captained by centre forward J.J. 'Jock' Davidson who led by example and finished as the club's leading goalscorer. He was also the penalty taker and notched several hat-tricks, including two in successive ties of the Middlesex Junior Cup.

Inside forwards Alec Tomkins and D. Southern provided fine support and Southern achieved the season's best individual performance in one match by hitting five goals against North Paddington in the London Junior Cup.

On the flanks T.L. Gliddon and Herbert (H.W.) Pike supplied the crosses and the latter, according to the reports at the time, was worth his place just for his accurate corner kicks which led to a number of Hampstead goals.

Hampstead conceded just nine goals in 12 League games. In J. Pells they had a reliable goalkeeper who had seven clean sheets out of 12 league matches. In front of him J. Southwell and Ernie Hudson were a steady pair of full-backs and G.A. Rathbone was an able deputy when either was missing. A.A. McKichan was solid at the heart of defence with C. Bowden and W. Murray both driving forces at wing-half.

A couple of weeks before Christmas, Hampstead took what turned out to be a decisive step in the title race by beating close challengers Greenhill 5–0 at their Line Path ground in Barnet. Davidson, Tomkins and Southern all scored and the tally was completed by two own goals from the Greenhill right back.

In February 1911 Hampstead completed the double over Greenhill with a fine 4–2 win and followed this up with big wins over Campsbourne Institute and Friern Barnet. The club were looking good for the title.

Before the last Saturday of the season, 29 April 1911, the top of the table was:

	P	W	D	L	F	A	Pts
Hampstead Town	11	7	2	2	37	9	16
Greenhill	11	7	1	3	18	17	15
Old Burghleyans	11	4	4	3	18	9	12
Friern Barnet	11	4	3	4	15	24	11

With two points for a win, neither Hampstead Town nor Greenhill could afford to slip up in their last game and both had home matches against top four opposition. Hampstead duly won 3–0 against third placed Old Burghleyans to make absolutely certain of the Division One championship so Greenhill's 2–0 defeat by the inconsistent Friern Barnet did not affect the final outcome.

Hampstead Town had now won Divisions Three, Two and One of the Finchley & District League in three successive seasons, and were now ready to move to a higher level of football.

1911–12

As well as participating in both the local Finchley and Willesden Leagues, Hampstead Town also entered Division Two of the London League. This meant a full and varied fixture list for the forthcoming season. Many of the players from the previous campaign were still with the club, with useful new acquisitions in left winger George (G.H.) Garlick and inside right S. Evans.

By the end of October, the fortunes of the team had been mixed, but between the posts Pells had suffered a loss of confidence and form after conceding a number of soft goals as Hampstead let in six at Finchley and seven at Wealdstone. He made way for E.C. East, and almost immediately the defence tightened up and the results improved as Hampstead lost just one game out of 10 to the end of 1911.

With membership of the club increasing, and a fair number of games to be played, it was decided that the very strong second XI would take over most of the remaining fixtures in the Middlesex and Finchley Leagues, while the first team would concentrate on the London League, as well as engaging in occasional friendly matches against senior clubs. In fact, on the afternoon of 27 January 1912, both teams played and won Middlesex League fixtures, with the first team defeating Hyde & Kingsbury 4–1 at Kensal Rise, while the reserves won 3–0 at Kilburn. George Hyde, who had been scoring consistently for the reserves, earned a first team call up, and straight away notched a hat trick, as Nunhead were beaten 3–2 in the London League. In the event a final mid-table placing in a strong London League was a pretty commendable debut, while the championship of the Willesden League was won, after a play-off with Deerfield Social.

1912–13: The Avenue Ground

The season began with a friendly at Chelmsford against Hoffman's Athletic, and after a narrow defeat at Barking in the London League, the first home match saw the opening of the club's new home, the Avenue Ground at Childs Hill, Cricklewood. It was to be the team's base for 14 years until 1926.

The club had moved into a developing area. From being a semi-rural area on the fringes of London, the development of the Northern Line underground service to Golders Green in 1907 had seen the start of the development of the suburban housing that dominates the area today. A map of Childs Hill in 1912 still shows much of the area as fields. There had been some earlier development in Cricklewood to house workers from the railway yards. A little further north, there was industrial development along the Edgware Road, including the early aircraft industry.

The team celebrated their first match at the Avenue in style as local player O. F. Neale marked his debut with a hat-trick, as Kilburn were thrashed 5–1 in the London League. A.H. Parker made a successful reappearance at right half, after being injured at the end of the previous season. The Kilburn defence was in a tangle and the Town led by three goals within the opening 20 minutes. Kilburn improved, but Matthews, in the Town goal, was beaten only once. The second half was interesting, but the Town were always on top and added further goals. Garlick and Sumner played well and the latter was unlucky not to get on the scoresheet. Missing from the Hampstead line-up were Billy Denham, and vice-captain, Ernie Hudson.

The club's Willesden League XI, who were going very strongly, were due to play an attractive Premier Division fixture at Cricklewood against Stonebridge Athletic.

On successive Saturdays, Hampstead were involved in all major cup competitions, but their debut appearance in the FA Cup, Amateur Cup and London Senior Cup unfortunately resulted in defeats against Maidenhead, Luton Albion and Page Green Old Boys respectively. Harry Pride's hat-trick against Polytechnic saw Hampstead through in the Middlesex Charity Cup. Seven of the next 10 league games were won up to the turn of the year, putting the club in strong positions in both the London and Middlesex Leagues. Highlights included a 6–0 London League hiding of Deptford Invicta, in which inside-left Ollie Sumner scored a hat-trick, and a 5–1 success against Barnet & Alston in the London League, where Sumner added two more.

The first Saturday in January saw a Middlesex Senior Cup exit against the 2nd Battalion Grenadier Guards, but a run was maintained in the Middlesex Charity Cup, and the Town reached their first senior cup final in the Middlesex Charity Cup, beating Southall 5-0 in a semi-final replay at the Avenue. In the final, Town lost 2–1 to Uxbridge at Staines, after taking a second half lead through Sumner. Uxbridge equalised almost immediately and then scored the winner. The *Ham & High* said that it as a "disappointing display...Town were not at full strength owing to injuries".

Meanwhile the league form had been excellent, and consistent centre-forward Herbert Pennifer hit hat-tricks in the Middlesex League against Walthamstow Grange and Page Green Old Boys. He finished the season with over 20 goals and was the club's leading goalscorer. Sumner and Gordon Marchant also got into double figures. A heavy schedule of league games in late April saw the club play six times in 11 days. In spite of this the club clinched the Middlesex League Premier Division title, but were pipped for the London League by Bronze Athletic after losing a crucial home fixture to them in the middle of a congested spell of games.

The strong reserve team picked up the Finchley League Division One title ahead of Friern Barnet, an overall excellent finish to the 1912–13 season for the club. However, a second team friendly match at the Avenue caused problems for the club. The visitors were Childs Hill, there was "considerable local interest" in the match according to the Ham & High, and Town won 6–1. However, the report continued: "Town did not bargain for the unsportsmanlike behaviour which caused the premature conclusion of the game. The Town owe an apology to their regular supporters for the unruly scenes at this match for which, however, they were clearly not responsible... The whole matter must go before the London Football Association."

Final Middlesex & District League Table

	P	W	D	L	F	A	Pts
Hampstead Town	14	12	0	2	42	12	24
2nd Battalion Scots Guards	13	9	1	3	34	20	19
Wood Green Town	13	7	0	6	25	30	14
Walthamstow Grange	12	6	1	5	44	25	13
Barnet Alston	14	6	0	8	28	42	12
Page Green OB	14	4	1	9	24	36	9
Waltham	10	2	2	6	15	28	6
Kilburn	12	2	1	9	12	28	5

At the Avenue on 26 April 1913, the *Willesden Chronicle* reported that Hampstead Town beat Wood Green Town 2–0 in the London League, Division One. Both goals were scored by H. J. Pennifer. Immediately following this match, the 2nd XI entertained Christ

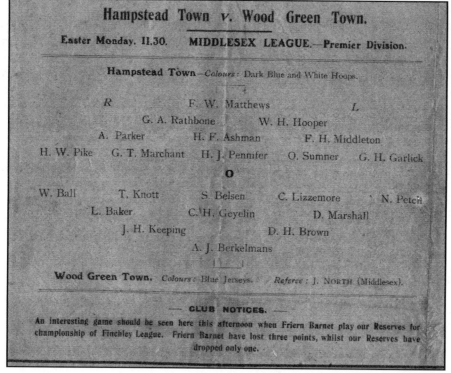

The Hampstead programme from Easter Monday 1913, a 2–1 win over Wood Green Town. The advert for E. Morris tea rooms on Pond Street says that 'footballers specially catered for' and offers a dressing room and baths.

Church Hampstead in a friendly. Christ Church put up a splendid fight, their goalkeeper giving a particularly good display, but the experience and better combination of the home team produced the inevitable result, the Town reserves winning a good sporting game by 2–0.

The annual club supper was held later in the evening at the Cricklewood Tavern, over 60 members and their friends being present. Charles Farrer, the president, occupied the chair, and when proposing the toast of 'the Club', complimented the players and officials on the excellent results they had achieved during the season. Mr C.E. Timms, the club's chairman, in reply, attributed this success to the splendid spirit of comradeship existing between the players, to the excellent work of the committee, and more especially to the untiring energy and enthusiasm of the secretary Walter Styles's remarks were endorsed by loud cheering and the toasting of the secretary with musical honours. An excellent musical programme was provided, and the evening finished with the singing of *Auld Lang Syne*, with great anticipation for next season.

The club applied for election to the Isthmian League for the first time at the end of the season, but did not receive any votes. West Norwood were elected.

1913–14

Once again, the club competed in two leagues, the Middlesex League and the London League, as well as various cup competitions.

Hampstead Town met Bronze Athletic four times this season, the following account is from the *Hendon & Finchley Times*, in February 1914: "Bronze Athletic, who visited the Avenue Ground on Saturday, sustained their first defeat of the season in the Premier Division of the Middlesex League, while the Town retained their unbeaten record in the competition. Keen rivalry exists between the two clubs, as they are running neck and neck at the present time in both the Middlesex and London Leagues, but Bronze were unquestionably second best on this occasion. As showing the Town's predominance, Matthews had not a single shot to save in the second half. The Town's first goal was one of the best seen on the Avenue ground this season. Following a splendid effort by J. Fearn, admirably repelled by Mayne, the Bronze goalkeeper, J. Schebsman made a grand volley from 30 yards range, which completely beat the opposition. The visitors equalised soon afterwards, when Smith, their centre-forward, netted with a capital shot. The brilliance of Mayne alone saved Bronze from a heavy defeat, and the Town forwards only managed on one other occasion, as Arthur (A.W.) Humphreys, with a brave effort, cleverly headed a goal from Garlick's centre."

The third meeting that season between Hampstead Town and Bronze Athletic was watched by 800 spectators and they saw Athletic gain revenge for their previous 2–1 defeat with a 3–2 win. The loss of those two points would ultimately prove costly to the Town. In the last month of the season, Hampstead undertook a total of 11 matches, in order to complete their fixtures in both leagues.

The most important win proved to be the London League success over Bronze Athletic at the Avenue on 11 April 1914. An excellent crowd of 1,500 spectators saw Garlick put Town in front at the interval, and midway through the second half Humphreys clinched a 2–0 win, which virtually wrapped up the London League title. Hampstead still had a chance of adding the Middlesex League championship too, but on the last day of the season, Page Green Old Boys put up a fine performance at the Avenue (in what was their home fixture), and Grant's 75th minute goal was a deserved

9

winner on the day. It meant that Hampstead to be satisfied with the runners-up spot in the league. Humphreys finished the season as the club's leading scorer with a fine tally of 31 goals in all competitions, while support came from Alfred Tomkins with 18 goals, and eight each from Oscar James and Gordon Marchant.

Goalkeeper F.W. Matthews played a couple of first team games for QPR in the Southern League at the end of the season, deputising for their regular goalkeeper. He kept a clean sheet on both occasions.

London League – Premier Division (Amateur)

	P	W	D	L	F	A	Pts
Hampstead Town	12	8	3	1	25	12	19
Walthamstow Grange	12	8	2	2	31	13	18
Bronze Athletic	12	5	3	4	24	14	13
Custom House	12	5	2	5	28	17	12
Barking	12	3	5	4	18	22	11
Woolwich	12	3	2	7	15	34	8
2nd Batt. Grenadier Guards	12	0	3	9	11	40	3

Middlesex League final table - Premier Division (top four)

	P	W	D	L	F	A	Pts
Bronze Athletic	14	11	2	1	43	9	24
Hampstead Town	14	11	1	2	38	15	23
Wealdstone	14	6	2	6	20	12	14
Liberty FC	14	5	4	5	34	29	14

In the London League, the Town played Fulham Reserves in the end of season championship play-off, but lost 4-1. Fulham Reserves had won the League's Professional Premier Division. The match was scheduled to be played at Highbury, but sadly the local paper did not have a report of it. In Division One, Town's reserve team finished fifth, with 10 points from 14 matches.

The *Ham & High* reflected on the club's progress: "In the space of two seasons the Town club has attracted and retained a following that is the envy of many older established senior amateur clubs." The season's record was played 46 matches, with 29 wins, four draws and 13 defeats. Town scored 101 goals and conceded 65. There were also plans to carry out "extensive work" at the Avenue Ground.

1914–15: World War One

Hampstead Town were elected to the Athenian League following the resignation of Townley Park, a Surrey based club who were formed in 1882, and elected to the league on 5 June 1914, resigning just 10 days later. Townley Park did not resume after the War.

War was declared on 4 August 1914, and would continue until 11 November 1918, with the loss of millions of lives in the trenches and hardship at home. The FA continued with the FA Cup and the Amateur Cup for the 1914–15 season, although it was criticised in some circles for this. The Football League continued to play, although clubs faced growing problems as the season progressed.

In September the desirability, or otherwise, of continuing association football during the War was the subject of debate. Many members of Hampstead Town Football Club had already joined various branches of the forces, and the club's celebrated centre half Eric (E.J.E.) Wright, was about to depart for foreign service. The War Office appeared to be in favour of the continuation of football, and in the circumstances, the officials of Hampstead Town decided that it was their duty to carry out the business of the club to the best of their ability, while urging every young fellow, who could do so, to join the forces. The club would also encourage an interest in sport for young people.

The season opened with a meritorious win by 7–2 in a friendly against Finchley at the Avenue Ground, before a considerable crowd. Wright, had the afternoon 'off-duty', and assisted his old club mates. He gave a polished display at centre half, and to the delight of the supporters scored the Town's opening goal. The other successful marksmen were Humphreys with four goals, T.B. Poltock and F.S. Rayner. The latter, who had had considerable football experience on the continent, was a clever and speedy outside-right. During the early part of September 1914 other Hampstead players signified their intention of joining the forces, but thankfully the club had some excellent reserve team players to draw on.

Hampstead Town had more players called to arms including George Garlick, P. Sperrin, Ernie Hudson, T. Gibbs and Vic Hough. Despite these losses, and previous depletions in their playing strength, the club successfully opened their Athenian League programme in September with a 2–2 draw at Barnet & Alston (who later became Barnet FC). O. Warren scored the goal by which Town led at the interval, and shortly after resuming, Humphreys put them further ahead. Barnet & Alston rallied in the concluding stages of the game and managed to draw level before the final whistle.

Another Athenian League draw was achieved, this time 1–1 at Summerstown, with a goal from Humphreys. In September, owing to serious depletions in the ranks of the clubs in membership due to the war, the Athenian League programme was abandoned for the season. Hampstead's debut season in the league had lasted just two games, but they were unbeaten. Being faced with very heavy liabilities at the Avenue Ground, the Town, who had an excellent reserve of players ineligible for the forces for various reasons, tried to continue to provide for their supporters harmless and reasonable recreation on Saturday afternoons throughout the season and a number of friendly games were arranged, including Millwall, who sent their reserve side to the Avenue. It was expected to be a tough game, but Town emerged with flying colours, only being defeated by more experienced opponents 6–4. Taking into account that two of Millwall's goals came from penalty kicks, and a third accidentally by one of the Town backs, the result was very satisfactory for the home side, and well received by the large crowd of over 600, including some Belgian refugees who for several weeks had visited the Avenue Ground, and appear to have become interested in football.

Humphreys opened the scoring against Millwall reserves with a fine goal which earned him considerable applause, but this was neutralised shortly after by a penalty kick awarded to Millwall, who later took the lead by the aid of Horbury, the Town's left back, who, to his chagrin, neatly beat his own goalkeeper. Hampstead equalised later with a clever effort by Garlick, who was enjoying an afternoon's leave from military training but at the interval, Millwall led 3–2. Play continued to be fast and vigorous through out the second half, during which Millwall added three goals, interspersed with two for the Town by Humphreys and Poltock. A feature of the game, and one which gave great pleasure to the crowd, was the magnificent display in the Hampstead goal by

11

W. Winyard, who was a youngster and had previously played in junior football. He saved the home side from a much heavier defeat and showed much promise as a goalkeeper. Although the Athenian League had been suspended for the season, it was agreed that the fixtures previously arranged by the clubs would be fulfilled as friendly matches.

A keen and interesting game resulted from the meeting with Croydon at the Avenue ground. The score was 2–0 in the Town's favour. The midfield exchanges were very even and the home goals came from two excellent individual efforts by Humphreys who was proving to be a prolific goalscorer. Winyard, the Town's new keeper gave another fine display in goal.

Town's next game, the FA Cup tie versus Yiewsley, was played at the Avenue. Yiewsley had choice of ground, but at considerable expense, the Town, in the interests of their supporters, arranged for the match to be at the Avenue.

Every credit is due to Yiewsley for the splendid fight they put up in the cup match, the result was a 2–2 draw. Over 700 local followers witnessed a keen and interesting game. Had the Town taken full advantage of their opportunities, they could have won by a big margin. Hampstead were constantly on the offensive. Yiewsley opened the scoring, indecision on the part of the Town backs allowed their inside-right, R. Warner to break through and cleverly beat Winyard. The Town were not to be denied, however and just before the interval, Humphreys equalised from a pass by Rayner on the right wing.

S. Brown, who played a fine game throughout in the Yiewsley goal saved what appeared to be certain scoring efforts by Warren and Poltock, but eventually with the ball placed nicely by Garlick, Schebsman headed into the net and gave Town the lead, with the result looking certain in their favour, Hampstead relaxed their strenuous efforts and, with only a few minutes to go, F.W. Smith, the Yiewsley captain, brought the scores level with a fine shot.

In the replay, at the Avenue ground, Hampstead Town won 3–0 and deserved their victory. The visitors again put up a splendid fight with a slightly improved team, but on this occasion failed to score, although one or two excellent chances came their way.

Warren opened the account for the Town, with a finely headed goal from Poltock's centre and later increased the score with a goal, an exact replica of his previous effort, the ball coming nicely to his head, this time from Rayner who played well on the right wing. Humphreys added the third goal in the second half with an excellent shot. The game was enjoyed by a local crowd of over 800.

Enfield were visitors to the Avenue Ground in October 1914 and won 3–2. They were only the second team to beat Hampstead that season. The home team helped them along the way with an own goal. The local paper took up the story: "Dale, the Enfield custodian, who gave a clever display throughout, had far more attacks to negotiate than the home goal-keeper. In the early stages of the game, during a period of pressure, the Town's centre-half, J. Schebsman, accidentally opened the Enfield score. This was quickly neutralised however, for immediately from the kick-off, F. Rayner forced a corner, and placed the ball beautifully for A.W. Humphreys to head into the net. The Town took the lead early in the second portion, O. Warren scoring a fine goal, after a clever individual effort. Enfield wore down the opposing defence in the concluding stages, and by the aid of McCormack and Duck, scored twice, in each case after a melee in the goal-mouth."

At Chelmsford on Saturday 31 October, Hampstead Town won 6–0 with a hat-trick from Humphreys, two goals by Warren and one from L. Fraser, while on the same afternoon the reserves defeated Kingsway Rovers 7–1 at the Avenue in the Paddington

Cup. The local paper reported that: "Numbers of our Belgian friends, now residing in the vicinity, visit the Avenue Ground every Saturday, a cordial invitation having been extended to them by club officials, and they seem keen to appreciate the recreation thereby offered. Hampstead Town have happy recollections of a visit to Ghent last season, where they were regally entertained by the local clubs."

Southall were the next visitors to the Avenue in the divisional qualifying final of the FA Cup. Kick-off was set for 2.30pm, to allow for extra-time if necessary. Southall were at that time renowned cup fighters and were expected to include many prominent players in their line up.

It was reported that Corporal T.L. Gliddon, one of Hampstead Town's players, was serving on the Western Front. The local paper said that "He is only a youth and played with great success at outside left for the Town. Thirteen other members of the club are now with the forces."

On the pitch, Hampstead Town confounded those who had forecast their early removal from the FA Cup by a decisive and well deserved 3–1 win over Southall. The visitors played well up to their great reputation throughout, but there was no mistake about the Town's superiority. They started and continued with great determination and after the Southall goal had several narrow escapes, Humphreys scored with a fine shot. This advantage was neutralised before the interval, Ballard at left half making a splendid drive through a crowd of players with Winyard unsighted. On resuming, the Town quickly took the lead, Garlick putting on the finishing touch to a clever move by the home forwards. Later on, Poltock was heavily fouled in the penalty area by a Southall defender and Bill (W.H.) Hooper scored from the spot-kick.

Southall made many efforts to score, but Winyard in goal, and Hooper and Horbury the Town backs, kept them out. The Town were fortunate in having the assistance of two of their old players, Wright at centre-half and Garlick at outside-left who both had an afternoon's leave from their military training. The attendance was well over 1,000.

A letter sent home to Hendon from a gunner in the Royal Field Artillery refers to a meeting on the Western Front with a couple of local lads, one of whom was O.F. 'Okay' Neale, the former Hampstead Town centre forward. They had just come from Antwerp in Belgium, apparently travelling on a fleet of omnibuses. Two of these had been blown up by enemy gunfire and another one they'd been on, had seen its staircase blown right off. It had all been a bit too close for comfort.

City of Westminster visited the Avenue Ground in November in the third round of the London Senior Amateur Cup. The local press reported it as: "A good sporting game resulted in the Town being easy winners by 4–0. Three excellent points were registered in the first half by F. Lucas, T. Poltock and O. Warren, while such a sound defence was exhibited by W.H. Hooper and C.J. Horbury that the visitors never had a chance of scoring. In the second period, the home team played a less vigorous game, O. Warren adding one more to the score. The latest members of the club to join the forces are O. Warren and L. Fraser, but their services will be available for the first few weeks of military training."

Another cup tie followed, this time in the fourth qualifying round of the FA Cup. The Town visited Guildford and honours were even at the end of 90 minutes play, each side having scored once. Both teams missed excellent chances in the early stages of the game, but after 30 minutes the Town took the lead, Humphreys heading through, following a scrimmage in the goalmouth. Guildford equalised shortly after the interval with a fine effort. The Town had a weakened team, and were stronger in defence than attack. Hooper and Lucas played well. A crowd of 350 turned up at the Avenue for the replay, Hampstead Town won 2–1. Hooper scored from the spot and H. Spiller got their other goal. In the next round Hampstead would face Bromley.

Another player, L. McCoy Hill, had joined the forces in Kitchener's Army. Warren, mentioned above, was in the HAC and Fraser was in the 7th City of London Rifles.

At the end of November, with a depleted team, Hampstead Town visited Page Street Old Boys in the Amateur Cup first round. Humphreys scored twice for the Town, but later missed a penalty in a 4–2 defeat. While the professional game at the time was attracting a good deal of unfavourable criticism, and regarded by some as having an adverse effect on recruiting, amateur football seemed likely to be suspended for the opposite reason. So many players, officials and supporters had joined the forces since the outbreak of war, including 18 members of Hampstead Town. Each week witnessed further depletions in the club's ranks.

Some clubs had dropped out of the Amateur Cup, and the number of qualifying rounds had been reduced from four to two. Five clubs who had had exemption to the competition proper dropped out at that stage.

At the start of December, Town met Bromley in a well contested and exciting FA Cup 5th qualifying tie, and achieved a highly creditable 1–1 draw. Hampstead put a very mixed team on the field, the home side were practically at full strength, including such well known amateurs as McWhirter, Peacock, Guthrie, Hill and Hutton. Losing the toss, facing a strong wind and sun, the Town were hard pressed in the first half, and great credit was due to Winyard who made many fine saves in goal, and played a sound game throughout. The shot with which Hutton opened the scoring for Bromley followed an exciting scrimmage in the Town goal. The Hampstead forwards played a resourceful game, but lacked the fine combination of their opponents. However, they continued to play with great determination in the second half and G.I. Fox equalised with a fine goal just on time.

The replay took place a week later at the Avenue. The local paper reported: "Hampstead Town made their exit from the English Cup competition somewhat unexpectedly, when Bromley defeated them in the fifth Qualifying Round replay. On the previous Saturday, the Town effected a draw away, but on this occasion Bromley had the services of several of their more notable players who have joined the forces, and unquestionably, the better team won. The Town showed excellent promise in the opening stages of the game, with G.I. Fox, on the left wing, making a fine start, and easily beating the opposing goalkeeper. After Bromley had equalised, the same player again secured the lead for the Town with a splendid individual effort, but the visitors continued to persevere and eventually crossed over at half-time with a one goal lead. They continued their winning way in the second period, the final score 5–2 in their favour."

Plumstead were the next visitors to the Avenue in what should have been a London Senior Cup 4th round tie. However they were only able to call on part of their team and under the circumstances it was agreed to play the match as a friendly with each side fielding nine men, and the Town lending their opponents a player. Hampstead won 5–3.

The cup-tie was played a week later at the Avenue on Boxing Day 1914. Incessant rain had made conditions treacherous, and the gate was considerably affected. Nevertheless, an interesting encounter was witnessed and the Town won 4–1.

By now, many amateur clubs in the south of England were finding it difficult to raise a team to play regularly.

Towards the end of February, Shepherd's Bush, then members of the Isthmian League visited the Avenue. Hampstead won 1–0. The local paper reported: "The Town's point [goal] was scored within a few minutes from the start by F.K. Gooding, a recent and useful addition to the Hampstead forward line. Although many excellent attempts were made by both sides, no further goals arrived. Some few weeks ago, the Sportsman's Battalion XI, which comprises of some of the leading footballers under military training visited Cricklewood and were defeated by 3–1, the Town being one of the very few clubs to beat them. As the result was not entirely acceptable to the visitors, a second encounter has been arranged."

That game took place during the early part of March and again the local paper reported it. "The 1st Sportsman's Battalion XI furnished an excellent attraction at the Avenue ground, and this fine combination of athletes provided an enjoyable and keenly contested game. Hampstead Town, however, confirmed the result of the previous encounter, being successful on this occasion by 3–0. The absence of points for the visitors was not due to any lack of skill or effort on their part, but mainly to the sound defence of the home team, and particularly W. Winyard in goal. This capable and improving player made two meritorious saves from Owers (late of Bristol City), worthy of the highest commendation. The Town were quickly on the offensive, and within 10 minutes from the start, G. Christie circumvented Higgins (late of QPR), and centred right into the goalmouth. Kirton successfully negotiated this attempt, but punted the ball to T. Poltock, who turned it into the net with a fine drive. Shortly after A.W. Humphreys, who was going nicely for goal, was brought down in the penalty area, but Hooper failed with the resultant kick."

The Town secured a two goal lead before the interval, with Gooding scoring cleverly, while the visitors, meanwhile, made continuous and valiant attempts to get on terms. Hampstead were fortunate in having the services of the well known amateur R.H. Jonas at centre-half, who played a sterling game throughout, and it was from one of his well judged passes that Humphreys was able to dribble through the backs, before beating the keeper with a shot into the corner.

Owers got well away on one occasion but shot over, and the same player, with the last kick of the match, made a brilliant attempt to score, but just failed to beat Winyard. The soldiers were good in all departments, Littleworth, Higgins, Owers and the brothers Hendren being particularly prominent. The Town, however, showed superior teamwork, and thus secured a well-merited 3–0 victory."

Over the Easter break, on the Saturday afternoon at the Avenue, the Town planned to play a team organised by the Belgian refugees now in the country. The whole of the proceeds would be given to the Belgian Wounded Soldiers Fund. On Easter Monday morning, the 2nd Sportsman's Battalion would be the visitors.

Two weeks later, Hampstead Town entertained the Footballers Battalion, now in training at the White City. The team to oppose the Town is composed entirely of professionals from English, Scottish and Southern League clubs.

Somehow the club managed to play a total of 29 games during 1914–15, which considering the difficulties of player availability, was an achievement in itself.

On Saturday 24 April 1915 Hampstead Town played their last game of the season, not realising that it was to be their last game for three years as the war took its hold, and toll. The Footballers' Battalion were the visitors to the Avenue. Their team was: P. Roney (Bristol Rovers), J. Robertson (Birmingham City), R. Reason (Clapton Orient), S. Ripley (Stoke City), S. Morris (QPR), H. Hogarth (Burnley), D. Grey (St Mirren), C. Bell

The Avenue Ground (Courtesy Richard Blackmore & Hendon FC)

(Woolwich Arsenal), J. Pennifer (QPR), W. Gerrish (Aston Villa) and W. Gallagher (Bristol Rovers). Hampstead lost 3–1.

The Middlesex County FA postponed their annual meeting but were still hopeful of playing their cup ties in 1915–16. It was also noted that over 2,500 Middlesex footballers had joined the forces.

The FA abandoned the FA Cup and Amateur Cup for the rest of the war. A handful of amateur clubs in the south of England continued to play friendly matches, but Hampstead Town did not take the field again until 1918.

2. 1918 to 1930: Into the Athenian League

In 1914, Hampstead Town had been elected to the Athenian League. But the commencement of the First World War meant that the competition was abandoned, and it was not until 1919 that the club would take its place in senior amateur football.

At the end of the war, much of Hendon was still semi-rural. The underground railway finished at Golders Green, and the extension to Edgware was not completed until 1924. This was an important factor in the development of the area between the wars. By World War Two, much of the area had been developed for housing, much of it for middle class commuters, although the London County Council (LCC) developed the Watling estate in Burnt Oak between 1926 and 1931. In the 1920s, there was important road development in the area, with the Hendon Way & Watford Way, Great North Road and North Circular all being completed. There were still important light industrial areas along the Edgware Road, and the Cricklewood area had a large railway sidings. Aeroplane production was given a boost by the outbreak of the war, and became an important part of the economy of the area. Cricklewood had become a busy shopping centre before the war.

Clitterhouse Farm on Claremont Road closed in 1926, and the Hendon Urban District Council had acquired the land for playing fields and to provide a new home for Hampstead Town Football Club.

The war ended with the Armistice on 11 November 1918. In 1922, a huge crowd assembled to watch the unveiling of the Hendon War Memorial at the junction of Watford Way and The Burroughs.

A month after the Armistice, Hampstead Town started playing again, with three friendly matches. The Athenian League did not run in this season, so the club entered the United Senior League for the rest of the season.

This was an eight team league, including Southall, Barnet & Alston, Tufnell Park and Wimbledon. There were some clubs that the club rarely played again, including Darracq, Catford Southend, and Great Western Railway.

Catford Southend had won the Athenian League in 1912–13, with Barnet & Alston as runners-up, and in 1913–14 Tufnell Park had been Athenian League champions. Of course, it is impossible to judge the real strength of clubs in this short season compared to their pre-war strength.

The club opened their campaign on 4 January 1919 with a 5–3 defeat at home to Southall at the Avenue. But only two more league games were lost, and at the end of April, Hampstead Town had won the League, with 10 wins and a draw giving them 21 points, two clear of runners-up Darracq.

T.B. Poltock was top scorer with 13 goals, followed by Charlie Allwright with six. Reports of the club's matches note that gradually some players who had played before the War were returning, including W.G. Darvill, R.H. Barratt and E.J. Wright.

As well as the League programme, the club played friendly matches, beating Bromley 2–1, and holding Oxford City to a 2–2 draw in the final match of the season. However, one report referred to Hampstead playing on 'their own mud patch' in Cricklewood Lane – evidently the club had pitch problems in those days as well.

17

1919–20: Athenian League debut

The Athenian League was founded in 1912, and had nine clubs in its first season, 1912–13. This was expanded to 12 for 1913–14. At the end of that season, four clubs left the League, and four new clubs were elected, one of which, Townley Park, resigned after only 10 days membership, and Hampstead Town were elected in their place. For the first post-war season, the League had 12 clubs. The club again applied for election to the Isthmian League, but again received no votes. The Casuals, Civil Service FC and Tufnell Park were invited to join. Curiously, the latter two clubs would – in the future – ground share with Hampstead Town or Golders Green.

Hampstead continued their success of the previous season in the Athenian League, and finished fourth, with 26 points from 22 matches, 11 points behind champions Luton Clarence, who only lost one league match all season. But it was a creditable start in senior amateur football.

A report in the *Hendon Advertiser* at the start of the season said that prospects for the club were "exceedingly propitious", and that "substantial financial support" had been received from local people. Also, the club's ground was "in the pink of condition" was "one of the prettiest in Middlesex" and was "certainly one of the most conveniently situated". Most of the club's players from the previous season had remained, although F.W. Congreve was on military service in Egypt and H.J. Dale had been recruited as 'custodian' (goalkeeper) to replace L.G. Mellish.

In November, the paper published profiles of the club's players. In goal, Dale had played for Shepherd's Bush before the war. At full-back, S. Dunstone was in his first season in first class amateur football, while his partner H.H. Allwright was "one of the best amateur backs... fast, a fearless tackler and sound kick". At half-back, J.H. 'Chummy' Parker was an experienced player but was still "vigorous and safe", Wright at centre-half had been club captain for a number of years, and left half H.F. Woodward came from the area, although he had played most of his senior football in Surrey. He was "a robust player with a sound knowledge of the game." The club had eight forwards to select from, including George Blackburn who was sought after by three professional clubs, David (D.R.) Bullough had played for Glossop in the Football League, and F.L. Burrage had played in South Africa. J.P. Croal, at inside left, had played for Southampton in the Southern League. Left winger Garlick was a veteran. The paper said: "Sometimes he is brilliant and always a trier with the best interests of the club uppermost in his mind."

The season opened in September with three league matches – defeats at Bromley and at home to Barnet, followed by a home win over Chelmsford. The next two months were taken up with FA Cup and Amateur Cup matches. Despite playing 10 games, the club failed to qualify for the competition proper in either cup. In the FA Cup, the club entered at the preliminary round stage. Victories over Southall, in front of considerably over 2,000 supporters – the largest ever crowd at the Avenue, Marlow and Windsor & Eton, all at the Avenue, were followed by a 4–1 win over Isthmian League Wycombe Wanderers in the third qualifying round. However, Gnome Athletic stopped the club's progress, with a 1–1 draw in Cricklewood followed by a 2–0 defeat for Hampstead Town in the replay. In the Amateur Cup, the draw also favoured Hampstead, with four home draws. But victories over Sutton Court, Botwell Mission and Napier were followed by defeat against Chesham United in the fourth qualifying round.

18

The club then resumed its league programme, putting together an unbeaten run of seven games to the end of the year. On 6 December, Hampstead won 4–2 at Chelmsford, who had famous amateur footballer Vivian Woodward in their team. Hampstead's defence managed to contain the great player, apparently without committing a foul.

The unbeaten run included matches on three consecutive days over the Christmas period. The *Hendon Advertiser* reported that over 300 supporters went to Southall on Christmas morning to support the team. They saw 'a splendid game'. On Boxing Day, a "huge crowd" saw Hampstead win the return match 2–1. The report said that the visitors play was "unduly vigorous and four of Hampstead's players were rendered hors de combat." These injuries meant that Hampstead's team was weakened for their third match of the holiday period, when "a very big attendance" saw a 3–3 draw with Cheshunt, Croal scoring a hat-trick for Hampstead.

At the end of January, Hampstead Town were top of the league, following a 3–1 win at Metrogas. Hall scored twice for Hampstead on their trip to the Old Kent Road. On 27 March, Luton Clarence came to the Avenue, and the *Hendon Advertiser* reported that the 2–2 draw was a fair reflection of the relative merits of the teams. Croal and Mallett with a penalty scored Hampstead's goals.

Their league form was fairly consistent until April, when three consecutive defeats ended their challenge for runners-up spot. George Blackburn and Croal were top scorers in the League, with 11 goals each.

The club did not enter any Middlesex cups, and in the London Senior Cup lost in the first round at Barnet. In the second half of the season, the club staged four friendly matches against reserve teams of London professional clubs. All four, against Queen's Park Rangers, Arsenal, Millwall and Watford were lost, but three only by one goal.

The *Hendon Times* reported that at the club's annual dinner in March, the president, Charles Farrer, said that "the season had been most successful. There had been fine games, large numbers of supporters and excellent weather. The club was popular far and wide because of its sporting fixtures, it being shown that no matter what the result might be, they were prepared to meet all comers." He pointed out that they were the youngest senior amateur club of the 24 clubs in the leading two amateur leagues and had had a competitive season. The question of the ground was obviously under consideration, as he denied rumours about its future, and said the club had a long lease.

After the last match of the season, a 2–2 draw at Kingstonian, the *Hendon Advertiser* reported that the club's players and officials had reflected on a successful season over dinner at the Kingston Hotel. Over 30,000 people had attended matches at the Avenue Ground, and only two amateur clubs, Barnet and Chesham had won there. The club was planning to run two senior teams in the 1920–21 season, by entering a team in the London League. The report concluded: "All the cups have been entered for and with plenty of the right talent available future prospects are exceedingly bright."

Once again, the club applied for admission to the Isthmian League, but again did not merit a single vote. Wimbledon and Wycombe Wanderers were elected.

1920–21: Another cup final

The next season, Hampstead Town built upon their success in 1919–20. In the league, they finished third, with 28 points, five behind champions St Albans City. And the club were runners-up in Middlesex Charity Cup, losing the final 3–1 to Botwell Mission (who later became Hayes FC) at Griffin Park.

The club entered a team in the London League. This was a senior competition, but the match programme for the match against Old Aloysians in February referred to "our reserve team... making steady progress in the London League" and it is clear that the Athenian League side was the club's leading team. A preview in the *Cricklewood & Willesden Advertiser* said that one team would enter the "Athenian League and the English [FA], Amateur, London and Middlesex Senior Cups, and the other in the London League." However, it did mean that there was football on offer every week at Child's Hill for the club's supporters.

The club had again improved its ground, with new dressing rooms and a clubhouse. The covered stand was being extended and more banking built around the pitch. On the playing side, the club said that 19-year-old George Blackburn was not turning professional (in fact he did so in December, joining Aston Villa), and that A.E. Mallett would captain the side. One of the most famous amateur players, the Rev. Kenneth R.G. Hunt was also available for the club in important matches. However, forward Llew Price had joined the professional game with Mansfield Town. He subsequently played for Aston Villa, Notts County and QPR.

George Blackburn went on to have a distinguished professional career. His best year was 1924, when he became the first former Hampstead player to play for the full England side, in a 3–1 win over France in Paris. Also in the England team were three amateurs, F.H. Ewer of the Casuals, and W.V.T. Gibbons and S.J.G. Earle of Clapton. He also played for Aston Villa in their 2–0 defeat to Newcastle United in the FA Cup Final. In 1926 he joined Cardiff City, and subsequently played for Mansfield Town and Cheltenham Town.

Another Hampstead player who turned professional around this time was Arthur Chandler. He joined QPR in September 1920, and after playing 78 games for the west London side, scoring 16 goals, he joined Leicester City in 1923. There he scored 273 goals in 419 games. He joined Notts County in 1935, but finished his career at Leicester in 1936.

Uxbridge Town and Cheshunt had lost their places in the Athenian League, and been replaced by West London Old Boys, who only lasted one season in the League, and Barnet, who were members until 1965. The autumn programme was again dominated by cup matches. In the FA Cup, an 8–0 victory over Polytechnic in the preliminary round, including four goals from Blackburn, was followed by victories over Luton Amateurs, Fricker's Athletic and St Albans City. In the last match, Blackburn played at centre-half, with Llew Price leading the attack. Over 800 Hampstead supporters travelled to the match, and the crowd of 3,500 was a record for St Albans. Hampstead lost 3–0 at Oxford City in the fourth qualifying round. There was less excitement in the Amateur Cup, where Hampstead lost 4–3 at Uxbridge in the first qualifying round.

In the London Senior Cup, Polytechnic were beaten again, this time 5–2, but the next week Green & Silley won 1–0 at Child's Hill to end Hampstead's progress. In the Middlesex Senior Cup, Limehouse Town were beaten 5–1, but Barnet won 3–0 at the Avenue in the second round.

There was more progress in the Middlesex Charity Cup. Hampstead entered at the semi-final stage, drawing 2–2 at Enfield in April, and winning the replay 2–0 the next week. Hampstead won the replay despite three of their players, F.L. Burrage, Cecil Wise

HAMPSTEAD TOWN v WEST HAM UNITED RES.
SATURDAY, MARCH 19th, 1921

HAMPSTEAD TOWN (Black & White Hoops)
R   C. B. Evans   L
W. Draper   S. Dunstone
W. E. Brewer   C. A. Burrage   H. F. Woodward
S. P. Briscoe   F. L. Burrage   G. H. Perry   C. Wise   H. S. White

Ruffels   Smith   Leaf   Bailey   Crowther
     Palmer   Carter   Lane
        Stanley   Turner
L   Jobbins   R
WEST HAM UNITED (Red and Blue Shirts)
Referee—Lieut. J. A. Old (Army F.A.)

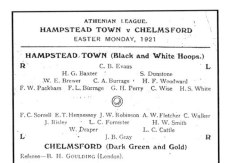

ATHENIAN LEAGUE.
HAMPSTEAD TOWN v CHELMSFORD
EASTER MONDAY, 1921

HAMPSTEAD TOWN (Black and White Hoops.)
R   C. B. Evans   L
H. G. Baxter   S. Dunstone
W. E. Brewer   C. A. Burrage   H. F. Woodward
F. W. Packham   F. L. Burrage   G. H. Perry   C. Wise   H. S. White

F. C. Sorrell   E. T. Hennessey   J. W. Robinson   A. W. Fletcher   C. Walker
J. Risley   L. C. Forrester   H. W. Smith
     W. Draper   L. C. Cattle
L   J. B. Gray   R
CHELMSFORD (Dark Green and Gold)
Referee—B. H. GOULDING (London).

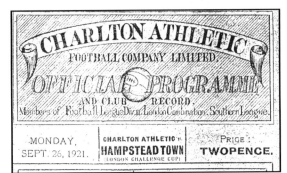

CHARLTON ATHLETIC
FOOTBALL COMPANY LIMITED
OFFICIAL PROGRAMME
AND CLUB RECORD
Members of Football League Div. II. London Combination. Southern League.

MONDAY,   CHARLTON ATHLETIC v.   PRICE:
SEPT. 26, 1921.   **HAMPSTEAD TOWN**   TWOPENCE.
                LONDON CHALLENGE CUP

Metrogas Athletic Club
SATURDAY, AUGUST, 27th, 1921.
Metrogas V Hampstead Town.
Athenian League.
Ground:- Devonshire Grove, Old Kent Road.

METROGAS.
Colours Red and Blue Shirts, White Knickers.
H. Steward.
F. Morgan.   W. Lawford.
J. Grant   J. Whitmarsh.   R. Howard.
F. Devlin.   G. O'Leary.   C. King.   J. Bryson.   W. Harding.
Referee: Mr. H. BART.
KICK-OFF   O   3.30 p.m.
H. White.   W. Bowers.   D. Saxby.   G. Prince.   J. Payne.
H. Woodward.   A. Thwaites.   W. Brewer.
S. Dunstone.   H. Baxter.
C. Evans.
HAMPSTEAD TOWN.
Colours: Blue and White Shirts, White Knickers.

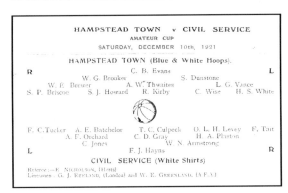

HAMPSTEAD TOWN v CIVIL SERVICE
AMATEUR CUP
SATURDAY, DECEMBER 10th, 1921

HAMPSTEAD TOWN (Blue & White Hoops.)
R   W. G. Brooker   L
          C. B. Evans
W. E. Brewer   A. W. Thwaites   S. Dunstone
S. P. Briscoe   S. J. Howard   R. Kirby   L. G. Vance   C. Wise   H. S. White

F. C. Tucker   A. E. Batchelor   T. C. Culpeck   O. L. H. Levey   F. Tait
A. F. Orchard   C. D. Gray   H. A. Plaston
C. Jones   W. N. Armstrong
L   F. J. Hayns   R
CIVIL SERVICE (White Shirts)
Referee—E. NICHOLSON, (Herts.)
Linesmen : G. J. REELAND (London) and W. E. GREENLAND, (A.F.A.)

SUMMERSTOWN F.C.
ATHENIAN LEAGUE
MATCH No. 33   K.O. 3 p.m.
SUMMERSTOWN
GREEN & WHITE
A. P. Roberts.
A. V. Howe.   H. McAuliffe.
E. Dorkins.   H. L. Pease (Capt.)   F. Lowton.
H. Cobb.   J. W. McEwen.   H. J. Gillham.   W. E. Clegg.   W. Jeffryes.
Referee : A. E. HATCHER (London).
H. S. White.   C. Wise.   Travers Day.   S. J. Howard.   S. P. Briscoe.
C. W. Durham.   L. G. Vance.   W. E. Brewer.
W. F. Mays.   W. G. Brooker.
C. B. Evans.
BLACK & WHITE HOOPS.
HAMPSTEAD TOWN.

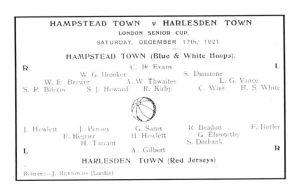

HAMPSTEAD TOWN v HARLESDEN TOWN
LONDON SENIOR CUP
SATURDAY, DECEMBER 17th, 1921

HAMPSTEAD TOWN (Blue & White Hoops).
R   C. B. Evans   L
          W. G. Brooker
W. E. Brewer   A. W. Thwaites   S. Dunstone
S. P. Briscoe   S. J. Howard   R. Kirby   L. G. Vance   C. Wise   H. S. White

J. Hewlett   J. Pewsey   G. Sams   R. Beadon   F. Butler
F. Regrier   H. Hewlett   G. Elsworthy
H. Tarrant   S. Deebank
L   A. Gilbert   R
HARLESDEN TOWN (Red Jerseys)
Referee :—J. REYNOLDS (London)

Programmes and team line ups from the early 1920s.

21

and H.G. Baxter playing for Middlesex in the final of the Southern Counties Championship.

But in the Final on 7 May, Botwell Mission proved to be too strong for Hampstead, winning 3–1. The Athenian League insisted on the club fielding a team for a League match on the same day, so a reserve team was sent to play Metrogas, and lost 7–0.

Botwell Mission 3 Hampstead Town 1
Middlesex Charity Cup Final

Botwell Town were pre-match favourites, having won the Middlesex Senior Cup the week before against Enfield. They were unbeaten in the Great Western League, with 41 points from 22 matches. Wise and Packham were prominent for Hampstead early on, and they took the lead when White crossed for Packham to score. Botwell applied pressure before half-time, but although Hampstead goalkeeper Evans was injured, he was able to continue playing, and with centre half Burrage 'showing remarkably good form', it remained 1–0 at the break.

Botwell were on top in the second half, and equalised after 65 minutes through F.C. Knight. His namesake, R. Knight, then gave them the lead. F. C. Knight added a third goal to secure the cup for the west London side, which was presented to them by the Brentford FC chairman, Mr H. Jason Saunders.

Hampstead Town: C.B. Evans, S. Dunstone, W.G. Brooker, W.E. Brewer, C.A. Burrage,
H.F. Woodward, F.W. Packham, F.L. Burrage, S.P. Briscoe, C. Wise, H.G. White.
Botwell Mission: H. Hart, J. Brooks, W. Ramsey, A. Sceeny, H. Pacey, J. Gore, H. Deamer, F. Long,
R. Knight, F.C. Knight, H. Smith.

After the excitement of the early season cup ties, league action had resumed just before Christmas with a 4–4 draw with Summerstown. On Boxing Day, "a record holiday crowd" came to the Avenue Ground for a 3–2 win over Luton Clarence.

After a draw at Southall, the team won six consecutive league matches before losing the return at Luton.

One creditable victory was over local rivals Barnet on 5 March, when a crowd of 3,000 saw Hampstead's goalkeeper P. Bruty taken to hospital after being kicked in the head early in the game. B.S. White went in goal, and F.L. Burrage scored from a free kick taken by his brother Cecil Burrage.

Cyril (C.B.) Evans took over as the club's regular goalkeeper, and the club staged a benefit match for their injured goalkeeper, to compensate him for his stay in hospital, which lasted for some weeks. The *Hendon Advertiser* said it was "the worst accident that has happened on a local ground for some years".

The final two homes matches of the season were seen by over 5,000 supporters. Champions elect St Albans drew 1–1 on Saturday 23 April, and Hampstead then beat Metrogas 4–0 two days later.

However, three defeats at the end of the season, including the one at Metrogas, prevented Hampstead Town from winning their first league title.

Forward Cecil Wise won two England amateur caps during the season, against Ireland and France, as well as appearing in other representative games. He was the first Hampstead Town player to win England honours while with the club.

Hampstead Town FC 1921–22

1921–22: Middlesex Charity Cup win

The third full season after the war was a successful one for Hampstead Town. New recruits included A.W. Thwaites at centre half, and O.H. Prince, a centre forward who had recently left the forces, and had played in the Navy versus Army match. D. Saxby joined the club from nearby Hendon Town, but on 10 September the club programme announced that he "hardly played up to expectations, and has returned to his old club".

The autumn fixtures, as before, were devoted to cup matches. The season had opened with four Athenian League fixtures – two defeats and two draws. Hampstead entered the London Challenge Cup for the first time, and the season's first victory was against Tufnell Park at the Avenue Ground. Wise and White scored for Hampstead in a game that the *Willesden Chronicle* said "was a splendid one to watch... the best seen at the Avenue Ground for a long time." Two weeks later, Hampstead travelled to Charlton Athletic, and according to the club programme "created considerable surprise in the football world by drawing with our formidable opponents." The London FA had said that the replay must take place on the Thursday afternoon, but as Hampstead's players had already taken time off work to play on the Monday, and three were playing for the Athenian League team on Wednesday, the club said they could not field a team. They offered to play the following Monday afternoon but this was not acceptable to the London FA, so Hampstead Town withdrew from the competition.

In the Amateur Cup, Hampstead reached the competition proper for the first time. After battling through four qualifying rounds, Hampstead beat the Civil Service 2–0 at Child's Hill with goals from Wise and White in front of nearly 3,000 fans before going down 5–0 in Cardiff to Cardiff Corinthians. The Cardiff programme said that Hampstead Town were "one of the strongest amateur sides playing in London this season."

In the FA Cup, Hampstead again failed to reach the first round proper. Barnet and Wealdstone were beaten at the Avenue Ground before St Albans City won 4–2 to end Hampstead's interest in the competition.

The club's luck in cup draws was also present in the London Senior Cup. Three home matches were won before an away draw at Bromley ended in a 2–0 defeat. Barnet got revenge for their FA Cup defeat in the Middlesex Senior Cup, defeating Hampstead 1–0 at Underhill.

But the club did win their first senior trophy. In the Middlesex Charity Cup, victories over Yiewsley and then a 6–5 thriller over Cheshunt in the semi-final at the Avenue Ground, with Travers-Day scoring a hat-trick, produced a final against Botwell Mission on 13 May at Griffin Park.

Botwell Mission 1 Hampstead Town 2
Middlesex Charity Cup Final

A large crowd watched the final, reports saying that "several char-a-bancs being run from Child's Hill" for Hampstead's supporters. Five of the Hampstead team had not played in the 1921 final between the two teams. Botwell Mission were the cup holders.

Hampstead scored first after 20 minutes, when a long shot from Howard beat Hart. They had the better of the first half, with White and Wise being prominent in attack. After the goal, Wise hit the bar, and then White put Hampstead Town 2–0 up just before half-time. Botwell Mission fought back after the break, and Finlator pulled a goal back.

Botwell Mission pressed for the equaliser, and Long hit the bar, but they could not break down Hampstead's defence and the club won its first senior trophy. Mr Sanders, the chairman of Brentford FC presented the cup to Hampstead's captain Cecil Wise, who accepted that Botwell Mission had been unlucky.

Hampstead Town: C.B. Evans, W. G. Brooker, W.F. Mays, W.E. Brewer, Lewis Smith, L.G. Vance, S.P. Briscoe, S.J. Howard, Travers Day, C. Wise, H.S. White.
Botwell Mission: H. Hart, T. Brooks, W.W. Ramsay, A. Sceeny, H. Pacey, Lesley, C.B. Ramsay, J. Brooks, F.C. Knight, F.J. Long, V.R. Finlator.

The Athenian League had been expanded to 14 clubs. West London Old Boys had lost their place, but Guildford, Cheshunt and Enfield had all joined the competition. Hampstead finished fourth, with 29 points from 26 matches, 12 behind champions St Albans City.

The team was very strong at home, only St Albans won at the Avenue, but only three matches were won away from home, and a further two drawn. Cecil Wise was top scorer with 14 goals, and he was the only player in double figures.

At the club's AGM in June, secretary Walter Styles said that in the three seasons of post-war league football, the club had not finished lower than fourth, and "in view of the admitted high playing strength of the Athenian League, this consistency gave cause for considerable satisfaction." He also said that the crowds had been very good, and the club was aiming to build up funds to purchase the ground.

The improvement in the club's facilities was shown when two Middlesex County matches, against Surrey and Essex, were staged at the Avenue Ground. Also, the Athenian League played the Middlesex League there.

Eight of the club's players, Brewer, Thwaites, Vance, Briscoe, Howard, Kirby, Wise and White, won representative honours during the season. One player, W.E. Brewer, had not missed a game since he joined the club in September 1920.

1922-23

In August the club announced that Isthmian Leaguers Civil Service FC were to share the Avenue Ground for the forthcoming season. A season ticket for 12/6d (62.5p) gave admission to both club's matches. The club was to stage a trial match against the Civil Service side to open the season.

On the playing front, pre-season reports said that Cyril Evans was still the first choice in goal, Brooker, the 'old war horse', was as sound as ever, W.F. Mays was recovering from a serious illness, and it would be some weeks before he could play; G. Hughes was a newcomer at left back, Brewer was vice-captain at right half, H. Pacey, a centre half had joined from Botwell Mission, the left half was L. G. Vance, G. E. Sampson had joined from Chiswick Town, Cecil Wise, the well-known inside left, was the captain, Travers Day, an Old Haberdasherian, was centre forward, S.P. Briscoe, was 'likely to be as popular as ever' in the right wing, while G.F. Howell, on the left wing, had also joined from Chiswick Town, following that club reverting to junior status. A new local player of great promise was inside right W.H. Lakin. Another recruit from Chiswick Town was forward Freddy (F.G.) Young, who would go on to have a distinguished career with the club.

In the Athenian League, there were now 13 teams in the League. Chelmsford and Metrogas had left, Windsor & Eton had joined. The reserve team moved to play in the Middlesex League from the London League. Prices for first team matches were 8d (3p) for adults, 4d (2p) for boys and 1/3d (6p) to sit in the stand.

For the opening Athenian League match at Barnet, the Hampstead Town team was announced as: C.B. Evans, G. Hughes, Brooker, Brewer, Pacey, Sampson, Briscoe, Lakin, Travers Day, Wise, Howell. In fact, Brooker did not play, as he was playing cricket for the Post Office. Hampstead managed a 2–2 draw, and this was followed by a 2–1 defeat at Luton Clarence, when Lewis Smith returned to the team, having had a trial for Aston Villa in the close season.

The cup matches soon started. In the London Challenge Cup, Hampstead were in the qualifying competition, and beat Enfield 6–0 at the Avenue after a 2–2 draw. Sterling Athletic were then beaten 7–1, having given up ground advantage to play at the Avenue. Cecil Wise scored a hat-trick. Tufnell Park were then beaten 3–2. The Town now had an aggregate score of 18–5 in four games in the Cup, but then lost 1–0 at Clapton, despite fielding a strong team that included two St Albans City players, the Millers, as guests.

In the FA Cup, Hampstead lost 2–1 at Enfield. "Hampstead Town will not be figuring in the FA Cup Final at Wembley Park next spring" said the *Hendon Times*. Enfield took the lead after 10 minutes, Wise scored from a corner just before half-time. Rawlings scored winner near end, but in the last minute Travers Day came close to equalising.

Returning to league action, it was 'Hampstead's Black day' when they lost 4–1 at home to league newcomers Windsor & Eton at home A new recruit was Arthur 'Billy' Baker, who had previously played for Brentford's first team. Stan Briscoe missed the game, having been injured in a bicycle accident. W.E. Brewer had not missed a game for two seasons, and was described in the *Hendon Times* as a 'keen and resourceful player, his spoiling tactics are frequently a feature of the games at Cricklewood Lane.'

The team's form now became erratic. Summerstown were beaten at home, with J. Brooks playing at right back, but then defeats followed at Cheshunt and 4–0 at home to St Albans, with over 1,000 away supporters travelling to the match by train.

25

Programmes from the early 1920s, including a joint Hampstead and Civil Service FC fixture list, and (right) a programme cover for the club from the early 1920s at The Avenue Ground.

26

Hampstead gave a very poor exhibition in front of their best gate of the season. Despite this result, Hampstead were still fourth in the league, but most teams had games in hand on them.

Further gloom followed at the start of November, with a 4–0 London Senior Cup defeat at Cheshunt. "'What is the matter with Hampstead Town' is the topic of the hour in senior amateur football," said the *Hendon Times*, adding that it was of great concern to hundreds of local enthusiasts. In the last four matches the team had conceded nine goals, and scored none. The report said the "Forward line was weak and ineffective in front of goal."

Two more league defeats followed, and in the Amateur Cup, the team lost 4–1 at Grays Athletic, in front of a 2,000 crowd. Travers Day equalised just before half-time. Cyril Evans broke a bone in his right hand, and missed the second half. But the *Hendon Times* report said that "drastic changes" were needed.

The club used a friendly against Luton Amateurs to give four new players a trial, including E.T. McCracken in goal, F. Cantrell, from Yiewsley, and D.H. Clark. Things improved on Boxing Day, with a 6–2 league victory over Luton Clarence. The *Hendon Times* said that 'the new players have added some excellent talent to the club.' A.B. Butcher played at right back, and Abrey on the right wing. The club also announced that they had been accepted as full members of the Football Association; only 13 other London amateur clubs had achieved this privilege.

At the end of the year, a 3–2 defeat at Enfield saw Hampstead Town fifth in the league, with 11 points from 14 games. But the club had played more fixtures than any other team in the league apart from Bromley, who were top with 14 wins from their 14 matches.

The club continued the search for new talent. Goalkeeper G.M. Boxall joined from Bishops Stortford, as Evans would be out for some weeks, and L.B. Evershed came in at half-back, and played well against Southall, although Hampstead lost 4–1 against unbeaten opponents.

Things improved with a 4–1 win at Sutton, Travers Day scoring a hat-trick, and W.C. Little returning to the club. To lighten the mood, the club held a Fancy Dress Ball (although fancy dress was optional) at St Peters Hall in Cricklewood. By the end of January, the team rebuilding was paying dividends, with a 2–1 against Kingstonian. The following week, Freddy Young scored a hat-trick, and Travers Day scored twice in a 5–1 victory over Old Lyonians in the Middlesex Senior Cup. Four weeks later, Hampstead went to Acton to play STD, a motor works team in the next round, and won 3–1, with Travers Day scoring twice. On 10 March, in the semi-final, Southall came to the Avenue Ground, and drew 0–0 in front of a big crowd. Reports say that Hampstead deserved to win, and had two goals disallowed. Hampstead lost the replay which was played in midweek 11 days later.

On 24 February, Guildford were beaten 2–0 at home. J.W. Cochrane, a Durham Varsity Blue and county player made his debut, but was injured in the first few minutes, so did not do himself justice. F.G. Butler played his first game on the right wing, and had joined the club from Walthamstow Grange. Brooker had played for the Athenian League team against Arsenal reserves, but the Athenians let in 11 goals. Hampstead were now third in the league table, but had played more games than any other club.

The Middlesex Charity Cup also provided some sustenance for the Town's fans. A 3–2 win over Tufnell Park, with Young scoring a hat-trick for the second week running, was followed by a 5–4 defeat in the semi-final against Botwell Mission. Wise got a hat-trick, but Hampstead were missing Lewis Smith and Howell who were playing for the Athenian League at Eastbourne.

Form improved in the league as well, and Hampstead finished eighth with 20 points from 24 matches. On 17 March, the Town beat Cheshunt 9–1, a record score for the Avenue Ground. It was 8–0 at half-time, and Young had been injured in the first half, otherwise the score may have been double figures. After this game, the team were third, but had played eight more games than some other teams. The last three league games were lost, and over the whole season, Hampstead lost six out of 12 home games, and away, won only three times.

Over Easter, the club went on tour to Jersey and Guernsey, and won the Victory Cup. The party left Paddington on Thursday evening, got to Weymouth at 2.30 am, and were on the boat to Jersey at 3am. A crowd of nearly 4,000 saw them play the next day, a 1–1 draw with a Jersey Amalgamated side, Travers Day scoring. On Easter Saturday, Hampstead beat a Jersey Island team 6–3, Young scoring twice, and then on the Monday, a 7,000 crowd saw a 4–3 victory over the Guernsey Island side to secure the Victory Cup. Travers Day scored twice, Lewis Smith and Young adding the other two.

A couple of interesting friendly matches were played at the Avenue before the end of the season. Civil Service FC were beaten 2–1, and then Charlton Athletic's reserve XI visited, and won 3–1, a respectable result against professional opposition. Also, the club hosted the Middlesex FA against the London FA match on 19 April, further recognition of their progress in amateur football.

At the club's AGM in June, Walter Styles reported that it was the first time in senior football that the club had won less games than they lost: 20 compared to 22, with five draws, scoring 106 goals against 101. He said that the season "held many disappointments" and was "a time when the loyalty of those interested was fully tested."

1923–24

At the start of the season, over 100 aspiring players were given trials by the club. The *Hendon Times* reported that the following had joined: F. Baker, F.A. and S. Blackburn, brothers, who are expected to uphold the family traditions in the game – presumably they were related to George Blackburn – A.T. Clayton, L. Elizaide, H.R. Tobin, T.W.B. West and Bill (W.H.) Lakin. A preview of the season said that the forwards and half-backs from the previous season were strong, but the defence needed strengthening. Two new full-backs, W.T. Field and W. Harry were signed. Field had played for the Hertfordshire County side, and Harry had played for Middlesex. Other new recruits were Bob Wardlaw, who was 'a fine young player' who had gone on the Easter tour to the Channel Islands, and played for Luton Clarence the previous season, Kenneth Seabrooke, Reg Kirby, who rejoined the club having been playing for Watford and Wealdstone, A. Isaac, a left winger from Ealing, and H. Blezard, a left winger who had played for the Westmorland County side.

In October, H.G.M. Barnes, a Suffolk County player, joined the club from Suffolk League side Leiston Works as he was now living in the Hendon area. On the debit side, Cyril Evans had left the club, with McCracken becoming the first choice goalkeeper. Later in the season Evans played in the Amateur Cup Final for Erith & Belvedere.

The season opened with a friendly against Luton Amateurs, which resulted in a 3–3 draw. But in the league, the first win was not until 29 September, a 3–1 victory over Kingstonian, with 'Hampstead Town gradually settling into a winning combination'.

The week before, Hampstead had taken 'the first step towards Wembley' with a 5–2 victory over Luton Clarence in the FA Cup preliminary round. But in the next round, a crowd of over 3,000 saw Tufnell Park draw 1–1 at the Avenue, Cecil Wise scoring for the Town. But Tufnell Park won the replay.

In the Amateur Cup, the club again faced a battle through the preliminary rounds. Three own goals helped Hampstead in an entertaining 6–4 victory against Hounslow at home, although two of them were 'certain to end up in the net'. Two weeks later, Harrow Weald drew 2–2 at the Avenue, Seabrooke and Young scoring. Cecil Wise returned for the replay, and Hampstead won 5–2, Seabrooke scoring a hat-trick. The *Hendon Times* reported: "One often hears that Cecil Wise is too slow for modern day football, but his presence in the team on Saturday made all the difference to it." Polytechnic FC were then beaten 7–2, Seabrooke bagging another three goals, with Wise and Kirby scoring two each.

In the Divisional Final, Hampstead travelled to Staines Lagonda. *A.V. Isitor* covered the match for the *Hendon Times*, having been told by a club official that he inevitably bought the team luck. He said that Staines would not normally extend an Athenian League team, and travelled to the match "from Waterloo with two or three ladies from Child's Hill who would not entertain the idea of defeat." The Hampstead Town team was: E.T. McCracken, W.F. Field, W.G. Harry, W.C. Little, Leslie F. Smith, R. Wardlaw, S.F. Briscoe, K. Seabrooke, R. Kirby, C. Wise, G.F. Howell.

Hampstead's visit attracted a good crowd to the 'somewhat primitive' ground, and former Hampstead player S.J. Howard gave Staines the lead in the first half. The home team's captain, Nicholas, added a second, and Hampstead could not recover. *A.V. Isitor* said that Staines' win was thoroughly merited.

In the London Senior Cup, Hampstead visited Edmonton. They were 1–0 down at half-time, Wise equalised, but then the home team scored twice in extra time played in semi-darkness, continuing the club's record of little progress in this competition.

Inevitably with the club's involvement in cup matches, little progress was made in the league programme during the autumn. Barking Town had replaced Guildford in the Athenian League compared with the previous season. In November, Hampstead 'ran riot' against Enfield at the Avenue, winning 8–1 with Cecil Wise scoring five, and 'exhibiting form reminiscent of his brilliant international year'. That record lasted only until Boxing Day, when Luton Clarence were beaten 9–0 on a 'terribly muddy' Avenue Ground. Howell got a hat-trick, and Travers Day and Wise both scored two goals. This victory gave Hampstead a 26–14 goal average, the best in the Athenian League, and a 'respectable' position in the table. The team were unbeaten at home, but erratic away from home.

There were a couple of unusual matches at the Avenue in January. The reserves, known as Hampstead Town Wanderers, played Lyons in the London Intermediate Cup, and won 7–2. The next week, with both senior clubs playing away, Old Haberdashers played Alleyn in the Southern Amateur League. And a week later, the London FA played the Middlesex FA there, with R.F. Brazier, Hampstead's reserve left back playing.

On 26 January, Botwell Mission came to the Avenue Ground in the Middlesex Senior Cup. Goals from Wise and Young gave Hampstead a 2–1 win, which was followed four weeks later by a 5–2 win over Enfield. Young gave Hampstead a 1–0 half-time lead. The *Hendon Times* said that "Cecil Wise being again an outstanding player, his well-judged passes and general footwork earning admiration from all. Apart from showing great discrimination in distributing the ball he never lost an opportunity when better placed than his colleagues, of shooting." Seabrooke, Lewis Smith and two more goals from Young for his hat-trick in the second half secured a memorable win. The ground was frost bound.

In the semi-final, Hampstead travelled to RAF Uxbridge to play Southall. The clubs had suggested using Fulham FC's Craven Cottage ground for the match, but Chelsea were at home the same day and objected, presumably they were concerned that fans may prefer an amateur match to the fare offered at Stamford Bridge! Hampstead had a strong wind in their favour in the first half, but it was Southall who led 1–0 at half-time. Southall then scored again, when a long shot went through McCracken's hands. Young pulled a goal back when he scored from a centre by Howell, but the equaliser would not come. Hampstead had played well, but should have made more use of the wind in the first half.

In the Middlesex Charity Cup, Hampstead lost to Barnet in the first round. The match had to be played in midweek, as Barnet were so far behind with their fixtures that they had only played five league matches by early February.

In the league, Hampstead finished fifth, with 26 points from 24 matches. The team were unbeaten at home, with seven wins and five draws. But they took only five points away from home, and lost nine out of 12 games. As late as Easter Monday, 21 April, Hampstead were still pressing for the runners-up spot, but only two points from the last four games meant fifth place, still an improvement on the previous season.

In April, the reserves played Hendon Town in a friendly to benefit the Hendon Cottage Hospital. Wise and Travers Day turned out, and Hampstead won 2–0, with goals from Travers Day and Smith.

Overall, the team played 42 matches, with 20 wins, nine draws and 13 defeats; 109 goals were scored and 71 against. W.G. Harry played in every game.

1924–25: Middlesex Senior Cup final debut

The development of the Hendon Way was causing the club concern, as the new road cut into the club's ground, and the Annual General Meeting discussed looking for a new home. But at the beginning of August it was reported that only a couple of yards would be lost from the pitch, and as it was well over the minimum size, the club could stay there for the present, although the lease only had two years to run.

On the playing front, McCracken had decided to stop playing football, as his career as a professional tenor singer did not allow him to play. Howell joined Erith & Belvedere and Lewis Smith had left London. C.F. Standish, a goalkeeper who lived near the Avenue joined from Barnet, and Barnes, who had played largely for the reserves the previous season, was expected to play for the first team at centre half. Another recruit was J. Weaver from Walthamstow Grange. In September, Ernie (E.F.) Goodwin joined the club and became the first team goalkeeper. His Life Guards regiment had transferred to London. The previous season he played for Windsor & Eton, and had also played for Army representative teams. Having failed to keep the first team slot, Standish joined Wealdstone in November. Syd Sweetman signed on after playing in the pre-season trial, having been in Fulham's reserves the previous season. However, he only stayed for a few months, returning to the professional game with Queen's Park Rangers in February, having signed for them as an amateur in December. He went on to play over 100 first team games for QPR before joining Millwall in 1929.

```
┌─────────────────────────────────────────────────────────────────┐
│ FOOTBALL ! !                          FOOTBALL ! !                │
│ AT AVENUE GROUND, CRICKLEWOOD LANE, N.W.2.                        │
│ BOXING DAY, DEC. 26th.  │  SATURDAY, DEC. 27th.                   │
│ HAMPSTEAD  TOWN         │  CIVIL  SERVICE                         │
│           v.            │          v.                             │
│ SUTTON   UNITED         │  NUNHEAD                                │
│ (ATHENIAN LEAGUE)       │  (ISTHMIAN LEAGUE).                     │
│ KICK-OFF 2.30.          │  KICK-OFF 2.30.                         │
│ Admission : ADULTS 6d.; SCHOOL BOYS 3d.; STAND 1/2 (including Tax).│
└─────────────────────────────────────────────────────────────────┘
```

December 1924 advert for football at The Avenue Ground

There were some new recruits after Christmas, V.F. Rowe who had played for Brentford's reserves, and Norris from Slough. There were also some promising reserve players who were expected to challenge for first team places. These included Ron (R.F.) Brazier, who had played regularly for the County junior side, Frank Iles, W.E. 'Taffy' Harris (who signed amateur forms with Aston Villa in February), S. Bloxham, and Eric Irwin from the Hampstead Garden Suburb team.

The Athenian League grew to 14 teams. Luton Clarence were not re-elected, and were replaced by West Norwood and Uxbridge Town.

The season opened with one of the most successful runs in the history of the club to date, being unbeaten until an FA Cup replay at Barnet in November.

In the FA Cup, Hampstead beat two teams from Luton, Luton Frickers 4–2 in the extra preliminary round, and then Luton Amateurs 5–0. Enfield were vanquished 7–0, with Wise scoring a hat-trick, before Hampstead faced a third Bedfordshire team with a trip to Waterlow's Dunstable. Hampstead had been drawn at home, but switched the game as the Civil Service FC had a game at the Avenue. Hampstead won the replay, but then faced Barnet at the Avenue. Nearly 2,000 fans saw a 2–2 draw on a very muddy pitch. Young and Wise scored for Hampstead, and it was the first time, on 1 November, that the team had failed to score three goals. Hampstead lost the replay 3–2.

The goals flowed as well in the Amateur Cup. Yiewsley left the Avenue on 25 October, having been beaten 9–0, with Wise scoring four goals, Young and Seabrooke two each and Sweetman just one. Yiewsley's neighbours Uxbridge were Hampstead's next victims, being beaten 5–1 at the Avenue.

In the league, by mid-November, Hampstead had only played five matches, with three home wins and two away draws. One memorable victory was over Bromley at the end of September. Travers Day missed the match as he was playing tennis in the London Country Club tournament. His place was taken by Eric Irwin. By Christmas, the club could look back on a very successful first half of the season. Of the first 22 matches, 15 were won and five drawn.

The New Year opened with a visit from The Casuals in the Amateur Cup to the Avenue. On a very soft pitch, Hampstead adapted better to the conditions. There were no goals at half-time, but in the second half Wise put Hampstead ahead following up after a shot from Seabrooke had been blocked. Irwin added a second goal to secure an important win. But two weeks later, London Leaguers Bostall Heath won 3–1 at the Avenue Ground, ending an unbeaten home record that had lasted nearly two seasons. The visitors were 1–0 up at half-time, and added a second after the break. Sweetman replied with a penalty, and 'for a time [Hampstead] looked good for an equaliser'. Bostall Heath's third goal came in the last minute, and the Hampstead supporters in a 3,500 crowd went home disappointed.

In the London Senior Cup, Hampstead beat Cray Wanderers, Edmonton and Mitcham Wanderers to reach the competition proper. Freddy Young scored a hat-trick against Mitcham, his second in the competition after achieving the same feat the previous week against Edmonton. In January, a crowd of 7,000 saw Hampstead lose 1–0 at Dulwich Hamlet in the first round. Wardlaw was injured and missed most of the second half. The *Ham & High* said that the second half was marred by the "unnecessary offside tactics" of the home side. Dulwich went on to win the trophy, so it was a creditable result.

The Middlesex Senior Cup bought more success. After beating Hanwell Town 4–1 at the Avenue, despite being 'much below their usual form', on 21 February, Hampstead had a 'somewhat unexpected though thoroughly meritorious victory' over Barnet at Underhill. It was the first time Hampstead had won there, despite many visits in league and cup matches. Hampstead were 3–0 up at half-time, and won 4–0, Wise and Reinke scoring two goals each. Three weeks later, Hampstead beat the RAF 3–0 at Uxbridge in the semi-final. Wise gave Hampstead a 1–0 half-time lead, and Young and Wardlaw added further goals in the second half. The *Ham & High* said the team had reached their first Middlesex Senior Cup Final 'in convincing style'. But the cup run ended in an anti-climax. The final against Southall was played on Easter Monday, 13 April, and with the first team on tour in Belgium, Hampstead fielded a reserve team and lost 5–0.

Southall 5 Hampstead Town 0
Middlesex Senior Cup Final

Hampstead Town's first Middlesex Senior Cup Final at Brentford's Griffin Park ended in defeat. Town's reserves were no match for Southall. However, Hampstead nearly took the lead early on, when a shot from Marks was inches wide with the Southall goalkeeper Holding beaten. Southall were, not surprisingly, on top, and took the lead after 15 minutes. But the *Hendon Times* said that Esser was being impeded when they scored their second goal on 40 minutes, making the half-time score 2–0. Southall dominated the second half, with Corben scoring twice and Goodwin once for a final score of 5–0. Esser, Clarke and Brooker all played well for Hampstead in defence. Rowe, Marks and Cowgill all came close to scoring for Hampstead. The *Hendon Times* said Hampstead's youngsters "never gave up trying" even though they were outplayed. However, the *West Middlesex Gazette* said: "The game proved to be little short of farcical... The result was as expected a walk-over for Southall. Many people had no doubt anticipated this and the crowd also affected by the wretched weather was the worst at a final for many years, the number being only a little over 2,000 and the gate receipts £136 compared with 8,877 when the game was last played at Brentford two years ago."
Hampstead Town: P Esser, R.S. Clarke, W.H. Brooker, A. Thornby, H. Dimmock, W.C. Little, J. Bingham, V. Rowe, H. Marks, C. Cowgill, V.C. Fennell.
Southall: T. Holding, E. Buttery, R. Gower, F.R. Johnson, R. H. Wenham, A. Vance, H. Jackson, D. Clarke, A.E. Corben, F. Goodwin, G. Howell

Hampstead Town FC 1924–25 in the Meuse Cup: Back: Kenneth Seabrooke, Harold Pease, Frank Iles, Ernie Goodwin, Bert Barnes, Bob Wardlaw, Cecil Wise, Harry Hughes (trainer). Front: Eric Irwin, Taffy Harris, Jimmy Elderton, Oscar Reinke, Ron Brazier, Stanley Smith.

In the league, the team finished fifth with 31 points from 26 games. The biggest wins were 6–0 against Cheshunt, and 5–1 against Summerstown and West Norwood, all at home. Another impressive result was a 5–2 victory on 28 March over champions-elect Redhill at the Avenue. The *Ham & High* said that 'Hampstead played in a manner more suggestive of championship honours than their opponents and the team work generally was excellent.' Only Barking won at the Avenue, 3–2 in April, when Young was injured in the first minute. But the team did not achieve any away victories, but did manage nine draws in 13 away fixtures.

Over Easter, a party of 30 players and officials went to Liege in Belgium to play in the Meuse Cup. On Good Friday the team beat Dover United 4–0 before travelling to Liege by ferry via Ostend. On Easter Sunday, in front of a 20,000 crowd, Hampstead Town beat Stad Francais 6–1. Their opponents had six French international players. Seabrooke got a hat-trick, with Wise adding two goals and Young one. The next day, Hampstead won the trophy beating Royal FC Liegeois 1–0 in a 'hard and gruelling game'. During the visit, the team put a wreath on the memorial to Liege club members killed in the War.

The future of the club's ground was still uncertain. The final game of the season against Enfield was won 2–0. The *Ham & High* reported that a "Bumper attendance expected for this final encounter, which may prove to be the last game to be played on this enclosure owing to the encroachment of the new Watford by-pass road".

At the Annual General Meeting in July, the club looked back on a successful season. Walter Styles said that he could not remember a season more enjoyable than the last one. The team had played 49 matches, winning 27, drawing 13 and only losing nine, with 139 goals scored and 55 conceded. Cecil Wise had been the top scorer with 37, and Seabrooke and Young contributed 30 goals each. There had also been progress by younger players, with Ron Brazier playing in all the first team matches, and Stanley Smith only missing one. The meeting also noted the death of Jack Wright, a life member and former player, who had never recovered from injuries sustained during the war.

It was also clear that the club's time at the Avenue Ground was coming to an end. The lease expired in September 1926, and the new road had cut a corner from the ground, meaning it was just possible to fit in a pitch. Also, the ground's owners, the Ecclesiastical Commissioners were planning to sell the ground at the end of the lease for building houses.

1925–26: Finale for the Avenue Ground

The club's final season at the Avenue was a successful one, with fourth place in the Athenian League and reaching the last 16 in the Amateur Cup. One change at the Avenue Ground was that the ground-sharing arrangement with the Civil Service FC had finished, as they moved to a ground in Chiswick. The reserves were to compete in the first division of the London League, where their opponents would include neighbours Hendon Town.

One new recruit was Harold (H.L.) Pease, who joined the club from Summerstown. He had played for the club on the Easter tour earlier in the year. In September, it was reported that a well-known Welsh international, Joseph, was likely to join. Also, George Bucci started playing in the first team. He remained a first team regular until the end of the Second World War, and went on to serve the club as a committee member.

The season started well, with four consecutive victories in the league. In the FA Cup, Hampstead beat Finchley 2–0, the first time the clubs had played since the war, Wise and Reinke scoring. Two more home matches followed. Berkhamsted Town were dispatched 8–1, with Oscar Reinke scoring four and Wise grabbing a hat-trick, and then Baldock Town left Childs Hill after a 10–2 defeat, Reinke scoring five. But at the end of October, Cheshunt won 2–0 at the Avenue in the Divisional Final, ending hopes of entry into the competition proper.

By the end of November, Hampstead were top of the league. But then the cup competitions took over the fixtures again. In the London Senior Cup, Sutton United and Wood Green Town were beaten; before Finchley got revenge for their FA Cup defeat with a 1–0 win in at the Avenue in the Divisional Final. The game attracted the best crowd so far of the season, and reports said that Finchley were 'greatly improved' from the previous game.

The Amateur Cup campaign started at the beginning of January, with a 5–3 win at Underhill against Barnet, Reinke scoring a hat-trick. Two weeks later, Isthmian Leaguers Wycombe Wanderers were due at the Avenue, but the match had to be postponed. The decision was taken in time to stop a train with 1,000 Wycombe supporters from having a wasted journey. The game was played the following week, but the kick off was delayed for half an hour when the referee decided that the team's shirts were too similar. Wycombe borrowed some white shirts so that the game could start. The light held, and Hampstead won 1–0 with a goal after 15 minutes, when Reinke scored from a good centre by Bucci.

Hampstead's reward was a trip to Ferryhill Athletic in Durham. The *Ham & High* recognised that the club was "One of the 16 remaining clubs out of the very large original entry embracing the whole of the Kingdom". Hampstead headed north on the Friday evening from Kings Cross. But it was a fruitless trip north. In front of a 3,000 crowd, Hampstead were beaten 4–0 by 'a much better team'. The Hampstead side was:
E. Goodwin, D. Clarke, S. Bloxham, A. Thorlby, H. Pease, R. Wardlaw, S. Cousins, J. Ashby, O. Reinke, C. Wise, G. Bucci.

In the Middlesex Senior Cup, Hampstead beat London League Millwall United 5–1 at the Avenue Ground before losing 4–3 at Barnet. There was more success in the Middlesex Charity Cup. Southall were beaten 6–2 at the Avenue, with Reinke contributing a hat-trick, then on 24 April, Barnet were beaten 1–0, so Hampstead faced Botwell Mission at Griffin Park in the Final. However, the match was postponed due to the General Strike, which was a great disappointment to the club which had hoped to celebrate their last season at the Avenue with a trophy. The match was played in September.

During the season, the club had secured a new ground at Claremont Road. The final matches at The Avenue Ground were full of goals. On 26 April, Cheshunt were demolished 9–3, with Cousins getting a hat-trick, and Ashby, Rowe and Wise scoring two each. Then on 1 May, Windsor & Eton were beaten 7–2. There was a big crowd for the game, and Ashby scored for Hampstead in the first minute. Windsor equalised, but by half-time, Hampstead were 6–1 ahead. Ashby completed his hat-trick, with Rowe, Cousins and Wise also scoring. The second half was more even. Windsor scored, but then Pease scored with a penalty. Ashby missed the second half due to an injury, and the *Hendon Times* report said that Goodwin played well in goal against his old club, and the balance of play was not reflected in the score. At the end of the game, the band played the national anthem and *Auld Lang Syne*. The final match was a schools fixture on 15 May between Hendon and Hampstead elementary schools.

In the league, Hampstead finished fourth, with 31 points from 26 matches. The team won six away games, but also let in five goals at Barking Town and Barnet. At the club's AGM in June, Walter Styles said that the club had lost four players at the start of the season, Brazier had suffered a serious injury, and Wardlaw had also been in and out of the team through injuries. He said that in view of these factors, fourth in the Athenian League was satisfactory. He said that the reserves had struggled in the London League as players had been selected for the first team, but the club's junior side had been unbeaten. In the next season, the reserves would play in the Athenian League's reserve section.

Moving to Claremont Road

In November 1925, it was reported that the club was negotiating for another ground in the area, but nothing had yet been agreed. In March, news came that the club had an option on a site on Claremont Road, a 10 to 15 minute walk from the Avenue. Clitterhouse Farm on Claremont Road had closed, and the Hendon Urban District Council had acquired the land for playing fields and to provide a new home for the club.

The club announced that £2,000 was needed to fit out the new ground, and started to raise the money. Lord Glendyne got the ball rolling with a donation of £100. There was also support from the Mayor of Hampstead and George Balfour, the MP for Hampstead.

Within two weeks, the appeal had raised £571, a considerable sum in those days. Local support for the club was clearly strong. A letter to the *Ham & High* from H.G. Pritchard said: "during the dreary winter months, when outdoor recreation is hard to come by, except for the wealthy, this club provides healthy pleasure to thousands of men and women." He went on: "By sending a subscription to the fund for equipping the new ground they would be making a real contribution to social welfare."

Hendon Council proposed to charge the club a rent of £225 a year for Claremont Road. In May, the club still had £200 to raise to reach the £1,300 it now needed to equip the ground, and launched a 5,000 shillings appeal. Supporters present at a meeting at the end of the season subscribed nearly 1,000 shillings straight away.

By the start of the 1926–27 season, the club had a new ground, which was nearly finished, and a new name, now being called Hampstead. This change had been agreed at the AGM.

On 18 September 1926, the ground had been declared open by Lt Col C.D. Crisp OBE JP, and there were many prominent people from the world of football present, along with representatives of the Hampstead, Willesden and Hendon District Councils.

The club had secured a new home which would serve it well for more than 80 years, and become one of the most famous venues in amateur and non-league football.

1926–27: A new home

As well as a new ground, the club also had some new players. Allen had returned to the club from Ilford, Burford joined from Sutton Court, McQueen from Southall, R.T. Sear from St Albans and Moiser from Gillingham. In October, G.P. Deeks joined the club from Barnet. Two departures were Goodwin and Ashby, who both joined Barnet. Cousins joined Tooting Town, and Reinke moved to Clapton, although he soon returned to Hampstead. Freddie Evans also joined the club from local junior club Burlington. Cecil Wise was still playing, and it was reported that although he had lost speed, "there are few deadlier shots in the League and he has the happy knack of getting the best out of his colleagues." In January, Jimmy Smy, who had been playing for Spurs' 'A' team made his debut for the reserves, and soon established himself in the first team. Ron Brazier missed the first half of the season through injury, returning to play for the reserves in January.

On 1 September, there was some unfinished business from the previous season, with Hampstead facing Botwell Mission in the final of the Middlesex Charity Cup at Southall.

Botwell Mission 4 Hampstead 3
1925–26 Middlesex Charity Cup Final

Botwell Mission had more support in a good crowd than Hampstead, but all the fans were entertained in an 'exceedingly interesting' game.

Botwell Mission were on top in the first half, and Allen showed excellent form in goal for Hampstead before being beaten by Long after 20 minutes. Atlee then scored again for Botwell, but Sear pulled a goal back before half-time. In the second half, Botwell went 3–1 up, Evans pulled a goal back, but despite pressure from Hampstead's attack, Botwell scored again for a 4–2 lead. Evans ran almost half the length of the field to score for Hampstead, but despite more pressure, could not equalise. Pease, Clark and Wise all played well for Hampstead; and of the new players, Brandon, Evans and Sear all had good games.

Hampstead: Allen, Clarke, Broadbridge, Thorlby, Pease, McQueen, Sear, Evans, Rowe, Wise, Brandon.
Botwell Mission: Waters, Purvey, Weddon, Scorsey, Farmer, Walker, C. Knight, Long, F.C. Knight, Atlee, Findlater.

The new ground opened with an FA Cup match against Berkhamsted Town. The season started with three away league matches, which were all lost. But things improved with a

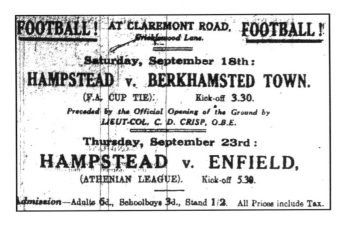

Top and middle: The farmhouse and farm buildings at what is now Clitterhouse Playing Fields, in 2005. (PL)

Left: Advert for the first matches at Claremont Road.

4–3 win against Berkhamsted, R.T. Sear scoring the first goal at Claremont Road. The teams for the match were:

Hampstead: R.S. Allen, R.S. Clarke, A. Parsons, A. Thorlby, H.L. Pease, R. Wardlaw, R.T. Sear, H.W. Shearcroft, F.P. Evans, C. Wise, G.F. Howell.
Berkhamsted Town: D.A. Patterson, W. Mothersole, Sam Ringsell, B. Bayliss, A. Gomm, S. Field, A. Wright, W. Boardman, R.J. Devlin, Stan Ringsell, W.H. Lloyd.

Two more FA Cup victories, both 2–1 at Claremont Road, against Letchworth and Enfield followed. Evans and Shearcroft scored against Enfield. The first defeat at the new ground was at the hands of Kingstonian on 23 October. The FA Cup run ended on 30 October with a 4–2 defeat at Waterlow's (Dunstable) in the qualifying Divisional Final, in front of a crowd of just over 1,000. Evans scored in the first half, but Hampstead were 2–1 down at the break, and lost 4–2. Deeks scored Hampstead's second goal. Reports say that the team's form was at least 50 per cent below that in the other FA Cup ties. The next week, Enfield won 6–1 at Claremont Road in the London Senior Cup. It was a 'melancholy day' for Hampstead. Howell scored in the second half, and it was Enfield's first win on a Hampstead ground.

The successful move to a new home was not replicated on the pitch. The team finished 13th - in the bottom two in Athenian League – and had to apply for re-election for the first time. The final tally was 16 points from 26 games. Although the club were confident they would be re-elected, which they were, it was very disappointing. In October to December, the team had eight successive defeats, including a 5–3 loss at struggling West Norwood, which gave Hampstead the worst record in the league. This disastrous run ended with a 10–0 revenge win over West Norwood on 18 December, with Shearcroft scoring four goals and Applebee three.

Over the Christmas break, Hampstead were forced to field weakened teams, and lost 2–0 at Underhill to Barnet on Christmas Day, but drew 1–1, despite fielding eight reserves, in the return at Claremont Road.

Things improved after Christmas, but not enough to avoid having to apply for re-election for the first time in the club's history. There had been constant changes in the team before Christmas, resulting in inconsistent performances. The club said at the end of the season that their supporters' patience had been severely tested. At home, apart from the West Norwood massacre, Hampstead won 6–3 against Windsor & Eton, and scored five twice. But away from home there was only one win and one draw in 13 games, with heavy defeats at Bromley, 6–0, and 6–1 at Enfield.

There was some excitement in the cup competitions after Christmas. In the Amateur Cup, the club had a bye to the first round proper, and drew 3–3 with Casuals on New Year's Day, in front of a 3,000 crowd at Claremont Road. The illustrious visitors were 2–0 up after 20 minutes, but then Howell and Applebee scored to make it 2–2 after 30 minutes. Hampstead went 3–2 up through Howell, and Deeks hit the bar before Casuals equalised with 13 minutes left. In the replay, Shearcroft and Wise gave Hampstead a 2–0 lead, and they were 2–1 up at the break, but Casuals fought back to win 3–2, the winner coming 12 minutes from the end.

The two Middlesex cup competitions provided some joy for Hampstead. On 22 January, Enfield were beaten 4–2 at Claremont Road on a pitch of hardened snow and in heavy mist. This was the fifth meeting between the clubs this season, and the crowd was considerably below normal, with doubt over whether the game would be played. Howell scored twice, with Deeks and Shearcroft also scoring to secure Hampstead's win.

A hat-trick from G.H. Smith helped secure a 4–3 win at Tufnell Park in the second round, but the semi-final took Hampstead to Southall, with the *Hendon Times* saying that 99 out of 100 people would expect them to lose. The writer's pessimism was borne out, with a 1–0 defeat. However, a big crowd saw Southall score just after half-time, which Hampstead's defence should have prevented. The game was hard fought, and given that Southall were top of the league, and Hampstead one from bottom, defeat was not unexpected.

In the Middlesex Charity Cup, Hampstead reached the final again. Botwell Mission were beaten 6–2 in the first round, with Shearcroft scoring a hat-trick. In the semi-final, Uxbridge Town were beaten 5–4, in a 'desperate struggle' and on 7 May, Hampstead travelled to Griffin Park to face Barnet in the Final.

Hampstead 3 Barnet 3.
Middlesex Charity Cup Final

A crowd of around 2,000 saw Hampstead and Barnet fight out a 3–3 draw. Due to the heat, it was agreed not to play extra time, but that the clubs would hold the cup for six months each. The Barnet team included former Hampstead players Goodwin and Cousins. Barnet scored first, and then quickly added a second. But Hampstead fought back, with Deeks crossing for Shearcroft to score with a header. Then from a corner by Deeks, Smith equalised for Hampstead. Howell scored just before the break to give Hampstead the lead. Play was even in the second half, with both teams having chances, but Barnet equalised with 13 minutes left. Trevers, Parsons, Wardlaw, Deeks, Howell and Shearcroft all played well for Hampstead, and Brazier had a good game given he had missed so much of the season. The captains tossed a coin to decide which club would have the cup first.

Hampstead: J.M. Trevers, R.F. Brazier, A. Parsons, A. Anderson, H.L. Pease, R. Wardlaw, G.F. Deeks, G.H. Smith, H.W. Shearcroft, J. Smy, G. F. Howell.
Barnet: E.F. Goodwin, F. Fletcher, F.R. Garrett, A. Snaith, G.A. Hughes, E. Casey, J. Garrett, S. Cousins, G. Sparrow, W. Davies, W.E. Aldone.

The second half of the season saw some changes in the team. Jimmy Smy made his debut for the first team in January, in a 5–3 win against Redhill at Claremont Road. He scored the first goal, and seems to have taken Cecil Wise's first team place, as Wise only played occasionally in the second half of the season, at times for the reserves. Another newcomer was A.L. Beckworth, who had been playing for Queens Park Rangers' reserves. In January, G.R. Smith joined from Cheshunt, and in March T. Morrell, who had recently left the RAF, signed up for the club.

On 19 March, Hampstead beat Bromley 2–1 at Claremont Road, their second league victory since Christmas. Hampstead were 12th in the league, with 14 points from 22 games, but Barking were only two points behind, having played only nine games. Summerstown also had 14 points, but had three games in hand on Hampstead. The final league game of the season, against Windsor & Eton, was won, and the club's record in all competitions was 15 wins and four draws from 42 games, with 113 goals scored but 129 conceded. The *Hendon Times* correspondent said in March: "I cannot but admire the loyalty of the Hampstead supporters. Many clubs who have played in such an in-and–out fashion as Hampstead have done this season would have found gates dwindling tremendously, but the same people turn up at Claremont Road week after week with the same smiling faces, all hoping for the best."

The club's other teams had more success. The reserve team reached the London Intermediate Cup semi-final, and the junior team won the Middlesex Minor Cup, beating Maypole 4–1 in the final, and the London Junior Cup, with a 4–3 win over Hoxton.

Harold Pease was awarded his county cap by the Middlesex FA, and along with Anderson, was selected for the Middlesex Wanderers Easter tour to the Channel Islands. Together with Bloxham, they were selected for Middlesex against Devon in February. Pease also played for Middlesex against Devon & Cornwall and Hampshire.

The club had accepted an invitation to tour Germany at the end of the season. Fourteen players and five club officials went on the tour at the end of May. The first game, played on 'softish concrete with granite chippings', was lost 4–1 to Barmen in front of a 1,500 crowd. The second game, played on a better surface, was a 2–2 draw with Düsseldorf, who had beaten Cambridge University and Middlesex Wanderers, and the final game was won 4–2 in Rheydt. The tour lasted a week, and the party travelled and went sightseeing between the matches.

Another new initiative taken by the club was running a social section in the summer, with tennis croquet and putting, and renting out the ground to the Hendon Traders Association to use for social activities. A cricket team also played in the summer. The income from these new activities helped offset the costs of the new ground.

At the AGM in July, the club reflected on a difficult season on the pitch, but noted the success of the junior team, who had been unbeaten. Mr Styles was presented with a gold watch in recognition of his many years work for the club. Charles Farrer resigned as president as he had moved away from the area, and Mr A. Gordon Raymond took his place.

A Hampstead hero: Cecil Wise

Cecil Wise joined the club in 1920, and was their first real star, as a goal-scoring inside forward. Little is known of his career before joining the club, although he also played for Kildare in a business league, and FA records list his club as Kildare when he played for England, although he was playing regularly for Hampstead Town at that time. He made his England amateur debut against Ireland in Belfast on 13 November 1920, and scored a hat-trick in a 4–0 win. He missed the next game against Wales, but returned for the final amateur international of the season, a 2–1 defeat against France in Paris on 5 May 1921. He also played for the Middlesex FA County side, and for the Athenian League side five times in 1921 and 1922. In October 1922 the *Evening Standard* wrote about him: "Hampstead Town's captain and inside-left Cecil Wise, is a very clever player who has already earned his amateur international cap. When he played for England against Ireland last season, he had the unique distinction of performing the hat-trick. He is exceptionally clever with his feet and is equally as good with accurate passing which his fellow forwards do not fail to take advantage of. Frequently his footwork is a feature of the games at Cricklewood Lane. Wise, who has also gained London and Middlesex caps, will possibly be the recipient of further honours before he has completed this season."

He played in three Middlesex Charity Cup finals for the club, including being captain in the 1921–22 winning team. He set a club record in senior football by scoring five goals against Enfield in November 1923. In 1924–25 he was top scorer with 37 goals, but was very much a team player. He finished playing for the club at the end of the 1926–27, having lost his first team place to Jimmy Smy. There is no record of him playing for another senior club after leaving Claremont Road.

1927–28

The new season did not start well, with a burglary at the club's ground. Shirts and other sports gear were stolen, along with 2,000 cigarettes, and several bottles of whisky.

Most of the previous season's players were available, except Jimmy Smy who had decided to play for Spurs, although in fact he played fairly regularly for the club. Goodwin had returned from Barnet to play in goal, F.T. Ryding, an inside left, joined from Brentford, W.J. Carter from Sutton Court, R. Warren from Old Johnians, and Ron Brazier was available again, having missed much of the previous season through injury. Oscar Reinke was also playing for the club again, but Freddie Evans was playing for Hendon Town. In September, H.H. Allwright returned to the club from Uxbridge. He had first joined the club eight years before. J.E. Harvey left to join Botwell Mission, and at the turn of the year, Warren and Smith left, and Anderson left as he was in business in Southend and needed a club nearer his home. Pease and Parsons also left during the season. Towards the end of the season, George Bucci played regularly in the first team.

The club had done further work to the ground, including building a dressing room for the referee and linesmen, and repainting the stand.

The FA Cup provided some entertainment in the first half of the season. A 7–1 win over Waltham Comrades in the preliminary round was followed by a 7–4 victory over Spartan League Welwyn Garden City, with Smy scoring five. In the next round, Hampstead were at home again, and drew 2–2 with Chesham. Five days later, Hampstead won the replay 3–2, with Reinke scoring twice. A crowd of 3,897 then saw a 2–1 win over Barnet at Claremont Road. But on 12 November, Hampstead lost the qualifying Divisional Final 3–2 at Southall. The home team were 2–0 up, but goals from Shearcroft and Smy made it 2–2 before Southall got the winner in the second half. Pease was injured in the first half, and had Hampstead had a full team for the whole match, could have made further progress. The Hampstead team was:
E. F. Goodwin, J. Shorland, A. Parsons, A. Anderson, H.L. Pease, R. Wardlaw, F.G. Young, H.W. Shearcroft, O. Reinke, J. Smy, D. Levy.

In the Amateur Cup, on 27 December Hampstead lost 2–1 at home to Royal Navy Depot (Chatham) in the first round, in arctic conditions. Hampstead were 1–0 up at the break through a header by Levy, but the 'sailor boys', as the *Hendon Times* called them, fought back to sink Hampstead's cup hopes in the second half.

At the turn of the year, Hampstead's only cup interest was in the two Middlesex competitions. In both Hampstead's first match was abandoned with them losing. In the Senior Cup, Cheshunt were leading 3–2 at Claremont Road on 28 January when the match was abandoned with 10 minutes left. There was a piercing wind and driving rain, and Cheshunt were down to eight players when the game was halted. Reports say that the players were in a 'pitiable state'. The next week, Hampstead won the restaged match 6–1, with Jimmy Smy scoring four times. Two weeks later, Hampstead beat Tufnell Park 4–0 at Claremont Road. The match was switched to Hampstead's advantage as London Caledonian, who shared the Tufnell Park ground, had a home match in the Amateur Cup on the same day. It was the first 'clean sheet' since the first day of the season. Smy scored twice, Sear and Reinke added the other goals.

The semi-final bought Spartan League RAF Uxbridge to Claremont Road. But hopes of another Middlesex Cup final were dashed when the airmen won 2–0. Hampstead missed a lot of chances, and the RAF deserved their victory, achieved in a gale and blinding snow in the middle of March.

In the Middlesex Charity Cup, Barnet were leading 6–1 at Claremont Road on 3 December, when the game was abandoned due to bad light. When it was played again at the beginning of April, Hampstead won 4–1, but then lost to Enfield in the semi-final.

In the League, Hampstead finished 11th, with 16 points from 26 games, the same points total as the previous season. The team had improved enough to avoid applying for re-election again, but remained inconsistent. In mid September, there were two consecutive wins, against Cheshunt and Uxbridge, but the next league win was on 21 January against Enfield. Percy (P.J.) Moody made his debut at centre half in this game and helped improve the defence. Overall, the team only won three games at home, but did win three away from Claremont Road. There were some heavy defeats, including 7–2 at Kingstonian in October, and 8–2 at Leyton in December, when Hampstead had some new, and inexperienced players. A 4–2 win at Claremont Road against Windsor & Eton made the club fairly safe from having to apply for re-election.

After a 4–1 defeat at Barnet in the final league match, the *Hendon Times* said that "Hampstead have provided few pleasant surprises for their supporters this season and the unexpected did not happen on Saturday."

The club arranged a couple of friendlies towards the end of the season. In March, Tottenham's 'A' team drew 1–1 at Claremont Road, and in April, Old Boltonians were beaten 3–1. Overall, Hampstead had played 42 matches, with 15 wins and six draws. Only 92 goals had been scored, down 21 from the previous season, but the defence let in only 104, an improvement of 25 on 1926–27. The most disappointing results had been the two matches against military opposition in the Amateur and Middlesex Senior Cups, both matches the club would usually have expected to win. And the team's poor form had been reflected in the gates – the committee had to pay the rent of £600 in March. At the AGM in July, the club reported a financial loss, with gate receipts down £124 from the previous year. The treasurer did say that bad weather had affected the crowds, and hoped that things would improve.

The club once more applied to the Isthmian League, but along with Bromley did not receive enough votes. Kingstonian were elected.

1928–29: League runners up

The committee made strong efforts to recruit new players to the club following two seasons in the lower depths of the league. The result was a remarkable rise – from 11th to runners-up. Hampstead finished with 35 points from 26 games, eight behind champions Leyton. Claremont Road became a fortress, with only one league defeat and 10 wins from 13 games.

Jimmy Smy became the captain, but in January, he turned professional with Tottenham. He made his debut for Spurs on 9 February, but although he played 17 first team games, scoring six goals, he never established a regular first team place and joined Sittingbourne at the end of the 1931–32 season. Had he stayed to the end of the season, it is arguable that Hampstead could have won their first Athenian League title. The new players included two internationals: left-winger Stan Moore, from Millwall United, who had won two England amateur caps the previous season and Ted (H.E.J.) Miller, who played for England in 1924, and had played for St Albans City and Clapton, and a couple of first team games for Watford. C. Fish from Millwall United and Harry (F.H.) Sherman from Cheshunt strengthened the forwards, a new half-back was Ronnie Rowe, who had played for Wimbledon and Brentford, and at the back, Freddy Webb joined from Southall. He was believed to be one of the best backs in the Athenian League. In December, Cecil Graves, an inside left known as 'the midget', joined from Tooting Town, and J. McKenzie came from Beckenham Town. Both had moved into the district. In March, H. Vanner, joined from Grays Athletic. He had a Royal Navy background, and had played for the Chatham Depot team who had knocked Hampstead out of the Amateur Cup the previous season. He had also played for the Royal Navy, Kent, Charlton and Watford. H.J. Mead, a centre half, joined in March on trial. Another link with the professional game came with George Bucci signing amateur forms for Arsenal near the end of the season.

The league campaign opened with a 1–1 draw with Bromley at Claremont Road. Goalkeeper Sid Smith missed a penalty for Hampstead in the second half. Hampstead lost the return at Bromley 2–1, but then beat Uxbridge twice and Kingstonian to be top of the league at the end of September.

On 13 October, Hampstead lost 1–0 at Amateur Cup holders Leyton in the league in front of a 3,000 crowd. But the team were then unbeaten until the end of the year, when a weakened team lost 6–1 at Enfield. This run included doubles over Barnet and Wealdstone, the latter over Christmas, a 6–0 win at Cheshunt, and a repeat 6–0 win over Windsor & Eton at home, with Shearcroft scoring four goals and Smy adding two.

Hampstead had been knocked out of the FA Cup in the first qualifying round 6–2 at Botwell Mission. This meant they could concentrate on league matches in the autumn. At the turn of the year, Hampstead were still top, four points clear of Leyton, who had five games in hand. Hampstead had 30 points from 20 games.

At the beginning of February, Hampstead beat reigning champions Sutton United 4–2 at Claremont Road. The team had only conceded 24 goals in 19 league matches, with

HAMPSTEAD HAMMER HENDON.

The Locals Meet in the Middlesex Senior Cup.

HAMPSTEAD 7, HENDON 0.

The *Hendon Times* headline from the Middlesex Senior Cup massacre.

much of the credit going to goalkeeper Sid Smith. Hampstead were still five points clear of Leyton, who had four games in hand. But the team were so far ahead with their fixtures that the last home league game was scheduled for 23 February, against Cheshunt. That game was drawn 1–1, and a 2–1 defeat at Windsor & Eton the next week considerably reduced the team's championship hopes. Three more away defeats, one at Leyton when the title was already decided, ended the title hopes, but it had still been a huge improvement on the last two campaigns.

In the Amateur Cup, Hampstead won 4–2 at Spartan League leaders Maidenhead in the first Round, with Smy scoring a hat-trick. In Jimmy Smy's last game for the club, Hampstead then lost 4–3 at Sutton United in the next round. Shearcroft with two goals and one from Bucci put Hampstead 3–1 up in the second half, but three quick goals from Sutton finished Hampstead's hopes for another year. The Sutton team included former Hampstead players G. H. Smith and D. E. Levy. Hampstead's team was: S.R. Smith, F.T. Webb, A. Owens, F.G. Young, P.J. Moody, R. Wardlaw, F.H. Sherman, G. Bucci, H.W. Shearcroft, J. Smy, S.J. Moore.

In the Middlesex Senior Cup, Hampstead had a rare local derby with Hendon Town on 26 January. Hendon switched the match from their Station Road ground to Claremont Road, to allow the 2,300 crowd to watch in greater comfort. The *Hendon Times* said that "relations between the clubs are of the happiest character", but Hampstead put a strain on the relationship with a 7–0 win.

Graves gave Hampstead the lead after four minutes, and it was 4–0 at half-time, with two goals by Moore and one by Shearcroft. Graves and Shearcroft both scored again in the second half, with Bucci scoring. Hendon's goalkeeper Miall was the 'hero of the game' stopping Hampstead reaching double figures.

But three weeks later, Hampstead lost 4–2 at Barnet in the second round. Hampstead were missing Sherman, Moore and Bucci who were playing for Middlesex. The semi-final and final were staged at Claremont Road, a new honour for the club. Finchley won the final 2–1, their first senior county cup win.

In the Middlesex Charity Cup, Hampstead reached the final again, once more facing Botwell Mission in the final. Hampstead had beaten Barnet 4–1.

Botwell Mission 1 Hampstead 0
Middlesex Charity Cup Final

Hampstead faced Botwell Mission on 12 May at Brentford's Griffin Park ground. Shearcroft was missing from the Hampstead team, having been injured the week before at Leyton. Also, George Bucci played after a severe attack of tonsillitis, and was not fully fit. Hampstead had the wind in their favour in the first half, but did not trouble the Botwell goalkeeper. The first corner came only a couple of minutes before half-time, but Young cleared Botwell's effort.

Botwell took the lead 25 minutes into the second half, with Harmsworth scoring from close in. Mead, Moore and Potter all came close for Hampstead, and, according to the *Hendon Times* "a good deal of vigour marked the closing stages". The players did not receive medals for their efforts, as the match was for charity.

Hampstead: S.R. Smith, J. Shorland, A. Parsons, F.G. Young, H.J. Mead, R. Wardlaw, F.H. Sherman, H. Vanner, G. Bucci, A.G. Potter, S.J. Moore.

Botwell Mission: W.H. Walter, J. Brooks, J. Stirling, A. Sceeney, R. G. Rowe, C. Powell, G. Kershaw, C. Knight, J. Harmsworth, G. Treasure, R. Joy.

With the league fixtures finishing early, Hampstead went on tour to the Channel Islands over Easter. All three games were won, with Guernsey Island beaten 1–0, Guernsey Northerners 3–1 and Jersey Island 3–0. At home, the reserve team beat Hendon Town 2–1 in a friendly. In April, Arsenal's reserves beat Hampstead 4–2 at Claremont Road in a friendly. Arsenal manager Herbert Chapman, who lived in Hendon, attended the match.

Hampstead were well represented in the Middlesex County team. Webb, Smy, Sherman, Moore and Bucci all played, with Sherman and Moore playing in the Southern Counties Amateur Championship final against Hertfordshire. In October, the club were represented on both sides in a county match, Ted Miller playing for Hertfordshire against W.C.H. Neil who was in the Bedfordshire side. Smy and Moore also played for the London FA in Germany in September.

The good atmosphere at the club was particularly shown on two occasions. In December, the reserve match against Enfield was a benefit for the family of Albert Parsons, who had lost a lot of time from work when he had been injured playing for the club in Germany. On Christmas Eve, Bob Wardlaw got married in Scotland. He had played for the club since March 1923, and had been captain for three seasons. He was presented with a canteen of cutlery, and was said to be "most popular with the rest of the players."

The club's overall record showed a considerable improvement on the previous two years. The first team played 41 matches, with 24 victories and 4 draws. Hampstead scored 103 goals, and conceded 72. Only three matches were lost before Christmas. The *Hendon Times* end of season summary said that "Jimmy Smy's departure for Tottenham Hotspur in February affected subsequent results." The report went on: "During the first half of the season few changes were necessary in the team, and although it could not be called a brilliant side, yet there was an even greater asset than brilliancy in the spirit of unity pervading the side. In short, they were a happy family and no discordant note was ever heard. Of the new players, Webb, Sherman and Moore have done well... A word of praise is due to George Bucci, who has surpassed himself no matter the position in which he has been placed."

The area around the ground was also changing. In November, the *Hendon Times* reported that houses were being built near the ground, and there would be an entrance from the Watford bypass to the ground. The club was also developing the facilities for other sports, including the bowling green, cricket and tennis.

At the club's Annual General Meeting in June, Arthur Crawley said that match receipts had actually gone down from the previous season, but this was due to only one cup match being played at home. There had been expenditure on the pavilion, tennis courts, and a new dressing room. He also said that he was a 'resident of Finchley' presenting the accounts for a Hampstead club that was situated in Hendon, showing the club's rather ambiguous link between its location and its name.

Mr Raymond said that the club were aiming to win the Athenian League title, and could have done so had Jimmy Smy not left. The club did not make any announcements about new players, but Percy Moody had to give up playing football on medical advice.

Despite their successful season in the League, the Isthmian League were not convinced of Hampstead Town's worth. The club were the only applicants apart from Leytonstone and Tufnell Park, who were applying for re-election, and the latter two were successful.

1929–30: Middlesex Charity Cup Finalists

In July, the club announced that all last season's players had signed on for the new campaign. New recruits included E. Thorne, a left back, formerly of Cheshunt & Swanley, V. Gardner, an inside right from Wealdstone, W. Morton, an inside left from Hendon Town, E. Mitsen, a left winger from Fulham's reserve team, William A. Drew, an inside forward from Tufnell Park, who had also played for Queen's Park Rangers, making one first team appearance in 1926, and A.E. Payne, a left back from Torquay United. The club said that all the new players were living in the locality, and claimed to have a higher proportion of local players than most clubs in suburban London. Another local recruit at the start of the season was J. Wilton from Hendon Town.

Captain Freddy Webb had recovered from an accident that had kept him out of team towards the end of the previous season. However, he joined Wealdstone in February.

Harry Shearcroft missed the pre-season trial and some early matches, as he was playing cricket for Richmond CC, and it was also unclear if Sherman would play for the club. He missed the first league match as he was playing for the Athenian League side against the champions, Leyton. In September it was announced that Tottenham Hotspur had persuaded him to play for Northfleet, their nursery team, but within a month he had decided to make playing for Hampstead his first choice. In October, he played in the FA Charity Shield match at Millwall, when the Professionals beat the Amateurs 3–0. A report of the game said he was "clever and entertaining".

There were also some changes in the local football scene. In the Athenian League, Windsor & Eton were replaced by Finchley, although controversially their membership was only to last one season. And Hendon Town had withdrawn from the London League for the season, as they had lost their Station Road ground to building development.

The first half of the season saw some excitement in the FA Cup. Hampstead beat old opponents Spartan League Hayes (formerly Botwell Mission) 2–0 in the preliminary round at Claremont Road, Moore and Shearcroft scoring in the second half. Two weeks later, Abingdon Town gave up ground advantage to play at Claremont Road, and went home defeated 7–0. A crowd of 2,000 saw Sherman play his first game for the club this season. He was the only forward not to score, the goals coming from a hat-trick by George Bucci, two from Shearcroft and one apiece by Moore and Gardner. Isthmian League Oxford City provided a sterner test in the next round, Hampstead winning 2–1 at Claremont Road in front of 3,000 fans. The *Hendon Times* said that: "Hampstead possess the will to win and that goes a long way. Though G. Bucci has not yet reached last season's form, there was a big improvement in his play. He is a popular player and when he can touch his old standard everyone will be happy." Shone played at centre forward instead of Harry Shearcroft. Now Hampstead faced a trip to Maidenhead United in the Divisional Final. Shearcroft was recalled, but in a surprise result, Hampstead lost 6–0, 'their biggest defeat in cup tie football for years" according to the *Hendon Times*. It was 4–0 at half-time, and the report said it was not necessary to describe the second half at length. After this, Shorland, Wilton, Seddon and Gardner were all dropped.

In the Amateur Cup, Hampstead also faced Isthmian League opposition, Woking visiting Claremont Road in December. Hampstead were a goal down after five minutes, but played brilliantly in the first half, winning 3–2 with a penalty by Moore after 65 minutes. The crowd was a disappointing 1,400, with the match report saying that access to the ground must be improved. But in January, Barking Town won 4–1 at Claremont Road to end the club's interest in the competition. The *Hendon Times* said that the 'backs were unreliable' and 'the forwards never got together'. Sherman and Parsons were injured during the game, but this was not an excuse for Hampstead's display.

The Middlesex County Cups bought some success. In the Senior Cup, Hampstead beat Staines at Claremont Road, but then lost 2–1 to Barnet in the next round. In the Charity Cup, Enfield were vanquished 6–0 at Claremont Road in November, then Hampstead took a rather hollow revenge on Barnet with a 5–2 win at Claremont Road in the semi-final. Due to fixture congestion, Barnet played two cup matches on the same day, and fielded a reserve team, their first team easily beating St Albans.

On 9 May, Hampstead once again travelled to Griffin Park for the Middlesex Charity Cup Final, this time to face Wealdstone.

Hampstead 1 Wealdstone 3 (after extra time)
Middlesex Charity Cup Final

Goalkeeper Sid Smith kept Hampstead in the game, with a "marvellous display". According to the *Hendon Times*, without him there would not have been extra time. Another Hampstead hero was Freddy Young, who had his best game of the season.

Hampstead started well, but Wealdstone were on top when Harry Shearcroft ran through after 20 minutes to put Hampstead ahead. Hampstead kept their lead until the break, despite Shearcroft having to go off injured for part of the first half. Butland was also injured, and had to play on the wing. Wealdstone equalised through Hannam to force extra time, and then scored twice in the second period of extra time to win the cup for the first time. Three days earlier, they had also won the Middlesex Senior Cup, beating Haywards (Enfield) at Claremont Road.

Hampstead: S.R. Smith, J. Shorland, J.P. Wilton, F.G. Young, F.R. Johnson, G. Bucci, V. Gardner, C. H. Walsh, H.R. Shearcroft, W.H. Butland, S.J. Moore.
Wealdstone: F. Poulson, R. Groves, C. Davies, F. Turner, H. Smith, D. Short, T. Maskell, E. Hannam, L. Hoskins, R.L. Clark, S. Hester

In the Athenian League, Hampstead finished 11th with 23 points from 26 matches. The season started well, despite fielding a young side. When the team played Finchley at Claremont Road in the second match of the season, the *Hendon Times* reported that the side was so inexperienced that there were rumours that old players would be recalled, and that "Cecil Wise, one of the greatest inside lefts the club has had, was asked when he would be taking the field again." Wise had retired in 1927. At the end of September, Hampstead drew 2–2 with Barnet at Claremont Road. The local rivalry was reflected in the *Hendon Times's* comment that: "While rivalry is as keen as ever, there is not that rancour which formerly marked the meetings of the clubs, and it is hoped that future games will be equally pleasant." The game itself was described as a 'grim struggle'. Hampstead were second after this match, with seven points from four matches, one point behind Leyton. On 16 November, Hampstead beat Cheshunt 5–1 at Claremont Road, and were second in the table on goal average. But in an unbalanced fixture list, six of our eight games had been played at home, and the team's inconsistency was shown in a 3–2 defeat in the return the next week, Cheshunt's first win of the season.

On 21 December, the return match at Finchley was abandoned due to bad light. Finchley were winning 2–0, the game had started late and spectators invaded the pitch to argue with the referee about his decision. Bad light was not an uncommon problem in these pre-floodlight days. In November, the *Hendon Times* had printed a letter from a Hampstead supporter saying that kick-offs should be earlier, matches should start on time, and the interval should only be five minutes. He said that the last 10 minutes of the match against Southall had been impossible to follow as it was too dark. Apparently the long interval was so the band could play. Interestingly, and 32 years before floodlights were installed at Claremont Road, in March the club programme said that it may be possible to play football at night, and estimates for the cost of equipping the ground with suitable lights were being obtained. The Football Association were not so enlightened, and banned the use of floodlights in the summer of 1930. Apart from occasional exhibition matches, the ban stayed in place until after the Second World War.

Over Christmas, Hampstead took only one point from three matches, which included fixtures on Christmas Day and Boxing Day with Wealdstone, a tradition that would continue for 40 years. Hampstead beat Redhill 5–4 on 4 January, with Freddie Evans returning at centre forward after an absence of three seasons. The team were now fourth in the table, but with 13 points from 13 matches. Although the return at Redhill was won, Hampstead continued to play inconsistently

By the beginning of March, Hampstead had only three home matches left. On 29 March, Leyton won 1–0 at Claremont Road, the match marking the return of Harry Shearcroft, who had been playing for Leytonstone in the Isthmian League for several weeks, but had decided that his heart was with Hampstead. The next week, Hampstead won the last home league match 1–0 against champions-elect Walthamstow Avenue. But Hampstead finished a disappointing 11th, a decline from the lofty heights of runners-up the previous season. At home, only six games were won out of 13 games, with the best win being 5–1 against Cheshunt. Away from Claremont Road, there were three wins and two draws. The best result was a 4–0 win at Uxbridge Town in September.

To fill some gaps in the fixture list, friendly games were arranged. Jimmy Smy played for a Tottenham team that drew 3–3 with Hampstead at Claremont Road in February, while goalkeeper Sid Smith missed a friendly at Redhill the next week as he had been injured playing for Arsenal. On Good Friday, Northern Nomads won 6–3 at Claremont Road.

Overall, Hampstead played 42 games, winning 17, drawing 7 and losing 18, scoring 89 goals, but conceding 91. But of the last 19 games played, only four were won and four drawn, "a sorry story" according to the *Hendon Times*. The newspaper's end of season report said that Hampstead must find forwards "who can score" and that Shorland and Wilton had served the club well at full back since Webb left in February.

The strongest part of the team was the half-back line, with Young, Johnson and Bucci. Percy Moody had been missed. Of the forwards, Moore had got slower, Evans had been injured after a long absence, and Gardner had not been consistently successful.

Smith, Bucci and Sherman all played for Middlesex during the season, with Bucci and Sherman being awarded county caps, and Smith a badge.

At the Annual General Meeting at the end of June, it was reported that the club's financial position was stronger, although some members had made loans to the club to support it. As more housing was being built near the club's ground, membership was growing. But the crowds were still not as high as hoped because of the lack of good transport facilities. However, it was recognised that it had been a patchy season. Freddy Young had played in every match, and Bob Wardlow and Harry Shearcroft were given life membership in recognition of their service to the club.

The Isthmian League turned down the club for the sixth time. Leytonstone (for the second consecutive season) and Clapton were re-elected. Cambridge Town, Maidenhead, Bromley and Walthamstow were also unsuccessful.

Three Hampstead FC players from the late 1920s or early 1930s

FINCHLEY FOOTBALL CLUB.

OFFICIAL OPENING of
GRAND STAND
ON
December 20th, 1930, at 2 p.m. sharp
BY
SIR FREDERICK WALL, Sec. Football Association.
Cr. VYVYAN WELLS, Esq., Cr. A. T. PIKE, Esq.
L. C. BOWKER, Esq., O.B.E., M.C.,
E. G. HAMMOND, Esq.

FINCHLEY v. HAMPSTEAD
KICK-OFF 2.30 p.m.

Come in your Thousands and Support the Club.

Advert for the December 1930 match at Finchley

3. 1930 to 1939: County Cup Finals

1930–31: Two Middlesex Cup Finals

By 1930, the Hendon area had changed considerably from when the club first moved to Childs Hill in 1911. There were new transport links – the Hendon Way, Watford Way and North Circular Road had all been completed by 1927. The underground railway had been extended to Edgware in 1924. In 1931, the inclusion of Edgware in Hendon Urban District gave the area a population of 115,682 which made it the largest urban district in the country and meant that it achieved borough status the following year. New services provided by the council included new schools, health centres and libraries. The Golders Green estate was built by builders Laing on land that had previously been used by the Cricklewood Aerodrome. The estate had Pennine Drive as its central road, and bordered Clitterhouse Playing Fields, much as it does today and provided more potential local supporters for the team. The area had lost the rural feel it had before the First World War and was now part of suburban London.

In football, local rivals Finchley had not lasted long in the Athenian League. They were removed from the League in a shock decision as their ground was deemed not to be up to standard. They had been admitted to the League on the basis of their new ground being completed, which had not happened. They rejoined the London League, and were replaced by Hayes.

New players included full back D. Blair from Gillingham FC, H. Buswell from Ealing Association, and J. Berry from Royal Navy Depot (Chatham). One notable name in the pre-season trial match was a 17-year-old Les Compton, playing for the reserve side at centre forward. He had been signed from a local junior side. He made his official debut for the reserves on 13 September, in a 7–1 win at Cheshunt, and scored a hat trick from centre forward. He made his first team debut against Sutton United on 3 January, and was established as the first team's left back by the end of the season. His younger brother Denis was playing for the Hendon Schools team at this time, including captaining them in the Middlesex Junior Final, which they lost 6–1 to Ealing.

In September, A.H. Elwell joined the club, but Shorland joined Wealdstone and Johnson moved to Enfield. In November, J.P. Wilton moved to Isthmian League Ilford, but the next month, there were two new recruits. Right winger T.P. Bruton joined from Cheshunt, and inside forward J. Hooper, who had played for St Albans and Tufnell Park, also came to Claremont Road.

In October, the club appointed their first professional trainer-coach, Mr W. Wilson, who had played for Notts County before the war, and had been involved as a trainer-coach with the Olympic Games.

The FA Cup qualifying rounds again provided some excitement in the early part of the season. The visit of Maidenhead United revived memories of the previous season's disastrous defeat, but this time Hampstead won 3–2, Moore getting the winner in the closing minutes in a thrilling match. Two weeks later, Bicester came to Claremont Road, having given up ground advantage. They went home with a share of a £60 'gate', but also with an 8–2 defeat, including a hat trick by Walsh and two goals from Butland. Hampstead captain and goalkeeper Sid Smith missed the game – he had been injured at work, in the machine room of *The Times* newspaper - on Friday night.

Advert for matches at Claremont Road in April 1931

In the next round, Hampstead recalled Shearcroft and Bloxham. The *Hendon Times* said that both players had been dropped from the first team many times, but remained loyal to the club. A crowd of over 2,000 saw a 2–2 draw, but Hampstead won the replay four days later 2–1 after extra time. Evans came into the team in place of Shearcroft at centre forward, and won the game with a goal five minutes from time.

Isthmian League Oxford City came to Claremont Road hoping to avenge their defeat the previous season, but this time were beaten 3–1, Gardner, Moore and Evans scoring Hampstead's goals. This meant that in the qualifying Divisional Final, Southern League professionals Guildford City stood between Hampstead and a debut in the first round proper. This was the first time the club had faced professional opposition in the competition, and Guildford proved too good - just - winning an exciting game 3–2, Evans scoring twice for Hampstead.

In the Amateur Cup, Hampstead's interest in the competition did not reach the New Year. Welton Rovers won 6–2 in the first round at Claremont Road in December. Hampstead lost Walsh with a rib injury just before half time, and Welton's goalkeeper had a brilliant game, but it was still a disappointing result.

The two Middlesex Cup competitions provided more success. In the Senior Cup, Hampstead beat Lyons 7–1, Evans scoring five goals and Enfield 4–1, with Evans scoring twice. In the semi-final, 4,000 fans saw Hampstead draw 2–2 with Barnet at Finchley; then 3,000 saw Hampstead win the replay 6–1 at Claremont Road. The *Hendon Times* said this result showed how much Hampstead had improved during the season.

Hampstead 1 Hayes 4
Middlesex Senior Cup Final at Wealdstone

The *Hendon Times* said that Hampstead did not deserve to lose by such a large margin. The match was played on Easter Monday, in front of a crowd of over 4,000. Hayes took the lead after 25 minutes through Knight, and then Lloyd scored to make the half time score 2–0. The pitch was very muddy, which restricted the play of both sides. Hampstead started the second half well, but Morgan scored again after 10 minutes.

Rowe made it 4–0, and then Morton pulled a goal back for Hampstead. Potter was badly injured 20 minutes from time, but by then the game was beyond Hampstead's reach.
Hampstead: S.R. Smith, F.H. Dean, L.H. Compton, F.G. Young, G. Bucci, W.H. Butland, W.G. Morton, C.H. Walsh, F. P. Evans, A.G. Potter, S.J. Moore.
Hayes: T. Holding, J. Maskell, H.H. Gower, E. Caesar, A. Wainwright, A. Butcher, C. Knight, R.G. Rowe, J. Morgan, T.D. Welsh, E.M. Lloyd.

Hampstead also knocked Enfield out of the Charity Cup, this time 3–1 in the first round. In the semi-final, a poor display by the forwards saw a 0–0 draw at Southall. Bucci, Evans and Walsh scored in the replay to give Hampstead a 3–1 victory and a repeat of the 1930 final against Wealdstone. The *Hendon Times* reporter said that "The best [shot] of all came from Compton from long range, and nothing would have given the onlookers greater pleasure than to have seen this promising young back find the net."

Hampstead 2 Wealdstone 3
Middlesex Charity Cup Final at Finchley

Wealdstone retained the cup with a goal in the last minute of the game. Although this was a much more respectable result for Hampstead than in the Senior Cup Final, the *Hendon Times* commented that it was a "feeble display" and that "neither side showed any brilliance".

Harry Sherman played on the right wing for Hampstead, having been playing for Bournemouth & Boscombe FC in the Football League for most of the season. Four of Hampstead's forwards were injured during the game, which did not help their cause.

Wealdstone took the lead after 15 minutes, Champion scoring from a corner. Freddie Evans equalised for Hampstead, and then had a goal disallowed. After the break, Groves put Wealdstone ahead again, but Evans equalised and Young hit the post. Bowyer won the game for Wealdstone. There had been numerous fouls during the game, and when Councillor A.T. Pike presented the cup and said that 'we have seen a very good sporting game', many fans shouted 'No, No'.

The final was Charlie Walsh's last match for the club, as he turned professional with Arsenal in the close season, subsequently joining Brentford.
Hampstead: S.R. Smith, F.H. Dean, L.H. Compton, F.G. Young, G. Bucci, W.H. Butland, F. Sherman, C.H. Walsh, F.P. Evans, W.G. Morton, S.J. Moore.
Wealdstone: F.E. Poulson, J.S. Shorland, C. Davies, C.G. Brown, C. E. Woodham, T.J. Turner, T. Maskell, E. Wilson, C. Bowyer, A.E. Champion.

In the Athenian League, Hampstead finished eighth, with 28 points from 26 matches. The season started well, with a 2–2 draw at home to Bromley followed by a 7–1 win in the return, with Moore getting a hat trick, and Evans scoring twice. This was followed by a 6–0 win over Cheshunt, with Hampstead missing two penalties. At home, Hampstead won seven out of 13 matches, but were inconsistent, with defeats by 5–0 against Walthamstow Avenue and 4–0 against Enfield. Christmas saw lots of goals, a 5–2 defeat at Wealdstone followed by a 3–0 win in the return at Claremont Road, and a 4–4 draw with Hayes two days later. Hampstead were then ninth in the league, with 10 points from 12 matches. The final position was an improvement on the previous season, and Evans had scored regularly to bolster the attack.

Overall, Hampstead played 44 matches, winning 21, drawing 9 and losing 14, scoring 125 goals but conceding 95. Hampstead failed to score in only three matches. Freddy

Young had played in every match, and the club awarded him with a gold medal to mark 150 consecutive appearances. The promotion of Dean and Compton into the first team had been successful, both players having developed through the Hendon schools team. It had been a transitional season, with some new players being introduced, and reaching two county cup finals was a good record.

At the Annual General Meeting at the end of June, it was reported that the club's financial position was not strong, due to bad weather on match days. There was discussion on the club's name, with Mr C.E. Timms saying it should be changed, as they had the name of a locality "which was a considerable distance away". He said that if the club had a local name, they would get local support. A few weeks earlier, Hendon Town FC had applied to change their name to Hendon FC.

1931–32

Three new recruits at the start of the season put Hampstead in a strong position to challenge for honours, and build on the improvement in the previous season. T. Welsh, a forward, joined from Hayes, A.R. Eagles from Civil Service FC, and B. Peck who had played for Cheshunt. Harry Sherman said he would also be available to play regularly for the club. In October, another forward, Alexander (A.D.) Buchanan, who had been playing for Thames FC in the Football League, came to Claremont Road. Welsh only stayed with Hampstead until November, when he joined Ilford, which was nearer his home. He had not been able to get a regular place in the attack, mainly due to the good form of Freddie Evans.

However, at the beginning of October, Freddy Young moved to neighbours Hendon FC. He wrote to the *Hendon Times* to explain why he had left Hampstead: "I am deeply sorry to think that after about 10 years playing I have to break faith with the Hampstead supporters, who have been as faithful to me in every way as any crowd of supporters could be. I have always done my best to give satisfaction, even to my last game for the club at Hastings [in a pre-season friendly], but evidently the selection committee – for some unknown reason – do not consider I am worth a place in the first team, or of any use to assist the reserve XI. I think I have been fair in waiting a clear month, before approaching any other club to see if I should be of any service still, but I find if I want to play (and I feel that I am far from finished) I must play elsewhere, hence I am signing for the Hendon club, to whose supporters I hope to give the same satisfaction. However, I wish the Hampstead team every success." Young had been one of the club's stalwarts for much of the 1920s, having joined as a forward in 1922, and later switched to the half-back position. In 1924–25 he scored 30 goals. He played in many Middlesex Cup finals for the team, and once for the Athenian League side.

Les Compton had successfully become established in the first team, but a professional career was clearly on the horizon. In November, the *Daily Telegraph* reported that Arsenal manager Herbert Chapman had agreed with Compton's father that he would stay with Hampstead for the rest of the season to get more experience. The report said that Mr Chapman hoped to make him an England centre half, which did happen – in 1950 – when Compton was aged 38. In January, Chapman had an article in a national newspaper when he wrote about a young amateur player on Arsenal's books who was currently playing for a London amateur club, and his concern that the player could join another club at the end of the season. It is not unreasonable to assume he was talking about Compton. Four weeks later, it was announced that Compton would be signing as a professional for Arsenal, and his last game was against St Albans on 20 February. The club made him captain as recognition of his progress at Hampstead. Two months later, he made his first team debut for Arsenal, at Aston Villa, deputising for Tom Parker, who was also a Hendon resident. Although often overshadowed by his younger brother Denis, Leslie had a good career in both professional football and cricket, where he was Middlesex's wicketkeeper for many seasons.

Hampstead lost L. Graves, who returned to live in the north in November. Near the end of the season, three new players joined: Jack Richardson, a left back from Uxbridge, A. Cole, who had played for Summerstown and was now with Columbia, and W. Minter, a veteran who had played for St Albans City, and once scored seven goals in a game.

In the FA Cup, Hampstead could not repeat the success of the previous two seasons. In the preliminary round, a 1–1 draw at Wealdstone was followed by a 5–2 win in the replay at Claremont Road, Freddie Evans scoring four goals. But two weeks later, Southall won 3–0 at Claremont Road to finish any hopes of a debut in the first round proper, and a chance to play against a Football League team.

The Amateur Cup campaign started in December. Keynsham Town, of the Bristol & District League, conceded home advantage to Hampstead, who repaid this generosity with a 7–2 win. Evans and Butland scored hat tricks, with Dean also scoring for the fourth consecutive match. Around 2,000 fans saw the match. It was 2–2 early in the second half before Hampstead took control. The *Hendon Times* said that Keynsham were one of the weakest clubs in the competition proper. But in the second round, Western League Portland United, supported by the MP for South Dorset, Lord Cranborne, drew 0–0 at Claremont Road. Extra time had been unable to provide a goal, and the sides met again the next week, Portland winning 1–0. They were undefeated at home for three years, partly, according to the *Hendon Times*, due to the slope of their pitch. Evans had missed the train from Waterloo, and had to be driven from Bournemouth, 40 miles to the ground, at speeds "not limited to 20 mph".

Hampstead had affiliated to the AFA, and were invited to enter their cup. Although some senior teams entered, many of the teams were 'Old Boys' or bank teams, below the standard of Hampstead's usual opponents. Hampstead beat Old Malvernians 5–1, Evans and Bramley scoring two goals each, then London Welsh 6–1, Evans bagging a hat trick. Two weeks later, St Albans were beaten 3–1 in Compton's last game, but then Hitchin Town won 2–0 at Claremont Road to end hopes of winning a new trophy.

The Middlesex Senior Cup provided more success. Hampstead won 5–1 at RAF (Uxbridge) in the first round, with Evans getting another hat trick, and then beat Hounslow 3–0 at Claremont Road. This produced a semi-final with Park Royal at Wealdstone. It was the first time the clubs had met in a competitive match. Park Royal won 1–0. Hampstead's forwards were disappointing, and Park Royal scored near the end to secure a final against Barnet. But the county's senior trophy still eluded Hampstead.
Hampstead: S.R. Smith, F.H. Dean, A.H. Elwell, J. Bloxham, P.A. Rees, G. Bucci, A.G. Potter, A.D. Buchanan, F.P. Evans, W.H. Butland, W. Bramley.
Park Royal: P. Bartaby, G. Clark, E. Balkwill, F. Wade, F. Mallett, W. Payne, E. Hannam, K. Davis, L. Copeland, J. Hewlett, S. Prout.

In the Middlesex Charity Cup, Hampstead had the misfortune to be drawn away to holders Wealdstone in the first round, and duly lost 6–3.

In the league, Romford replaced Cheshunt. Hampstead finished fourth, 32 points from 26 games, seven behind champions Barnet. This was a considerable improvement on the previous season, and at the beginning of January, Hampstead were top of the League. There were only two home defeats, but Hampstead were never consistent enough to challenge for the title. Evans dominated the goal scoring, and if he was missing, or off form, the attack could struggle. Hampstead scored five on four occasions, against Bromley, Enfield, Leyton and Uxbridge Town. Away from home, there were four wins, including 8–2 at Redhill at the end of the season, and 6–1 at Wealdstone on Christmas Day. Evans had a particularly good Christmas, scoring four at Wealdstone, and repeating the dose in a 4–3 win in the return on Boxing Day. He scored his 100th goal for the club in the 8–2 win at Redhill.

Compton and Evans were both selected for the Athenian League side, and Compton played for the AFA. Evans was also selected for Middlesex in the final of the Southern Counties Championship against Ilford at Essex, George Bucci being chosen as reserve.

Frank Dean was selected for the Casuals. In April, it was announced that Mr H.E. Compton – Leslie's father, would be running a junior team for the club, made up of former Hendon schoolboys.

On Easter Monday, Hampstead played Hendon at Claremont Road in a benefit match for the club's trainer, Mr Wilson. Hendon won 3–2, but Hampstead won a return match 1–0, the match being played to help Hendon's finances.

The club did not forget the social side, running a party on New Year's Eve for 45 children, followed by one for the 'grown ups'. And a new bus service to Claremont Road via The Vale helped supporters reach the ground.

The overall record was similar to the previous season, although the league position had improved. Hampstead won 22 games, drawing seven and losing 15, scoring 116 goals and conceding 81. Freddie Evans scored a remarkable 48 goals, Bill (W.H.) Butland and W. Bramley scored 13 each. The *Hendon Times* reflected that "if the attack had proved as strong as the defence, Hampstead probably would have won the League championship as well as a cup or two." Richardson had proved to be a good replacement for Compton, and Joe Bloxham had replaced Graves when he left the club. In attack, both wings had not been as strong as had been hoped, although Minter had been a good recruit towards the end of the season.

The Annual General Meeting was told that gate receipts had increased by 25 per cent to £1,539 for the season. The club were negotiating with Hendon District Council to extend the lease at Claremont Road. Improvements to Claremont Road itself, and the development of more housing near the ground had all helped increase support.

1932–33: Athenian League runners up

Hampstead continued to improve in the Athenian League, but could not win their first championship, finishing runners up to Walthamstow Avenue by just two points, with 36 points from 26 matches. Hampstead were top scorers in the League with 82 goals, an average over 3 per game, and had the second best defence, conceding 35 – less than 1.5 per game.

Hampstead kept the first team players from last season, and recruited inside right R.G. Rowe from Hayes, half back K. Tibbett from St Albans City, A. Butler from Walthamstow Avenue, and Bill (A.J.) Breagan, a right winger from Southall. However, Bill Butland left the club in the autumn to join Enfield.

The league campaign started badly, with a 3–2 defeat at Barking. Hampstead took revenge in October, with a 7–1 win in the return, one of the club's best home performances since moving to Claremont Road. Barking were soon immersed in controversy; in November 19 of their players were declared to be professionals following an FA enquiry.

Two weeks after putting seven past Barking, Hampstead won 3–0 at Barnet, beating the champions in one of their best away performances for months. E.G. Gibbs made his debut, having joined the club from Windsor & Eton.

Freddie Evans was still scoring regularly in a forward line largely rebuilt from the previous season's attack. A hat trick against Barking was followed by five against Hayes in a 6–1 win at Claremont Road. The next week, on 2 December, Hendon put six more past Sutton, Herbert Knott, a 17 year old from Goole in Yorkshire, who had played for the Arsenal 'A' team several times, marked his debut on the left wing with two goals, and making some of the others.

After a Christmas double over Wealdstone, Hampstead were second at the turn of the year, with 19 points from 13 matches. The team were unbeaten in the league since the first match at Barking.

The goals continued to flow. On 4 March, Romford left Claremont Road after a 7–1 defeat, with an Evans hat trick, two from Rowe and goals from Spalton and Knott completing the rout. But then Walthamstow won 1–0 at Claremont Road, Jim Lewis scoring the winner in the last five minutes, and then Hampstead were 'soundly beaten' 3–2 at Redhill, making it difficult to win the title.

On 8 April, struggling Bromley came to Claremont Road. All Hampstead's forwards scored in a 10–1 slaughter. Evans led the way with four, Rowe and Spalton got two each, and winger Porritt and Breagan also scored. Hampstead then did the double over Enfield at Easter, and were top of the league. But a midweek 2–1 defeat at lowly Uxbridge Town ended hopes of the title. Hampstead were unbeaten in the last four games, including a 1–0 win over Barnet, completing the 'double' over the previous season's champions.

The Reserves won the Athenian League reserve section for the first time, finishing one point clear of Sutton United. A young Denis Compton played for the reserves, scoring a couple of goals.

The cup competitions provided lots of goals and mixed fortunes. The elusive target of a first appearance in the competition proper of the FA Cup was missed again. A 6–1 win over Uxbridge Town at Claremont Road, Rowe scoring a hat trick and Evans getting two was followed by a 5–2 home win over Bicester Town. This time Evans scored three, Rowe being content with two. But then Spartan League Slough shocked a 3,000 crowd by winning 2–1 at Claremont Road.

The forwards had a rare off day in the Amateur Cup. Hampstead lost 4–0 at Barnet in the first round in December. It was the first time this season that Hampstead had failed to score.

Hampstead again entered the AFA Cup. In December, Bristol University were vanquished from Claremont Road 13–3, with Spalton scoring five times, and every forward finding the net. Then Hampstead won 6–0 at Midland Bank. No admission fee was charged, and Hampstead's supporters stood on the touchline to watch the game, as there was no stand. A 2,500 crowd saw Hampstead win 5–1 at Southern Amateur League Hastings, then Cambridge Town were beaten 4–1 at Claremont Road after a 0–0 at Cambridge.

In the semi-final, Hampstead faced St Albans City at Leyton. The forwards were 'impotent' for once and a goal after 30 minutes was enough to stop Hampstead reaching the final.

In the Middlesex Senior Cup, Hampstead lost 3–2 at Uxbridge in the first round, the winner coming in the last minute. The *Hendon Times* complained that "Hampstead have a lamentable record in knock out competitions since emerging from the junior ranks" which maybe was slightly unfair.

There was a better showing in the Middlesex Charity Cup. Southall were beaten 9–0, then Enfield 7–2, both at Claremont Road to take Hampstead into the final.

SATURDAY, MARCH 18th, 1933   Kick-off 3.15 p.m.

Hampstead v. St. Albans City
(A.F.A. CUP—SEMI-FINAL).

HAMPSTEAD
(Blue and White Hoops).

RIGHT]   GOAL   [LEFT

S. R. Smith

2 F. H. Dean   3 J. W. Richardson

4 J. W. Bloxham   5 G. Bucci   6 H. Butt

7 A. J. Breagan   8 R. G. Rowe   9 F. P. Evans   10 J. G. Spalton   11 H. Knott

Referee   O   Mr. J. C. BATTISON.

12 J. Gill   13 C. Ette   14 A. Nurton   15 C. Bunce   16 H. Figg

17 H. Williams   18 H. Runchman   19 W. Haycock

20 S. Hughes   21 R. L. Clark

22 W. C. Gatwood

LEFT]   GOAL   [RIGHT

St. ALBANS CITY
(White Shirts).

Linesmen—Messrs. A. PERRY & E. J. LE GASSICKE

Hampstead 2 Hayes 3
Middlesex Charity Cup Final

Hampstead had beaten Hayes twice in the League, but could not repeat this to win the Charity Cup at Wealdstone. Breagan scored after 10 minutes to put Hampstead ahead, and Hampstead were on top in the first half. But Hayes equalised through Flint. Porrett missed a good chance to put Hampstead ahead, and Hayes broke away to go ahead through Lethbridge, and kept their lead until half time. Groves secured the game for Hayes midway through the second half, with Hampstead unable to take advantage of playing down the slope. Rowe pulled one back for Hampstead, and Evans came close to an equaliser, but once again Hayes had frustrated Hampstead in a county cup final.
Hampstead: S.R. Smith, F.H. Dean, J.W. Richardson, J.W. Bloxham, G. Bucci, A. Broadis, A.J. Breagan, R.G. Rowe, F.P. Evans, J.G. Spalton, L.C. Porrett.
Hayes: T. Holding, J.W. Ward, W.J. Harrison, E.J. Caesar, A.W. Wainwright, G. Murphy, W. Miller, C. Lethbridge, W.C. Flint, R.C. Brown, L.G. Groves.

Overall, despite some disappointments in cup matches, it had been a successful season. Hampstead won 25 out of 43 matches, with seven draws and 11 defeats. A remarkable 157 goals were scored, and only 63 conceded. Evans was top scorer again, with 44 goals, but was better supported, with Jimmy Spalton getting 35, Rowe 30, Knott 15 and Breagan 14. The second team won 23 out of 34 matches.

The club's lease on the ground had been renewed, although without a reduction in the rent. But the population of Hendon was growing, and the club was confident of increasing its support.

In 1931, the club had discussed – and rejected – the idea of changing its name. But with the lease at Claremont Road being renewed, it was clear that the club now had few links with Hampstead. In April, the club held a meeting to discuss a new name. Hendonian FC was recommended by the committee, but this was felt to be too similar to the Old Hendonians club. Hendon Borough, Golders Green, Cricklewood and Hendon Central were all considered, and after Cricklewood was defeated, Golders Green was accepted by a substantial majority. The change was agreed at the club's AGM in June.

At Christmas, it was announced that Walter Styles, the long serving club secretary, was giving up the post as he was moving to Brighton. Former Hayes FC secretary S.D. Bradburn took over the position, but at the AGM, a proposal to confirm him in the post was rejected, and Stan Greene was chosen in his place.

The gate receipts had gone up again, and the club ended the year in a slightly stronger financial position than the previous year – a balance of £2/14/4 compared to a similar deficit the previous year. The main items of expenditure were:

Rent, rates, taxes, lighting & insurance	£329
Match expenses	£534
Groundsman's wages	£133
Entertainment tax	£239
Share of gates to opponents	£379
Repairs to stand	£63
Playing requisites	£45
Printing, posters, advertising	£123
Postage, telegrams, telephone	£35

A new name did not make the club any more attractive to the Isthmian League. The club was turned down – yet again – along with Epsom Town, Hitchin Town, Leyton, Maidenhead, Metropolitan Police and Walthamstow Avenue. Woking and Clapton were re-elected.

1933–34: Middlesex Senior Cup triumph for Golders Green

A major change occurred in the local football scene with Hendon FC not being re-elected to the London League, and withdrawing from activity for a year. The club had not been certain of renewing the lease on their Welsh Harp ground, and had provisionally withdrawn from the League. This problem seemed to be resolved, but the League said they had to seek re-election, which they did not achieve. The club had ceased playing for a season before, but this time the break was final, and a club with a history dating back to 1900, and a name to the 1880s died.

It is interesting to speculate whether the Hampstead club would have changed its name to Hendon in 1933 had the original Hendon FC collapsed a few months earlier. But there could have been no certainty that it would not arise from the ashes again, so the scenario is only conjecture.

Some of Hendon's players: A. Ellis, a right-back, A. White, a right-half, Charlie Drinkwater, a left-winger, goalkeeper Arthur (A.C.) Godding, and forwards Bramley and Lawrence joined Golders Green. But half-back Joe (J.W.) Bloxham left the club for Wealdstone. Drinkwater was selected for the Athenian League XI to play Walthamstow Avenue in the annual Champions versus the Rest of the League match. With Breagan, he signed amateur forms for Arsenal, and played in their midweek league side.

In November, three new players joined: right back D.W. Lennard who previously played for Bromley and Nunhead, Short, a centre half and former captain of St Albans City, and Leishman, an inside left who had played for Barnet.

There were changes in the cup competitions. Three seasons of poor form in the Amateur Cup was reflected in the club having to enter the qualifying competition again. The Committee also decided to enter the London Senior Cup, but pulled out of the less prestigious AFA Cup.

In the FA Cup, the team failed to emulate previous seasons with a good run, losing 4–3 at Oxford City in the preliminary round, with Spalton missing a penalty.

In the Amateur Cup, the Civil Service waived ground advantage to play at Claremont Road, and were beaten 7–3, Evans scoring four goals and Rowe two. Uxbridge and Hayes were both beaten, before 'The Green' as the team became known, lost 2–1 at Tufnell Park in the final qualifying round. The quality of the Amateur Cup at this time was shown, with an Isthmian League side playing in the qualifying competition. The London Senior Cup also bought little joy, with a 1–0 defeat at Clapton in the first round.

However, the Middlesex Senior Cup bought more success, with the club finally winning the competition. In the first round, Golders Green travelled to Waltham Cross to face Hoxton Manor, winning 1–0, then beat Southall 6–1 at Claremont Road, Evans scoring a hat-trick and having two goals disallowed.

In the semi-final, 4,000 supporters saw Golders Green beat Barnet 2–1 at Finchley to reach the final. Barnet only scored in the last minute, and the *Hendon Times* said that Barnet's attack, which included amateur international Lester Finch, "was held in a vice-like grip by a defence which was both powerful and constructive."

There was no score at half-time, but then goals from Evans and Drinkwater won the game for Golders Green. Barnet's goal came from a shot by Finch which deflected off Ellis into The Green's net. But, according to the *Hendon Times*, the best moment of the match was a 40 yard shot by Knott that hit the bar with the Barnet goalkeeper 'hopelessly beaten'. One national newspaper said that Golders Green were "probably the strongest amateur club in the country at the present time".

Golders Green: S.R. Smith, H. Ellis, J.W. Richardson, R.G. Rowe, A. Broadis, G. Bucci, A.J. Breagan, J.G. Spalton, F.P. Evans, H. Knott, C.J. Drinkwater.
Barnet: F. Painter, M. Wade, F. Garrett, A.T. Barber, A. Snaith, W. Martin, M. Marchant, W. Charlton, A. Morris, F.G. MacDonald, L. Finch.

For the final, Golders Green returned to Finchley, to face Park Royal, who had beaten them in the semi-final stage the previous season.

Golders Green 2 Park Royal 0
Middlesex Senior Cup Final

Golders Green won the Middlesex Senior Cup at Finchley in front of a crowd of 5,200 with a dramatic own goal near the end of the second half. Knott, who had been injured and was limping on the left wing, went through unchallenged while Park Royal's players appealed for offside. He sliced his shot which was going wide, but White, Park Royal's left half, thought it was going in, and in trying to clear diverted the ball into his own net.

Park Royal had lost three players to Bromley the week before the game, and their inside left, Howlett, was injured in the first half. Evans secured Golders Green's win with a second goal late in the match. The *Hendon Times* reported that the match was a poor spectacle, with both teams playing "kick and rush" in windy conditions.

The club applied for Jack Richardson to be given a medal as he had missed the final through injury. It was the first time the club had won the Middlesex Senior Cup.

Golders Green: S.R. Smith, R. Ellis, J. Weeks, R.G. Rowe, A. Broadis, G. Bucci, A.J. Breagan, J.G. Spalton, F.P. Evans, H. Knott, C. Drinkwater.

Park Royal: P. Bartaby, W. Hewlett, P. Petrie, A. Russell, R. Walker, R. White, J. Judge, C. Ette, C. Darby, J. Hewlett, G. Willshaw.

The Middlesex Charity Cup also bought success for the club. On 17 March, Enfield were beaten 4–2 at Claremont Road in the semi-final, Rowe, Knott and Evans with two scoring the goals. Hayes were their opponents in the Final at Brentford FC on 12 May.

Golders Green 1 Hayes 2
Middlesex Charity Cup Final

This was the fourth time the teams had met this season, with The Green winning the previous three encounters. Cyril Drinkwater missed the match, and Jack Weeks, who normally played at half-back or full-back, took his place. It was so hot that it was agreed that no extra time would be played if the teams were level on 90 minutes.

Golders Green had plenty of chances in the first half hour, but failed to score. There was no score at the interval, then after 20 minutes of the second half, Groves gave Hayes the lead. Knott equalised soon afterwards. Evans was injured and played on the wing. It looked as if a draw in the heat would be the result, but then Pullen scored the winner for Hayes in the last minute. The *Hendon Times* said that "For Golders Green it was a disappointing end to a successful season. Hayes certainly deserved their win, but had the match been played a month ago, Golders Green would certainly have won this cup as well as the principal county trophy."

Six coach loads of The Green's fans came to the game, including former Hampstead player George Blackburn, who had turned professional with Aston Villa in 1920.

Golders Green: S.R. Smith, R. Ellis, J.W. Richardson, R.G. Rowe, A. Broadis, G. Bucci, A.J. Breagan, J.G. Spalton, F.P. Evans, H. Knott, J. Weeks.

In the Athenian League, Golders Green finished third, with 34 points from 26 matches, seven behind champions Walthamstow Avenue. The Green scored 80 goals, and were joint top scorers with the Walthamstow club. At home, nine matches were won, including an 8–1 slaughter of Hayes. The Green were equally successfully away from home with a 9–2 win at Bromley and a 6–1 triumph at Redhill, but there were heavy defeats as well; 4–0 at Romford and 6–2 at Enfield.

The season started with two defeats against Walthamstow Avenue, 2–1 at Claremont Road and 1–0 in the return. Golders Green's first victory in the league (and any competition under the new name) was against Uxbridge at Claremont Road on 23 September. Only three more league games – all lost – were played before a Christmas double over Wealdstone signalled a return to form. Evans scored twice in the 3–2 home win on Boxing Day, and got another double against Romford on 30 December. In the first half of the season, Golders Green had played 20 games, winning 11 and drawing one. Only 46 goals had been scored compared to 93 in the first half of the previous season, but there had been some matches then against weak opposition.

But any doubts about goal scoring vanished in the next few weeks. The Green scored six at Redhill, then beat Hayes 8–1 at Claremont Road, with seven coming in the second half, Evans and Knott scoring hat tricks. The Green were now fourth in the League. At the end of January, a 4–0 defeat at Romford set back hopes of a league challenge, but on the same day, Freddie Evans made his debut for England against Wales. A 5–3 win at Hayes was followed by a 4–1 win over Barnet at Claremont Road, Rees and Drinkwater both scoring two goals in front of a 3,000 crowd.

The previous season, Bromley had let in 10 goals at Claremont Road. They had taken revenge for this humiliation with a 2–1 win in the autumn, but The Green repaid the favour with a 9–2 win at Bromley on 24 February. Knott and Breagan scored hat tricks, Evans got two and Spalton one to complete the rout.

On 10 March, Barking Town were beaten 5–0 at Claremont Road, Evans and Knott both scoring twice. The Green now had 13 wins in their last 14 games, and since losing to Southall on 9 December had scored 59 goals while conceding only 14.

The Green beat Army Wanderers 5–1 in a friendly on 24 March, with a hat-trick from Knott. In the league, Golders Green could not afford to drop a point if they were to have a chance of the league title, as Walthamstow Avenue were doing so well at the top of the table. The next two league matches with Enfield, on Good Friday and Easter Saturday finished Golders Green's title hopes. A 6–2 defeat at Southbury Road, the biggest defeat of the season, was followed by a 0–0 draw at home. A 2–0 win over Leyton on 7 April saw Golders Green third, with 27 points from 21 matches, four behind Walthamstow Avenue with a game in hand. The next week saw a 2–0 win at Barnet, the third victory over their local rivals this season. But hopes of the league title finished with a 2–2 draw at Uxbridge Town. Knott hit the post in last minute. Two 5–1 wins followed. Knott and Broadis both scored twice in a victory at Leyton, one of The Green's best displays of the season against the Amateur Cup finalists. On 28 April, Knott scored four as Sutton United were vanquished by the same score. But a 4–3 defeat in the return match at Sutton saw Golders Green finish third. A victory would have secured second place on goal average.

One important development this season was the setting up of the Supporters Association in September. A meeting was held at the Trades Hall on Cricklewood Lane, organised by Mr Bates. This led to the formation of a body that still exists today, and has played an important role in the history of the club, particularly with its fundraising and providing of volunteers for match days in recent years. Mr Bates became the secretary, and at the end of the season appealed for help from supporters in building the terracing at Claremont Road. Membership at the end of the season was nearly 300, and they had held weekly whist drives to raise funds. A meeting at the end of the season was addressed by Mr A. Williamson, secretary of the National Federation of Football Supporters Clubs. Mr Bates had become secretary, and the chairman was Mark Rutherford, a post he held until the 1960s.

Among honours won by the club's players, Freddie Evans played for England, Middlesex and the Athenian League side, and was awarded his county cap. A presentation in recognition of his achievements was made to him before the home match against Sutton United at the end of April. Jimmy Spalton and Bill Breagan played for the Athenian League against the Spartan League. The Athenians won 10–3; Breagan scored once and Spalton twice. In March, a guest player, E.L. Henry played for the reserves. He was described as the finest footballer in the Malay States, and was on a visit to England to study football.

The *Hendon Times* said that the club had made "wonderful progress" in the league after a poor start, and but for two defeats at the end of the season could have been runners-up in the League and holders of both Middlesex County cups. Herbert Knott ended up as top scorer with 36, followed by Freddie Evans with 31. The first team won 27 out of 42 matches, with three draws and 12 defeats.

The Annual General Meeting in July was told that the gate receipts had fallen to £1,268, mainly because of so many cup matches being away from home. The president, Mr Raymond, said that the rent charged by the Council was very high compared to that paid by Finchley FC, although he preferred to see "a bad balance and a good team, as was the case, rather than vice-versa."

1934–35: The FA Cup first round

The season opened on 25 August with a 3–3 draw with Hitchin Town at Claremont Road in a friendly. Five players left the club: Sid Smith went to Redhill, Jimmy Spalton to Hayes, Rowe to Uxbridge, and Ellis to Park Royal. Herbert Knott had turned professional with Arsenal and joined Margate, their nursery club. New recruits included Tommy Evans who joined from Post Office Engineers, R. White from Park Royal, K. Jones from Lincoln City and T.H. Berry from Millwall Albion. Frank (F.H.) Dean expected to return to play for the club. He had played in the first few games of the previous season. At the ground, new banking had been erected by the Supporters Association. One early season honour was Charlie Drinkwater being selected for the Athenian League team against champions Walthamstow Avenue.

On 1 September, another friendly was played at Hitchin, this time resulting in a 4–4 draw. In the league, the next week, a visit to Sutton United resulted in a 6–2 defeat. A. W. Scarboro played at inside-left and J. Long at right back. Long formerly played for Hitchin Town and was disappointing, moving to the forward line in second half. Scarboro moved to full-back in his place and also failed to come up to expectations.

Another defeat followed, 2–1 at Barnet. T.E. Edwards, who had recently been captain of Tufnell Park played at inside right, Bill (W.G.) Boston was given a trial at right back and Fred (F.S.) Boston played on the left wing. All three new players made a good contribution. White and George Bucci collided, clashed heads and White was taken to hospital. He had four stitches, but rejoined his colleagues after the game. J.P. Wilton, a former Hampstead player was playing for the reserves.

The first home league match of the season saw another defeat, 1–0 at Claremont Road against Enfield. Fred Boston stood down from the next match, at home to Redhill as he preferred to play for his works team. At last the team found some form with a 7–0 win. Edwards, Breagan and Freddie Evans each scored twice with Drinkwater adding the other goal. Sid Smith was playing in goal for Redhill against his former club and prevented them conceding double figures.

The next week saw The Green draw 3–3 with the Brigade of Guards in a friendly at Claremont Road. Clearly the team was now settling down, as four consecutive Athenian League victories followed, with home wins against Barnet and Sutton, the latter 7–1 with a hat-trick from Tommy Evans, then wins at Hayes and Enfield. After the Hayes match, Golders Green were fifth in the table with eight points from seven games. One honour for the players was that Drinkwater and Richardson were selected for Middlesex against Essex at Ilford.

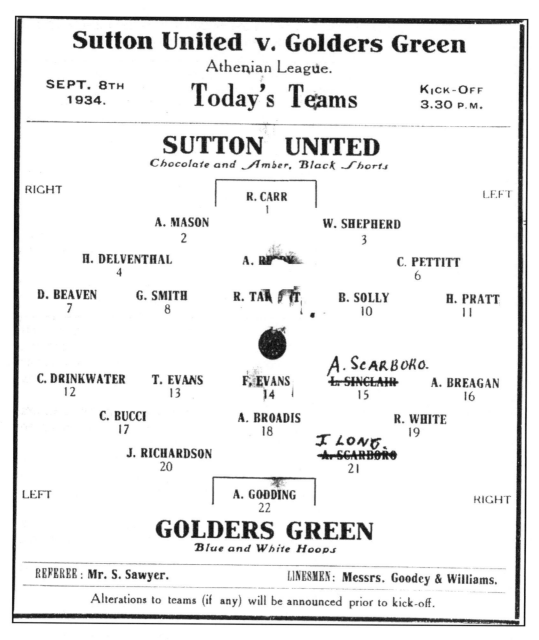

Sutton United v. Golders Green

Athenian League.

SEPT. 8TH 1934.

Today's Teams

KICK-OFF 3.30 P.M.

SUTTON UNITED
Chocolate and Amber, Black Shorts

RIGHT

LEFT

R. CARR
1

A. MASON
2

W. SHEPHERD
3

H. DELVENTHAL
4

A. R....
5

C. PETTITT
6

D. BEAVEN
7

G. SMITH
8

R. TAR.TT

B. SOLLY
10

H. PRATT
11

A. Scarboro.

C. DRINKWATER
12

T. EVANS
13

F. EVANS
14

~~L. SINCLAIR~~
15

A. BREAGAN
16

C. BUCCI
17

A. BROADIS
18

R. WHITE
19

J. Long.

J. RICHARDSON
20

~~A. SCARBORO~~
21

LEFT

A. GODDING
22

RIGHT

GOLDERS GREEN
Blue and White Hoops

REFEREE: **Mr. S. Sawyer.**   LINESMEN: **Messrs. Goodey & Williams.**

Alterations to teams (if any) will be announced prior to kick-off.

The teams from the match programme at Sutton. Golders Green lost 6–2.

The club had been given a bye to the fourth qualifying round of the FA Cup, and on 10 November drew 1–1 at Isthmian League Ilford. The home team took the lead in the first half, and Freddie Evans equalised with 20 minutes left.

Five days later, Golders Green won the replay 2–0, with Freddie Evans scoring twice. White was The Green's best player, and only a good display by Tietjen in goal for Ilford kept the score to 2–0. A 2–1 defeat at Barking Town in the league followed before

Golders Green made their long awaited debut in the FA Cup first round proper. A visit to Football League Third Division South side Southend United was a tough draw.

Southend United 10
Golders Green 1

After many years battling through the qualifying rounds of the FA Cup, often to fall at the final hurdle before reaching the competition proper with the chance to face Football League opposition, Golders Green's players and supporters must have wondered if it was all worthwhile after conceding 10 goals to Southend United.

SOUTHEND'S BIG SCORE

Golders Green Outclassed

The *Southend Times* reported that this success was "scarcely expected" and that Golders Green "are no easy opponents for any Third Division team". In the *News Chronicle*, 'Crusader' reported that Southend were "in an inspired mood" and that Golders Green were "hopelessly outclassed from the beginning... completely overwhelmed by the speed and purposeful movements of the professionals."

Southend got a penalty in the first minute, but goalkeeper Godding saved Lane's shot. The *Southend Times* said that Godding, who was on Arsenal's books as an amateur, "put on a superb exhibition [and] saved at least six certain goals.

After the penalty miss, the game was fairly even for 20 minutes. Johnson put Southend ahead, and three minutes later Cheesmur made it 2–0. A minute before half-time Deacon put the home side 3–0 up. In the second half, Carr scored a penalty on 49 minutes, and it was 8–0 when Drinkwater replied for Golders Green with 10 minutes left. But Johnson, who already had a hat-trick, scored two more in the last 10 minutes. This win is still Southend United's record score, although they did equal it in 1968 against Brentwood. The *Hendon Times* report could not recall a similar defeat for the club.

There was some compensation for Golders Green in their share of the £531 gate receipts from a crowd of 8,640.
Southend United: Moore, Morfitt, Kelly, Mackay, J. Wilson, Carr, Lane, Johnson, Cheesmur, Deacon, Oswald.
Golders Green: A.C. Godding, W.G. Boston, J.W. Richardson, R. White, A. Broadis, G. Bucci, A.J. Breagan, T.E. Edwards, F.P. Evans, T.E. Evans, C.J. Drinkwater.

The defeat at Southend seemed to knock the team's confidence for the rest of the season. However, the next week Hounslow Town were beaten 4–0 at home in the London Senior Cup, with goals from Broadis, Freddie Evans, Drinkwater and J. Edwards. Golders Green had been drawn away, but the match was switched to Claremont Road by Hounslow. The covered terracing was available for use for the first time at this match. Mr Raymond had paid for it, and it protected 1,000 people from inclement weather. It was formally opened at a 3–3 draw against Romford on 15 December. The Mayor and various councillors and aldermen attended the ceremony.

The week before, Uxbridge had drawn 2–2 at Claremont Road in the Middlesex Charity Cup. Ronnie Rowe played for Uxbridge against his old club.

On the Saturday before Christmas the club played two first team matches on the same day. In the AFA Cup one team got a 4–4 draw at Winchmore Hill, while there was also a friendly against the University Athletic Union at home. The latter match had been arranged some weeks before and presumably the club did not want to cancel it.

The now traditional clashes with Wealdstone at Christmas saw a 6–4 defeat at Lower Mead with Golders Green taking revenge with a 6–0 home win on Boxing Day. On 29 December, Winchmore Hill were beaten in the AFA Cup replay 3–1 in conditions more suitable for water polo.

It was reported that Denis Compton and Eddie Holton were playing for Nunhead. Denis was the mainstay of the Hendon Schoolboys team for sometime, and "promises to make as big a name for himself in the football world as has his brother Leslie." This proved to be correct, although he achieved more in cricket, being one of England's post-war stars and most flamboyant batsmen ever. He was on Arsenal's books, but had little chance of a first-team place at Claremont Road at this time, so moved to Nunhead.

The team's record in the first half of the season was nine wins and seven draws from 23 matches, with 65 goals scored and 55 conceded.

Two home defeats in the first two weeks of January finished any hopes of progress in the London Senior Cup and Amateur Cup. In the former, Nunhead won 3–0 at Claremont Road, and in the latter, old enemies Enfield won 2–1. Denis Compton and Eddie Holton both played for Nunhead, with Compton scoring. Both played well, and the *Hendon Times* said that Compton "was a thorn in the flesh to the defence and received a good cheer from his old-time admirers when he got the second goal." In May it was reported that he had turned professional with Arsenal, and was also on the MCC ground staff.

Writing many years later in *The Denis Compton Annual*, in a chapter titled *Football matches I will never forget*, Compton recalled this period: "Before becoming a professional I played first for Hampstead [it was actually Golders Green] but evidently they didn't think I possessed sufficient ability, for I was unable to hold a regular place in the first team. Father felt that I was destined for something better than reserve soccer, though personally I enjoyed a game whatever the standard of play. As I was on the Highbury ground-staff at the time, father approached the late Mr Herbert Chapman – then the manager – who immediately arranged for me to join the Isthmian League side, Nunhead, Arsenal's nursery club. I was put into the first team straight away. Not many weeks afterwards Nunhead were drawn away against Hampstead in the London Senior Cup... I longed to do well against my former colleagues and fortunately everything seemed to go right. Nunhead won 3–0 and I managed to score twice. I must say the Hampstead club took the defeat in the best spirit and their officials were the first to visit our dressing-room to congratulate us." Nunhead reached the semi-final, losing to the Metropolitan Police.

In the Amateur Cup, The Green's display was better than against Nunhead, but "There was again a lack of punch in the team" according to the *Hendon Times*.

It was reported that the selection committee were being 'severely criticised' after the first defeat, but said that the club had been unlucky with injuries since the Southend game. One new recruit was Joe Bloxham, who rejoined the club from Wealdstone.

By 2 February, the club had also been knocked out of the AFA Cup and the Middlesex Senior Cup. In the AFA competition, a 1–0 win at Worthing was followed by a 5–1 defeat at Harwich and Parkeston. In the Middlesex Senior Cup, London Caledonians won 4–3 at Claremont Road after extra time.

After the defeat at Harwich, of the last 14 games, four had been won and three drawn. The local paper was wondering if the club had reached rock bottom. Apparently not, as a 6–0 defeat at Romford in the league followed. It was the third time this season the team had conceded six in the League away from home, although apparently they played better than at Harwich. The Green were now ninth in the League with 13 points from 13 games. Some people felt that they were missing Breagan who had been injured at Southend. The defence continued to ship goals at Southall with a 7–3 defeat. The *Hendon Times* said that "To say Golders Green were disappointing is to put it mildly."

There was a slight improvement at Uxbridge in the Middlesex Charity Cup replay with a 2–2 draw after extra time. Some good news was that Middlesex County Council had accepted a proposal that Hendon Borough Council could reduce the rent to the club from £225 per annum to £175.

Over the years various Middlesex cricketers played for the club. Len Muncer, who was on the ground staff at Lord's, had been playing for the reserves and was selected to play against Walthamstow Avenue, although he did not actually play in the match. Golders Green drew 2–2. T. Berry, who had played for the reserves earlier in season and a few times for Tilbury, and Mike Fallon played in place of Tommy Evans and Freddie Evans. T.E. Edwards was called away to Gloucester to play for the Middlesex FA.

On 9 March, The Green drew 2–2 at Leyton. The Leyton goalkeeper was injured, and Len Muncer played. The team had not won in 1935 except in the AFA Cup match at Worthing. In another 2–2 draw, at home to Southall, T.E. Edwards and Tommy Evans played, although Freddie Evans was still missing.

On 23 March, Leyton were beaten 4–0, it was the first home win since 29 December. But the next week, The Green's last hopes of a cup success ended with a 1–0 defeat at Uxbridge in the Middlesex Charity Cup. Uxbridge scored from a corner after 30 minutes. Freddie Evans was still not available to play.

April saw some improvement in the team's fortunes. A 2–0 home win over Barking saw Golders Green eighth in the league with 20 points from 19 matches. H.P Lawrence was elected secretary of the Supporters Association. The club also announced that Bernard Joy was to play at centre half on Easter Monday. He usually played for the Casuals. He was the last amateur to play a full international for England.

The next week, The Green won 2–1 at Walthamstow Avenue. Johnny Browne made his debut aged 15 and scored. Then Uxbridge Town were beaten 6–2 at home with a hat-trick from Fallon. Golders Green were now playing better than at any time since August.

In the League Golders Green finished sixth, six points behind champions Barking, with 29 points from 26 matches. They were top scorers with 70 goals, but conceded 56. Despite the miserable mid-season run, there were only two league defeats at Claremont Road, but there were only four away victories,

The season finished with a 5–2 win in a friendly against Deerfield, the Hendon League champions. The *Hendon Times* reflected at the end of the season that the defeat at Southend "seemed to have a depressing effect on the side for some time." George Bucci and Bill Boston stood out over the season, and the team had missed Bill Breagan for several weeks through injury after the Southend match. Only 18 matches were won out of 46 played, with 13 draws. 117 goals were scored, but 107 conceded.

In June, it was reported that the supporters had started work on terracing behind the top goal at Claremont Road.

The AGM at the end of June reflected that the season had been 'patchy' although much of this was due to injuries. The meeting also agreed to reduce the size of the committee from a 'cumbersome' 20 to 11 members. A more cheerful part of the meeting was the presentation to Leslie Compton of a canteen of cutlery, as he was soon to be married.

A Golders Green hero: Freddie Evans

Freddie Evans was the second player from the club to win an England amateur cap. He played against Wales on 27 January 1934 in a 5–3 win at Bangor. He scored, but was not selected again. He was the only player to be capped while the club played under the Golders Green banner. He also played for the Middlesex County FA side, being awarded his county cap, and five times for the Athenian League side.

He originally joined Hampstead in 1926, from local junior side Burlington. However, he was unable to establish a regular first team place, and the next season joined Hendon Town. He returned to Claremont Road in January 1930, but was injured in the second half of the 1934–35 season and seems to have left the club at the end of the season. He was a prolific goal-scorer. He scored five goals in a match twice, against Lyons in 1930–31 and Hayes in 1932–33. He scored 48 goals in 1931–32, 44 in 1932–33 and 31 in 1933–34. He played in six Middlesex Cup Finals for the club, scoring four goals. Only one was won, the Middlesex Senior Cup match against Park Royal in 1934.

Freddie Evans was a key part of the club's attack in the first half of the 1930s, and one of the most prolific goal-scorers in the club's history, with 176 goals for the first team.

1935–36: London Senior Cup finalists

This season saw a recovery from the poor form of the previous year. Golders Green reached the final of the London Senior Cup for the first time, won the Middlesex Charity Cup and reached the semi-final of the Middlesex Senior Cup.

On the playing front, Johnny Browne had gone to Northfleet, Tottenham Hotspurs' nursery club, with the aim of turning professional. Fred Boston was planning to play for the club, having played occasionally the previous season.

The season opened on 31 August at Southall with a 5–2 Athenian League win. Cyril Drinkwater missed the game as he was in Birmingham having a trial with Aston Villa. Arthur Godding had lost his place in goal to David Miles, and said he was leaving the club. Despite the win at Southall, the next week a visit to Leyton ended in a 9–0 defeat, the heaviest league defeat in living memory. Leyton scored in the first minute, and it was 5–0 at half-time.

It was announced that Browne would play against Barnet, despite his plans to play for Northfleet. Maybe he made a difference, as a 2,000 crowd saw a 7–0 League win. The club had painted the roof of the new stand, which it was claimed could be seen from the North Circular Road.

Golders Green FC 1935–36: Back: Dave Walker, Jimmy Shorland, Bill Boston, David Miles, Joe Bloxham, Bert Broadis. Front: Billy Breagan, Johnny Browne, George Bucci, Tommy Evans, Fred Boston.

In the FA Cup, The Green visited Finchley and lost 3–2. Over 3,000 supporters saw Drinkwater score twice for The Green in an exciting match. But in the league, the team's form was more consistent, with a 4–1 win at Redhill and then a 5–4 victory over Hayes at Claremont Road. Walker scored two goals for the second week running in this match, which saw The Green third in the league with eight points from five matches.

Joe Bloxham and Albert Broadis were both selected for the Civil Service representative side against the Royal Navy at Portsmouth. Jimmy Shorland returned to the club from Wealdstone, but a significant loss was Cyril Drinkwater turning professional with Aston Villa.

The team's erratic form continued with a win over Bromley, with Browne scoring, a draw with Barking and then defeat at Bromley in the return. A new recruit was goalkeeper Gerry (G.L.) Kimber, who joined the club from Finchley. On 2 November, Enfield were beaten 10–1 at Claremont Road. The Green's scorers were Walker with four, Fred Boston with two, Fallon, Bloxham, Breagan and Browne. However, Enfield's goalkeeper was injured in the first half, and was replaced by Ellis, their left back.

Golders Green were now second in the Athenian League, level on points with Walthamstow Avenue, with a game in hand. But the next week, Walthamstow beat The Green 11–2, and Golders Green had now let in 33 in 10 games in the League.

The second cup match of the season saw a 1–1 draw with Finchley in the Middlesex Charity Cup. Kimber played in goal, with Jimmy Shorland at left back. Cyril Drinkwater scored a goal in his debut in the First Division for Aston Villa.

The return against Walthamstow resulted in a 5–0 defeat. New recruits included T. Goslin, from the Army. Cliff (C.V.) George, a Welsh international, who had played for Epsom & Ewell and Park Royal. J. W. Richardson was playing for Uxbridge. W. Wilson was replaced as trainer by H. Pedder from Guildford City. The club also announced that an 'A' team would be run again.

A 5–0 win against Uxbridge at Claremont Road meant that the club were the second highest scorers in the league, but they had let in 38. Browne was chosen for the Athenian League team to play the Isthmian League.

Two draws followed, at Sutton and at home to Romford, before the latter won the return 4–0. Over Christmas, there was more cheer for The Green's supporters. On Christmas Day, The Green won 6–3 at Wealdstone, with Fred Boston scoring a hat-trick, and making two others. In the return on Boxing Day, The Green won 3–1. They were now second in the League, but had played more games than the other teams. Two days later The Green won 4–1 at Hayes before starting a run of cup matches.

In the Amateur Cup, a home tie with Leyton attracted 2,500 fans to Claremont Road to see a 2–2 draw. Fred Boston scored both goals and The Green were twice ahead. In the replay, The Green won 3–0 with goals from Walker, Browne and Fred Boston before a crowd of 5,000. It was the best performance of season so far. However, it was announced that Dave Walker was leaving to play for Northfleet, the Tottenham nursery club. He had scored 20 goals this season, and the local paper said "There are scouts for professional clubs at most amateur matches and a promising player has to have a strong mind to withstand these advances."

Two weeks later, Golders Green won 2–1 at Barking in the second round with goals from Fallon and Breagan. The Green played in green, rather than usual colours of blue & white hoops. But hopes of a Wembley appearance ended in Cheshire, with a 4–2 defeat by Northwich based ICI Alkali. Duffield replaced Fallon in the Golders Green team which undermined the team understanding. This decision was made at the 11th hour. Broadis and Evans scored for Golders Green. One hundred Golders Green supporters saw a disappointing display.

The run to the final of the London Senior Cup started with a 4–0 win at London League side Leavesden. Tommy Evans got a hat-trick. This was followed in February with a 4–0 win over Isthmian League Clapton. The fog lifted just before the game. Evans scored twice, with Fallon and an own goal completing The Green's scorers. The next week, Finchley were beaten 5–2 at Claremont Road in the third round in front of a 2,500 crowd. Evans got a hat-trick, with Broadis and Fallon also scoring. The semi-final came on 10 April, Ilford were beaten 2–1 at Leyton.

Golders Green 0 Walthamstow Avenue 1
London Senior Cup Final at Ilford

The final was on 9 May at Ilford FC. Golders Green faced Walthamstow Avenue and lost 1–0 in the last minute of extra time, despite having only 10 men for most of the game. Tommy Evans was badly injured early in the game. He tried to return to play, but stood isolated on the wing, scarcely able to walk.

Hundreds of Golders Green fans had travelled to watch the game, joining a crowd of over 4,000. The Green had conceded 16 goals in two matches to Walthamstow this season, but this match was far closer.

70

The *Hendon Times* said it was "a magnificent performance" by The Green to only lose in the very last minute to a header by Collins. The Green held out, but with Fallon ineffective at centre-forward, and Evans injured, had little to offer in attack. Fred Boston had a good shot in the second half of extra time, but the match was sealed with Avenue's late winner.

Golders Green: G. L. Kimber, W. Boston, C.V. George, J. Shorland, A. Broadis, G. Bucci, A. Breagan, J. Browne, M. Fallon, T.E. Evans, F. Boston.
Walthamstow Avenue: S.A. Barlow, F.R. Hicks, E. Childs, J.W. Lewis, H.A. Oliver, C.F. Mercer, E.C. Collins, W. Magner, A. Green, V.J.L. Vincent, F.A. Davis.

In the Middlesex Senior Cup, The Green won 4–1 at Wood Green. Broadis and George missed penalties. This was followed by a 4–0 win against Wealdstone at Claremont Road, with two goals from Bill Breagan. The supporters had a collection for a wedding present for George Bucci at half-time. He had played for club for 12 years. At the wedding, the bride and groom left church through an archway of corner flags, with football boots suspended from them. A presentation was made at the club the next week. The newly weds were given a suite of furniture, although this was not actually presented to them at the ground.

But this good form could not be maintained in the Middlesex Senior Cup. In the semi-final on 7 March, Finchley won 3–1 at Claremont Road in front of over 3,000 fans.

In the Middlesex Charity Cup, The Green won 1–0 at Finchley in a first round replay, George Bucci scoring. The semi-final saw a draw at Hayes, with a 5–0 win in the replay on 25 April taking The Green into another cup final. Evans with a hat-trick and Fallon with two were the scorers. In the final, The Green faced London Caledonians at Finchley on 4 May.

Golders Green 2 London Caledonians 0
Middlesex Charity Cup Final

Goals from Broadis, with a penalty, and Fallon sealed a disappointing match for Golders Green. Bucci, George and Fred Boston played well for The Green. A large crowd saw Broadis put The Green ahead after only four minutes. Then after 15 minutes, a cross from Fred Boston was headed home by Fallon. The Green had two more goals disallowed before half time. A dull second half saw Golders Green once again win the Middlesex Charity Cup.

Golders Green: G. L. Kimber, W. Boston, C.V. George, J. Shorland, A. Broadis, G. Bucci, A. Breagan, J. Browne, M. Fallon, T.E. Evans, F. Boston.
London Caledonian: M. Best, R. Caira, D. Blair, W. Masters, J. Garden, D. Wright, A. Conners, J. Bird, R. Blair, R. Bateman, A.J. McAlpine.

On 14 February, Golders Green were second in the Athenian League, one point behind Enfield, having played one game more, with 23 points from 18 matches. They finished fifth, with 31 points from 26 matches, seven points behind champions Romford. The Green were the third highest scorers, but conceded 60 goals. The second half of the season did not really see a challenge for the top places, with eight points from the last eight matches.

The first team's record was 22 wins from 44 matches, with eight draws. 118 goals were scored, with 81 conceded. Tommy Evans was the leading goal scorer with 25, followed by Dave Walker.

On the representative front, Bill Boston and Tommy Evans were selected for Middlesex against Sussex in the Southern Counties Amateur Cup semi-final. Evans was also selected for the Athenian League team to play in Brussels on Easter Saturday. Gerry Kimber was selected by the FA for an amateur team they were sending to tour New Zealand in 1937.

One other new development was that in January, the Strollers (the third team) started playing friendlies. The club AGM in June heard that 37 young players had played for the team under the direction of Vic Rowe. Increased gate receipts meant a loss on the season of only £1/2/11 (£1.15). Mr Raymond said that the team had shown 'wonderful spirit' during the season. He said that the dressing rooms needed to be improved.

The Supporters Association had more than doubled their membership to 376, and had run coaches to all away matches except at Barnet and Finchley. They had also paid for an insurance policy to cover the club's players while playing or training.

1936–37

After the cup highlights and improved performance in the Athenian League, this was a poor season at Claremont Road. Golders Green dropped to 10th from fifth the previous season, their worst since 1927–28, with 21 points from 26 games. The team scored 58 goals, but conceded 56. The FA Cup provided some victories in the first half of the season, and the club made a further appearance in the London Challenge Cup, but a first round defeat in the Amateur Cup to London Paper Mills was very disappointing.

The poor form was more surprising as most of the previous season's squad stayed with the club. Fallon left to join Bromley, having said he intended joining Barnet. Reg Hayward joined from Spartan League Hertford. Other early signings included A. Ottaway, a 16-year-old six foot tall defender whose father had played for Southampton, a German goalkeeper from Berlin who had come to live in England, Corporal E. Mallinder of the Royal Engineers, who had played for the Army's representative team and A.R. Greig from Old Aloysians. George Bucci was named as captain for the season.

An early season honour came for Tommy Evans, who was selected for the Athenian League team to play Romford, and thus missed the first league match, a 4–0 win at Barnet. There was news of a former Golders Green player, Herbert Knott, who had left the club to join Margate, an Arsenal nursery club. He had a leg injury, which it was thought would finish career, but he had played a successful trial for Brentford, who were then in the First Division. He is in the club team photograph for that season, but never played for the first team.

The season's cup ties started on 5 September with a 9–0 victory over Bushey United at Claremont Road in the FA Cup extra preliminary round. Fred Boston got a hat-trick and Eric Duffield scored twice against weak opposition, with The Green's defence not really tested. It was announced that the club's treasurer Arthur Crawley was ill. He had been associated with club since its beginnings in 1908, and was unlikely to come to ground for a long time. Happier news was that the club's committee said that they intended to complete the covering of popular side terracing.

The early season good form continued with a 6–1 win over Southall, and then a 5–1 win over Pinner in the next round of the FA Cup. Johnny Browne and Fred Boston scored twice, with Duffield getting the third. The *Hendon Times* said that "Claremont Road was packed with a crowd of deliriously delighted fans". Pinner had waived the right to play at home.

The FA Cup campaign continued on 3 October with a 6–2 win over Barnet at Claremont Road in the first qualifying round. It was Cliff (C.V.) George's last game for the club as he was going to work in Manchester. Fred Boston and Green both scored twice in front of a 3,550 crowd. At half-time it was 2–2, with amateur international Lester Finch having played brilliantly for Barnet. But they fell apart when Golders Green went 3–2 ahead. The Green's best forward was Browne, who the *Hendon Times* described as "a brainy player who is more effective this season because he has dropped some of his embroidery work... [and] now passes the ball with more judgment and shoots more frequently."

Another big crowd came to Claremont Road two weeks later for the next round in the FA Cup to see St Albans City vanquished 4–0. A 3,000 crowd included 600 visiting supporters. Green scored a hat-trick, while St Albans performance was better than the scoreline suggested. Browne shone again for The Green. On 31 October hopes of another appearance in the first round proper ended with a 2–1 defeat at Enfield in the qualifying divisional final. Enfield were 1–0 up at half-time, Breagan equalised after 80 mins, but Enfield got the winner with three minutes left. Hayward was The Green's outstanding player, and the team were missing Tommy Evans, who was still injured.

The chance to face league opposition did not materialise in the London Challenge Cup either. On 21 September Golders Green drew 1–1 with Enfield, with Eric Duffield equalising 12 minutes into the second half. A week later, Golders Green went to Southbury Road and lost 2–0 in a very poor game. It was the first time they had failed to score that season. The prize for the winners was a home match with Brentford.

In the League, the team's promising start continued with a 5–0 thrashing of Bromley at Claremont Road. L.C. Green, formerly of Nunhead, played at centre forward. The *Hendon Times* proclaimed that the team "Have found a centre forward at last. His play was constructive and thrustful." Three Bromley players M. Fallon, F. Centa and Jack Weeks had previously played for Golders Green. But defeats followed at Bromley, then at home to Barnet and Hayes. The gloom of these defeats was lifted with a 2–0 win on 14 November over local rivals Wealdstone at Claremont Road in the Middlesex Charity Cup. Browne and Green scored in one of the best games of the season.

Inconsistent form continued, with a 6–0 defeat at Walthamstow Avenue, including two own goals, and then a 7–0 win at Uxbridge. Fred Boston got a hat-trick and Green scored twice. George Bucci sent a telegram saying that he could not play, so W. Morton, who had played for the club a few years ago, came on after 10 minutes.

A 2–2 draw at Hayes followed, with Fred Boston scoring twice. But the club received bad news when Tommy Evans had to give up playing football on medical advice. He had been to a Harley Street specialist and the local Manor House hospital.

In December, Sutton United were beaten at Claremont Road. W.T. Lawson from Cockfield was given a trial at centre forward. He had played for Willington and Cockfield in the north.

Any hopes of more success in the London Senior Cup ended in the first round just before Christmas. Leyton won 1–0 with a penalty at Claremont Road. A 1,650 crowd saw the match on a heavy pitch.

Christmas was not very cheerful for The Green's supporters, with both matches being lost to Wealdstone, 1–0 on Christmas Day, and 4–3 at home on Boxing Day, when the pitch resembled a plate of porridge.

At the end of 1936, the team had won 10 out of 21 matches, but lost nine, seven by the odd goal. The defence had kept seven clean sheets, but the attack had been weak. The club announced that Billy Blyth, 'the famous Arsenal Scottish international half-back had become an honorary vice president, and had offered 'to give the players the benefit of his wide experience with weekly lectures'.

The team's inconsistency was shown in the first match of the New Year, with an 8–0 victory over Redhill, who must have dreaded their visits to Claremont Road. Bill Breagan scored four times, Soden got a hat-trick and Reg Hayward got the other one. Sid Smith, the former Golders Green goalkeeper was in goal for Redhill. A collection was held for Joe Bloxham, who was getting married. Apart from a short spell at Wealdstone, he had played for the club since 1932.

Any hopes of progress in the Amateur Cup ended at the first hurdle, with a disastrous 3–2 defeat on 9 January in Dartford to London Paper Mills. George Bucci missed the coach as he was visiting his wife in hospital. He tried to travel by train, but couldn't get to the match. The Green took the lead early on through Browne, but were 3–1 behind early in the second half. Broadis scored, but The Green's forwards could not break down the home defence again. Undoubtedly the team missed George Bucci, but the *Hendon Times* report said that Fred Boston was given few opportunities to attack from the wing.

More bad news followed. Adding to the gloom of a home defeat against Romford was Reg Hayward breaking his leg playing for Northfleet at Folkestone. His place was taken by Bill Smellin of Tufnell Park. Three other players were also injured: Gerry Kimber, Joe Bloxham and Len Birch.

Any hopes of success in the Middlesex Senior Cup ended at Southall in the first round, with a 6–2 defeat. It was 4–0 at half-time, and the visitors were overshadowed by greater size and height of their opponents. The same opponents ended Golders Green's interest in the Middlesex Charity Cup, with a 1–0 victory on 20 February.

A return to Athenian League action on 30 January saw a 2–0 win over Uxbridge at Claremont Road. Soden and Bucci scored, but the *Hendon Times* said that the "play was still too individual in style." A tour to the Channel Islands was being planned for Easter, as the early exits from the cup competitions had left some gaps in the fixture list.

At the beginning of February The Green travelled to Beckenham for a 3–1 win in an unusual friendly with Lloyds Bank. One new recruit was A.C. Huggins, a left-back who had played for Ilford and Kingstonian.

The team continued to drift in the league, with two defeats against Barking in February. After the first, a 3–2 home loss, the *Hendon Times* said that they had a "Good deal of misfortune through injuries, fundamentally, the team is sound, so that if only they would use tactical thought combined with first time kicking, they could win."

The problems at the club were exacerbated at the end of February when Albert Broadis and Bill Boston announced their resignations. The club committee refused to comment. Team captain George Bucci said that "it was a great pity" that the two players had left. There was criticism of the club committee in the local paper. The Supporters Association said that the resignations would hit the club's attendances.

Further defeats at Romford and Southall followed. The team were now in ninth place in the league. But on 20 March a 2–1 win over Spurs 'A' team revived the club's spirits. Johnny Hill and F. Alaway were lent to Spurs for the match. It was the best performance by the team since Christmas. Browne and Bucci scored. Bill Boston played to mark his return to the club.

The tour to the Channel Islands was a break from the league action, with a 2–0 defeat to a Guernsey Island Representative XI, a 1–0 win over Guernsey Island, with a goal from Soden two minutes from time and a 2–2 draw with a Jersey Island XI, Bloxham and Soden scoring.

In the league, there was a slight improvement with draws at Sutton and at home to Enfield. The team were not in danger of finishing in the bottom two and having to face re-election. Further defeats followed at Enfield and Redhill. It was announced that Uxbridge were resigning from the league due to difficulties with their ground. On 23 April, The Green drew 3–3 with Walthamstow Avenue at Claremont Road. The performance was better than for some time, although the visitors played five reserves, as they had players missing due to a tour to Australia. Then on 28 April, Golders Green beat Leyton at Claremont Road, their first league win since 30 January. A draw at Leyton the next day meant a final league place of 10th, with 21 points from 26 matches, from eight wins and five draws.

The season ended with a 2–1 victory over London Caledonians in a friendly. Two bright points at the end of the season were the Middlesex Charity Cup Final being played at Claremont Road, Southall beating Finchley 2–1; and Golders Green winning a six-a-side competition at Finchley FC, beating Barnet 6–2 in the final.

Despite the disappointing season, some players still won representative honours. Gerry Kimber and Johnny Browne played for Middlesex and the Athenian League side. Broadis and Fred Boston were also chosen for the county team.

One change at the club's AGM was the departure of treasurer Arthur Crawley, who had served the club for 29 years, but stood down through ill health. The question of having a professional trainer was raised, but the meeting decided to continue with trainers for each team and Billy Blyth as honorary coach.

The Supporters Association AGM looked back on a successful season for the association, with a growth in membership, and that they had built a new headquarters. Their treasurer, Jack Innes was resigning as he had been appointed as the club's treasurer. The Association was taking responsibility for the club's programme, and expected to sell 50,000 during the forthcoming season.

1937–38: Another Middlesex Charity Cup Final

This season saw a revival in the club's fortunes, with another appearance in the Middlesex Charity Cup Final, and a climb up the league table to fifth place.

Albert Broadis returned to the club, along with Reg Hayward, who had recovered from his broken leg. New recruits included Peter (P.S.) Leahy, a Welsh international right winger from Southall; Dave (D.C.) Walker, who had played for the club in 1935–36, before joining Northfleet and then Romford and A.H. Snazel, who came from Finchley FC. H. Preston was another new recruit.

The club also announced that, despite the decision at the AGM in July, Bertie Smith was to be a professional trainer-coach. He had played for Huddersfield, Bradford City and Bournemouth. The *Hendon Times* said that "There is gradually making itself felt throughout the club a new atmosphere of confidence, fellowship and goodwill, which does so much to inculcate the team spirit and will to win and which appeared so lacking in the closing weeks of last season."

The season started with a 3–2 league defeat at Tooting & Mitcham. The first win came against Southall at Claremont Road, where Dave Walker was a 'steadying influence' at centre-forward in a 4–2 triumph. Three days later, Hayes were beaten at Claremont Road by the same score. Fred Boston got a hat-trick, but the referee had to intervene several times in incidents between players. Southall got revenge in the return match with a 1–0 win, J. Jacobs playing in goal for The Green, replacing Hill who had been injured against Hayes. A more promising result was a 4–4 draw at high-flying Walthamstow Avenue in front of a crowd of over 3,000.

The first cup campaign of the season was in the FA Cup. Northmet were beaten 3–1 at Claremont Road in the preliminary round, with goals from Walker, Broadis and Soden. But on 2 October, the best crowd of the season so far saw Enfield win at Claremont Road, with Broadis scoring for The Green. One new arrival was goalkeeper Stan (S.A.) Barlow from Walthamstow Avenue.

In the league, on 25 September the team lost 5–2 at Romford. The match included three penalties. One went to Golders Green, Broadis scoring. Two draws followed, at Sutton and at home to Walthamstow Avenue. After this game, The Green were sixth, with seven points from eight games. A win over Romford at Claremont Road in 'shocking conditions' with driving rain and high wind was followed by another at Leyton. This was the club's first visit to Leyton's new ground on Lea Bridge Road, which had formerly been used by Clapton Orient. Another player tempted by the professional game was Fred Boston, who signed amateur forms for Chelsea. He celebrated by scoring twice against Bromley in a 5–0 win at Claremont Road. Two draws with Barking were followed by a defeat at Barnet. Middlesex cricketer Harry Sharp was playing regularly at this time.

The enthusiasm for football and the club was shown when over 200 supporters attended a meeting and film show on a Tuesday on 23 November. The team's trainer, Bertie Smith explained the side's tactics, including the role of the full-backs in starting attacks. The film show included Middlesex Wanderers matches, and the previous Christmas encounter between Wealdstone and Golders Green. The evening finished with a talk from George Allison, the Arsenal secretary-manager. He outlined various plans for players in defence and attack, and hoped that he would be able to assist Golders Green in the future.

Cup ties returned with a 4–0 win over London Caledonians in the Middlesex Charity Cup. But the match was abandoned six minutes from time, having been played in a blinding snow storm. There were requests from the Caledonian players for the abandonment after the fourth goal, and they accepted the result, but the Middlesex FA decided that the match had to be replayed. It was reported that "Conditions were so bad that anything might have happened."

Ron Graves came into the problematic centre-forward role against Barnet on 11 December. The Green won the local derby 4–2 at Claremont Road. The club launched an appeal to build an extension to the covered area on the popular side.

The week before Christmas a 4–1 defeat at Nunhead ended The Green's interest in the London Senior Cup. Ward scored and Barlow injured his shoulder. There was little cheer for Golders Green supporters at Christmas, with a 4–1 defeat at Wealdstone on Christmas Day. George Bucci returned from injury for the return match two days later, which was a draw.

The New Year opened with a thrilling 5–4 win over Sutton United at Claremont Road. The team was showing 'much improved form' and were fourth in the Athenian League, with 20 points from 18 games, six behind Walthamstow Avenue, who were top with 26 from 15 games. The good form continued with a 3–0 win at Redhill, Ron Graves scoring twice. After 20 matches, Golders Green had won seven, drawn seven and lost six, scoring 49 goals with 42 conceded, excluding the 'win' over London Caledonian. Already the team had one more point than the whole of the previous season.

In the Amateur Cup, a 'huge crowd' saw Barking beaten 2–1 at Claremont Road, Fred Boston and Graves scoring for The Green. Barking took the lead after 15 minutes, Boston equalised in the second half, and Graves scored the winner in extra time. But hopes of further progress in the cup ended on 5 February, when Leyton won 2–0 at Claremont Road in front of a crowd of over 4,000. Former Golders Green player Snazel scored for Leyton. The *Hendon Times* said that "Golders Green had an off day. There was lamentable weakness in attack and the defence should have put up a stronger show than they did."

Between the two Amateur Cup matches, Hayes won 2–1 at Claremont Road to end The Green's interest in the Middlesex Senior Cup. Fred Boston scored, but Hayes netted twice near the end.

In the league, a home defeat against Redhill was followed by a great 6–3 win at local rivals Enfield. Sexton got a hat-trick, Walker scored twice and new signing, inside left William 'Tagge' Webster scored. The latter had played for Cambridge University, Corinthians and the England amateur international team, and later became president of the MCC in 1977 and Middlesex CCC in 1980. He was also member of the FA Council, and chaired the finance committee for 12 years. At cricket, he played 45 first class games for Middlesex. Brian Sexton, a former Colchester Town player, was also making his debut. At centre-half was A.S. Peverell, who had been playing for the 'A' team. His progress in the first team was stopped when he broke his ankle later in the season.

At the end of January, Dave Walker had come close to moving to Wealdstone, but had changed his mind. The transfer forms had not been signed and he decided to stay at Claremont Road. Two players who did leave were Albert Broadis – again – and Johnny Browne, who both joined Finchley.

London Caledonians returned to Claremont Road to 'replay' their Middlesex Charity Cup match. The Green won again, 4–2 this time, with two goals from Dave Walker and one each by Fred Boston and Jerry Marrable.

Walker again scored twice in a 2–0 win against Tooting & Mitcham. The local paper noted that left-back Tommy Caswell had "improved wonderfully this season".

With few cup matches, friendlies were again arranged. In March, Chelsea 'A' were beaten 1–0 at Claremont Road. Johnny Browne played as Finchley had no game. The covered stand extension fund had now raised £30, which would be matched by Mr A. Gordon Raymond.

On 12 March, a Middlesex Senior Cup semi-final was played at Claremont Road. Wealdstone beat Uxbridge 6–0. The next week, Golders Green won a far closer semi-final in the Middlesex Charity Cup, winning 2–1 at Finchley with goals from Breagan and Fred Boston. A crowd of over 2,000 saw The Green clinch their win in the second half after the teams had been drawing 1–1 at the break.

Spurs 'A' team returned for a friendly, and lost 1–0. £136 was needed to extend popular side cover; the total was now £70. Another professional club's 'A' team came to Claremont Road the next week, The Green beating Fulham 4–1.

League action returned with two defeats, 4–2 at home to Leyton, then 6–0 at Hayes on Good Friday. Enfield were beaten 3–0 at Claremont Road on Easter Saturday in the final Athenian League match of the season. On the bank holiday Monday, Army Wanderers won 6–1 at Claremont Road in yet another friendly match.

While Golders Green were winning a friendly 3–2 at Isthmian League Oxford City, a crowd of nearly 3,000 saw the Middlesex Senior Cup Final at Claremont Road. Wealdstone beat Tufnell Park 5–1.

On 27 April, the famous Casuals came to Claremont Road in the Will Mather Cup and won 3–0. This cup continued to be played for against various opponents until the 1960s. Its formal title was the Golders Green Hospitals Cup for Manor House. It was presented by Mr Will Mather, who presented the cup to the Casuals captain.

One cup that did come to Claremont Road was the AFA Junior Cup. The Green's reserves won the final at Eastbourne, beating Hastings & St Leonards Reserves 2–0. It was the first time the club had won this competition.

Some familiar names returned to Claremont Road on 4 May, when the Present team beat a Past team 6–2. The match raised money for the ground improvement fund. Prolific scorer from the early 1930s, Freddie Evans, played for the Past team. The referee was former player Tommy Evans, and Arsenal player and former Hampstead star Leslie Compton ran the line.

Wealdstone 4 Golders Green 0
Middlesex Charity Cup Final

The season ended on 14 May. The match was closer than the score showed. The half-time score was 2–0, and The Green were hit by an injury to Marsden, who had to move to the wing. Graves played very well at centre-half, and provided some resistance to a Wealdstone team who were "certainly more clever" than the Golders Green team.

Potts gave Wealdstone the lead on 10 minutes. Dyke added a second and Wealdstone came close to increasing their lead before half-time. Morriss scored for Wealdstone after the break, and their final goal was a penalty by Ellis, who had been fouled by Pidgeon.

Golders Green: S.A. Barlow, T. Caswell, W. Pidgeon, G. Bucci, R. Graves, F. Davis, A.G. Breagan, R. Marsden, J. Lambie, D. Walker, F. Boston.
Wealdstone: R. Lewis, A.W. Loveday, R. Ellis, W.F. Showler, S. Friday, D. Scott, C. Brown, H. Dyke, T. Morriss, J. Wilson, K. Potts.

In the Middlesex Intermediate Cup, Golders Green Reserves lost the final 3–1 in a replay to Yiewsley.

Loyal servant George Bucci marked 15 years for the club at the end of the season. He also played for Arsenal and Watford's reserve teams. He had played in practically every position for the first team.

On the goal-scoring front, only two players reached double figures. Dave Walker got 19, including two in friendlies, and Fred Boston contributed 16. Various players won representative honours. In March, Fred Boston was a reserve for the England Amateur team in their trip north of the border to face Scotland. Bill and Fred Boston won their county caps for Middlesex, which were awarded after seven appearances for the county side. Johnny Browne, before his move to Finchley, and Dave Walker also played for the Middlesex team. Dave Walker and Fred Boston played for the Athenian League team.

The club's AGM at the end of June took the historic decision by 36 votes to 21 to change the club's colours to green shirts, with white collars and cuffs. The club's colours until this time were blue and white. There was much debate, and when the vote was announced, there was a shout of "most of the players against".

The meeting heard that there had been a loss of £40 for the year, reflecting the lack of progress in the major cup competitions. The team had improved, but once again injuries had held back their development. It was the club's 30th anniversary, and there had been huge progress from being a junior church-based side in Hampstead in 1908.

After the AGM, there was also discussion with the Hendon Borough Council about the future of the ground. There were two proposals – to improve the stand, dressing rooms and pitch drainage at a cost of £5,000; or to move to a new site at Highfield Avenue off Hendon Way. The Council meeting agreed to ask the borough treasurer to report on both schemes.

1938–39: Middlesex Senior Cup winners

This was the club's 21st consecutive season in the Athenian League, including the abandoned season in 1914-15, and their last before the Second World War. At the end of the season, Barnet had competed for 23 seasons in the Athenian League, followed by Golders Green, Bromley and Southall who had all been members for 21 seasons.

Apart from welcoming the new club colours, supporters' enjoyment of matches at Claremont Road was increased by the introduction of a loudspeaker system for announcements and music. On the pitch, new arrivals included a centre-forward, C.V. Lewin and C.J. Donovan from Harwich & Parkeston.

The season opened with a home league match against Tooting & Mitcham, which was lost 3–1. Fred Boston missed the game as he was playing for the Athenian League side against the champions.

The cup campaign opened with a visit from Pinner in the FA Cup preliminary round. R.H. Brown, a new recruit from Hayes, made his debut in a 4–1 victory. Two weeks later, in the preliminary round, Golders Green won 1–0 at Tufnell Park, with a goal from Lewin. In goal for Tufnell Park was Reg Hill. The *Hendon Times* looked at a Golders Green team from September 1937. The only players from that side still with the club were the Boston brothers, with George Bucci now playing for the reserves. A 3,000 crowd saw Wealdstone draw 0–0 at Claremont Road in the first qualifying round. In the replay, Breagan and Fred Boston scored to take The Green through 2–1, with Boston's winner coming seven minutes from time. Fred Davis had been called up to the armed forces and missed the match, a sign of things to come.

Two weeks later, there was another FA Cup local derby against Barnet. In front of a 5,000 Claremont Road crowd, The Green were 2–0 down in the first half. Breagan replied, then Coppola equalised before Long scored the winner 10 minutes from time. Hopes were building of another appearance in the first round proper, but on 29 October, Golders Green lost 2–1 at Spartan League Apsley in the Qualifying Divisional Final. Graves scored for The Green. The *Hendon Times* reported that the pitch had a steep slope sideways, but that could not be blamed for the defeat. The wing halves were weak and the defence not strong enough.

In the league, only two of the next six matches were won, at Tooting and at home to Southall. After losing at home to Barnet, Golders Green were ninth in the table. After another defeat the next week, 2–1 at Southall, the *Hendon Times* pointed out that the first team had scored 18 goals in 13 games, but the reserves had scored 37 in only 12, and that it would be worth trying some of the reserves in the first team.

On 19 November, Barking won 4–0 at Claremont Road. The team changes introduced by the committee had not worked. It was the poorest display of the season, and was followed by a 5–1 defeat at Enfield in the Middlesex Charity Cup, the fifth defeat in succession.

On 3 December there was an official visit to the club by the Mayor of Hendon Councillor H.G. Potter. He spoke about the Christmas Appeal for distressed families, and kicked off the game. In a change of fortune Golders Green beat Redhill 3–1. Three new recruits made their debuts: A. Lovell, from Southall, L.A. Ellison from Barnet and Ted (E. M.) Owen, a Welsh junior international who had played for Bangor City. Another new arrival was E. Pomfrey from St Albans City. On the same day, the reserves drew with Kenilworth in AFA Junior Cup 6–6 after being 5–1 up.

A 3–1 league defeat at Romford was followed by a 3–1 first round exit in the London Senior Cup at Hayes. Coppola scored for Golders Green. Claremont Road was now being used by Tufnell Park for their matches, as their ground was covered in ARP (Air Raid Precaution) trenches. A. Lowry, a former Leytonstone centre-forward and W.S. Cosker, a former Blyth Spartans centre half were having trials for the 'A' team.

There was more gloom when all the Christmas games were cancelled as the grounds were under nine inches of snow. Supporters had been looking forward to the traditional battles with Wealdstone and a friendly against Fulham.

The weather had improved by New Year's Eve when Golders Green beat Leyton 4–2 at Claremont Road. It was an action packed second half as the half-time score was 0–0. But any hopes of a revival of form were dashed when Walthamstow Avenue won 5–0 at Claremont Road. The Golders Green team was:

S.A. Barlow, W. Boston, T. Caswell, A. Lovell, R. Graves, G. Bucci, A. J. Breagan, L.A. Ellison, R. Thomas, A. Wilson, F. Boston.

The Amateur Cup brought some cheer to the club. In the first round, a 0–0 draw away to London Caledonians, at a large, gloomy ground with few spectators, fog and failing light was followed by a 2–0 win in the replay. Lovell was The Green's star player, with second-half goals from Breagan and Thomas clinching the match.

Two weeks later, Golders Green beat Southwick 2–1 after extra time at Claremont Road, after being behind at half-time. Breagan equalised and Fred Boston scored the winner. In the third round, Golders Green faced a difficult trip to Sutton. The pitch was 'a shining sea of mud'. Graves and Thomas scored for The Green, but the home team won 4–2 after extra time.

Once again the Middlesex Senior Cup was the club's best hope of cup glory. In the first round, a 1–1 draw with Hayes at Claremont Road was followed by a 1–0 win in the replay. This was followed by a 4–0 win over Hoxton Manor at home. Both Boston brothers scored, along with George Bucci and Ellison. On 25 March, Finchley came to Claremont Road for the semi-final. Golders Green won 3–1 after being 1–0 behind with 30 minutes left. The game was played in high wind, hail and snow. Thomas, Breagan and Ellison scored the goals that clinched another County Cup final.

On 4 March there was a break from first team action as Claremont Road staged the South versus North schoolboy trial. The South won 6–1. Golders Green were ninth in the Athenian League with 10 points from 13 games, having scored 16 goals and conceded 28. The team's league form continued to be inconsistent, with a home draw with

Wealdstone followed by defeat in the return match. On Good Friday, Golders Green drew 3–3 at Enfield, but won the return the next day. On Easter Monday, 10 April, Golders Green faced Wealdstone again in the Middlesex Senior Cup Final at Finchley. Last season The Green had lost the Charity Cup final 4–0 to their old rivals. Could they now take revenge?

Golders Green 4 Wealdstone 0
Middlesex Senior Cup Final

Golders Green were "easy and worthy winners" of this match at Finchley against local rivals Wealdstone. Veteran George Bucci was their best player. Fred Boston gave The Green the lead after 11 minutes with a great cross shot. Ellison then scored following a free-kick to make it 2–0 on 15 minutes. Breagan made it 3–0 on 33 minutes, and three minutes later Thomas made the score 4–0. Golders Green had been playing up the slope, therefore there was little chance of Wealdstone recovering. A crowd of 4,000 watched the match.

Golders Green: S.A. Barlow, W. Boston, T. Caswell, A. Lovell, R. Graves, G. Bucci, A.J. Breagan, L. Ellison, R. Thomas, E.M. Owen, F. Boston
Wealdstone: R. Lewis, A. Loveday, R. Ellis, L. Green, S. Friday, D. Scott, C. Brown, K. Baldwin, C. Bunce, G. Gaze, C. Barker.

In the league, Sutton United were beaten at Claremont Road. Roy Evans played for Golders Green, he had not been eligible for the Middlesex Senior Cup matches. The team had improved since Christmas, winning nine and drawing five out of 17 matches. In the Middlesex Senior Cup they had scored 13 goals and only conceded two. They hoped to climb the table in the last few weeks of the season.

However, fixture congestion finished any hopes of a challenge for the top positions in the table. A run of six games in eight days saw only one victory – 2–1 at Hayes when Ron Graves had to play in goal as John Jacobs did not arrive at the match. The final position in the league was eighth, with 24 points from 26 games. Again the attack was the weakness, with only 42 goals scored, compared to 57 conceded.

There were two end of season matches in the Will Mather Cup. A small crowd saw Casuals win 2–0 at Claremont Road in one of the best matches of the season. The season finished on 13 May at Barnet, with a 4–2 defeat.

Towards the end of the season Bob Thomas was fined 2 guineas by the FA after being sent off at Wealdstone on 1 April. A letter of protest was sent by H.P. Lawrence, the club's press secretary.

The *Ham & High* said that "If Golders Green had played in first half of season as well as they have in this latter half, they would have finished well in the top half of the Athenian League. Much of The Greens improvement is noticeably due to the introduction of Thomas, Ellison, Lovell and Owen. I consider Lovell has had the greatest effect; he has put that punch into the half-back line without which the forward line would have failed to function with any success. I must mention that... George Bucci, (may he never grow old) will not play again this season – his cut forehead necessitating his retirement."

The writer continued the following week: "The team has chopped and changed considerably. Barlow, Bill Boston, Tommy Caswell and Ron Graves have, apart from injuries, been ever present... Barlow is equal to any goalkeeper in amateur soccer on his day. Bill Boston has had few lapses from form and his turn of speed still surprises many an unwary forward, Tommy Caswell, after a shaky start… settled down to a safe, if not spectacular game. Skipper Graves has played himself into the centre half position for the rest of his days, apart from a tendency to dribble in front of goal (a relic of his forwards days?) he is as good a centre half as The Green are likely to have for many days.

In the wing half positions we have seen Donovan, Davis, Bucci, Ward, Lovell, Button and even Breagan and R.H. Brown (now departed). Donovan [was] a great disappointment… Fred Davis had the misfortune to be dropped before he could settle down, Bucci… settled down to play like a brilliant schoolboy. Button made a brilliant debut, Ralph Ward started well, but he did not appear to be fit…

Fred Boston, Fred Long, Billy Breagan, R.H. Brown, Lewin, Coppola, Johnnie Hill, Davis, Morgan, Owens, Ellison, Thomas, Pinkham, Evans, Marcantonio – it seems a never-ending list yet all these people have played in the forward line this season. Boston had an unaccountable loss of form …he is now shooting as well as ever. Long deputised for him exceedingly well on occasions, R.H. Brown had a touch of class, which unfortunately, he knew only too well and consequently there was little sighing when he [left], Bill Breagan gave his 90-minute non-stop act every week and was a revelation at inside-right; Lewin came with a reputation, but was knocked off the ball too easily, Coppola came from Fairey Aviation FC as a goal getter… Johnnie Hill I personally rate, Morgan is young enough to do well, unless he grows lazy with age; Ellison is fast, Thomas is a centre forward and The Green have needed him for a long time. Evans's midfield play improved. Maracantonio is not quite good enough these days. If The Green can keep this team together, they should finish much higher in the table next year."

Of 45 matches, 19 were won and nine drawn. Thomas was top scorer with 17 goals, Breagan got 15, Ellison 11 and Fred Boston 10.

The ground now held 4,000 under cover. Mr Raymond said that the target of the Athenian League title was possible. However, Bob Thomas had turned professional with Brentford and would need to be replaced. Dominic Bucci, after 32 years service to the club, had been elected as an honorary life vice-president. All the players except Thomas had rejoined. Jack Innes, the treasurer reported a profit of £3 2s 11d, compared with loss of £40 the previous season. However, gate receipts were down £200. Bill and Fred Boston, Graves and Brown had all played for Middlesex.

The club was clearly now established as a force in amateur football, ready to challenge for the Athenian League title and the Amateur Cup. But world events would intervene, and it would be six years before these challenges could be resumed.

4. 1939 to 1945: The War Years

1939–40

In the summer of 1939, war clouds were gathering over Europe as the international situation became more serious. But the club continued its pre-season preparations as usual, as occurred throughout football. Local rivals Finchley were rejoining the Athenian League after a long spell in the London League. New players included A. Wright, a centre-forward who had previously played for Enfield, and Roy Stroud, who was on Arsenal's books, and had played in a schoolboy international trial the previous season. In the club's trial match on 18 August, other newcomers included former Barnet goalkeeper W. Painter, John Griggs who had scored 40 goals in junior football, and A. Page, a left winger from Woodford Town. However, Lewin left the club to join Tufnell Park.

The club had been trying to persuade the London Transport Passenger Board to run a bus up Claremont Road for supporters on match days, but their request had been refused. It was not until the late 1970s that this battle was won, with a bus route that served the Brent Cross Shopping Centre on the other side of the North Circular Road.

The club's ground facilities were being improved, and it was announced that the covered area on the popular side would be opened on 9 September. In fact, due to the war, the stand was finally opened in 1946.

During the war and the Blitz, the area was extensively bombed, but not as badly as central London. Both the industrial areas along the Edgware Road and residential areas were affected. The worst incident was in February 1941, when 80 people were killed and 1,500 made homeless in a rocket attack on West Hendon.

Athenian League abandoned

Golders Green had played two matches when the Athenian League was abandoned when war was declared on 3 September 1939. There had been one win and one draw, Golders Green were fourth in the table with three points. They had beaten Barnet at home 6–4, with Barnet scoring three goals in the last seven minutes. Brothers Bill and Fred Boston played at full-back in that game. The team also drew 0–0 at Southall. On Saturday 2 September, as they were not involved in the FA Cup extra-preliminary round, the club arranged a friendly at Hastings & St Leonards. However, this was cancelled due to transport problems. The reserve team played at Claremont Road, and the club expected this to be their last match for some time to come.

On Friday 8 September, five days after war had been declared, the Football Association suspended all football it controlled. Only games involving the Army were allowed. However, 15 days later, there was a partial lifting of the suspension, although no competitive games were allowed. Matches were allowed in non-evacuation areas, and the club's committee met on 16 September to decide what to do.

Amateur clubs north of the Thames were allowed to organise competitive football on a regional basis, limiting journeys to save fuel. There was a meeting of teams in the north-west and west areas of London and the home counties to arrange a fixture bureau to have matches among themselves. As well as Golders Green, Barnet, Enfield, Finchley, Hertford Town, Hitchin Town, St Albans City, Southall and Wealdstone participated. On 23 September Golders Green played a friendly at Wealdstone, losing 2–1. Ward scored for The Green, and J. Cochrane, the son of a former Sunderland manager, made his debut. The match was played with the 'dash and enthusiasm of a cup tie', and members of HM Forces in uniform were admitted for half price.

The next week, another friendly was arranged, Hertford Town being beaten 3–2 at Claremont Road, Graves scoring a hat-trick. The club hoped that Jack Weeks, who had played for the club before the war at centre-half, as well as playing for Bromley would play. The club had only one team running, but hoped to have a reserve team. Reflecting the problems the club faced, it decided that everyone as far as possible would get a game, with some players standing down if necessary. Wealdstone withdrew from the fixture bureau, and were replaced by Tufnell Park. Their ground was unavailable, so it was agreed that they would share Claremont Road for the duration of the War. Their secretary was former Hampstead goalkeeper Cyril Evans.

From the beginning of October, the clubs involved in the fixture bureau formed the Herts & Middlesex Combination, which the next season was renamed as the Herts & Middlesex League. This was the league that sustained the club during the war years.

However, a note of caution should be raised about the importance of results and league tables in war-time football. The main aim seems to have been to provide entertainment for the public and a game for the players. Some club suspended activities altogether, and obviously the needs of the forces, war-time production and the blitz on London all affected the club's activity. Also, rationing gradually got more severe as the war went on, for example from 1942 no petrol was available for private motorists. It is to the club's credit that they kept going, but the results were almost secondary to providing public entertainment to keep morale high. However, the war period did include the club's first Wembley final, and the establishment of players such as Bill Fisher, Laurie Topp and Roy Stroud.

Golders Green made a great start in the new league, which had 10 clubs competing, winning 5–2 at Hertford Town on 7 October. This was followed by two draws with Southall, Len Bustard playing in the first match. On 28 October, Hitchin Town won 7–3 at Claremont Road. The game kicked off 30 minutes late, and the few supporters present who had braved the bad weather were entertained by the Childs Hill band. The next week, in the return match at Hitchin, a depleted Golders Green side lost 14–2. Barlow and Painter could not play, and The Green had a replacement goalkeeper. Bustard and Lovell scored for The Green.

Two wins over Enfield, with W.E. Barnes keeping goal in the second, were followed by two defeats against Finchley. On 9 December, Tufnell Park were beaten 4–3 at Claremont Road. Hart played in goal for The Green, and it was announced that Bustard had joined Tufnell Park. The next Saturday, 16 December, Golders Green made the short trip to Colindale to face the Metropolitan Police, and lost 3–0. The ground was next to the RAF base, and the *Ham & High* report said that the ground was not suitable for senior football, and the game was interrupted by the continual zoom of aeroplanes that were so low that a skied ball could have hit one of the wings.

Over Christmas, two friendlies were played with Wealdstone. Golders Green lost both: 2–1 away on Christmas Day morning and 4–2 at Claremont Road on Boxing Day. Bustard had returned to the club from Tufnell Park. On the last Saturday of 1939, Barnet won 4–1 at Claremont Road in the league in arctic conditions. Very few people watched the game, which was played 35 minutes each way, with no half-time break.

The bad weather continued, and only one game was possible in January, Tufnell Park being beaten 3–1 in the Middlesex Red Cross Cup, H.V. Tomlinson scoring a hat-trick. This competition replaced the Middlesex Charity Cup during the war.

Only one league match was played in February, Hertford Town being beaten 9–0 at Claremont Road. Hertford had a weakened side, and Golders Green lent them H.T. Martinson. The 14-year-old Roy Stroud played well for The Green. The next week, on 17 February, Golders Green lost 3–1 at Walthamstow Avenue in the London Senior Cup. But seven days later, Southall were beaten 7–3 at Claremont Road in the Middlesex Red Cross Cup. Victories over Tufnell Park and St Albans followed in the league, and then Hayes were beaten 2–1 in the Middlesex Red Cross Cup semi-final at Claremont Road. Tomlinson put The Green ahead after 22 minutes, and Breagan made it 2–0 after 37 minutes. Hayes scored on the hour, but the Green hung on to reach the final. Since the turn of the year, The Green had won six out of seven games, scoring 28 goals and only conceding nine.

On Easter Saturday, The Green held the champions-elect Metropolitan Police to a 1–1 draw at Claremont Road, J. McCaulay and G. Coleman making their debuts. The next week, R. Ward missed the league return at Hertford Town, as he had been injured colliding with railings in the blackout.

By the middle of April, Golders Green were sixth in the Herts & Middlesex League, with six wins and three draws from 18 matches. The team finished the season in seventh place. One honour for the club was Fred Boston being selected for the Athenian League XI to play the Isthmian League at Wimbledon. However, at the end of April it was announced that the Athenian League had disbanded for the duration of the war, and the Herts & Middlesex Combination would continue and possibly expand. A new name was being considered: The North London Senior Amateur League, although this was never actually adopted.

At the end of April, Golders Green drew with Tufnell Park 0–0 in the Middlesex Senior Cup. The replay was on 11 May, and Golders Green lost 2–1. However, before then, Golders Green travelled to Wealdstone for the Middlesex Red Cross Cup Final on 4 May.

Wealdstone 4 Golders Green 1
Middlesex Red Cross Cup Final

The home side went 2–0 up in the first half, Baldwin scoring twice. Fontana pulled one back for The Green, who put pressure on the Wealdstone defence, but could not score. Wealdstone then added a third through Bunce, and Barker's penalty in the last minute meant Golders Green lost 4–1. A crowd of 3,000 watched the match, which raised £128 for the Red Cross.

Golders Green: A.E. Hart, W. Boston, F. Boston, A. Lovell, J. McCaulay, G. Bucci, A.J. Breagan, L. Fontana, H.V. Tomlinson, A. Cochrane, G. Coleman
Wealdstone: R. Lewis, A. Loveday, C. Barker, A. Doig, C. Edmonds, D. Scott, W.W. Parr, K. Baldwin, C.E. Bunce, J. Wilson, S. Schofield.

The season finished with a friendly at Finchley on bank holiday Monday. In the league Golders Green finished seventh, with 15 points from 18 matches.

1940–41

In July at the club's AGM, Alfred Murray was elected as President. He replaced Mr A. Gordon Raymond, who stood down due to ill health. The match receipts were down to £449 10s 4d compared to £1,305 the previous year. It was reported that the activities of the Supporters Association were practically nothing and there were liabilities to Hendon Borough Council of £123.

Alfred Murray

In August, the club was ready for the new season, which started on 31 August. The new league was ready except for a final decision on its title. The Herts & Middlesex League was finally agreed, although the Senior Amateur League was used early in the season. It was an extension of last year's Herts & Middlesex Combination, and comprised some of the strongest clubs in the home counties, with 12 clubs. The club had enough players to cover most positions. H.V. Tomlinson was out of London for work, and A. Lovell was in the army. Collections were to be held for Hendon Four Fighter Fund at home games, which raised money to buy four Spitfires. The club's posters advertising games were curtailed due to defence regulations. At the club's trial match, D. Bustard, the brother of former club player Len showed enormous promise.

The season opened with a 1–0 league defeat against ground-sharers Tufnell Park. The next week, a 4–0 defeat in a friendly at Tooting & Mitcham was brought to a premature end by the sound of air raid sirens. The blitz was now hitting London hard, and although the club played the next week, a 4–3 league defeat against Slough at Claremont Road, the next match was on 12 October, when Southall were beaten 3–2 at Claremont Road in front of a very small crowd. The club made an appeal to the public: "Golders Green are trying to keep the flag of senior amateur football flying, in spite of difficult conditions. The response from public is most disappointing. The club has heavy financial commitments. Unless there is a better public response, the club will close down. The public must patronise games. On 26 October, we are at home against the Metropolitan Police. The attendance will do much to decide the future of the club."

The club lost that game 4–0, and then the following week, 'a fine Hitchin Town side' won 9–0 at Claremont Road. The club again outlined its problems: "The club is still in a serious position, due to lack of support. If the public do not have a desire for the recreation offered to them, the club will have no alternative but to suspend its activities."

Hayes had dropped out of the league, so the next match was a 4–4 draw with Enfield at Claremont Road on 30 November. Bill Pidgeon had joined the army, but Fred Boston managed a rare game at left-back. A new recruit was D.W. Rowe, but the report said he was inexperienced for this level of football. The game was played in a heavy mist, and restricted to 35 minutes each way, with no half-time break. Golders Green won the return the next week 4–3, the team's first away win of the season. The next week, Wood Green Town were beaten 2–1 in the London Senior Cup. There were no Christmas matches, and the year finished with a 4–2 home defeat against St Albans City, although The Green lost four players at the last minute. In January, Joe Bloxham returned to the club. The club committee decided to continue playing to the end of the season.

In February, league wins against Finchley and Barnet were followed by a 7–1 defeat at Barnet in the London Senior Cup. After a 4–0 league win at Finchley on 22 February,

Golders Green were eighth in the league with 12 points from 16 matches, having won five games and drawn two.

Towards the end of March, with the league matches nearly completed, a couple of friendlies were arranged against forces teams. On 22 March, an Army XI, captained by Spurs' Arthur Rowe, won 3–2 at Claremont Road, but the next week The Green beat an RAF XI 6–2. At the beginning of April, Wealdstone were beaten 4–3 in the League, but the club lost L.A. (Jock) Ellison who was moving north for business reasons. Two more forces friendlies were held, an Army & RAF XI were beaten 9–1, and then an Army XI were beaten 1–0.

Golders Green then had a 2–2 draw with Tufnell Park for the Will Mather Cup. The club had now played for the Will Mather Cup four times, and never won it. Two friendly matches were arranged to complete the season, a 4–2 defeat at Tooting & Mitcham, and a 4–0 defeat at Walthamstow Avenue. The Golders Green side for the game at Walthamstow on 7 June was:

A.E. Hart, W. Boston, T. Kay, A. Breagan, A. Lovell, H. Kay, R. Stroud, L. Pulling, G. Gray, A. Birbeck, A. Cochrane.

Lovell was on leave from the Army, and played one of his best ever games for the club.

In the league, the club had played 20 matches, winning six and drawing three, ending up with 15 points and a final place of eighth. Three cup matches had been played, with a win, a draw and a defeat. Out of five friendlies, three had been won. The overall record was 10 wins and four draws from 30 matches, with 78 goals scored and 98 conceded. J. Griggs was top scorer with 17, and Roy Stroud got 13.

The club was having difficulties fielding a team, as apart from players in the forces, many players were involved in work of national importance and not available to play regularly. The club had been forced to field younger players, but were aiming to play in the 1941–42 season.

1941–42

The new season opened on the last Saturday in August, with two friendlies against Tooting & Mitcham United. The *Ham & High* reported that: "Golders Green look forward with confidence to third season war time football. The whole of the team that finished last season are available, there are vacancies for promising local players. The club is competing in the Herts & Middlesex League. The Metropolitan Police have withdrawn, Walthamstow Avenue, Leyton and Wood Green are new. With clubs from Essex and Buckinghamshire, it is a step nearer to the United London League that officials of The Green endeavoured to form as a war measure at end of the 1939–40 season. In the cups, the Middlesex Senior Cup, and Middlesex Red Cross Cup are to be run, and Golders Green are to compete in both. No decision has been made on the London Senior Cup, but the club will enter if it runs. The management of club sincerely hope that all who can support their efforts to keep senior amateur football going will do so, and trust that all members will forward their annual subscriptions as soon as possible. Finance is a vital factor."

Tooting won both the friendly matches. The Green were 2–0 up in the first, Lovell and Cochrane scoring, but then faded to a 7–2 defeat. In the return at Claremont Road, Tooting won 4–1, but the match was notable for the debut of Bill Fisher. For the first league match at Wood Green, the club's selectors made drastic changes after the friendly matches. Fontana played after almost a season's absence. The *Ham & High* said that "The forward line was remodelled to cut out the 'fiddling' canker which has been the bugbear of the side. J. Bradshaw made his first appearance at centre forward, Cochrane went to inside left and at outside left C. Shorland played, who was the nephew of former club player Jimmy Shorland. The match ended 2–2, Shorland and an own goal being The Green's scorers. The team was:

A. Hart, W. Fisher, A. Ebert, G. Bucci, A. Lovell, A. Mundy, R. Stroud, L. Fontana, J. Bradshaw, A. Cochrane, C. Shorland.

The team's form was erratic, probably due to continual changes in personnel. Two matches with St Albans resulted in the home team winning each time, then Wood Green were beaten 6–2 at Claremont Road, with J. Wreford playing in goal, and Ebert, a young Hackney schoolboy partnering Bill Fisher at full-back, and 'showing distinct promise'. But two weeks later, along with Bucci and Weeks, he missed a 5–4 defeat against Walthamstow at Claremont Road as he had been called up. Golders Green had been 2–0 up after 20 minutes against a team with famous amateur international Jim Lewis and four other pre-war Avenue stars, and lost when Lewis scored the winner with four minutes left. Cochrane got a hat-trick for Golders Green.

Supporters who did manage to attend matches were entertained. Three weeks after the Walthamstow match, Golders Green beat Finchley 7–4 at home, after being 3–0 down in the first half. Goals from Fontana, Stroud and Birbeck levelled the scores at half time. Finchley went ahead, but two goals from Pulling and two more from Birbeck, completing his hat-trick, secured The Green's win.

The next three league matches were lost. L. Page made his debut – his father A.L. Page had played for the club back in 1920. Against Slough, Tony Munday, E. Munday and J. Munday all played. A sad piece of news for the club was that Major G.P. Aldridge, the President of the Supporters Association had died.

On 6 December, Joe Bloxham played, as he was home on leave, and helped Golders Green beat Edgware Town 7–2 in the Middlesex Senior Cup. But this was followed by a 6–1 defeat at Barnet. Frank Alexander and C. Stockwell made their debuts, although Alexander was injured after 15 minutes. Stockwell had played for the club's pre-war 'A' team. Ted Owen had arrived unexpectedly on leave, and was allowed to play in the second half, and scored The Green's goal near the end.

There were no extra matches over the Christmas holiday, but on 27 December, Tufnell Park were beaten 5–2. Wreford was in the Army, so H. Crisp played in goal, and S. Benham played at right back so Fisher could play at centre half. But the next week, Hart was back in goal, and in top form in a 3–3 draw with Barnet at Claremont Road.

On 10 January 1942, Golders Green reached the semi-final of the Middlesex Senior Cup, beating Napier Athletic 4–0 at home. Stockwell scored twice, and it was the team's first clean sheet of the season. The good form continued with a 1–0 win at Enfield, with M. Leniston in goal. Golders Green were now sixth in the table, level on points with St Albans, but with an inferior goal average.

Tufnell Park were vanquished 3–0 in the Middlesex Red Cross Cup. Shorland was home from the Navy on leave and scored. But Finchley ended the club's interest in the London Senior Cup and Middlesex Senior Cup. On 14 February, Golders Green lost 5–0 at Summers Lane, with 'few of the players showing their normal form'. There was an improvement the following week, but a 2–1 defeat meant there would be no repeat of the previous season's final appearance. F. Long was home on leave and played, and

Cyril Goodchild got The Green's goal. Finch scored Finchley's winner in the second half, although Long hit the bar near the end.

Golders Green: M. Leniston, G. Bucci, C. Rodwell, A. Breagan, W. Fisher, A. Munday, R. Stroud, L. Fontana, L. Pulling, F. Long, C. Goodchild.

The team's improvement continued, when Hitchin Town were beaten 3–1 at Claremont Road. Golders Green had struggled against the Hertfordshire side in the past, but this victory was no fluke. Fontana had put The Green ahead, and it was 1–1 at half time. A brilliant goal from Stroud restored The Greens' lead, and Alexander secured the win with a third. H. Perrith played in goal, the team's fifth goalkeeper this season.

Many professional players had joined the forces, as Golders Green found to their cost the next week, when RAF (W) beat them 3–1 at Claremont Road in the Middlesex Red Cross Cup. The rules allowed professionals to play, and the RAF had seven, as well as amateur international Lester Finch. Lovell, Weeks and Bucci were missing from The Green's side. Stroud equalised in the first half after the airmen had taken the lead, but they won the game in the second half.

Golders Green: H. Perrith, W. Fisher, C. Rodwell, A. Breagan, A. Munday, F. Alexander, R. Stroud, L. Fontana, L. Pulling, A. Cochrane, C. Goodchild

RAF (W): Clack (Birmingham City), Forder (Crystal Palace), McNickle (Linfield), McGregor, Hall (Bishop Auckland), Johnson, (Newcastle U), Critchley (Everton), Blastock, Needham, Mulligan (Aston Villa), L. C. Finch (Barnet).

Another military team visited Claremont Road two weeks later. Golders Green faced a Polish Air Force XI, in aid of Hendon's Warship Week. The Green won 7–2. The Polish flag was displayed on one end of the stand and the Union Jack on the other. Supporters listened to martial music from the Middlesex Regiment. The teams were introduced to the Mayor of Hendon. Pulling scored five goals and Alexander two for The Green.

The problems of war-time football were shown the next week, with a 6–0 defeat at Finchley. Golders Green started with nine men, as Bucci and Fontana had not arrived. A tenth man was found, but the side was not completed until five minutes before half time. The match was reported as being a fiasco. The next week, on Easter Monday, three new players helped Golders Green beat Tufnell Park 1–0. One honour for the club was Roy Stroud being selected for a Herts & Middlesex League XI in a match at Barnet.

The last league match of the season was against Leyton on 25 April at Claremont Road. Golders Green lost 3–2, if they had won, the team would have finished fifth in the league. The following Wednesday, Hampstead Wardens FC played Ascot Gas Water Heaters at Claremont Road in aid of the Red Cross. The result was a 2–2 draw.

On 2 May, the club finally won the Will Mather Cup, beating Tufnell Park 2–1 after extra time. Fontana missed the game as he was now in the Navy. Pulling put The Green ahead, then got the winner in extra time. The season finished with two friendlies with Edgware Town over the Whit weekend. The Green won the first 8–3, with R. Webb, a Middlesex County schoolboy giving a great display, but lost the return 2–1.

So Golders Green had completed their third war time season. A report in the *Ham & High* at the end of the season said that it had been 'fraught with difficulties, but has been enjoyable and has kept the flag of amateur soccer going strongly at Claremont Road.' The club had difficulties in having a settled team, and the continual loss of personnel due to calls of services. During the season, The Green had four regular goalkeepers. However, there had been a considerably fuller fixture list than before, but playing results only moderately successful.

In the league there had been eight wins and four draws from 24 matches, producing 20 points and a finish in eighth place. In the cups, there had been five wins from nine games. Two friendlies out of five had been won. Overall, 102 goals had been scored, with 105 conceded. Les Pulling was top scorer with 32, Roy Stroud got 20 and A. Cochrane 11. The report said that "Stroud and Pulling had been equal in middle of March with 17 goals each, latterly Stroud gave others the chance to score instead of shooting himself, perhaps with beneficial results for the team."

One problem for next season was travel to away matches, as coach facilities were now severely restricted. There were negotiations between the FA and the Traffic Commissioners, and it was hoped to find a solution.

1942–43

The new season opened on 29 August with a friendly at Tooting & Mitcham. A preview in the *Ham & High* said that the club were "making a determined effort to keep the amateur football flag flying at Claremont Road and the club was hoping for increased support." In the Herts & Middlesex League, there would be only 12 teams, as Enfield closed down. The club were also entering the Middlesex Senior Cup, London Senior Cup, Middlesex Red Cross Cup and the Herts & Middlesex League Cup if it took place. The majority of last season's players were available. Roy Stroud was selected for the League XI against Walthamstow Avenue, the champions.

However, The Green went down 8–2 at Tooting, against a team containing a lot of the home club's pre-war stars, including former Golders Green player Dave Walker. Bucci and Munday were not available, and Breagan had joined Southall, due to travel problems. Stockwell, who was home on leave, did play.

The league season started the next week with a 5–0 home defeat against Barnet. Golders Green fielded an inexperienced team, and were 3–0 down at half time. The Golders Green side was:

A. Stidder, W. Fisher, C. Rodwell, G. Meakin, F. Alexander, A. Munday, R. Stroud, E. Worthington, L. Pulling, C. Stockwell, C. Goodchild.

Things improved the next week, with a 1–1 draw in the return match at Underhill. Roy Evans and W. Page, two of the club's pre-war players, played; and Evans scored the equaliser. A league victory against Wood Green Town at home was followed by the return friendly against Tooting & Mitcham. A 2–2 draw saw £5/0/1 collected for the Mayor of Hendon's Aid to China fund. Ted Owen, who was home on leave, played.

A 5–2 defeat at Walthamstow was followed by a 7–1 defeat at Claremont Road against Finchley. The Green were 1–0 up at half time, when it was discovered that thieves had got into the unlocked dressing room and the players' wallets had been stolen. Between £15 and £20 was lost (£600 to £800 today). The visitors' dressing room was not touched, and club officials were amazed that the thieves had not been seen. The return match was also lost, but only 3–1, with Lucas playing in goal. By the end of October, things were improving. A. Cochrane was home on leave and put on a 'magnificent exhibition' in a 4–2 win at Hitchin Town. Also, it was announced that the club was planning to run a reserve XI.

Continual team changes meant the side's form was inconsistent. A 5–1 home defeat against Southall was followed by a 2–1 win at Leyton, their first home defeat of the season. The same day, 21 November, the reserves played their first match of the season, losing 5–2 at Pinner.

December brought some cup matches. In the Middlesex Senior Cup, a home match against Pinner was abandoned as a 0–0 draw in extra time. A fortnight later, Golders Green lost the replay 3–1 on a quagmire, Stroud scoring The Green's goal. In between, a 2–1 defeat at Barnet ended the club's interest in the London Senior Cup. Pulling scored after the game had been scoreless at half time. Only five players appeared in both matches, and some of them played in different positions. But things improved over Christmas, with two victories over Wealdstone, including a 9–2 extravaganza on Boxing Day at Claremont Road. A. Rogers, yet another new recruit, was an immediate star.

Inconsistency continued in January and February, with only one win in five league matches, and an early exit in the Herts & Middlesex League Cup against Tufnell Park. The gloom of that defeat was lightened after the game, with a meal for 60 people, who were welcomed by club president Alfred Murray, and an outing to the Golders Green Hippodrome. Things improved in March, with a 3–0 win at Wealdstone in the Middlesex Red Cross Cup, Stroud scoring twice, and a 3–0 win in a friendly against an RAF XI, Chappell scoring a hat trick.

On 10 April, Golders Green visited Finchley for the Middlesex Red Cross Cup semi-final. Goals from Bucci and Goodchild put The Green 2–1 up at half time, but Finchley fought back, and Finch got the winner a minute from time. The *Ham & High* said that Golders Green played the better football, but lacked punch up front. The Golders Green side was:

A. Sale, W. Fisher, F. Alexander, A. Rogers, C. Sealey, A. Munday, R. Stroud, G. Bucci, L. Pulling, R. Mitchell, C. Goodchild.

Roy Stroud played for Arsenal on 17 April, missing The Green's 3–0 defeat in a friendly against Leyton. The league season finished on Easter Monday, 26 April, with an exciting 5–4 win against Wood Green Town at Claremont Road, Stroud getting the winner in the last minute. It gave the team fifth place in the league, their best since the start of the war. The team won nine and drew five of the 22 league matches, ending up with 23 points. The campaign ended with a 3–1 friendly win against Handley Page, and an 8–2 win against Tufnell Park to secure the Will Mather Cup.

A report in the *Ham & High* said that it had been a season of ups and downs, with some striking performances and some bad failures. Golders Green were the first side to defeat Hitchin, Leyton and St Albans on their own grounds in the league. But the club had fared badly in cups, losing in the first round in all of them except the Middlesex Red Cross Cup.

The team's record was 14 wins and six draws from 36 games, with 79 goals scored and 89 conceded. Roy Stroud was top scorer with 22 goals, followed by Dave Chappell with 14, George Bucci 10, Eddie Yates 8, and Les Pulling 5. Chappell scored his 14 goals in only 10 games. Fifty players appeared in the first XI, showing the club's problems in fielding a consistent team. Bill Fisher was the only ever present, for the second consecutive season. Other players who lead the appearance charts were Tony Munday with 30, Les Pulling and Cyril Sealey 25 each, Frank Alexander 23, and George Bucci 22.

After a shaky start, the inclusion of Sealey and Keen had strengthened the side. Chappell, Mitchell and Webb also played towards end of season, and the side showed a vast improvement.

The reserves played 16 games, all friendlies except one, won six and drew three, scoring 54 goals and conceding 44.

1943–44

The new season started again with a friendly with Tooting, which was becoming a war-time tradition. Roy Stroud and Keen were now in the forces, otherwise the same players were available. F.R. Johnson was appointed as coach. The reserves were playing in the Finchley and District League, the same competition the club had originally entered in their first season in 1908.

A 3–2 defeat at Tooting was followed by a 3–0 defeat at home to Grays and then a poor 5–0 defeat at Hitchin, when Chappell, Bucci and Sealey were all missing. On 25 September, The Green won 3–0 at St Albans, with Chappell, Bucci and Stroud scoring, but the first home win only came on 30 October, when Wood Green Town were beaten 2–1, with McCann in goal winning the game for Golders Green. But the next week, in the return match, The Green lost 4–2., their first war-time defeat against their Tottenham based opponents. Goodchild and Worthington put The Green 2–1 up at half time. The Golders Green side was:

R. McCann, W. Fisher, C. Sealey, E. Currie, R. Gallacher, A. Munday, A. Rogers, E. Worthington, E. Ridley, R. Mitchell, C. Goodchild.

The gloom continued with a 7–0 defeat at home to Barnet, and a further defeat against Tufnell Park. At the beginning of December, Finchley came to Claremont Road and secured a 4–4 draw. F. Barker, in his first game at centre forward for The Green got a hat trick. Roy Stroud was home on leave and played. The Boston brothers were playing for Finchley – they had been with Golders Green at the start of the war, and later rejoined the club.

In the London Senior Cup, The Green got a creditable 3–3 draw at Underhill, but Barnet won the replay 4–1 on 1 January. Sealey had joined the forces, but R. Gallacher and F. Gallacher played in the first game. In the Middlesex Senior Cup, Eversheds were beaten 7–1 at Claremont Road, despite Golders Green playing the first 25 minutes with 10 men. F. Barker got another hat trick. He repeated this feat in the next round, a 4–2 win at Southall after extra time. But hopes of a final appearance ended with a 3–1 defeat against Acton United at Claremont Road in the semi-final. The club were fielding their weakest side for some weeks, and the forwards' passing and shooting were wild. Cyril Goodchild scored an equaliser in the first half, but the visitors were 3–1 up at half time and kept their lead.

In the Middlesex Red Cross Cup, Golders Green lost 2–1 to Tufnell Park, but it was reported in the *Ham & High* that young Laurie Topp was "a fine wing half".

The team's league form improved around Christmas. After beating Clapton 6–1 on 4 February, of the last eight league matches, four had been won and three drawn, with 32 goals scored and 21 conceded. The return match at Clapton, on 19 February, was notable for being Bill Fisher's 100th consecutive game. On the same day, the reserves reached the final of the Middlesex Intermediate Cup, beating the holders, Ordnance (Feltham) 2–1 in the semi-final.

After three league wins in March, Wealdstone won 6–2 at Claremont Road in the first round of the Herts & Middlesex League Cup to end the season's cup campaigns. The next week, Tufnell Park were beaten 3–1 at Claremont Road. The Green only had nine men at the start of the match, so their opponents lent them Len Bustard and J. Fennell. The next week, Slough won 3–0 at Claremont Road on Easter Saturday in front of one of the best crowds of the season.

An unusual honour for the club was R. Worthington, the reserves' regular centre forward, being selected for England in an Air Training Corps international against Scotland on 15 April. He had played for first team over Easter.

On 22 April, The Green lost 2–0 at champions-elect Walthamstow Avenue. Golders Green lined up:

A. Simmonds, B. Buckle, P. Bossoms, L. Topp, W. Fisher, R. Gallagher, R. Stroud, G. Bucci, G. Cox, E. Worthington, C. Goodchild.

The league season finished with a 1–0 win at Finchley on 6 May. Fair scored for The Green, and Bucci missed a penalty. In the league, Golders Green finished tenth, with 22 points - nine wins and four draws - from 26 matches.

On 13 May, Golders Green retained the Will Mather Cup, with a 4–3 win against Tufnell Park. Mickey Lane, who had an illustrious career with Hendon after the war, made his debut for Tufnell Park. Cox and Bucci put The Green 2–0 up, but at half time it was 2–2. Bucci made it 3–2, Tufnell Park equalised, then Henocq scored the winner in the last few minutes. The same day, the reserves won the Highwood Charity Cup, beating Highwood 8–0.

In March, the Secretary of Herts & Middlesex League had proposed that Isthmian and Athenian Leagues should work together after the war to run three divisions, including promotion and relegation. The idea had first been raised 30 years earlier, was not accepted then or this time, and it would take 30 years before a proper pyramid system was established for amateur football. Had it been, the club would have played in the top level from the early 1950s, if not before.

1944–45: Three Cup Finals

In July it was reported that the club was preparing for the forthcoming season, but it had not been possible to hold an Annual General Meeting, so the committee would continue for another year. Alfred Murray continued as president, with Mr Mungo Chapman as chairman, and Stan Greene as secretary, with his brother Claude as assistant secretary and first team secretary. Training would start in early August, and the club expected most of last season's players to be available.

In August the club believed that the following players should be able to play regularly: Bill Fisher, Peter Bossoms, Laurie Topp, R. Gallacher, Cyril Goodchild, F. Barker and C. Barnard. The club would be competing in the Herts & Middlesex League again, the three county cups and the league cup. An important recruit was centre forward Mervyn Griffiths, who was a regular scorer in the second half of the season.

The season opened at Claremont Road on 26 August, with Tooting & Mitcham visiting in a friendly. The team was announced as:

P. Martinson, P. Bossoms, L. Topp, W. Fisher, R. Gallacher, R. Stroud, C. Fair, F. Barker, R. Mitchell, C. Goodchild.

Martinson had played for club before the war, and was now available again. Jack Weeks was serving in the Middle East, and had played at centre half for the British Army against the Polish army. He saw action at El Alamein, and recently got his 'second pip'.

Golders Green won the friendly 5–1, the club's first victory against the south London club since the war started. McCann played in goal, and Mitchell scored two of the goals.

Tufnell Park FC war-time programme at Claremont Road.

The league season opened at Barnet with a 2–1 defeat, but five consecutive victories followed, despite regular changes in the team. Joy played in goal in the 3–1 win at St Albans on 16 September, but the next week R. Roberts was between the posts in a 6–1 win over Grays Athletic at Claremont Road. Cambridge University right winger F. Finch played instead of Roy Stroud, who could not get leave from the Army. Stroud returned the following week, in a 4–1 win at Southall, who fielded three former Golders Green players: Stidder, Breagan and Snazel. The Green were now second in the league, with a game in hand on leaders Hitchin Town. But after beating St Albans 3–2 in the league, Golders Green lost 4–2 at Hitchin, but "were not outplayed" and "put up an excellent fight". Bossoms and Finch scored for The Green.

The team's form then became more erratic. A 3–1 win over Leyton at Claremont Road was followed by a 6–1 defeat at Walthamstow Avenue, when the home team had an inspired day. After a 1–1 draw with Barnet and then a 6–3 defeat against Tufnell Park, The Green were sixth. Stroud returned the following week to score twice at Wood Green in a 3–2 victory 'in the mud'. But a 3–1 defeat at home to Clapton, when Roberts had an excellent game in goal and kept the score down, and a 2–1 defeat at Finchley, when The Green's team included Lamb at centre half and Harry Robshaw, who later joined Spurs, at inside-right, meant that The Green had taken only three points from the last six games, and were now eighth in the league.

The team's form improved in the cup competitions. On 9 December Golders Green travelled to Dulwich Hamlet in the London Senior Cup. J. Maloney played at left back, as Bossoms did not turn up. The Green's star was Laurie Topp: "wherever there was trouble and he was needed he was there." Also, Lucas had a brilliant game in goal. Dulwich were 3–0 up after around 30 minutes. But on 35 minutes, Topp scored with a lob, then Finch scored, so it was 3–2 at half-time. Dulwich then missed a penalty, and on 75 minutes, Fair scored with a penalty to make it 3–3. The next week, Handley Page came to Claremont Road in the Middlesex Senior Cup, and won 2–1, Robshaw and Long scoring. At the beginning of January, Dulwich won the London Senior Cup replay 1–0.

The *Ham & High* reviewed the first half of the season at the beginning of January: "In contrast to the first half of last season, Golders Green made a fine start to the 1944–45 campaign, winning seven of the first nine games. At this stage, they were second to Hitchin Town, who then led the Herts & Middlesex League table. But of the next 12

94

games, there were only two wins, six defeats and four draws. The defence as good as ever, but the forward line, deprived of the services of Cox and Goodchild, has lost its scoring ability. In the first nine games the team scored 34 goals, in the next 12 only 19. The club is still in the Middlesex Senior Cup, Middlesex Red Cross Cup and the League Challenge Cup. It will need an improved forward line which can score goals to have any chance of success in these or their remaining nine league games. Golders Green are eighth in the league table with 17 points from 17 games. This compares with 10 points from 15 games in the same period last year."

The scorers at this stage were: C. Fair 18, C. Goodchild 7, R. Gallacher and P. Bossoms 5, R. Stroud 4, G. Cox 3, R. Mitchell and E. Finch 2, A. Cochrane, L. Topp, E. Worthington, V. Henocq, H. Robshaw, F. Long and C. Street 1 each.

Cup competitions dominated the second half of the season. In the Middlesex Senior Cup, Golders Green beat Tufnell Park 3–2 in a replay after a 1–1 draw in the first game. This was described as one of the finest games seen at Claremont Road for many seasons. Golders Green were 2–0 down after 17 minutes, but changed their forward line at half-time, moving Griffiths to centre-forward. Fair scored after 70 minutes, then 10 minutes later Laurie Topp equalised with a header, and then got the winner with a few minutes left. In the semi-final, Golders Green beat Uxbridge 4–1 at Claremont Road, with The Green's half-backs, Topp, Malcolm and Gallacher dominating the game, but lost the final on Easter Monday 3–1 to Southall at Wealdstone.

Golders Green 1 Southall 3
Middlesex Senior Cup Final

This was a hard fought game in front of a good crowd. Southall won the toss, and played with the wind and the slope. They scored twice in the first 16 minutes, through Paynter and Pyne. Just before the break, Stroud broke through and crossed, but Cox's header just went wide. Cochrane scored for Golders Green after the break, but then Stroud injured his knee and was a passenger for the rest of the game. Southall secured the cup with a third goal from Pyne near the end.

Golders Green: R. Roberts, W. Fisher, J. Maloney, L. Topp, H. Malcolm, R. Gallacher, R. Stroud, H. Robshaw, M. Griffiths, G. Cox, A. Cochrane.

The Middlesex Red Cross Cup provided the club's first Wembley appearance. Golders Green beat Wood Green Town 8–3, Finchley 3–0 after a replay, with goals from Griffiths, Robshaw and Bucci, and then Wealdstone 3–0 in the semi-final to reach the final against Tufnell Park at Wembley Stadium on 16 May. Golders Green won 4–1 before a large crowd. The Green soon gained the ascendancy, and the result was seldom in doubt after Golders Green took the lead. On 15 minutes, Stroud passed to Griffiths who set up Cochrane to score. Five minutes later, Griffiths put Cochrane in possession. He passed to Bucci who made it 2–0, which was the score at half time. Three minutes after the break, Bucci scored with a header from Stroud's centre, despite having been injured earlier. Tufnell Park fought back, and after 75 minutes scored a "great goal" through Richards. Their forwards were kept at bay by a dour, solid Golders Green defence. Five minutes from the end Cochrane scored from a fine pass by Griffiths to make it 4–1. The *Ham & High* said that Griffiths "played a most unselfish game". Tufnell Park took their revenge by winning the Will Mather Cup 3–1 on Whit Monday.

In the Herts & Middlesex League Challenge Cup, Golders Green also reached the final. Golders Green won 4–1 at Finchley, 1–0 at Slough United and then beat Hitchin Town 4–2 after being 2–0 down, Cochrane with two, Griffiths and Fair scoring the goals. In the final, Golders Green faced Barnet on 28 April at Finchley. It was a 'magnificently fought encounter', Barnet winning 3–2 in extra time. Barnet had taken the lead in the third minute, and Thomas had equalised with barely a minute of the match left. Barnet took the lead in the second period of extra time, Griffiths equalised, but then Barnet got the winner. The *Hendon Times* report said that Laurie Topp "dominated the play".

Golders Green: R. Roberts, W. Fisher, P. Bossoms, L. Topp, H. Malcolm, R. Gallacher, C. Fair, H. Robshaw, M. Griffiths, G. Bucci, C. Thomas.

Barnet: H. Powell, E. Bunker, A. Farrar, W. Weightman, L. Pullen, F. Pymm, J. Jordan, D. Kelleher, A. Green, E. Brogdale, P. Reilly.

In the league, The Green finished ninth, with 24 points from 26 games, scoring 58 goals and conceding 59.

A Golders Green hero: George Bucci

George Bucci was one of the mainstays of the club from the mid 1920s to 1945. His father was Dominic Bucci, one of the club founders. He first played for the first team in the 1925–26 season, and finished his first team playing career in 1945, having played regularly during the war years, when he must have been in his late 30s. He later served the club as a committee member and officer.

During his long career he played in every position, even once in goal when the regular goalkeeper failed to arrive at a match. However, he played in the latter part of his career at half back. In 1928–29 he signed amateur forms for Arsenal, and played for their reserve team and Watford's reserves. He captained Golders Green in 1936–37, completed 15 years at the club just before the war, when the *Ham & High* said he was their best player, and the "Grand old man of The Green".

He won a county cap for Middlesex, and played three times for the Athenian League side. He played in 12 cup finals for the club, including the Middlesex Senior Cup wins in 1933–34 and 1938–39, and in the Red Cross Cup Final against Tufnell Park at Wembley in 1945, when he scored two goals.

So as the war in Europe came to an end, Golders Green could look back on their most successful season during the war. The club had continued to play, despite all the difficulties, survived, and recruited three players, Bill Fisher, Laurie Topp and Roy Stroud who would play a significant role in the club's post war successes.

On 23 April 1945, the Athenian League Council met, and decided that the League would start again in the summer with the same clubs in membership as in 1939. So Golders Green could look to build on their successes in the latter period of the war.

5. 1945 to 1955: Champions at last

1945–46: Finale for Golders Green

The war was only just finished when the new season started for Golders Green. Many men and women were still in the forces or in war-related work, the general election had just seen Labour sweep to power, and in Hendon, the local council faced the task of repairing bomb damage, and overcoming the many shortages and austerity that people faced.

But for sport, the post-war period was a 'golden age'. People were desperate for entertainment after the war years. Television was still in its infancy, and it would be the early 1950s before it became common in people's homes. So every major sport saw huge attendances.

The club had survived the Second World War intact, playing in the Herts and Middlesex League, and various cup competitions. The Athenian League had been suspended in 1939 when war was declared. The same 14 clubs contested the 1945–46 season. This gave Golders Green new local rivals, as Finchley FC had been accepted for League membership in 1939. Isthmian League side Tufnell Park continued the war-time arrangement of sharing the Claremont Road ground.

The club's Annual General Meeting, held in July, anticipated many difficulties in the coming season, with some players still in the forces, and others being called up for military service. The treasurer, Mr Innes, reported that the club had struggled financially during the war. In 1940–41, the gate receipts had been £93, compared to £1,330 in 1938–39. The club's late president, Mr A. Gordon Raymond had left the club £100 in his will, and had liquidated some other loans he had made to the club. Jack Innes said that the club's balance was £400, but without the bequests it would have been £3. Alfred Murray continued as president, with Mr Mungo Chapman as chairman, and Stan Greene continued as secretary.

The players included three who would be crucial to the club's development in the post-war period: Pat Lynch, Bill Fisher and Laurie Topp. Another star was forward Roy Stroud, who would eventually turn professional with West Ham. The problems of players being in the forces was reflected when the club programme in March welcomed back Ted Owen, who had played before the war, and was now a 'civvy' again.

The season opened with a trial game, with new players G. Burtenshaw in goal, and forwards C. Thomas and H. Fletcher. Centre half Gallacher missed the game as he was having a trial with West Ham United.

This was a period of great attacking football, with Athenian League matches averaging over five goals a game. Golders Green averaged over two per game in attack, with 56, but conceded over three a game with 84, to finish 10th in the final table with 17 points. Entertainment was certainly provided for the supporters, with 22 goals in the first three games – but all were lost 7–2 at Sutton United on the season's opening day, 5–3 at home to Barking the following week, and 3–2 at Bromley. A run of five victories followed, including a 5–1 victory over Hayes, when Lynch and Alf Williams, who had both joined the club from Tufnell Park, made their debuts and strengthened the team's left flank. Topp had a brilliant game and Glaser scored two goals. This was followed by a 5–0 win in the return match against Barking, who had to play all their matches away from home. In the 2–1 win at Finchley, A. Hart was home on leave from Germany and played, Roberts standing down to give him a game. After that run, the team struggled, and only won two more league games, against Finchley in January, and Hitchin in March. The 2–0 win over Finchley in January marked Bill Fisher's 175th consecutive game for the club. One disastrous defeat was against Hitchin Town on 3 November, when Golders Green lost 8–2 at Claremont Road, although reports said that the score did not reflect the run of play.

Cup competitions

The team found a little more success in the cup competitions. In the Amateur Cup, a 2–1 victory over Ford Sports at home on a hard, frozen pitch was followed by a 3–1 defeat against Leyton at Claremont Road. Wood Green ended any hopes in the Middlesex Senior Cup with a 3–2 win in the first round. The pitch was a sea of mud, rain and a burst water main creating the quagmire. Hicks, a 15-year-old reserve, scored both goals. In the London Senior Cup, Athenian League Champions-elect Sutton United drew 0–0 at Claremont Road, but Golders Green won the replay 2–1 at Gander Green Lane, one of the best results of the season. Mervyn Griffiths scored both goals, the winner coming two minutes from time when he headed home a corner from Roy Stroud. But in the next round, the team crashed 4–1 at Bromley.

The best results of the season were reserved for the Middlesex Charity Cup, which the club had won at Wembley Stadium the previous season under its war-time title of the Middlesex Red Cross Cup. In the first round, Enfield were beaten 8–1 at Claremont Road. Floyd and Lynch with a penalty made the half-time score 2–1 and Lynch scored again in the second half. Griffiths and Fair, with two each and King completed the rout. Finchley were then beaten 3–2 after extra time to produce a semi-final with Isthmian League Tufnell Park. Griffiths put Golders Green ahead in the second half, Tufnell Park equalising near the end. Four weeks later, on 27 April, Golders Green won the replay. A. Williams put Golders Green ahead on 38 minutes, but within five minutes Tufnell Park were level. Griffiths got the winner on 62 minutes.

In the final, Golders Green faced fellow Athenian leaguers Southall at Brentford's Griffin Park. The match programme said that members of H.M. Forces in uniform would be admitted at a reduced price – a reminder that the war was not long over.

Golders Green 3 Southall 2
Middlesex Charity Cup Final

This was to be the club's last match as Golders Green, and it was a winning departure, with a 3–2 victory. The stands were packed, and early on Jerry Marrable put Griffiths through, but he shot over the bar. But on 15 minutes, Mitchell put The Green ahead when he scored from a corner by Ted Owen. On the half hour, Topp passed to Owen who centred for Griffiths to head home. It was 2–0 at half-time, and despite losing King with a broken leg in the second half, leaving Golders Green with 10 men for the last half hour, Golders Green went 3–0 up with a second goal for Griffiths. Southall scored twice in the last 15 minutes, but could not equalise. One Golders Green official was critical of the decision to play at Griffin Park, feeling that an amateur game should be played at an amateur ground. The teams in the match programme were:

Golders Green: A. Godding, P. Lynch, A. King, L. Topp, W. Fisher, F. Williams, E. Owen, G. Marrable, M. Griffiths, A. Mitchell, A. Cochrane.

Southall: R. Saunders, C. Parker, D. Sutton, A. Chudley, R. Gasdon, W. Hill, A. Breacon, R. Sentence, D. Pyne, E. Francis, R. Christopher.

Melvyn Griffiths receives the Middlesex Charity Cup – Golders Green's last trophy

In May 1946, the club held a general meeting, and changed its name to Hendon FC. The chairman, Mungo Chapman, in proposing the change, quoted Shakespeare's *Romeo and Juliet*: "A rose by any other name would smell as sweet", said that the club's ground was in the borough of Hendon, and that Golders Green was not sufficiently comprehensive. The change had been discussed with the Council, and it was felt that the club's name should reflect the whole district. The name of Hendon Borough was rejected as 'not snappy enough'. There was also discussion on the team's colours, and whether the current green and white kit should be kept, or the club should revert to blue and white. After some debate, it was agreed to keep the green kit, although club secretary Stan Greene said he had only managed to acquire the shirts by "combing nearly every shop in London."

1946–47: Two Middlesex Cup finals

The newly named Hendon's fortunes improved in 1946–47, with a final place of eighth in the Athenian League table, with 26 points from 26 games. Goals scored had improved by six from the previous season, but it was in defence that progress was made with goals conceded falling from 84 to 59. Mervyn Griffiths was captain, and Pat Lynch vice-captain.

The club planned to field three teams in new season. The 'A' team would play friendlies, and the reserves in the Athenian League reserve section. Ted Drake was

99

appointed as coach. He was a former England and Arsenal centre forward. The club said that "the prospects of training and advice from him have already bought in a large number of applications for trials." He would go on to manage Chelsea to their first Division One title in 1955.

Ted Drake

Most of the 1945–46 season players were staying with club: Pat Lynch, F. Langdale, Arthur Godding, J. Wharton, A. Bent, Laurie Topp, J. Sibthorpe, J. Hemming, Jerry Marrable, Bill Fisher, A. Lovell, F. Williams, A. Williams, J. Maloney, Roy Stroud, R. Martin, Mervyn Griffiths, M. Gasman, R. Mitchell and Ted Owen.

New players included Cyril Sealey the club's war-time centre-half, who had been demobbed from navy, A. Hart, who had played in goal in early war-time matches, and was out of the army in September, H. Poulton, a left-half from Arsenal, Bill Reay, an inside forward from Erith & Belvedere, G. Chaney, a left winger from the RAF, and R. Carter, an inside forward from Chelsea. The club was also making alterations to dressing rooms which would make them the best in the Athenian League. Bernard Bryant was another new forward, scored a hat-trick in a private trial game, and was an excellent recruit, ending as the club's top scorer with 34 goals.

Three new players appeared at the club's trial game, all from Leyton. Bert Gibbs was a goalkeeper, and his colleagues Jock Watson and A. Nash also played. Cyril Goodchild, who had played for Golders Green before going into the forces, was back from India for the start of the season.

The season started well, with five consecutive league wins, so when Hendon faced Sutton United at Claremont Road on 12 October, the club proudly sat top of the league. This game was notable for the opening ceremony of the Gordon Raymond Stand – the covered terracing on the 'popular' (Clitterhouse Playing Fields) side of the ground, which was named after the club's former President. The President of the Middlesex FA, Lieutenant-Colonel C. D. Crisp and Councillor A.W. Curton JP, the Mayor of Hendon, did the honours. A special souvenir programme was issued for the occasion. Work on the stand had started in 1934, when terracing was put in to half the length of the side by members of the Supporters' Association. Mr Raymond then arranged for covering to be put up. Further work was done before the war, and the programme had a long list of 'credits' to people who helped the complete the work after the war, including skipper Mervyn Griffiths whose architectural skills were invaluable. The club claimed it was one of the best facilities of its type in amateur football. The club now claimed that 5,000 supporters could watch the game 'under cover'.

In the Athenian League, Hendon were leading the League in the first half of the season, and at the beginning of January were top with 21 points from 16 games, but a severe winter and some success in the county cups meant fixture congestion in the second half of the season, and the team eventually finished eighth, with 26 points from 26 games. At the beginning of February, there were still 10 league games to play, and the team were in three cups, but only 15 dates, including Easter, were available. At the end of April, a 5–2 defeat at Redhill diminished the team's championship hopes, they were six points behind leaders Sutton United with two games in hand. The government discouraged midweek games due to the economic crisis, so the last league match was on 14 June. Hendon still had a say in the title as they faced Barnet at Claremont Road. If

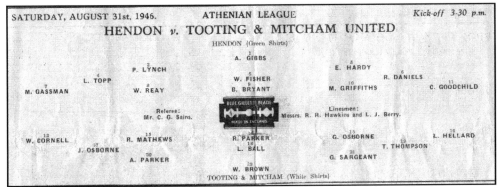

SATURDAY, AUGUST 31st, 1946.   ATHENIAN LEAGUE   *Kick-off 3·30 p.m.*

HENDON *v.* TOOTING & MITCHAM UNITED

HENDON (Green Shirts)

A. GIBBS

P. LYNCH   E. HARDY
        L. TOPP   W. FISHER   R. DANIELS
M. GASSMAN   W. REAY   B. BRYANT   M. GRIFFITHS   C. GOODCHILD

        Referee: Linesmen:
        Mr. C. G. Sains.   Messrs. R. R. Hawkins and L. J. Berry.

W. CORNELL   R. MATHEWS   R. PARKER   G. OSBORNE   L. HELLARD
        J. OSBORNE   L. BALL   T. THOMPSON
                A. PARKER   G. SARGEANT
                            W. BROWN
                TOOTING & MITCHAM (White Shirts)

The teams from the match programme for the first home game as Hendon

Barnet won, they were champions, if it was a draw or Hendon won, Sutton United took the title. Barnet won 5–1 to take the title.

The club started at the very beginning in the FA Cup, winning 3–2 at Pinner, after being 3–0 up, in the extra preliminary round. In the preliminary round, they lost 3–1 at Finchley, after being 3–0 down after 24 minutes. At the end of April, no doubt fed up with fixture congestion, the club announced that they would not enter the FA Cup in the 1947–48 season. The *Ham & High* reported that: "they feel it is a waste of valuable Saturdays to take part in a competition they cannot possibly win." This boycott only lasted one season.

In the Amateur Cup, Isthmian League Ilford ended Hendon's interest in the first round with a 2–1 victory. Griffiths was playing against his old club, and was the best forward on the pitch. Roy Stroud gave Hendon the lead on 18 minutes, but Ilford had taken the lead before half-time, and injuries to Bryant, Griffiths and Hardy in the second half saw Hendon knocked out.

In the London Senior Cup, Hendon beat Finchley 4–1 at Claremont Road, the match having been switched from Summers Lane because of drainage work, and then the Metropolitan Police 3–2 on 15 March in a blinding snowstorm. Two weeks later, Isthmian League Wimbledon ended the run, with a 5–2 win at Plough Lane, after Griffiths had put Hendon ahead on 21 minutes. Reay also scored for Hendon.

In the Middlesex Senior Cup, Wealdstone were beaten after a replay and then Edgware Town were vanquished 4–0 in the second round. In the semi-final, Hendon faced Hayes at Wealdstone, and won 4–2 after the scores had been level with seven minutes left. Prior had put Hendon ahead, then Bryant with 2 goals and a penalty from Pat Lynch in the last minute secured a place in the final against Enfield

Enfield 1 Hendon 0
Middlesex Senior Cup Final

The game was played at White Hart Lane on Whit Monday, 26 May. Hendon lost 1–0 under a grilling sun. The winner came late in second half, Rawlings scoring after 79 minutes. Laurie Topp had a great game, he and Roy Stroud did not deserve to be on the losing side. The game went from end to end, and after 10 minutes Bryant hit the bar. In second half Enfield used the offside trap. Hendon had chances to equalise, with Bryant and Prior coming close.

101

Hendon: R. Kemp, P. Lynch, J. Watson, L. Topp, W. Fisher, E. Hardy, R. Stroud, W. Reay, B. Bryant, A. Wharton, W. Prior.
Enfield: R. Bennett, A. Rosser, H. Rawlings, W. Heal, A. Warren, A. Marchant, P. Steed, J. Chappell, C. Wade, J. Rawlings, L. West.

Hendon 5 Southall 0
Middlesex Charity Cup Final

Hendon won the Middlesex Charity Cup for the third season running, beating Finchley and Wealdstone to reach the final. Having played in finals at Wembley Stadium and Brentford's Griffin Park, Hendon now faced Southall at Highbury on 7 June. Southall had beaten Hendon twice in the league, but were no match for them in the final. Hendon won 5–0 before a small crowd, the match having been arranged at short notice. A hat-trick from Bill Reay and two goals from Roy Stroud gave Hendon victory, but Topp and Prior were Hendon's outstanding players according to match reports.
Hendon: R. Kemp, P. Lynch, J. Watson, L. Topp, W. Fisher, E. Hardy, R. Stroud, A. Wharton, W. Reay, D Russell, W. Prior.
Southall: R. Saunders, C. Parker, T. Parker, D. Cornish, R. Gadsden, D. Sutton, H. Farrow, R. Sentence, J. Prout, H. Tillyer.

In cup matches, Hendon had played 15 games, winning 10, drawing one and losing four, scoring 36 goals and conceding 22. Overall, the top scorers were Bryant with 34 and Reay with 18. Bill Reay played all 41 games, Lynch and Stroud 39 each, Hardy 38, Watson and Topp 35, Fisher 34, Bryant 32, Kemp 30.

At the club's Annual General Meeting in July, Laurie Topp was presented with a gold watch in recognition of his five appearances for England during the season. It was also announced that Ted Drake had moved to manage Reading.

1947–48: League runners up

One change on the playing front was the arrival in the first team of Dexter Adams, who would be one of the club's key players over the next few years. Other new players were Ken Scott from Sutton United, Jack Weeks, who rejoined the club, J. Russell and G. Garrigan from Wealdstone and R. Owens, a goalkeeper from Edgware Town. George Wakeman also played regularly at centre forward. In February, Mickey Lane joined the club from Tufnell Park.

In the league, Hendon's improvement since the war continued, with the club finishing runners-up in the table, five points behind champions Barnet. By now, the number of goals per game in the league had fallen to around 3.5, and this was reflected in Hendon's record – only 30 conceded, just over a goal a game, but only 45 scored, less than two a game, and almost half Barnet's 86.

After an opening day defeat at lowly Barking, eight of the next 10 league games were won. At the end of September, Hendon were top of the league after a 1–0 win at Redhill, and were leaders for much of the autumn. However, the two defeats were against Barnet, 1–0 at Claremont Road on 4 October, and 3–2 at Underhill a fortnight later. Taking only one point from the two Christmas matches against Wealdstone did not help the campaign, although on 24 January, Hendon was only two points behind their Underhill neighbours, but had played three games more. Barnet was one of the top amateur clubs at this time, so to finish runners-up was no disgrace, and a considerable improvement on 12th place two years earlier.

When the club decided not to enter the FA Cup to reduce fixture congestion, the committee could not have anticipated an Amateur Cup saga against Barking. Hendon's campaign had opened with an impressive 2–1 victory at Isthmian League Kingstonian with goals from Reay and Fontana, followed by a 3–1 triumph over Western League Poole Town at Claremont Road. The third round brought Barking to Claremont Road. The visitors earned a 2–2 draw, equalising in the last minute. Barking were "quick tackling, [and] faster on the ball, according to the report in the Ham and High, and "would not let Hendon settle down to play good football" Bob Avis was marked by Prince, but still scored 2 goals. Fontana was also marked, and could not do his usual defence splitting passes. This was followed by a replay which saw Hendon 3–0 up with 10 minutes left when the game was abandoned due to snow and frost. The referee could not follow the ball in the snow. Avis had scored two goals again, and Stroud added the third to put Hendon 3–0 up after 28 minutes. It was Hendon's best display of the season, but did not count for anything.

(Courtesy Arsenal FC)

The match was staged again on the following Tuesday afternoon. A heroic performance by Hendon's defence resulted in a 0–0 draw after extra time. With Bill Fisher injured and hobbling on the wing, centre half Weeks was knocked out twice during the game, and keeper Kemp made save after save. After all this, Roy Stroud nearly won the game for Hendon in the last minutes, forcing Barking's international goalkeeper Wilson to save to keep his team in the tie. After the game, the team went to the Golders Green Hippodrome to see a show there, as guests of comedian Harry Mooney, who was a supporter of the club.

The *Ham & High* announced that "Hendon - Barking Marathon to continue at Arsenal." The following Saturday, the teams resumed battle at Highbury, in front of 16,000 supporters. Bob Avis put Hendon ahead, only for Barking to equalise within a minute. After half an hour they took the lead, only for Fontana to equalise for Hendon just before half-time. Two minutes after the break, Bill Reay scored the winner for Hendon, a lead the Greens kept to end 410 minutes of hectic football. The *Ham & High* reported that they showed flashes of fine football and "some of their forward inter-passing movements would not have disgraced some of the professional teams which appear on the ground."

Maybe exhausted by all this, Hendon lost 4–1 to Isthmian Leaguers Leytonstone at Claremont Road the next Saturday. It was the first time the club had reached the Amateur Cup quarter-final, and showed they were now in a position to challenge for the trophy. Leytonstone were the cup holders, and the club had made the match all ticket. The prize had been a trip north to face Bishop Auckland in the semi-final. Hendon's goal came in the last minute, an own goal set up by Roy Stroud.

The week after the Leytonstone game, Hendon's interest in the London Senior Cup also finished, with a 7–1 defeat at Dulwich Hamlet. It was only 2–0 at half-time, but Hendon had four players injured. Prior dislocated his shoulder, Jock Watson had concussion and missed most of the second half, Fontana was limping for most of the game, and Ray Kemp broke a bone in his right hand.

In the Middlesex Senior Cup, Edmonton Borough had won 3–2 at Claremont Road in the first round. Hendon had been 2–0 up at half-time, with goals from Wakeman and Reay, but eased up and threw the game away. But Hendon made more progress in the Middlesex Charity Cup, beating Tufnell Park and Finchley to reach their fourth consecutive final, including the 1945 Red Cross Cup match, against Hayes at Wealdstone on 8 May.

Hendon 3 Hayes 2
Middlesex Charity Cup Final

This was a far closer affair than the previous season's Final, but Hendon won 3–2, with a Roy Stroud goal 11 minutes from the end of extra time. The *Ham & High* reported that Hendon were fortunate to be all square at the end of normal time, but were the better team in extra time. Cochrane put Hendon ahead, Hayes equalized through a penalty to make it 1–1 at the break. Two minutes after half-time, Hayes went ahead. Bob Avis equalised for Hendon on 53 minutes.

Hendon: R. Kemp, P. Lynch, J. Watson, L. Topp, D. Adams, E. Owen, R. Stroud, L. Fontana, R. Avis, W. Reay, J. Cochrane.

International matches

The club played international friendly matches this season, beating Utrecht from Holland 4–2 at Claremont Road in September, and then winning an international tournament in Belgium over Easter. Both the teams they faced were professional. On Easter Sunday, Hendon beat Vervetors 4–2, after being 1–0 down at half-time. Hendon's goals came from Reay with two, Avis and Laurie Topp, who scored with a shot from 30 yards. The next day, Hendon beat Daring Club 4–1, after leading 2–0 at half-time, with two goals from Reay, and one apiece for Avis and Cochrane.

At the end of the season, Arsenal came to Claremont Road in the Will Mather Cup, Hendon losing to their prestigious north London neighbours 4–1. Arsenal fielded their first team attack. Denis Compton was injured, but kicked off the game for Hendon, and Leslie Compton played for Arsenal. The match was played to support Manor House Hospital, a trade union hospital in Golders Green.

At the end of July, the Chinese team trained at Claremont Road before taking part in the Olympic Games. In September, Claremont Road had been used to make a coaching film for amateur and youth clubs. Laurie Scott, Stanley Matthews and Ronnie Rooke were among the professionals taking part. Schoolboys from Golders Green and Cricklewood rushed to ground to see these football heroes. The players were paid £3 per day for taking part.

Roy Stroud made his debut for the England amateur team against Wales, scoring in a 7–2 win at Bangor, and also played against Luxembourg and Holland in an Easter tournament. Laurie Topp played in an international trial, but did not add to his total of England caps. He did play for the Athenian League.

The club's AGM was held on 19 July. Chairman Roger Raymond reported that the club was planning improvements to ground with the aim of staging international matches. They wanted to make Hendon one of the best three amateur clubs in country. President

Alfred Murray said that Arsenal would use the ground for midweek coaching and staged four midweek league matches. He stressed that Arsenal would not interfere in Hendon's affairs, and that Hendon would not be an Arsenal nursery club. Roy Stroud was presented with a gold watch recognition of his achievements – he had played for England. Stroud said that he hoped to beat the record of George Bucci, the club's press secretary, who had played 21 years for the club. Stroud had joined the club in 1939. The players who had represented Hendon in the 1946 and 1947 Middlesex Charity Cup finals received spoons from the Middlesex FA.

1948–49: League runners-up - again

So near – yet so far. For the second season running, Hendon finished the season as runners-up in the League, with 37 points from 26 matches, four behind champions Bromley. Only 4 matches were lost, and the attack improved to net 55 goals, over 2 per game. The strength of the Athenian League was shown by Bromley winning the Amateur Cup, in the first final at Wembley, beating the Isthmian League's Romford. Remarkably, Hendon had lost 6–0 at Bromley in the league in September, with only a brilliant display by Reg Kemp keeping the score down. Hendon played consistently, and at the beginning of April, after winning 3–2 at Hayes, were only a point behind Bromley. After a 1–1 draw at Southall, and a 1–0 win over Enfield at Claremont Road, they were level on points, but had a worse goal average, and Bromley had three games in hand. By the time Hendon beat Bromley 3–0 in the league in early May, their opponents had secured the title – and the Amateur Cup – and did not have their strongest team out.

Three new players appeared in the club's trial game: C. Windrup, a right-half, centre-forward A. Parsons and inside-forward M. Green. At the AGM, the club had announced that left-winger Ted Hornsby and left-half Glyn Hinshelwood were to join, but Hornsby decided to stay with Edgware. However, he did join the club at the end of November, and netted twice on his debut in a 2–0 league win at Barnet.

Bill Fisher had fully recovered from his broken ankle in the Barking cup-tie. A Spurs junior, P. Woodward, played in the second half of the trial game, but it was decided he needed more experience and would play in the reserves. Prospects for the season looked good, with two good goalkeepers and a good selection of backs, although one loss was Jock Watson telling the club he was going abroad for work from September to January, and therefore asking to play in the reserves.

In September, Billy Dare joined the club from Kingsbury Town. He was a regular goalscorer, but was already on amateur forms for Brentford, and joined them in December. He played for Brentford until 1955, making 222 first team appearances with 64 goals, then joined West Ham United in a £5,000 deal. He made 111 first team appearances for West Ham, scoring 44 goals. One departure from the club was goalkeeper Bert Gibbs, who joined Tufnell Park in September.

The club's boycott of the FA Cup only lasted one season, but having not entered the previous season, the team had to battle through two preliminary rounds, beating Welwyn Garden City 3–0 and Hoddesdon Town 2–1, before reaching the first qualifying round. There, nearly 4,000 people saw a 2–1 victory at Finchley, goals from Avis and Stroud, both made by Dare, seeing Hendon through. Enfield were dispatched 3–0 at Claremont Road in the next round, then Wealdstone were beaten 4–2 at Claremont Road after extra time in the Divisional Qualifying final before Barnet ended the run with a 5–4

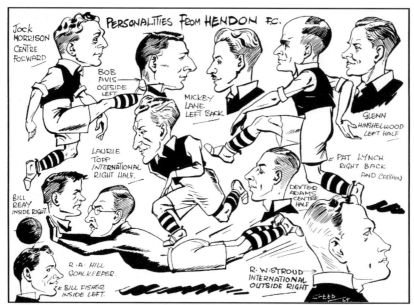

Left: The Hendon players in 1949 in cartoon format.

Middle: Hendon players line up at the Verviers tournament in 1949.

Bottom: The teams from the 1949 Will Mather Cup programme.

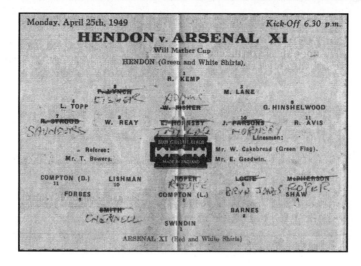

106

victory in the fourth qualifying round. It was Billy Dare's last game for the club, and he scored twice, his second putting Hendon 4–3 up in extra time. But Barnet equalised three minutes later, and got the winner in the second half of extra time.

In the Amateur Cup, Hendon had an outstanding 5–1 win at Isthmian League Ilford in the first round. Hornsby and Avis gave Hendon a 2–0 half-time lead. The Isthmian League side pulled a goal back after the break, but a further goal from Hornsby, and two from Roy Stroud, clinched the victory. The game was meant to be shown on television, but this had to be cancelled due to poor visibility.

This success was followed with a 1–0 win away to Poole Town, Stroud scoring in a poor game where good football was at a premium. The trip was a difficult one for Hendon's supporters because of fog. 350 fans were at Claremont Road at 8.30am, but the buses only got there at 9.30am. The fog cleared in the New Forest, and they arrived at the ground 10 minutes before the kick off. They left for home at 5.30pm, but at Staines the fog came down again. Some got to Hammersmith at 10.45pm, where their buses gave up. The more unlucky supporters got home at 2am.

But in the third round, the long trip to the north east to face Billingham Synthonia Recreation resulted in a 2–1 defeat. Billingham went 1–0 up, Roy Stroud equalised, but Billingham scored again to lead 2–1 at half-time. A sensational save by the home goalkeeper, Armstrong stopped an equaliser, and Hendon were unlucky to lose. Hendon had travelled north on the Friday evening, and had a tour of the factory which the home team was named after on the Saturday morning. Hendon were out of pocket on the trip, with a gate of under 3,000 and expenses that were heavier than usual.

Clapton knocked Hendon out of the London Senior Cup in the first round, with a 2–1 victory at the Old Spotted Dog Ground on New Year's Day. It was one of the team's worst performances of the season, but was played in dreadful conditions. In the Middlesex Senior Cup, Hendon beat Willesden 3–0 with goals from Hornsby, Avis and Reay before going out to Yiewsley 2–1 at Claremont Road after extra time. Avis had scored for Hendon, but missed a chance in the last minute to equalise. In the Middlesex Charity Cup, Hendon beat Tufnell Park 6–2 before a 1–0 defeat at Enfield ended the season's cup outings, and the club's hold on the Charity Cup. It was their first defeat in the competition for five years.

At Easter, Hendon again visited Belgium, entering the Verviers Tournament., beating Urainia (from Geneva) 4–2, and losing to Florisdorf by the same score after extra time. Roy Stroud scored three goals in the two matches, Bob Avis got two and Hornsby one.

Once again, the Will Mather Cup provided an end of season treat. Despite having beaten Chelsea two days earlier, and with a match against Manchester City two days later, Arsenal sent a team to Claremont Road with nine first team regulars. A crowd of 7,500 saw an Arsenal side including George Swindin in goal, the Compton brothers, Wally Barnes, Alex Forbes and Bryn Jones. Hendon faced this team missing Laurie Topp, Roy Stroud and Pat Lynch. Despite this, Bob Taylor gave Hendon the lead in the first half. But Don Roper soon equalised, and three more goals in the second half gave Arsenal victory – and the cup – by 4–1. It was reported that after the match, the teams had dinner together. The professional Arsenal players were drinking orangeade, while Hendon's amateur players could enjoy a beer.

Work on the ground was still a priority for the club. In October, the club announced the launch of a stand and pavilion improvement fund, anticipating the lifting of some of the restrictions on building work, where repairing war damage and building housing was still a priority. In November, the club said they were planning to build a training track at the ground at the end of the season, using grit from White City Stadium, which had been run on by some of the world's most famous athletes.

Laurie Topp played for England against France, and was selected as reserve for the Scotland match at Hampden. He was also selected for the Athenian League side three times, and goalkeeper Ray Kemp won his only Athenian League representative honour, playing against the Eastern League at the end of the season.

1949–50

Hendon could not maintain the high standards of the previous two seasons in the League, falling back to seventh place, with 28 points from 26 matches. The attack still averaged over two goals a game, with 54, but the defence conceded almost as many, 48. Hendon had started the season well, with a 5–0 victory at Hitchin followed by a 3–1 victory over champions-elect Tooting & Mitcham at Claremont Road on a freezing cold August afternoon. At the end of September, Hendon were top of the league, but after a 2–0 defeat against Redhill at Claremont Road on 15 October, Bromley regained top spot.

Tooting got their revenge for their Claremont Road defeat earlier in the season with a 5–1 win at Sandy Lane in February, as Hendon's season declined. One remarkable game was a 5–4 defeat at Barking in November. The game against Barnet at Claremont Road in November was shown on television. The team's form was erratic. Part of the problem was the lack of a regular centre-forward. Around Christmas, there was an unbeaten run of six matches, but this was followed by four defeats in the next five games.

Goalkeeper Reg Hill rejoined the club from Wealdstone, replacing Ray Kemp who joined Grays Athletic. He played in glasses, which he taped to the side of his head with sticking plaster and weighed around 16 stone. He was injured at Christmas, and lost his place to reserve keeper Cashman. Hornsby left the club, and two centre-forwards who played in the trial game, J. Ward and G. James were not of first team standard. Morrison started the season at centre-forward, but Billy Dare and Hornsby were missed. Pat Austin, Dennis Pacey from Woking, and two brothers, J. and Len Berryman, also played in the first team. At the end of the season, Pat Doyle and Albert Meek were recruited from Berkhamsted. Football journalist Peter Lorenzo played for the first team at Southall towards the end of the season.

The cup competitions

In the cups, Hendon were knocked out of the Amateur, Middlesex Senior and Middlesex Charity Cups by Finchley. In the Amateur Cup, Bowater's Lloyd were beaten 3–0 in the first round at Claremont Road. The *Hendon Times* said the club were 'expecting a record crowd', but why there should have been such interest in relatively obscure opponents is unclear. Stroud, Reay and Avis scored for Hendon, and 17-year-old Danny Shreeves had a good game. In goal, Cashman saved a penalty. But two weeks later, any hope of a Wembley trip finished at Summers Lane, where Finchley scored the game's only goal after five minutes on a bone-hard pitch. In the FA Cup, Hendon lost 4–0 at Wealdstone in the first qualifying round. Hendon dominated the first half hour, but Glyn Hinshelwood broke his arm, and after being 1–0 down at half-time, Hendon were easily beaten by the end of the game.

In the London Senior Cup, a 7–0 win at Imber Court over the Metropolitan Police, including a Roy Stroud hat-trick, was followed by the season's second television appearance in the next round, Hayes being beaten 3–2 at Claremont Road. Shreeves scored the winner 10 minutes from time. The game was Bill Reay's 150th consecutive first team appearance. The club record was 175, held by Bill Fisher. A 'huge crowd' enjoyed the game. After London League Woodford Town were beaten 5–0 at Claremont Road, Hendon faced Dulwich Hamlet in the semi-final at Wimbledon's Plough Lane home. Hendon's performance was 'ragged' in the first half, but the game was goalless at the break. In the second half, Hendon were on top when Dulwich scored after 17 minutes. Then with 12 minutes left, three goals from Dulwich Hamlet in four minutes settled the match. Arthur Phebey scored his second goal in the final minute to complete a 5–0 rout. Gornall, Connett and Green were Dulwich's other scorers.

Hendon: R. Hill, P. Lynch, M. Lane, L. Topp, W. Fisher, P. Austin, R. Stroud, W. Reay, D. Gittus, E. Owen, W. Birrell.

Dulwich Hamlet: A. Freeman, D. Eastman, W. Thrussell, B. Dacey, R. Cowley, T. Brown, D. Davies, A. Phebey, L. Gree, A. Connett, J. Gornall.

In the Middlesex Senior Cup, Metropolitan League Twickenham were beaten 3–1 in the first round at Claremont Road, although the first half was "pathetic to watch" according to the *Hendon Times*. In the second round, Finchley won 6–4 at Claremont Road after extra time, the lead changing hands five times. Finchley had equalised in the last minute of normal time to make the score 3–3. Stroud, Reay, Joyce and Shreeves were Hendon's scorers. Finchley's 'sensational victory' was achieved with four reserve players, and they were missing their England international forward George Robb. The game had kicked off at 2.45pm, but the weather had deteriorated, and the whole of extra time was played in darkness. In the *Evening News*, one of three London evening papers at the time, cartoonist Roy Ullyett drew a cartoon about the match, and the sports editor used it to campaign for floodlighting for football matches, which was eventually accepted by the game's authorities.

The drama was not repeated in the Middlesex Charity Cup, Finchley winning 1–0 at Claremont Road in a 'battle of defences'. The Strollers (third team) did win a cup, beating Letchworth Reserves 2–1 in the AFA Junior Cup Final, Dupont and Shreeves scoring.

Arsenal played London Midweek League matches at Claremont Road during the season. On 1 May, they sent a strong team for the annual Will Mather Cup match, from which the proceeds went to Manor House Hospital. Arsenal had just won the FA Cup, and paraded the trophy at half-time. Both the Compton brothers played, although Les was in the unfamiliar role of centre-forward. The famous former Arsenal amateur, Dr Kevin O'Flanghan and Scottish international Hugh Miller played as guests for Hendon, who lost 2–1. An own goal from Bill Fisher and Lishman scored for Arsenal, Avis replying for Hendon. Bill Reay missed the game – had he played he would have achieved a run of 164 consecutive appearances and four seasons without missing a game.

Towards the end of the season, the club were hoping to arrange a 'Past versus Present' friendly. Possible choices for the 'Past' team included: Harry Robshaw (Tottenham Hotspur), the Comptons, R. Mitchell (East Fife), Roy Evans (Enfield), Bob Thomas (Fulham), Billy Dare (Brentford) and Jack Cross (Bournemouth).

The less formal nature of amateur football was shown on Easter Saturday, when five Hendon players – Bill Fisher, Roy Stroud, Pat Lynch, Bill Reay and Ted Owen – played as guests for Hounslow in a Corinthian League match, as Hounslow were saving their players for the Middlesex Senior Cup Final on Easter Monday.

In November, the Italian national team trained at Claremont Rod prior to playing England at Tottenham. Laurie Topp was the only Hendon player capped by the England Amateur team, playing against France at Grenoble in May. He also played three times for the Athenian League. Roy Stroud played once for the Athenian League team.

Stroud, Topp and Adams were selected for Middlesex against Worcester on 1 April, but had to withdraw as the match clashed with the London Senior Cup semi-final. They did play for the County side against Essex in the Southern Counties Championship final. Adams and Stroud joined Middlesex Wanderers on their end of season tour to Holland.

At Christmas, George Bucci resigned as press secretary due to ill health. He had played in every position for the club, including in goal, and had retired as a player in 1945. His last game was the Middlesex Red Cross Cup Final at Wembley.

1950–51: Semi-final agony

The *Hendon Times'* summary of the season was headed 'A Memorable Season – But Hendon's Trophy Cupboard is Bare'. These few words barely tell the tale of one of the most exciting seasons in the club history. To be fair, the report does say that "For years Hendon had toiled in the obscurity of the Amateur Soccer world, but 1950–51 saw Hendon referred to as the 'Glamour team,' the 'team of the year,' the 'South's premier hope for the Amateur Cup' and many superlatives were generously handed out ..."

The season started with an unbeaten run of 18 games – 13 wins and five draws. However, the highlight of the season was the Amateur Cup. The first round bought Smethwick Highfield from the Worcestershire League to Claremont Road. Hendon's reward for a 2–0 victory, which was shown on television, was a trip to Suffolk & Norfolk League Bungay Town. Six coaches of supporters made the trip east, to a ground on low lying marsh land, which three weeks before had been under a foot of water. Also, the club had no grandstand. A 3–0 victory then saw high-flying Isthmian Leaguers Walthamstow Avenue come to Claremont Road. A capacity crowd saw a 0–0 draw on a barely playable muddy pitch, although the Walthamstow defence 'withstood what was probably their hardest fight this season. Hendon won the replay 2–0, with two goals from Bob Avis. It was Walthamstow's first home defeat of the season. A crowd of 9,000 included Prime Minister Clement Atlee, the local MP, and Secretary of State for Overseas Trade Arthur Bottomley. Hendon were 'superior

in every department' and the *Ham & High* said that Reg Ivey was becoming one of the best amateur goalkeepers in the country.

In the fourth round, Hendon faced a difficult trip to Plough Lane, the home of Wimbledon, at that time one of the country's leading amateur sides. A goal from Johnny Westmore gave Hendon the lead in front of a 12,000 crowd, but Wimbledon were on top in the second half and equalised for a 1–1 draw. In the replay, another goal from Westmore, and penalty from Bob Avis gave Hendon a 2–0 win, and a semi-final place for the first time in the club's history.

In the semi-final, Hendon faced Pegasus at Highbury. Only formed in 1948, and fielding a team made up of players from Oxford and Cambridge Universities, the club had been given a special bye to the Amateur Cup fourth qualifying round in their inaugural season. They reached the fourth round before losing to eventual winners Bromley, and had shown they could compete with the top amateur sides.

To reach the semi-final, the students had beaten Gosport Borough Athletic, Slough Town, Brentwood & Warley and Oxford City – all away from home.

A crowd of around 26,500 saw a dramatic encounter in the Highbury mud. With 20 minutes left, Roy Stroud gave Hendon the lead with a 25 yard shot into the top corner. With four minutes left, Tanner equalised for Pegasus. Then, with two minutes left, Hendon winger Avis was tripped in the penalty area. Dexter Adams hit the penalty firmly, but Pegasus goalkeeper Brown pushed the ball over the bar. Geoffrey Green's report in *The Times* says that "Hendon should have won", but the final result meant a replay the following week at Crystal Palace's Selhurst Park.

Hendon: R. Ivey, P. Lynch, M. Lane, L. Topp, D. Adams, W. Fisher, J. Westmore, A.H. Phebey, R. Stroud, G. Hinshelwood, R. Avis.

Pegasus: B. R. Brown, J. Maughan, R. Cowan, J. Platt, K. A. Shearwood, D. F. Saunders, H. J. Potts, J. A. Dutchman, J. D. P. Tanner, J. S. Laybourne, R. Sutcliffe.

The replay also saw Hendon so near – yet so far – from a Wembley final. Both teams made tactical changes for the match, and Roy Stroud, who had moved to the right wing, gave Hendon the lead; Tony Pawson equalising to make it 1–1 at half-time. In the second half, Avis gave Hendon the lead after the Pegasus players believed the ball had gone out of play.

Pegasus pressed desperately for an equaliser, and with six minutes left, Dutchman scored. Surely now extra time would follow. But with a minute left, Dutchman scored again to take his team to Wembley, and end a magnificent semi-final. In the final at Wembley, Pegasus won the cup, beating Bishop Auckland 2–1 before a 100,000 crowd.

Hendon: R. Ivey, P. Lynch, M. Lane, L. Topp, D. Adams, W. Fisher, J. Westmore, A. H. Phebey, R. Stroud, G. Hinshelwood, R. Avis.

Pegasus: B. R. Brown, R. Cowan, J. Maughan, J. Platt, K. A. Shearwood, D. F. Saunders, H. A. Pawson, J. A. Dutchman, J. D. P. Tanner, D. B. Carr, H. J. Potts.

Players

An important signing was goalkeeper Reg Ivey, who had played for Tufnell Park when they shared Claremont Road during the war. Phil Reilly was recruited from Barnet. Bill Reay left Claremont Road to join Bromley. In September, Middlesex cricketer Fred Titmus joined the club, having been playing for Watford's reserve team in the London Combination.

In November, another cricketer, this time from Kent, came to Claremont Road when winger Arthur Phebey joined from Dulwich Hamlet. In January, Roy Evans returned to the club from Enfield. He was a Welsh international forward. He was 29 years old and had last played for the club in the Golders Green days before the war.

London Senior Cup

In the London Senior Cup, Dagenham British Legion came to Claremont Road in the first round. Goals from Stroud, Reilly and Phebey saw Hendon into the second round.

111

Corinthian Casuals were beaten on 3 February, with Roy Evans making his first appearance. The Claremont Road pitch had mud that almost reached to the players' knees, and mist reducing visibility to 75 yards, keeping the crowd down to 1,500. Evans made a goal for Avis after three minutes. Avis scored again to take Hendon into the third round. Leytonstone were dispatched 3–2, although Hendon were defending for most of the game, and in the semi-final, Wimbledon were beaten 2–1 at Ilford. Stroud had given Hendon the lead just before half-time, and Avis took Hendon into their first post-war London Senior Cup Final with a header in extra time.

Bromley 4 Hendon 3
London Senior Cup Final

Hendon returned to Highbury for the final of the London Senior Cup, losing 4–3 to Athenian League champions Bromley after extra time, Welsh international winger Roy Evans scoring a hat-trick. Hendon played better than for many weeks, but the Kentish team were a little too strong for them. Hill, playing in goal in place of Ivey who was injured and failed a pre-game fitness test, had a fine game.

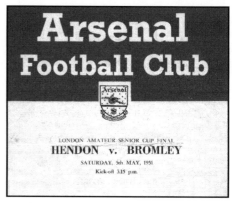

The two teams were regarded as having the best defences in amateur, so a seven goal thriller had not been expected. Hooper gave Bromley the lead early on, Evans replied five minutes later with a long shot into the top corner. On 17 minutes, Lane sliced a clearance and Gregory scored to put Bromley ahead again, a lead they kept until the break. On 54 minutes, Stroud crossed for Evans to head home. Three minutes later, he gave Hendon the lead with a 'full-blooded' shot. On 63 minutes, Fuller equalised to send the game into extra time. Thirteen minutes into extra time, Gregory intercepted a back pass from Dexter Adams and slid the winner home. The 11,078 crowd, which included the Mayor of Hendon, Alderman J.L. Freedman, had been well entertained.

Hendon: R. Hill, P. Lynch, M. Lane, L. Topp, D. Adams, W. Fisher, R. Evans, A. Phebey, R. Stroud, R. Avis, J. Westmore.

Bromley: T. Cornthwaite, L. Wager, D. Cameron, K. Yenson, C. Fuller, R. Sheen, T. Hopper, J. Gregory, G. Brown, R. Dunmall, R. Merrifield.

(Programme courtesy Arsenal Football Club)

In the Middlesex Senior Cup, Hendon lost 3–2 in the first round at Edgware, after being 2–0 up with five minutes left. The game was played on 7 April, due to fixture congestion, and four senior players were absent due to international calls and an injury. In the Middlesex Charity Cup, Yiewsley and Hayes were beaten at Claremont Road, both games being won 1–0. Hendon lost in the semi-final 3–1 at Wealdstone. The game was squeezed in at the end of the season, and Hendon fielded a below strength team, including 16-year-old third team goalkeeper Tom Mason.

The two 'open' cup competitions the club entered also provided great excitement. In the FA Cup, Hendon fought through the qualifying rounds, beating Barnet 3–2, with goals from Avis, Russell and Stroud, then Edgware were beaten 7–1 in front of a 7,000 crowd. Hendon were 'vastly superior' in all departments to their local rivals, Stroud and Avis scored hat-tricks, with Owen also scoring. In the second qualifying round, Hayes were beaten 1–0 and two goals from Avis helped Hendon to win 4–2 at Enfield to reach the fourth qualifying round. With the incentive of reaching the first round and a possible of a money-spinning tie with Third Division opposition, Hendon visited Southern League Tonbridge. More than 600 supporters made the trip, and with 15 minutes left, Hendon were 3–0 down. But goals from Stroud, Adams (a penalty) and Avis secured a 3–3 draw in a spectacular recovery. The replay was the following Thursday afternoon, and Hendon lost 2–1. Hendon had gone 2–0 down at half-time, before Westmore pulled a goal back.

The same week, the club's run in the London Challenge Cup had finished. This competition was open to the capital's professional sides, who usually fielded a reserve team, and the four semi-finalists from the previous season's London Senior Cup. Hendon beat Walthamstow Avenue 3–1 at home, won 4–0 at Millwall, and then held Charlton to a 0–0 draw at Claremont Road. Forced by the London FA to play the game on a Monday afternoon after the match at Tonbridge, Hendon fielded a largely reserve team and lost 1–0, Charlton's winner coming in the last minute, a highly respectable result against Charlton's reserve side.

The league

All this progress in cup competitions produced a season of 50 competitive matches, and inevitable fixture congestion. The league campaign started well, and the team were unbeaten in the league until 16 December, when Walton & Hersham won 2–1 at Claremont Road. However, a challenge for the league tailed off as the pressure of the cup competitions grew. After beating Corinthian Casuals in the London Senior Cup on 3 February, the club had 13 league matches to play, and were still in four cups, with 15 dates left, including the Easter weekend. Adding to the club's problems, the League had expanded to 16 teams, so there were four extra fixtures to fulfil. Towards the end of the season, the reserves fulfilled a first-team fixture at Enfield on Good Friday, drawing 0–0 with Enfield's first team.

On Easter Monday, the club played two first team matches, mixing the first team and reserves. In the morning, Hayes won 2–0 at Claremont Road, in the afternoon, another team won 1–0 at Leyton. Hendon's end-of-season tour to Hong Kong added to the problems, removing two possible Saturday dates. On 20 April, two first team games were played simultaneously: the first team drew 1–1 with Leyton at home, the reserves lost 3–0 at Redhill.

In a frantic end to the season, matches were played on 1, 2 and 3 May. Hendon did well to finish fourth, with 36 points, scoring 45 goals and conceding 40. One highlight of the league season was a 3–1 victory in front of a full ground at Bromley, who went on to win the championship.

On the international scene, Dexter Adams won his first cap for England, being chosen at right back against Ireland at Coventry on 3 February. He also played against Finland at the end of the season, this time at centre half. Laurie Topp and Roy Stroud were also capped for England, and on 19 January, Hendon had Laurie Topp playing for England against Wales at Leicester, with the Welsh team including his club team mate Roy Evans. Topp also played for Middlesex Wanderers in Holland.

Hong Kong

In January, Hendon announced that they were planning a tour to Hong Kong. In April, the squad was announced: Dexter Adams missed out due to an architectural exam, and Arthur Phebey was playing cricket for Kent. The players included: Reg Ivey, Reg Hill, Pat Lynch, Mick Lane, Reg Nelmes, Laurie Topp, Bill Fisher, Pat Austin, Glyn Hinshelwood, Colin Morley, Roy Stroud, Bob Avis, Johnny Westmore, Phil Reilly, Ted Owen, Des Gittus and Roy Evans. Trainer Jerry Marrable, Stan Greene, Roger Raymond, and referee L. A. McKay also joined the party. They left from Northolt on 6 May, the day after the London Senior Cup Final.

Hendon played Hong Kong Selection and Hong Kong Combined teams, winning the first 2–0 with goals from Topp and Evans, and drawing the second with goals from Stroud and Avis. The visit to Hong Kong lasted a week, and included Tiffin at Shek O Golf Club one day and Castle Peak the next. The team then spent another week in Manila. Seven matches were played, four won and one abandoned when the floodlights failed. Evans was the top scorer with six goals, Stroud and Austin got two each. It was reported that "wherever they went the players were received with kindness and hospitality." The party flew back to Heathrow to end one of the club's most successful seasons, but one which had not resulted in any trophies.

Above: The Hendon tourists to Hong Kong. Below: Match action on the tour

Hendon line up before one of the Hong Kong tour matches

A banquet on the tour

A Hendon line up from the late 1940s

Three team groups from the early 1950s

Laurie Topp is third from the right in the back row. Pat Lynch is in middle of the front row. Ted Owen is on the right of the front row.

Jerry Marrable is on the left, back row, Mickey Lane, Bill Fisher, and Dexter Adams next to the goalkeeper. Front: From right: Roy Stroud, Ted Owen and Pat Lynch.

The 1951–52 team:
Back: R. Evans,
P. Austin, A. Phebey,
R. Ivey, D. Adams,
M. Lane, J. Marrable;
Front: R. Avis, R. Stroud,
P. Lynch (c), L. Topp,
B. Fisher.

1951–52: Runners up again

Runners up again! Hendon finished in second place in the Athenian League for the third time since the war, two points behind champions – and local rivals – Wealdstone. This was despite the local press being pessimistic at the start of the season, saying the trial match was 'gloomy' and that the club's reserve strength was weak. Apparently the 1–1 draw with Leyton at Claremont Road that opened the season was so poor that fans were leaving well before the end. But things improved, and by the end of September, Hendon were top of the table with 13 points from nine games. The squad was largely the same as the previous season, although Glyn Hinshelwood had left. England international Eric Beardsley came to Claremont Road from Eastbourne. A rare overseas recruit was Wallace 'Shoehorn' Johnson, from the Gold Coast, who made his first team debut at Bromley in September, but he left the club in February to play for Civil Service FC. A further recruit with an international background was Roy Shea, who had played for the Singapore FA when serving there in the army. He had joined Hendon with Cliff Nock, and both players had been recommended to the club by Colonel Prince, the Secretary of the Army FA. In March, left-winger Alan Beningfield joined the club from Wealdstone.

Hendon only lost two matches in the league, at Hayes and Walton & Hersham. But eight points dropped through draws saw Wealdstone narrowly take the title. On 1 December, Hendon were top of the league, with 27 points from 17 games. Remaining unbeaten in the rest of the season was not good enough; the final 13 league matches produced eight wins and five draws.

The goals flowed – Hendon failed to score only once, in a 0–0 draw at Wealdstone, and beat Barking 8–0 and Hitchin 7–0 at home. The Barking result was a post-war club record, with the goals coming from a Roy Stroud hat-trick, two each for Roy Evans and Avis, and one from Phebey. Against Hitchin, Stroud and Avis both scored hat-tricks.

Cambridge City, Enfield, Redhill and Sutton United all left Claremont Road having conceded five goals. Hendon finished with 84 goals from 30 games – three more than Wealdstone, and conceded 32, which Wealdstone bettered by three, with 29.

London Challenge Cup

Success in the league was reflected in the cups. In the London Challenge Cup, Hendon made their first appearance under floodlights, and beat an Arsenal side at Highbury with a number of players with first team experience. The match was reported as the first competitive cup tie in England under floodlights, so Hendon had the honour of winning it! Southampton's reserves had played Tottenham a week earlier at The Dell to claim the honour of the first competitive floodlit match.

Hendon won 1–0, but it was a hollow victory, Arsenal played most of second half with nine men. Grimshaw went off with concussion, then Shaw was carried off with a leg injury. However, the *Ham & High* said that this "should not detract from Hendon's fine

(Courtesy Arsenal FC)

performance. Dexter Adams, Pat Lynch and Mickey Lane kept Arsenal forwards, led by international Reg Lewis well under control." Two minutes from time, Stroud crossed for Arthur Phebey to score past Kelsey for the winner. Arsenal manager Tom Whitaker visited the Hendon dressing room after the game to congratulate them on their victory, and said not to worry about the injuries to his players.

Hendon: R. Ivey, P. Lynch, M. Lane, L. Topp, D. Adams, W. Fisher, R. Evans, A. Phebey, R. Stroud, P. Austin, B. Avis.

Arsenal: Kelsey, Roper, Wade, Wills, Healey, Chennals, Ryan, Grimshaw, Lewis, Shaw, Robertson.

In the next round West Ham, with eight of their team having first team experience, were eliminated. Phebey scored the winner again, and it was reported that 'West Ham obviously underrated Hendon's ability and indulged in too much close passing and fancy work. Hendon played direct football and looked the more dangerous in front of goal.'

In the semi-final, on 5 November, Hendon drew 1–1 with Charlton. The professionals were 'outclassed in midfield' and Hendon deserved to win. Westmore put Hendon ahead five minutes after half-time, Charlton equalised 13 minutes later. Roy Shea, a 21-year-old national serviceman, made his Hendon debut.

In the replay, Hendon lost 2–1 in extra time at The Valley. Charlton, who fielded a team with eight players with first team experience, won through a goal from left-winger Barry, whose shot hit Dexter Adams leaving goalkeeper Reg Ivey helpless. Roy Evans came close to equalising, only for a 'wonder save' from Charlton keeper Gill to preserve his side's lead. Shea had scored for Hendon, who were missing Avis and Austin who couldn't get time off work to play.

Charlton Athletic: Gill, Campbell, Firmani, Forbes, Phipps, Hammond, Fell, Lumley, Townsend, Cullum, Barry.

Hendon: R. Ivey, P. Lynch, M. Lane, L. Topp, D. Adams, W. Fisher, R. Evans, J. Westmore, R. Stroud, C. Nock, R. Shea.

These matches were interesting tests for Hendon, facing players of professional standard. Charlton manager Jimmy Seed accepted after the game that Hendon "did not deserve to lose; you are a great side" and hoped Hendon would win the Amateur Cup.

Hendon missed out on another match with professional opposition when the team's FA Cup run ended at the first attempt at Aylesbury in the fourth qualifying round. Hendon lost 4–3, Evans, Avis and Adams scoring. Aylesbury faced Watford in the first round proper.

Jimmy Seed's hopes for Hendon in the Amateur Cup were not borne out. After a 3–2 win at Corinthian League leaders Slough in the first round, with goals from Stroud, Evans and Avis, Northern League giants Bishop Auckland came to Claremont Road in the second round. A 'record crowd crammed into Claremont Road' to witness a 1–1 draw. Stroud put Hendon 1–0 up in the second minute, but the northerners equalised in the second half. Eight coaches of Hendon supporters left at midnight on Friday for the replay, but witnessed a 5–1 defeat in the replay, in front of a 12,000 crowd. Dexter Adams scored Hendon's goal from a second-half penalty.

In the London Senior Cup, Hendon reached the semi-final, knocking out Wimbledon, Enfield and Corinthian Casuals before losing 4–2 to Finchley at Southall after extra time. Westmore and Stroud scored for Hendon. Finchley also ended Hendon's interest in the Middlesex Senior Cup, winning 3–2 at Claremont Road, with Nock and Phebey scoring for Hendon. In the Middlesex Charity Cup, Southall beat a Hendon side including five reserves 3–1 in January. It was Hendon's first home defeat of the season.

Laurie Topp became the club's first Olympian when he played for Great Britain against Luxembourg in Helsinki. However, Great Britain lost 5–3 after extra time. The only other Athenian League player in the team was George Robb from Finchley. Topp and Dexter Adams played for England against Northern Ireland in February. Mickey Lane, Roy Stroud, Arthur Phebey and Pat Lynch all played for the Middlesex County side. Roy Evans played for the London FA, and Tommy Mason played for the Middlesex FA Youth team on a tour to Germany. Roy Stroud had a further taste of the professional game, playing for West Ham's reserve team on Easter Saturday. He scored four goals and made a fifth. He then played for the first team against Notts County on Easter Monday. The Hammers lost 1–0, but Stroud 'played well'.

With Reg Ivey and Bill Fisher, Stroud returned to the Far East with an Athenian League side at the end of the season. He scored six goals, including a hat trick against the Singapore AFA side. Fisher and Ivey played in six matches each, Ivey saving a penalty in one game.

Hendon may have missed out on a place in the Middlesex Senior Cup Final, but the match between Enfield and Finchley was played at Claremont Road. Finchley won 3–0.

The club were also looking to improve their facilities. In November, it was announced that Hendon Borough Council had approved plans for 300 more seats by building an extension of the stand right along northern side of ground, and a new clubhouse. The club was also considering floodlights, but the problem was how to install them. They could not be put on top of the stands, which were not tall enough. An alternative was to mount them on all poles, but club secretary Mr Greene said: "there would be disadvantages in that. They might be an eyesore and you might get little boys climbing up them."

1952–53: Champions at last!

Champions at last! After coming so close - five times runners-up - the Athenian League title finally came to Claremont Road. The league returned to 14 clubs, Bromley and Barking having left to join the Isthmian League. Hendon finished with 42 points from 26 matches, with only 2 defeats and 6 draws. Second placed Wealdstone trailed five points behind. So in two seasons, over 56 league matches, Hendon only lost four times – surely one of the most consistent records over two seasons in amateur football. Only one match was lost at Claremont Road, Leyton winning 3–1 on 15 November, the first defeat of the season to amateur opposition. Away from home, the only defeat was at Wealdstone, 2–0 on Christmas Day.

Once again, supporters saw plenty of goals at Claremont Road. On 3 April, Redhill went home having conceded 11, with Hendon's goals coming from Stroud with four, two each from Snaith, Nock and Beningfield and one from Phebey. It was 6–1 at half-time, having been 1–1 early in the game. It was the club's record Athenian League victory. Three weeks later, Finchley was beaten 7–1, although they were fielding a weak side with guest players due to fixture congestion. In October Barnet had been beaten 6–0. Away from home, the 4–0 win at Hayes, with goals from Nock with two, Potton and Stroud was the club's best away win since the war. After this game, the *Hendon Times* said that Hendon were set for the Championship.

One memorable match was a 0–0 draw at Finchley on 14 April. Apparently Golders Green station was swamped by Hendon supporters trying to get to Summers Lane for the 5.15 kick-off. Finchley had reached the third round of the FA Cup, but now were having to field a team almost every day to catch up on a fixture backlog. The star of the Finchley team was George Robb, who was soon to turn professional with Tottenham Hotspur. Bill Fisher had a great game for Hendon to keep him quiet, and the point gained was an important one in the march to the title. Wealdstone lost at Barnet, so the 1–1 draw with Tooting & Mitcham United at Claremont Road on 25 April which confirmed Hendon as champions was academic as the team couldn't be caught at that stage. The *Hendon Times* reported on its front page that the title triumph had been celebrated with Champagne. Roy Stroud led Hendon's goalscorers with 29, following by Bob Avis with 16, Arthur Phebey 11 and Cliff Nock 10.

Players and honours

The title had been won under a new full-time coach, Ted Gaskell, who joined the club after 15 years with Brentford FC. He took over from Ted Drake at the start of the season. He was 35 years old, and it was his first coaching appointment. He had turned professional with Chesterfield in 1936, briefly played for Buxton, and then joined Brentford. He had never had a regular first team place at Griffin Park.

On the playing front, a new recruit from Eastbourne was Eric Beardsley, an England international. Pat Lynch had left to join Epsom FC as player-coach, although he later returned to Hendon. Roy Stroud was the new team captain, with Dexter Adams as vice-captain. Stroud, Adams and Topp made regular appearances in the England amateur team. At the end of the season, Topp and Adams toured Norway with England.

Other international honours included Roy Evans playing for Wales, although he left the club during the season to play for the Metropolitan Police side; David Evans played for the England Youth team against Northern Ireland at Molineux in March, and turned professional with Aston Villa at the end of the season; and Jim (Jock) Ward played for Scotland. Ward had played for Customs & Excise in a match at Claremont Road, and had been watched by Hendon officials, who then found out he could play for the club while working in London. In Scotland, he played for the famous amateur club Queen's Park.

Other new recruits included inside forward Maurice Potton, who joined the club in February from Irish club Bohemains; winger Bill Amor from Newbury, although his commitments with the police prevented him playing regularly, and football journalist Peter Lorenzo, who played a few games for the reserves. Departures included Danny Shreeves who joined Southall in September, and in the second half of the season included Johnny Richards to Walthamstow Avenue and Dutch goalkeeper Koper.

One problem Gaskell faced was players doing national service. In February, new winger Derek (Ken) Snaith was expected to play at Walton & Hersham, but at the last minute could not get away from his army duties, so trainer Jerry Marrable had to play. However, the club was assured by his CO (Commanding Officer) that he would be available for future matches.

FA Cup

A successful run through the qualifying competition gave Hendon an exciting first round match against Northampton Town at Claremont Road. Victories against Wealdstone, St Albans City – after a replay – Uxbridge and Dartford had produced this reward. It was the first time Hendon had faced Football league opposition in the FA Cup at home.

Hendon 0 Northampton Town 0
FA Cup First Round proper

A remarkable crowd of 9,000 crammed into Claremont Road, an attendance record that will never be beaten. Supporters queued for one and a half hours to get in. Northampton were second in the Third Division South and were the top scoring team in the Football League. With a heavy

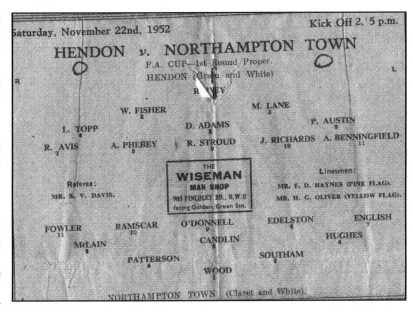

pitch, and Hendon in great form, there were great hopes of a giant killing. In the Northampton team was Ron Patterson, who in 1968 would become Hendon's coach.

Hendon started well, and a run from Roy Stroud ended when Patterson cleared his pass. Then Bill Fisher cleared off the line from a Northampton corner. Both teams continued to attack, and full back Pat Austin went close with a lob. Then Maurice Edelston, a former amateur international, and later a famous football commentator, missed giving the visitors the lead from four yards out. Then just on half-time, Bob Avis had a shot kicked off the line by Northampton's Gwyn Hughes. As conditions worsened in the second half, fewer chances were created. A Stroud header grazed the post, and with a few minutes left, the same player was fouled on the edge of the penalty area. But Hendon could not score from the free kick, and a goal-less draw was the final result.

Former Hendon player Denis Compton covered the match as a journalist, and said that "Hendon can be proud of their performance... They gave a tremendous display." He said that the Hendon defence was outstanding throughout the game.

Hendon: R. Ivey, W. Fisher, M. Lane, L. Topp, D. Adams, P. Austin, B. Avis, A. Phebey, R. Stroud, J. Richards, A. Beningfield.

Northampton Town: Wood, Southam, Patterson, Hughes, Candlin, McLain, English, Edelston, O'Donnell, Ramscar, Fowler.

Northampton Town 2 Hendon 0

The replay was held the following Thursday, with a 2.00pm kick off. The Northampton programme – which said the match was in the 'English Cup' said that Hendon had put up "A splendid fight" in the first match, and testified to "the excellence of their defence, for our forwards gained very few chances." A trip to Swindon was the prize for the victors. The teams were the same as in the first match.

Hendon held their professional opponents to 0–0 at half-time, but two goals in the last five minutes, saw Northampton home 2–0. The game was played on a treacherous surface caused by melting snow. Hendon had chances in the first half, but the game was goalless at the break. Five minutes from time, Ramscar put Northampton ahead after Ivey had saved a shot from Edelston. With a minute left, Fowler scored from a corner. The crowd of 6,120 gave Reg Ivey a great ovation at the end of the game. Freddy Debenham, writing in the next Hendon programme, said that the players "were a credit to Hendon Football Club and amateur football generally." He also said that the press had lavishly praised the team's performance in the two matches.

Cup competitions

In the Amateur Cup, Boldmere St Michael's, from the Birmingham & District League visited Claremont Road in the first round, and lost 4–0. Roy Stroud scored two of Hendon's goals. The game was shown on television, and the *Hendon Times* speculated whether the "poor crowd [of 3,500] was to be blamed on the weather or television." But in the second round, Hounslow Town won 2–1 at Claremont Road to end hopes of a Wembley trip for another year. Arthur Phebey scored for Hendon, who were handicapped by an injury to Bill Fisher, who had to move to the wing. Hounslow won the game near the end, Hendon having missed chances to score.

Hendon entered the London Challenge Cup, losing 3–2 at Claremont Road in October to a strong Tottenham team, including former Hendon player Harry Robshaw. Hendon were 3–0 down with eight minutes left, before a goal from Roy Stroud and penalty from Dexter Adams made the score respectable. Spurs manager Arthur Rowe said that Hendon gave a great display.

In the county cups, Hendon lost in the first round in both competitions. In the London Senior Cup, a 3–2 defeat at Southall was reported as a 'lack lustre display', Beningfield and Nock scoring for Hendon. In the Middlesex Senior Cup, Hendon went out 1–0 at Southall, who scored the only goal after 20 minutes. Hendon were missing Stroud, Topp and Adams, who were playing for England.

Maybe these defeats were a blessing, as it avoided the inevitable fixture congestion that could have cost the league title. There was more success in the Middlesex Charity Cup, with victories over Hayes (after a replay – Hendon had started the first game at Hayes with nine men after arriving late) and Wealdstone leading to a final against Hounslow Town at Hayes.

Hounslow 2 Hendon 1
Middlesex Charity Cup Final

Hendon took the lead on 24 minutes, when a shot from Avis hit Briggs and beat the Hounslow goalkeeper. But the game was decided around the half-time break: Hounslow equalised two minutes before the interval, and went ahead two minutes after it. Hendon were close to equalising near the end. Hendon had shuffled their forward line, with Potton on the wing and Stroud at inside-right, but the change had not been effective.
Hendon: D. Archer, B. Fisher, M. Lane, L. Topp, D. Adams, P. Austin, M. Potton, R. Stroud, J. Ward, R. Avis, A. Beningfield
Hounslow: A. Parsons, D Rickard, E. Emmins, L. Cope, R. Briggs, D. Evans, T. Fidler, H. Pope, A. King, D. Page, F. Peake.

Hendon played an Arsenal XI on 21 March in a friendly and lost 0–2. It was hoped to revive the Will Mather Cup, but it was not played. However, Hendon did play at Wealdstone in a Coronation match, one of many staged to celebrate the event. There was also an announcement that the club was to run a cricket section in the summer, with matches on Sundays at Clitterhouse Playing Fields. Laurie Topp, Bill Fisher and Roy Stroud were all expected to play.

Once again, the club were well represented at international and county level. On 15 November, three Hendon players were in the England team against Holland, a record for the club. Laurie Topp and Roy Stroud started the game, Dexter Adams came on for an injured player in the second half. Five Hendon players were selected for Middlesex against Kent on New Year's Eve at Wealdstone: Bill Fisher and Johnny Richards joining the three England stars. Roy Evans, Adams, Stroud and Topp all played for the Athenian League side.

1953–54: Anti-climax

Following the triumphs of the previous season, this campaign was an anti-climax. In the league, Hendon slipped to fifth, with 29 points from 26 games. Local rivals Finchley won the title, nine points clear of Hendon. The defence was – with Hitchin Town – the best in the league, conceding only 32 goals, but the attack managed only 40. After the goal feasts of the previous season, the biggest victory was 3–0, against Leyton and Walton & Hersham. In November, the club programme spoke of "an air of defeat and despondency at Claremont Road", and in February, Hendon found themselves 12th in the league, with 13 points from 14 games, although Southall in fourth place had played six games more, and was only 10 points clear of Hendon. A 3–2 victory at champions-elect Finchley towards the end of the season was reported in the club programme as seeing the "return of the Hendon fighting spirit which has been so sadly lacking." Three wins over the Easter weekend, without conceding a goal, strengthened Hendon's position, but Finchley won their first Athenian League title with a 3–1 win at Claremont Road towards the end of the season.

The club programme reflected towards the end of the season that "it is in attack that we have suffered our disappointments. Match after match we have territorially outplayed our opponents, only to fail in the all-important factor – G-O-A-L-S! The approach work has been brilliant, but far too often that extra devil and snap finish has been lacking. Injuries and team changes have been a contributory factor, but, this apart, let's face it, we have missed chances and this we cannot afford to do if we are to maintain our status as one of London's premier amateur sides."

In fact, the club had not managed to field the same team two matches running throughout the season. In the first match, at Leyton, Alan Beningfield broke his leg after only eight minutes play and was out for the season. Laurie Topp and Dexter Adams were regulars for the England amateur side, and missed three matches in the first two months of the season, the third being an FA Cup match against Yiewsley, when they were selected for an FA Amateur XI against Trinidad. By the end of September, the club had used 21 players in the first team.

Forwards John Core, an Army Sergeant who had been playing for Halifax Town, Charlie Hawes from Brentford and Frank Penn were new recruits early on in the season. Penn had a back injury, and missed the whole season, although he used to send 'good luck' telegrams to the team before matches regularly. Johnny Westmore left to join St Albans City. In October, Colin Murchison joined, along with Danish goalkeeper Paul Ahm.

At the end of September, full-back Mickey Lane retired, no longer being sure of a first team place and to concentrate on running his pub in West Ham. He was given life membership of the club in recognition of his service.

But the major set-back, particularly for the attack, was the departure of Roy Stroud and Bob Avis in November. There had been talk of Stroud turning professional for a couple of years, and he joined West Ham United in November. He was turning professional at the age of 28, late in his career. The club did not adequately replace Stroud for the rest of the season.

A Hendon hero: Roy Stroud

From making his debut as a 14-year-old in 1940 to turning professional with West Ham United in November 1953, at the age of 28, Roy Stroud was the mainstay of the club's attack. He started his career as a right-winger, but later moved to centre forward.

He was born in West Ham, but at the age of two moved with his family to Hounslow. He was a schoolboy with Arsenal, played for London and Middlesex Boys before joining Golders Green. He was also capped as a youngster by the England boys team.

He played regularly during the war, despite being called up in 1943. He was top scorer in 1942–43 with 22 goals. In 1945–46 he played four matches in the Brentford first team in the Football League South. International honours soon came his way, and he made his England debut on 24 January 1948, scoring in a 7–2 win over Wales in Bangor. He won nine England caps, scoring four goals. He played 18 times for the Athenian League side, including matches on tour in 1952 in Hong Kong and Singapore. He also played for the Middlesex County team.

For Hendon, he was captain, and top goalscorer, with 29, of the 1952–53 team which won the Athenian League. He played in two Middlesex Charity Cup winning teams, and was a runner-up in the Middlesex Senior Cup three times.

He made his West Ham debut while still a Hendon player on Easter Monday 1952, in a 1–0 win over Notts County. He then played in some floodlit friendlies, including a 7–0 win over Hearts. He turned professional with West Ham in November 1953, and Hendon struggled to replace his goal-scoring power for the rest of the season. His career at Upton Park was blighted by injury, and he made 13 appearances for the first team, scoring four goals. He left West Ham in 1957 to join Southern League Chelmsford City, but after breaking his leg retired from football.

Bob Avis joined former Hendon stalwart Pat Lynch at Epsom, having complained about barracking by the Hendon supporters.

In December, Johnny Bartholomew joined the club from Hayes, but Arthur Phebey left to join Dulwich Hamlet. The club signed Reg Gillett as a replacement on for the left wing. In March, Surrey cricketer Mickey Stewart joined the club from Isthmian League Wimbledon. The club programme welcomed "a most accomplished footballer," although in April he had to stop playing to take up his duties with Surrey. Another forward to play in the first team again while in London was Scot Jim Ward. A player who returned to the first team in April was Roy Shea. He had been aboard the *Empire Windrush* when it sank in the Mediterranean.

Cup campaigns

In the FA Cup, Hendon's interest in the competition ended in the third qualifying round, with a 2–0 defeat at Yiewsley in a replay. In the Amateur Cup, the first round draw took Hendon to Wealdstone on 19 December. A 3–3 draw at Lower Mead was followed by the traditional Christmas matches with Wealdstone – both teams winning their home games – and then the Amateur Cup replay at Claremont Road on 2 January, which Hendon won 2–0. Four consecutive local derbies musty have left supporters of both teams exhausted.

A 4–2 win over Hayes in the second round, which was watched by two Syrian visitors to England who were observing amateur football and were 'very impressed', was followed by another tough local derby with Finchley. A 1–1 draw, when Bartholomew had put Hendon ahead and Finchley equalised in the closing minutes, was followed by a 2–1 defeat in the replay. However, Hendon had fought back from 2–0 down, and club secretary Stan Greene had written to Dexter Adams congratulating the team on their "magnificent fight" in the game and said that Hendon did not deserve to lose. A crowd of 7,000, including Sir Stanley Rous, had seen Finchley reach the quarter finals for the first time in their 70 year history. Nock scored for Hendon in the second half, and a 'superb display' by Barham in the Finchley goal took his team through.

The London Senior Cup also produced a marathon. Two 2–2 draws with Southall in the first round were followed by a 7–2 win for Hendon at Claremont Road in the second replay, with inside-forward John Core scoring five goals, the best by an inside forward for the club since Jimmy Smy scored five in the 1920s. In the second round, Barking were beaten 2–1 at Claremont Road, but then hopes of another final appearance ended in the third round with a 4–1 defeat at Leyton. The defence was reported as being 'below form'. In the Middlesex Senior Cup, a 3–2 defeat at Hounslow after extra time in the first round ended Hendon's interest in the competition.

Hendon were invited to enter the London Charity Cup for the first time, but lost 3–1 at Carshalton in the first round. The Middlesex Charity Cup produced more success, victories over Enfield and Edgware Town seeing the team through to the final. The lead up to the clash with Edgware in January, a local derby, according to the *Hendon Times* was "exciting thousands of local soccer fans". Hendon won comfortably with goals from Core and Nock.

Hendon 1 Southall 0
Middlesex Charity Cup Final

Hendon won the Middlesex Charity Cup again at Hayes on 8 May. The game went into extra time, and a goal from John Core near the end won it for Hendon. He beat three defenders to score. But the defence deserved most of the credit. Goalkeeper Don Archer had injured an eye at the start of the second half, and Colin Edwards took over in goal. Archer returned for extra time, playing at centre forward. Ron Stanton was also injured in the second half and was a passenger for the rest of the game.

Hendon: D. Archer, B. Fisher, E. Beardsley, C. Edwards, D. Adams, P. Austin, R. Stanton, C. Nock, Peter Terry, J. Core, C. Hawes

The season also saw some high profile matches at Claremont Road. In the second match of the season, Spurs Reserves won 3–1, scoring two goals in the last 10 minutes. Then as champions, Hendon hosted an Athenian League XI, and drew 2–2, with goals from Core and Stroud. The distinguished guests included the Mayor of Hendon and Sir Arthur Morse CBE, President of the Hong Kong FA, who had welcomed Hendon to Hong Kong in 1951. On 29 April, Arsenal came for the Will Mather Cup match, and won 3–1. The Arsenal team included Brian McGreevy, who they had signed from Hendon earlier in the season.

One honour for the club towards the end of the season was Laurie Topp winning the Athenian League 'Player of the Year' award.

Another point of interest was the links between Hendon and county cricket. Two first class cricketers – Arthur Phebey and Mickey Stewart played for the first team during the season, and the club programme advertised benefit matches for Len Muncer and Leslie Compton, both former Hendon players. Of course, Phebey and Stewart both missed matches due to cricket commitments, and this combined with injuries and representative matches at international, county, FA XI and Athenian League XI for various players, plus players being selected for Army matches, must have caused the club's selectors continual headaches in what had been a difficult season.

1954–55: A Wembley Final

Wembley! Following the club's first Athenian League championship in 1953, two years on, Hendon reached the FA Amateur Cup final. There they faced northern giants Bishop Auckland. Hendon lost 2–0, before a 100,000 crowd, and despite the result, it was a great day for the Claremont Road club. After the pre-season trial match, Bill Fisher had confidently predicted that "we have the material to get to Wembley for our first Amateur Cup Final" and he turned out to be right.

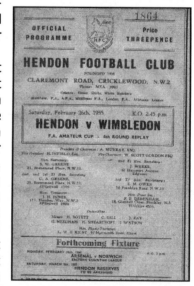

The road to Wembley nearly finished in the first round at Dartmouth United from the Plymouth & District League on 18 December. Hendon were 3–1 down with 15 minutes left before fighting back for a 3–3 draw. The Greens won the replay at Claremont Road 2–1 and then beat Cambridge City 4–3, with a last minute winner from Cunningham to progress to the third round. There, the draw did Hendon no favours, sending them to Green Pond Road to face Walthamstow Avenue. The Isthmian Leaguers were one of the strongest amateur sides in the country, but a 1–0 Hendon win, from an own goal by Brahan produced a further tough encounter, a visit to Plough Lane to face Wimbledon. A 1–1 draw at Plough Lane, when Hendon were "lucky still to be in the competition" according to the *Hendon Times*, was followed by a 4–1 victory in the replay, with Eric Parker scoring a hat trick. A crowd of 6,500, including Sir Stanley Rous, saw the replay. Wimbledon had gone down to 10 men after Gauntlett was injured when scoring the equaliser.

126

Two weeks later, on 12 March, Hendon faced Hounslow in the semi-final at White Hart Lane. In 1951, Hendon had gone out to Pegasus at this stage after two dramatic matches, but this time a 2–1 victory saw Hendon through. Parker put Hendon ahead after 37 minutes, but after an hour, Harper equalised for Hounslow. Beardsley scored the goal that took Hendon through from a free-kick after 73 minutes. The kick was indirect, and must have grazed a Hounslow player on its way into the net.

Hendon: R. Ivey, W. Fisher, E. Beardsley, L. Topp, D. Adams, P. Austin, G. Saffrey, R. Hvidsten, J. Bahler, G. Cunningham, E. Parker

Hounslow: D. Dawson, A. Eagles, E. Emmins, L. Cope, D. Rickard, E. Evans, R. Bickley, R. McDuell, A. King, D. Page, J. Harper.

Bishop Auckland 2 Hendon 0
F.A. Amateur Cup Final

The final attracted enormous interest. Bishop Auckland had won the cup seven times – a record – and in 1954 had been runners-up to Crook Town after 2 replays. Their team included eight amateur internationals, and most of their players had previous Wembley Amateur Cup final experience. Among their stars were stalwart half-back Bob Hardisty, goalkeeper Harry Sharratt, inside left Seamus O'Connell, who had played regularly for the Chelsea first team and their captain, left-back Tommy Stewart. However, they had never won the cup at Wembley, although they had been runners up three times since the final moved to Wembley in 1949. Their strength was shown by a 12–3 victory in the third round at Isthmian League Kingstonian.

Wembley was full, with the final attracting a 100,000 capacity crowd for the fifth year running. Laurie Topp remembers the supporters queuing down Claremont Road when the club put tickets on sale.

Dexter Adams was interviewed on television's *Sportsview* programme a couple of days before the final. The second half of the game was shown live on television. To help their preparations, Hendon played Arsenal in a practice match. Arsenal included former England centre-forward Tommy Lawton and won 4–0.

In the final, Lewin scored twice for Bishop Auckland. The first goal came after 25 minutes. Lewin beat Ivey to the ball and knocked it past him. It was 1–0 at half time, and Bishop Auckland made certain of their win after 21 minutes of the second half. Ivey caught a high ball, bounced it, but Lewin got possession and scored. Topp came close to scoring near the end.

Hendon's defence played well, but Ivey, according to reports, should have saved both goals. Hendon's attack did not threaten Bishop Auckland enough. Graeme Cunningham said after the game: "I just can't understand what went wrong with the attack. We have played far better games." Hvidsten admitted that he should not have played, as he was carrying a shoulder injury. Laurie Topp accepted that Bishop Auckland were the better team on the day.

The income for the Football Association from the final was £29,687.

Hendon: R. Ivey, W. Fisher, E. Beardsley, L. Topp, D. Adams, P. Austin, G. Saffrey, R. Hvidsten, E. Bahler, G. Cunningham, E Parker

Bishop Auckland: H. Sharratt, D. Marshall, T. Stewart, R. Hardisty, C. Cresswell, J. Nimmins, J. Major, D. Lewin, R. Oliver, S. O'Connell, B. Edwards.

The 1955 Amateur Cup Final

Top: The pre-match line up.

Middle: The presentations.

Bottom: Bishop Auckland's second goal

Programme courtesy Wembley National Stadium Ltd

New players

In the Wembley programme, *Hendon Times* journalist Fred Harris described the team as a 'United Nations' side. Although built around the defence of Fisher, Beardsley, Topp, Adams and Austin, the forward line had an international look. Right winger Gerry Saffery had joined the club in October 1954 from Tooting & Mitcham. At inside right, Norwegian international Rajnar Hvidsten had joined the club in January after coming to work in London. He had won 20 caps for Norway. At centre forward, 22 year old Swiss 'B' international Erwin Bahler flew to London to play in the final. He had joined the club earlier in the season while studying in London. At inside left, Scottish international Graeme Cunningham was another new recruit; he joined Hendon from Romford, and had previously played for Queen's Park. On the left wing was Eric Parker, a further new recruit from Southall. He preferred playing in the centre, and was a regular goalscorer. William Harrington, an Irish half-back, was another newcomer.

There were other changes among the playing squad during the season. Frank Penn had overcome his back injury and was available for selection, but left the club in October. Derek Snaith was out of the army, but in September suddenly announced he was returning home to his native Penrith.

The same month, Tommy Darling joined from Edgware Town, and Mickey Stewart started training at the end of the cricket season, only to decide to give up football in November after being injured in a match at Walton. In October, Paul Ahm left to join Corinthian Casuals, and reserve Ron Talbot also left.

Another international signing was Raphael Garcia, a Costa Rican international centre forward. And a Jamaican and a Chinaman also played for the club – not unusual today, but exotic in 1955. A further signing in February was defender Keith Imlah from Queen's Park. Bob Avis and Johnny Westmore also returned to the club at the same time. In April, Horace Meadows joined from Edgware Town, but returned there in September, having failed to win a regular place at Claremont Road.

John Core was hit by injury problems, and in December had a knee operation that meant he expected to miss the rest of the season. However, he did return to first team action in March, earlier than expected.

On 11 April, Jimmy Quail scored his first goal for the first team in a 5–0 win against Leyton at Claremont Road. He would go on to become one of the club's most famous players.

One problem for Hendon was the goalkeeper position. Don Archer started the season in goal, having taken over from Reg Ivey, who had left the club to play Rugby Union for the Metropolitan Police. However, an injury crisis saw Ivey return to the club in January He regained his first team spot, and played at Wembley in his 40th year. In December, goalkeeper George Locke had joined the club from Hounslow, played one game and went back to the west London club.

At the start of the season, the club staged a benefit match for Alan Beningfield, who had badly broken his leg the previous season. It raised £143–10s, and it was reported that he had been off work for a year.

The club also had a new coach, former Arsenal full-back Laurie Scott returning to the club, and taking over from Arsenal and Wales player Wally Barnes, who resigned in October.

London Senior Cup

As well as reaching the Amateur Cup Final, Hendon also were runners-up in the London Senior Cup, losing 3–2 to Walthamstow Avenue in the final at Highbury. In the first round, Leytonstone were beaten 3–0 at Claremont Road. The second round draw took Hendon to Champion Hill to face Dulwich Hamlet, and a rare appearance live on television, when the BBC showed the second-half of the match. There was debate among the amateur clubs about whether they should allow matches to be shown on television, but Hendon said they never turned down the chance to be 'on the box'. Hendon won 4–2 after extra time, and then won 2–0 at Finchley to reach the semi-final. There they faced Dagenham at Ilford's Newbury Park. Hendon were far too strong for their Delphinian League opponents, and won 7–1, with Bob Avis scoring a hat trick. In the Final, at Highbury, Walthamstow Avenue took revenge for Hendon's earlier Amateur Cup victory, winning 3–2.

Hendon 2 Walthamstow Avenue 3
London Senior Cup Final

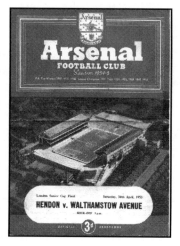

Hendon's second major final of the season could hardly have had a worse start; Julians and Bee put Walthamstow Avenue 2–0 up in the first five minutes. Roden pulled one back for Hendon at the start of the second half, but Julians restored Avenue's two-goal lead. Cunningham scored in injury time to make the score more respectable. Maybe Hendon's long season had caught up with them, the *Hendon Times* reported that in the second half "Hendon showed little fight. Laurie Topp has rarely been so off colour. Pat Austin was below form, Cunningham was a shadow of his former self and Core never got beyond the potential danger stage. Eric Parker, restored to centre-forward, did little to help the forward troubles."

Hendon: D. Archer, W. Fisher, E. Beardsley, L. Topp, D. Adams, P. Austin , D. Roden, J. Core, E. Parker, G. Cunningham, R. Avis.
Walthamstow Avenue: S. Gerula, D. Clarke, T. Farrer, E. Harper, L. Brahan, J. Jeffrey, R. Groves, J. Julians, J. Bee, G. Lucas, D. Flanaghan.
(Programme courtesy Arsenal FC)

Cup competitions

In the FA Cup, a 3–0 win at Berkhamsted Town was followed by a 2–1 victory over Yiewsley at Claremont Road, with a penalty from Core and a last-minute winner from Nock. But in the next qualifying round, Hendon drew 3–3 at Hayes, when Mickey Stewart returned to the team, but then lost the replay four days later 3–2.

In the Middlesex Senior Cup, a 4–1 win over Wembley was followed by defeat at Southall. In the Middlesex Charity Cup, after a home 1–1 draw, Hendon beat neighbours

Finchley 7–4 in the replay on 6 November. In the next round, played on 20 April, four days after the Amateur Cup Final, and when another match had been played two days earlier, Hendon lost 2–0 at home to Hayes.

In the FA Youth Cup, the 'Strollers' had a creditable 1–0 victory over Brentford's junior team.

The league

Although the Athenian League still only had 14 clubs, the number of cup matches Hendon played meant inevitable fixture congestion, with 11 games (almost half the programme), played in April and May. The Amateur Cup Final, London Senior Cup Final, a Middlesex Charity Cup match and the Will Mather Cup game against Arsenal, a narrow 3–2 defeat in Reg Ivey's final game for the club, were also played in this period, which finished on 7 May. For those five weeks, supporting the team must have seemed like a full-time occupation. Of the 11 league games in April and May, only five were won, not surprising for a squad for whom exhaustion must have been a problem.

Hendon finished a respectable fifth in the league, with 27 points. Only seven games were lost, but 11 were drawn. The attack scored 51, just under 2 per game, but the defence conceded 45. One remarkable game was a 5–4 defeat at home to Cambridge City in November. Hendon were 4–0 down after 15 minutes, and the local paper speculated whether goalkeeper Don Archer had lost his confidence, after making several mistakes in recent games, although it acknowledged he had had some injuries. Cambridge had also beaten Hendon 2–0 in Cambridge in October. These were the only two defeats in the league before Christmas, but after a 5–1 win over Wealdstone on 27 December, the next league match played was on 26 March.

At the end of the season, the club announced plans to spend £14,000 on ground improvements, including a grant of £12,000 from Hendon Borough Council. The plans included a new pavilion, reconditioning the stands and new dressing rooms.

Laurie Topp captained the England team at Crystal Palace in September, replacing Dexter Adams who was dropped. Eric Beardsley was selected for England against France on 8 May. Adams, Beardsley and Topp also played for the Athenian League side. Adams also played in a first team friendly for Spurs in the autumn, but assured the club that his future lay in amateur football. Another notable anniversary was Stan Greene completing 21 years as club secretary. The club also announced that they would be running a cricket team in the summer break.

HENDON FOOTBALL CLUB

Celebration Opening
of the

New Pavilion

CLAREMONT ROAD, N.W.2

SEPTEMBER 14th, 1957

by
THE WORSHIPFUL THE MAYOR
OF HENDON
Councillor STEWART E. ARRIDGE

President - ~ - - - A. MURRAY, Esq.

Sir Stanley Rous opens the new pavilion in 1957

6. 1955 to 1963: Wembley winners at last

1955–56: Champions again

Champions again! For the second time in four seasons, Hendon won the Athenian League championship. The final table showed Hendon three points clear of Hounslow Town, who were new recruits to the League from the Corinthian League, bringing the competition's membership to 15 clubs.

Most of the British players from the previous season stayed with the club, but Bahler and Hvidsten had returned home, while Don Archer moved to Hitchin Town. Cliff Nock moved to Finchley and Gerry Saffrey to Wealdstone. In November, Ron Stanton joined Tooting & Mitcham, and Brian Daley moved to Enfield. Eric Parker retired in the same month due to work commitments, but this was offset by Jeff Darey joining the club.

Notable recruits included inside-forward Jack Rawlings, an England international who joined the club from Hayes, and Gorden Holden from Tooting & Mitcham United. A new goalkeeper arrived, Bob Chambers, who had moved to London from Birmingham, and had been on West Bromwich Albion's books as an amateur. Another former West Bromwich Albion player was Alan King, who had won England Youth international honours.

In September, left-winger Miles Spector, who had been training with the club for 18 months, finally joined. The move was supported by Ted Drake, Chelsea's manager and former Hendon coach. Spector had played for Chelsea's first team as a young amateur, and won an England amateur cap. He made his debut in September against Tooting & Mitcham. He was 21-years-old, and as well as his football honours, had represented Hendon and Middlesex in athletics.

However, a blow was John Core being forced have another operation at the start of the season and eventually retiring through injury. Dexter Adams also missed the early weeks of the season following a cartilage operation. In January, Jim Ward again came to London from Scotland for work, and rejoined the club, winning further honours for Scotland while at Claremont Road. Jimmy Quail made a few first team appearances towards the end of the season.

Middlesex wicketkeeper John Murray left the club in December to join Hounslow Town, feeling there was little chance of first-team football at Claremont Road. Before his departure, the *Hendon Times* pointed out that a complete team (in either sport) of first-class cricketers who had played for Hendon could be fielded. The paper suggested: John Murray (Middlesex), Denis and Leslie Compton, Harry Sharp, Fred Titmus, William Webster (Middlesex), Harry Malcolm (Middlesex), Arthur Phebey (Kent), Mickey Stewart (Surrey), Andy Wilson (Gloucestershire) and Len Muncer (Middlesex and Glamorgan).

The club's international reputation was clearly well established. At a time when foreign players were almost unknown in the professional game, and rare in the amateur set-up, players applying for trials at the start of the season included: P. Linka, a Czech goalkeeper, who had played for Prague in representative games, Rene Muller a half-back from Switzerland, who played for Zurich juniors, Louis Cuturier, a Swiss right-winger, Y.M. Soofi, a left-winger from Sudan, S. Abrahams, a Hungarian right-winger and a German player called Habener from Hamburg

The club had worked on the pitch during the close season, and reroofed the popular stand. There were also plans to build a new pavilion.

The League campaign

The season did not start well, with a 3–3 draw at Hayes followed by a 4–2 defeat at Tooting & Mitcham. By the end of September, Hendon had played eight league games, with three wins, two draws and three defeats. But then the team performed remarkably consistently. Partly this was due to having a bye to the first round of the FA Cup, and except for three midweek cup matches, league fixtures were played every Saturday until 19 November. In October, Hendon won three and drew one game in the league, and at the end of the month were top of the table, with 15 points from 12 games. On 12 November, the team lost 1–0 at Leyton, but then, starting with a 4–0 Boxing Day victory over Wealdstone, won 11 consecutive league games. This run lasted until the end of March. In the club programme on 25 February, Freddie Debenham analysed the "terrific struggle for Athenian league honours". Hendon had seven matches left – three at home and four away. However, he felt that Tooting & Mitcham, who also had seven games left, which included five at home, posed the greatest threat. Enfield had 10 games to play, including four at home.

However, Debenham had underestimated the threat from Hounslow Town, who on 25 February were in fifth place, nine points behind Hendon, but with four games in hand. On 14 April, Hendon faced Hounslow at Claremont Road. Hendon were four points clear of Enfield, and a win would give the Greens 40 points with a superior goal difference and two matches left. Enfield could only reach 40 points. A resounding 3–0 win over Hounslow in reality gave Hendon the league title. A 4–4 draw at Finchley, after being 3–0 down, gave a final total of 41 points. The attack averaged over two goals a game, with 63 goals, and the defence conceded only 35. To lose only two league matches after the end of October was a remarkable achievement, and one of those, the 3–0 defeat at Hitchin on 21 April, was after the title was already won.

The cup campaigns

Freddie Debenham had been quite correct in his programme analysis of the championship race when he said that the title would make up for disappointing cup campaigns.

As Amateur Cup finalists, Hendon had a bye to the first round proper of the FA Cup. The draw offered the chance to play against one of third division teams from the Football League. Instead, it sent Hendon to Birmingham league Halesowen Town. When the Hendon supporters arrived in Halesowen, cows and sheep were grazing on the pitch. One local told the Hendon supporters that the town was the largest producer of nails in the country. Despite facing a packed ground, Hendon took an early 2–0 lead, and although Halesowen fought back to make the score 2–2, further goals from Spector and Edwards saw Hendon through to the second round. There, the chance to play Football League opposition did arise, but Exeter City proved too strong for Hendon, winning 6–2. Hendon had gone ahead after 17 minutes with a header from Spector, but the professional side were 3–1 up at half-time, having scored twice in 90 seconds just before the break. Avis scored for Hendon in the second half.

Hendon also faced League opposition in the London Challenge Cup, with a Monday afternoon trip in October to Stamford Bridge to play Chelsea. A 6–3 defeat against the Football League Champions' reserve side was a respectable result. Hendon's goalkeeper Chambers had dislocated his thumb, and couldn't save some goals he would usually have stopped. Chelsea had taken the lead in 40 seconds. Roden equalised on seven minutes. Jim Lewis & Seamus O'Connell (who had played for Bishop Auckland in the 1955 Amateur Cup Final) played for Chelsea. It was 4–1 at half-time, with Holden and Cunningham scoring for Hendon in second half.

In the Amateur Cup, Hendon lost 2–1 at Tooting & Mitcham in the first round. Hendon lost Eric Beardsley with an injury, and felt they could at least have got a draw with a full team.

Two weeks later, Hendon's interest in the London Senior Cup ended when Delphinian League Wembley won 3–1 at Claremont Road in the third round. Hendon had previously beaten Leyton and Dagenham. In the Middlesex Senior Cup, Hendon found more success. Wins at Yiewsley and at home to Tufnell Park Edmonton were followed by a 3–1 semi-final triumph over Finchley at Wealdstone. Hendon returned to Lower Mead for the final, and took revenge on Wembley with a 5–1 victory.

In the London Charity Cup, a 5–2 win at Ilford on 1 October was followed by a semi-final with Walthamstow Avenue in May. Avenue won after a replay, and went on to win the Cup. Enfield ended Hendon's hopes in the Middlesex Charity Cup, with a 1–0 win at Claremont Road.

The end of the season saw a strong Arsenal side visit Claremont road for the Will Mather Cup. The Gunners won 1–0 with a goal from Ward. FA Cup Final referee Alf Bond refereed the match.

Easter Tour

The relative lack of fixture congestion meant that the club could once again undertake an Easter tour to Luxembourg. Hendon beat Spora, Luxembourg's top side 4–2, and then lost to a German side Neuendorf 3–2 after extra time. Spora's president attended Hendon's match against Hounslow Town.

Wembley return

Despite the team failing to reach the FA or Amateur Cup finals, there was another Wembley appearance for the club. On 27 September, the first team and reserves played a match at Wembley Stadium to test out a new floodlighting system that had just been installed at the cost of £46,000. Sir Stanley Rous and other leading FA officials were present. Two different sets of lights were used. Apparently the first team beat the reserves 1–0, Gordon Holden scoring. It was not the first time that Hendon had played under floodlights – a London Challenge Cup tie at Arsenal in 1951 was their debut.

The Wembley floodlights were first used in the evening for an official match a month later, when London played Frankfurt in the Inter-Cities Fairs Cup, a forerunner of today's UEFA Cup. The Wembley authorities invited a party of Hendon players and officials to attend the game as their guests.

Honours

Eric Beardsley and Laurie Topp were selected for the Great Britain Olympic team against Bulgaria in the qualifying competition. Beardsley played in the away match, Topp in the home one. Great Britain lost 5–3 on aggregate, but were then given a place in the Melbourne games due to various teams withdrawing through political boycotts.

Beardsley played for England against Ireland in September, and Germany in November at White Hart Lane. Dexter Adams won one more cap, against Wales, and Laurie Topp played in the last England match of the season, a 3–1 win over France.

Six Hendon players were selected for Middlesex against Surrey, which was a club record: Bill Fisher, Laurie Topp, Dexter Adams, Dave Roden, Jerry Rawlings and Miles Spector. However, Roden withdrew through injury. Adams, Beardsley, Rawlings, Spector and Topp all played for the Athenian League team.

1956–7: Middlesex Charity Cup again

A season that promised much, and included two county cup finals, ended with Hendon winning the Middlesex Charity Cup in the last match of the season. Despite an opening day 3–0 victory over a Rest of the League XI, Hendon could not repeat the previous season's success in the Athenian League, slipping to fourth in the table. Hendon were top scorers in the league with 85 goals, which included nine against Hitchin Town at Claremont Road – revenge for a 6–2 defeat at Hitchin earlier in the season – an 8–2 win at Barnet, and six goals on three occasions. But three league defeats at Claremont Road and six on their travels resulted in 34 points from 28 games in the league.

To be fair, Hendon were missing Dexter Adams and Laurie Topp for six weeks from the end of October, as the two stalwarts were in the Great Britain squad in the Melbourne Olympics. A great honour for the club – club physiotherapist Len Kilby was also selected as masseur for the Athletics team – but three games were lost while they were away. And Dexter Adams was injured at the Olympics, and had to have an operation on his return. Laurie Topp played in both the team's matches – a 9–0 win against Thailand followed by a 6–1 defeat against Bulgaria.

New players

There were some significant changes in the playing squad during the season. Centre forward Tommy Lawrence, who was also on Arsenal's books, joined from Barnet during the summer, and two new goalkeepers were recruited: John Adamson and Brian Howarth.

Later in the season, another goalkeeper, Peter Shearing, joined the club from Tottenham Hotspur, and made his first team debut in December. Other new regular players in the first team were Jimmy Quail and Peter Terry, the latter having rejoined the club, although Terry was now playing at left back, having previously been a centre forward. Douglas Orr, a Scottish amateur international signed from Queens Park.

Jim Ward left the club at the start of the season, as work commitments took him to Stoke on Trent. He rejoined on his return to London in February, having been playing for Crewe Alexandra in the Football League Third Division North in the meantime. Jeff Darey played a few games for Brighton & Hove Albion in the Third Division South. Dave Roden broke his leg in November, and missed the rest of the season. In March, the club announced another international signing – refugee from the 1956 Hungarian uprising Jules Kluge, but under a FIFA ruling that applied to all Hungarian refugees, he was not allowed to play for the club for 12 months.

Programmes from the mid–1950s

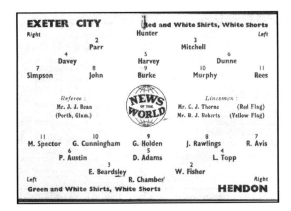

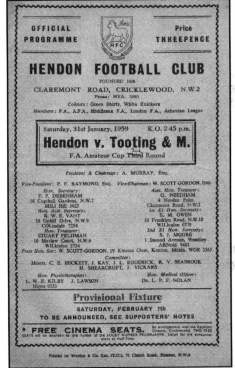

Representative honours, apart from the Olympic call-ups, while recognition for the club and players involved, often put a strain on club's playing strength. Sometimes the needs of international teams even influenced the club's team selection. A note in the club programme for 29 September said that for the match at Leyton on 22 September: "Alterations to the team were made at the request of the Football Association; Dexter Adams moved to right back, Eric Beardsley to left back and Colin Edwards to centre half". It didn't seem to hold Hendon back, as they won the match 5–2.

Cup competitions

Outside of the Middlesex cup competitions, Hendon had little success this season. In the FA Cup, they fell at the first hurdle, losing 1–0 at Yiewsley. Interest in the Amateur Cup was over by the end of January. A 1–1 draw at Delphinian League Ware Town was followed by a 4–0 win in the replay at Claremont Road. But in the second round, despite having 20 coaches of supporters urging them on, Hendon lost 4–3 at Briggs Sports.

In the London Senior Cup, Hendon also fell in the first round, Isthmian Leaguers Leytonstone winning 1–0 at Claremont Road.

There was more success in the Middlesex Senior Cup. A week after the defeat at Briggs Sports, the club welcomed back Pat Lynch, who was coach of neighbours Wingate FC. A 13–1 win, after being 2–1 up at half-time, saw Hendon into the second round. Two players scored nine goals for Hendon: Tommy Lawrence with five and Miles Spector contributed four. This equalled Hendon's highest first-team score. A 4–2 win at Hayes was followed by a 5–3 win over Yiewsley in the semi-final at Wealdstone. Hendon had been 4–0 up at half-time, with goals from two goals from Lawrence, and one each from Quail and Thomas. In the second half, Hendon rested on their laurels. Lawrence completed this hat-trick, but Yiewsley scored three times to make the final score more respectable. Claremont Road staged the other semi-final. Hounslow Town beat Edgware to reach the Final.

Hounslow 1 Hendon 0
Middlesex Senior Cup Final

Match reports say that Hendon gave a listless performance at Wealdstone. The team started with the initiative, but chances went astray, and with the exception of Thomas, the whole forward line blundered badly. The only goal was a disaster for Hendon. Centre-half Dexter Adams, who was outstanding in defence, gave away a penalty 18 minutes into the second half. Dennis D'Arcy converted to give Hounslow victory. Peter Shearing had saved a penalty earlier in the season from D'Arcy, having been advised by Hendon centre forward Tommy Lawrence who had played with D'Arcy at Barnet. But this time D'Arcy's shot inside the post beat Shearing.

Thomas had a good chance in the closing minutes, but Hounslow keeper Derek Dawson made an outstanding save.

Hendon: P. Shearing, W. Fisher, P. Terry, L. Topp, D. Adams, P. Austin, R. Thomas, J. Rawlings, T. Lawrence, J. Quail, M. Spector.

Hounslow: D. Dawson, G. Taylor, E. Emmins, B. Wales, A. Woodhouse, D. Evans, R. Hickley, H. Pope, R. Burns, D. D'Arcy, R. McDuell.

In the Middlesex Charity Cup, victories at Enfield and at home to Finchley saw Hendon play Southall in the final at Hayes.

Hendon 4 Southall 2
Middlesex Charity Cup Final

A report of the final said: "Hendon faded away after a promising start against Southall... Fortunately it was only a temporary lapse and Hendon fought back in extra time to salvage one senior trophy from a mediocre season." Hendon had taken the lead through Jimmy Quail, who was on sparkling form. Southall fought back to lead 2–1 at the break, with goals from Merry and Dyke. Right winger Roy Thomas moved to centre forward and scored the equaliser, beating two defenders and scoring with a terrific shot. Two further goals won the game for Hendon in extra time. The third goal was fortunate, the Southall goalkeeper punching the ball onto Tommy Lawrence's head, and then Miles Spector scored the fourth from a corner by Thomas. Hendon had really come to life in extra time.
Hendon: P. Shearing, W. Fisher, P. Terry, L. Topp, D. Adams, P. Austin, R. Thomas, J. Rawlings, T. Lawrence, J. Quail, M. Spector.
Southall: D. Clarke, T. Prior, R. Short, S. Casaly, C. Mears, D. Williams, G. Underwood, K. Merry, A. Dyke, D. Gittus, T. Bright.

In the London Charity Cup, Hendon beat Isthmian League Corinthian Casuals 2–1, with goals from Quail and Peter Terry, but then lost 3–2 in the semi-final at Claremont Road to eventual winners Dulwich Hamlet. The programme for this game commented: "Our players have served up some grand football in both League and Cup competitions, and are to be congratulated on their fine showing, particularly when one considers how depleted our team has often been through representative calls and a heavy crop of injuries." More generous words than the report of the Middlesex Charity Cup Final.

In the Will Mather Cup, Hendon held a strong Arsenal side, including nine players with first team experience, to a draw at Claremont Road, and shared the trophy. A crowd of 6,000 saw a 'feast of football'. Bloomfield put Arsenal two goals up, but Quail scored just before half-time, and Peter Terry scored from a penalty for the equaliser. Hounslow's left half Derek Evans played as a guest for Hendon, replacing the injured Pat Austin.

Administration changes

At the beginning of March, the club announced that Stanley and Claude Greene were moving to the south coast, and therefore retiring from their positions with the club. Stanley had been the club secretary since 1932, having joined the club in 1920. He was also a member of the Athenian League Council. Claude was assistant secretary and first team secretary. Freddie Debenham took over as club secretary, with Ted Owen becoming first team secretary. The Greenes had jointly served the club for over 50 years, and a collection was held for them at the match against Finchley in March.

On a sad note, committee member Mr Boyett died on the way home from the match at Leyton on 22 September. He had been a committee member since 1920, and was the first team trainer in the 1920s.

139

Supporters

The club's supporters remained as active as ever. As well as recruiting members, fundraising and running away travel, the club Social Section's Ladies Darts team entered the Cricklewood and District Ladies Darts League and won both the League and the Cup in their first season.

Representative honours

As well as Dexter Adams and Laurie Topp going to Melbourne with the Great Britain team, the club's players won various other honours. Laurie Topp was the only player to represent England, winning two more caps. Adams, Jeff Darey, Jack Rawlings, Miles Spector and Topp all played for the Athenian League side. On 5 September at Wealdstone, all five players played against a touring Uganda team, the Athenian League winning 10–1. The Ugandans' cause was not helped by playing barefoot in the first half, and being 8–0 down at half-time. Peter Shearing had been playing regularly for Tottenham's Midweek League side, and qualified for a championship medal as Spurs won the title.

1957–58: Middlesex Senior Cup victory

For once, there were not many changes in the club's playing squad. Peter Shearing was in the RAMC, although he managed to continue playing regularly. National Service did continue to cause some problems for the club – in October the club announced that new player John Slater was in the Army Pay Corps. In April, the club reported that he was stationed in Wiltshire and was not available on Saturdays, although he was "distinguishing himself" in Army football. In November, inside-forward Mickey Moore joined the club from Bromley, and quickly established himself in the first team. However, Jack Rawlings retired during the season on medical advice. Douglas Orr had a one-year trial with Queens Park Rangers. He played five first team games before continuing his career at Claremont Road.

The club had carried out work on the pitch to try to improve the drainage on the 'popular side' – an ongoing struggle – and had opened the new pavilion. Work was also being carried out to improve the terracing.

The league campaign

In the league, Hendon finished third, an improvement of one place on the previous season, but six points behind champions Sutton United. Hendon had the second best defence, conceding 40 goals in 30 games, but the attack scored 12 less goals than the previous season, despite playing two more games. The League had expanded to 16 teams, with Maidstone United joining from the Corinthian League. The Kent side quickly adapted to Athenian League football by finishing as runners-up. Hendon's best result was an 11–1 win over struggling Cambridge City, described as "one of the finest displays seen on this ground for some very considerable time" in the club programme. Another high score was an 8–1 win over Hounslow at Claremont Road. But in October, the club programme appealed for supporters not to 'slow handclap' the players, and to "give the players the right encouragement and the good old Hendon roar." The team were top of the league at the time, but had already lost at home to lowly Hitchin Town. Two other league matches were also lost at Claremont Road, against Carshalton Athletic and Wealdstone. Tommy Lawrence finished as third highest scorer in the Athenian League with 22 goals.

Cup campaigns

Once again, it was only the Middlesex County cups that provided much interest for Hendon's followers. In the FA Cup, a 5–0 win at Wealdstone was followed by a resounding 4–0 defeat at Finchley. There was a similar record of triumph quickly followed by despair in the Amateur Cup. A home 5–1 win over Isthmian League Dulwich Hamlet was followed two weeks by eventual winners Woking winning 3–1 at Claremont Road.

The team also made little progress in the London Senior Cup. In the first round, Corinthian League Wembley were beaten 4–1 at Claremont Road, revenge for a giant-killing act in the same competition in 1955–56. But in the next round, Sutton United won 2–0 at Claremont Road in the first match of 1958 to finish Hendon's interest in a competition they had never won.

The Middlesex Senior Cup provided more fruitful territory. A rare match against Parthenon League Twickenham saw Hendon through 4–1 in the first round, followed by wins over Wealdstone and then Wembley in the semi-final. In the final, local rivals Enfield were beaten 4–0 at Finchley.

Hendon 4 Enfield 0
Middlesex Senior Cup Final

Hendon took the Middlesex Senior Cup back to Claremont Road after a convincing win over Enfield. Jimmy Quail found some of his early season sparkle, and scored once in each half. Roy Thomas often had beating of former Hendon full-back Keith Imlah. On the other wing, Miles Spector's pace always gave Enfield's right back Yell problems

Enfield were always under pressure, although in one period in the second half the Hendon goal was under severe pressure, with Enfield having shots blocked on the line. Hendon took the lead after 14 minutes with a controversial goal. A free kick by Austin went to Thomas, who crossed for Quail to score with a header. Enfield thought the ball had crossed the goal line before Thomas crossed.

On 36 minutes. Hendon went two goals ahead. A heavy charge by Miles Spector took ball and goalkeeper Sanson into net, following a lob by Lawrence, and Hendon led 2–0 at the break. In the second half, Lawrence scored with a shot that went in off the crossbar. Hendon added a final goal when Lawrence crossed from the right wing for Quail to score.

Hendon: P. Shearing, B. Fisher, P. Terry, L. Topp, D. Adams, P. Austin, R. Thomas, M. Moore, T. Lawrence, J. Quail, M. Spector

Enfield: E. Sanson, D. Yell, K. Imlah, D. Sparrow, J. Collins, A. King, D. Potter, R. Aris, D. Taylor, L. Davey, A. Cornelius.

In the Middlesex Charity Cup, victories over Hounslow Town and Hayes were followed by defeat in the final against Finchley. As Finchley's semi-final went to two replays, the Final

Hendon's third goal in the 1957–58 Middlesex Senior Cup Final against Enfield
(Courtesy Mr & Mrs Hutton)

Arsenal's first goal in the 1957–58 Will Mather Cup match (Courtesy Mr & Mrs Hutton)

was played at the start of the 1958–59 season on 1 September. However, a County ruling that only players who had been registered with the club in the 1957–58 season were allowed to play, Hendon were able to field only four regular first teamers, due to various arrivals and departures. Miles Spector missed the game due to an ankle injury.

Hendon 1 Finchley 2
Middlesex Charity Cup Final

The club programme claimed that the team was "extremely unlucky" to lose 2–1. Hendon took the lead after 30 minutes. Laurie Topp passed to Lawrence, who flicked ball to Wyatt who scored. Don Walton equalised for Finchley just before half-time. The game was played with only 40 mins each way, as there were no floodlights.

Dixon won the game for Finchley seven minutes from time. Wright hit bar from a corner, and Dixon followed up to score. Hendon fought back, and missed chances to equalise.

Hendon: C. Warren, P. Terry, J. Westmore, L. Topp, F. Wilson, R. Ellison, A. Wyatt, M. Moore, T. Lawrence, J. Quail, D. Viddicombe

Finchley: D. Smith, A. Sandell, D. Wright, J. Jeffrey, A. Wastell, A. Wilkinson, R. Alder, T. Oliver, J. Dixon, P. Shreeve, T. Walton.

In the Will Mather Cup, an Arsenal team in which every player had First Division experience won 4–1 at Claremont Road at the end of April. An unusual friendly match was the first visit of Oxford University to Claremont Road in November. The match was one of series played by the university club in preparation for the annual Varsity match against Cambridge University at Wembley. Hendon were the only amateur club played by the University side, and the match ended as an honourable 2–2 draw.

Munich collection

Two sad events towards the end of the season – in March, the club held a collection for the survivors of the Munich aeroplane crash involving the Manchester United team. And at the end of March, club treasurer Jack Innes died. He had been club treasurer for 21 years, and had previously been treasurer of the Supporters Association.

For the first time for many seasons, no Hendon player represented England, although Dexter Adams and Laurie Topp both played for the Athenian League side.

1958–59: Cup excitement

After relative stability in the playing squad, this season saw extensive changes. Dexter Adams had retired through injury, Pat Austin and John Adamson moved to Southall, Roy Thomas joined Enfield, although he returned to Hendon in October and goalkeeper Peter Shearing was on National Service in Cyprus. In goal, Derek Dawson joined from Hounslow, and the half-back line was strengthened by Ray Kingsland and John Hannam joining from Wealdstone. Derek Snaith returned to the club, and other new recruits included Jimmy Watts, Derek Westley, Tony Walters, Johnny Wall, Ray Foster, Roy Cannon and Ray Pemberton, who arrived from Leyton Orient. The club also had a new coach, Alex 'Jock' Weir, who had formerly played for Preston North End, and coached the Swiss national team. In January, amateur international Terry Robinson joined the club, and Danish international Richard Neilsen, yet another international player, was also recruited.

Tooting & Mitcham

Undoubtedly the most prominent amateur club this season was Isthmian League Tooting & Mitcham. They reached the FA Cup third round, beating Football League opposition in Bournemouth and Northampton on the way, and then held First Division Nottingham Forest to a 2–2 draw at Sandy Lane. They lost the replay 3–0, a very commendable result, given that Forest went on to win the Cup. Hendon faced Tooting twice – in the Amateur Cup and the London Senior Cup.

In the Amateur Cup, Hendon won 3–1 at Vauxhall Motors in the first round, and a crowd of over 6,000 squeezed into Claremont Road on 31 January for the second round tie against their illustrious south London visitors.

Reports say that it was very wet, and the pitch was deep in mud. Hendon took the lead in the first minute, with a header from Mickey Moore. Despite pressure from Tooting, Hendon increased their lead later in the first half, Moore scoring when Tommy Lawrence won a header from a Miles Spector corner. Hendon controlled the game in the second half for an important victory. But after a 1–0 win at Hallam in the third round, Hendon lost 2–1 to Leytonstone at Claremont Road in a fourth round replay, having drawn 3–3 at Leytonstone.

In the London Senior Cup, Hendon reached their first final since 1955. Wins over Corinthian Casuals – at Surrey CCC's Kennington Oval ground, Kingstonian (after a replay), Carshalton and Wembley in the semi-final resulted in a final at Highbury against Tooting. But this time the Isthmian League side were too strong for Hendon, winning 5–2. Hendon skipper Laurie Topp missed the final with a shoulder injury.

Hendon 2 Tooting & Mitcham United 5
London Senior Cup Final

Tooting took the lead after two minutes, when Ray Kingsland, a former Arsenal ground staff player, marked his return to Highbury by turning a centre from Flanagan into his own net. Bill Fisher and John Harwood kept the Tooting attack at bay after this, but Hendon's forwards, with Spector at inside right and new player Brian Hamilton on the wing, were ineffective. The *Hendon Times* report said that Hendon's attack "hardly registered" against the powerful Tooting side.

After 28 minutes, Sells handled in the penalty area, but the referee only gave Tooting a throw-in. From it Hasty crossed for Grainger to put the Isthmian League side 2–0 ahead. On 40 minutes Bennett blocked a shot by Thomas, and Hendon were given a penalty. Thomas took it and scored. But seconds later, Holden restored Tooting's lead to 3–1, which they held until the break.

(Courtesy Arsenal FC)

144

Four minutes after half-time, a further penalty for Hendon, again converted by Thomas, made the score 3–2, but goals from Grainger and Hasty resulted in a final score of 5–2. A crowd of 6,286 saw the game, paying £540. So for the third time in the 1950s, Hendon had lost a London Senior Cup Final.

Hendon: J. Harwood, F. Sells, W. Fisher, J. Quail, R. Kingsland, J. Hannam, R. Thomas, M. Spector, T. Lawrence, M. Moore, B. Hamilton

Tooting & Mitcham United: R. Secker, J. Harlow, G. Edwards, G. Holden, B. Bennett, E. Murphy, A. Grainger, A. Viney, J. Blizzard, P. Hasty, D. Flanagan.

In the London Charity Cup, Ilford ended Hendon's interest in the competition in the first round. Hendon could not continue the success of the past two seasons in the Middlesex County cups. In the Senior Cup, they lost at Southall in the first round. In the Charity Cup, a 2–2 draw against Wealdstone was abandoned in extra time at Claremont Road in September due to bad light. Hendon lost the replay on 20 April 2–1 at Wealdstone.

The FA Cup, however, did provide some excitement in the first half of the season. A 3–2 win over Finchley at home was followed by victories over Dagenham and Hornchurch. The fourth qualifying round bought Isthmian League giants Wycombe Wanderers to Claremont Road. Hopes of a place in the First Round proper were dashed by a 3–1 defeat.

League campaign

As was inevitable in the days before floodlights were in common use, runs in the cup competitions produced fixture congestion at the end of the season. From Saturday 18 April to Monday 27 April, Hendon played six games – five league matches and one in the Middlesex Charity Cup.

Hendon finished fourth in the league, a drop of one place on the previous season. They were eight points behind champions Barnet. But it was their form at Claremont Road that let the team down, with seven defeats at home. Only two league matches were lost on their travels. Hendon were third highest scorers, with 69 goals, but let in 56, including four or more at home on four occasions. The biggest league win was 8–1 against struggling Redhill. An enjoyable outing for Hendon followers was a 5–1 midweek win at Enfield in September, with Tommy Lawrence and Jimmy Quail both scoring twice.

Only 640 supporters attended the match against Finchley at Claremont Road, due to a clash with the Amateur Cup Final. It was Hendon's lowest crowd since 1955, when only 293 loyal fans saw Hendon play Sutton United, when there was a clash with the FA Cup Final. The FA agreed to move the Amateur Cup Final to later in the season so that clubs could play a match in the early evening if they wanted. End of season fixture congestion meant that the Will Mather Cup match against Arsenal was not played.

Once again, no Hendon players won England caps. Derek Dawson and Mickey Moore played for the Athenian League side. Tommy Lawrence was the Athenian League's leading scorer with 27 goals.

1959–60: The Amateur Cup at last

One of the most dramatic finals in the history of the competition saw Hendon beat Kingstonian 2–1 at Wembley to win the Amateur Cup at last.

145

The road to the final started with a 3–0 win over Vauxhall Motors. Three weeks later, Isthmian League Wimbledon were beaten 2–1 at home. An easy 6–0 win at Redhill in the third round was followed by a tough draw at Northern League West Auckland Town, who were to reach the final in 1961. A creditable 1–1 draw was followed by a 2–0 win at home. The semi-final was much more local affair, Enfield at Brentford's Griffin Park. Five Enfield players had previously played for Hendon, but in front of 14,000 fans goals from Laurie Topp and Brian Figg took Hendon to Wembley.

Goals from Topp were rare. His future at the club had been uncertain at the start of the season, but after 32 minutes he put Hendon ahead with a left foot shot from 20 yards out. Hendon had come close to taking the lead after five minutes, when Jimmy Quail hit the bar. After Topp's goal, Enfield missed an open goal, leaving Hendon 1–0 up at the break. Six minutes into the second half, Quail set up Figg to put Hendon 2–0 ahead, and Hendon's well organised defence contained Enfield for the rest of the game to guarantee a return to Wembley. Fred Harris's report in the *Hendon Times* said that Hendon "played some dazzling football in a spectacular first half and if they continue this form no amateur team will be able to live with them."

Enfield's former Hendon goalkeeper Derek Dawson must have been particularly disappointed – it was the second time Hendon had knocked his team out at the semi-final stage. He had been in goal for Hounslow in 1955 when Hendon beat them at Tottenham in the semi-final.

Hendon: P. Shearing, R. Widdowfield, J. Harris, L. Topp, W. Fisher, C. Murphy, M. Candey, B. Figg, M. Spector, J. Quail, T. Howard.
Enfield: D. Dawson, P. Terry, R. Bambridge, D. Ridley, R. Kingsland, A. King, R. Thomas, R. Agar, T. Lawrence, B. Ridley, A. McDonnell

At Wembley on 23 April, Hendon would face Isthmian League Kingstonian, who had beaten Crook Town 2–1 in the other semi-final at Newcastle. Kingstonian had made one previous final appearance. In 1933 they beat Stockton 4–1 in a replay at Darlington after a draw at Dulwich Hamlet. Their only current international was inside-left Hugh Lindsay, who was a member of the Great Britain Olympic side. Their captain Jim Coates played for Great Britain in the 1956 Olympics. Their centre-half was John Ashworth, who later joined Hendon.

Hendon 2 Kingstonian 1
Amateur Cup Final

"One of the finest finishes to a match, professional or amateur, ever seen on Wembley's turf" was how the *FA Yearbook* started their report of Hendon's dramatic win. In *The Sunday Times* Brian Glanville said that the match's "crescendo would have graced the finest of professional matches". In the *Daily Telegraph*, David Miller wrote that "Not since Matthews lifted the FA Cup for Blackpool in 1953 has Wembley seen such a victory as Hendon's in the Amateur Cup Final on Saturday. The match had skill and suspense, with the tables twice turned, and a climax worthy of double the 60,000 crowd."

Hendon had three survivors from the 1955 Final: Laurie Topp and Bill Fisher in the half-back line, and Dexter Adams as coach. Laurie Topp had said before the game "When we win the 1960 Cup it will be the greatest thrill of my footballing life." But he could not have predicted the dramatic last three minutes of the match. Hendon dominated the first half, Brian Glanville saying that they "played Kingstonian off the field.

Their thinking was twice as quick, their movements twice as clever, their confidence immense." But Hendon could not score. Quail headed just wide of the post, Murphy and Howard forced Groves into saves, Spector beat the keeper, but his shot was kicked off the line. But five minutes before the break, Kingstonian took the lead. Harris crossed and Johnny Whing scored with a header. And they had another goal disallowed for a foul on Peter Shearing before the break.

It took Hendon the first 15 minutes of the second half to recover from the shock of being behind. Quail, Spector and Topp all created chances, but Hugh Lindsay missed a chance to put Kingstonian two up.

There were just three minutes left when Hendon equalised. Howard, on the left wing, passed to Quail. He passed to Miles Spector who set up Laurie Topp to smash home an unstoppable shot from 20 yards. "Laurie is the Tops!" as the *Daily Mirror's* headline put it. Then, with a minute left, Terry Howard was put through by Spector, and beat Groves to take the cup to Claremont Road for the first time. There was still time for Oakes to hit the post for Kingstonian, but Hendon held on to win.

The *FA Yearbook* concluded that "All 22 players should remember this match with pride, for they combined to make it memorable for its skill, incident and sportsmanship."
Hendon: P. Shearing, R. Widdowfield, J. Harris, L. Topp, W. Fisher, C. Murphy, M. Candey, B. Figg, M. Spector, J. Quail, T. Howard.
Kingstonian: R. Groves, B. Davies, D. Bird, D. Richards, J. Ashworth, L. Gilson, K. Harris, J. Coates, J. Whing, H. Lindsay, R. Oakes.

The start of the season had seen the usual turnover in players. Tommy Lawrence moved to Enfield, with goalkeeper Derek Dawson, and Pat Terry. In December, Ray Kingsland followed them round the North Circular to Southbury Road. Freddie Sells and Frank Warn also departed – Sells to Bromley and Warn gave up football for work reasons. An important recruit was left winger Terry Howard from Harwich & Parkeston, allowing Miles Spector to play at centre forward to cover for Lawrence's departure. Peter Shearing returned from National Service to reclaim his place in goal. Derek Wright, who had won Athenian League and Middlesex County honours, joined from Finchley, 17-year-old Jeff Harris joined from Arsenal on George Swindon's recommendation, Johnny Nichols from Wealdstone, Brian McLaughlin from Kilmarnock and Queen's Park, continuing Hendon's link with the Scottish amateur side. In October, Mike Candey followed Terry Howard to Claremont Road from Harwich & Parkeston. In December, Derek Godwin and Ron Widdowfield were signed. However, Godwin had played for Gosport in the Amateur Cup, and thus could not play for Hendon as well. Both regularly played for the Royal Navy team. In the same month, Brian Figg made his debut. Another player to establish himself in the first team was Charlie Murphy, who had been signed from local junior side St Mary's in 1958–59, and made his first team debut at the end of that season. In February, Welsh international Gordon Griffiths made his debut.

Laurie Topp decided to stay with the club, despite speculation that he would leave. Veteran Bill Fisher, at the age of 38, was coaching the reserves, but remained in contention for a first team place. For the first team, Dexter Adams returned to Claremont Road at the start of the season as first team coach. It was reported that Jock Weir left for financial reasons, but he said he had resigned. Adams had been offered a coaching role at Wingate, but preferred to take the Hendon position.

1960 Amateur Cup Campaign

Top: Miles Spector (right) scores against West Auckland Town in the fourth round replay. (Courtesy Miles Spector)

Middle: Action from the semi-final against Enfield at Griffin Park. Miles Spector challenges Derek Dawson. (Courtesy Miles Spector)

Bottom: Presentations at Wembley: Hendon captain Charlie Murphy introduces the Hendon players to the Earl of Derby. (HT)

Cup Final programme courtesy Wembley National Stadium Ltd

Action from the match:

Left: Captains Jim Coates and Charlie Murphy shake hands as referee J.W. Hunt looks on

Middle: Laurie Topp's equaliser

Bottom: Terry Howard's winner

(All photos *Hendon Times*)

Top: Charlie Murphy
receiving the Cup

Middle: Hendon's
Cup at last.

The Hendon team.
Back: Terry Howard,
Ron Widdowfield, Laurie Topp,
Peter Shearing, Bill Fisher,
Jeff Harris; front: Mike Candey,
Brian Figg, Charie Murphy,
Miles Spector, Jimmy Quail.

(All photos *Hendon Times*)

Middlesex Senior Cup

Hendon made it a cup double when they beat Enfield 2–1 in the Middlesex Senior Cup final at Finchley. To reach the final, Hendon had won 3–0 at Staines, 1–0 at Wembley and then beaten Uxbridge 3–0 in a semi-final replay, after the teams had drawn 1–1. Corinthian League Uxbridge gave Hendon a hard fight. After the 1–1 draw in the first match, it was 0–0 at half-time in the replay at Hayes before Terry Howard gave Hendon the lead early in the second half. Two goals from Jimmy Quail secured Hendon's win.

Hendon 2 Enfield 1
Middlesex Senior Cup Final

Enfield took the lead after 10 minutes through Tommy Lawrence, but two goals from Jimmy Quail won the game for Hendon. He equalised with a shot from the edge of the penalty area from a Terry Howard corner after 31 minutes. Twelve minutes into the second half, Peter Terry gave away a penalty and Quail hit the post with his shot. But two minutes from full-time, Miles Spector set up Quail to score the winner. Enfield had a goal disallowed at the end of the game, but reports say it was 'well offside'. Ron Widdowfield had withdrawn from the match so that Derek Godwin, who had been ineligible for the Amateur Cup final could play, and Johnny Harwood played in goal as Peter Shearing was injured.

Hendon: J. Harwood, D. Godwin, J. Harris, L. Topp, W. Fisher, C. Murphy, M. Candey, B. Figg, M. Spector, J. Quail, T. Howard.

Enfield: D. Dawson, P. Terry, R. Bambridge, D. Ridley, R. Kingsland, A. King, R. Thomas, R. Agar, T. Lawrence, A. Brace, A. McDonnell.

Cup competitions

In the FA Cup, Hendon won 2–1 at Ford United (formerly Briggs Sports) and Edgware before going out 2–0 at Hornchurch. As finalists in the previous season's London Senior Cup competition, Hendon were entitled to enter the London Challenge Cup, but lost 2–0 under floodlights to West Ham at Upton Park. There was little progress in the London Senior Cup – a 3–2 second round defeat at Walthamstow Avenue, or in the London Charity Cup, when Tooting and Mitcham won 3–1 in the first round at Claremont Road.

The league

Not surprisingly, Hendon's league form suffered due to commitments in the cup competitions. The team finished eighth, their lowest place since the 1946–47 season. Only nine games were lost, the same as Enfield who finished third, but 12 draws meant Hendon finished with 30 points from 30 games. Only three opponents won at Claremont Road – a considerable improvement on the previous season, but there five home draws, and only 48 goals scored in the league showed that the attack lacked punch at times. Only three league games were played in the first three months of 1960, and the first league win in 1960 was on 9 April against Finchley. A fixture list of 10 matches in April, including the Amateur Cup Final and the Middlesex Senior Cup semi-final replay and final saw only two out of seven league games won. At Hitchin on Easter Saturday, Hendon fielded a complete reserve side – it was the week before the Wembley Final, and there had been a first team match on Good Friday. And the Athenian League even scheduled two first team matches for the same evening – Leyton at home and Redhill away. In the event, the Leyton match was changed to 7 May. Despite being bottom of the League, and having to start the match in their shirts as their kit had not arrived, Leyton won 2–1. After 19 minutes, the game was stopped so Leyton could change into a set of shirts borrowed from local Sunday team Ciro Chic Casuals.

A further three league matches were played in early May. At the turn of the year, Hendon had been fourth, but with a record of seven wins and seven draws from 17 games.

Honours

Jimmy Quail and Terry Howard had trials for the Great Britain Olympic squad for the 1960 Rome Games. Bill Fisher was the Athenian League player-of-the-year. Peter Shearing was selected for the Athenian League team.

In May, Dexter Adams won an unusual honour for someone who was a famous amateur footballer – he was an accomplished club cricketer and was selected for the MCC to play Sandhurst at Lords.

End of season tour

Hendon visited France and Luxembourg for a three day end of season tour in May. The club had chartered a plane for the trip, and there was drama at the airport when it touched down only to take off again. Reports say there was a 'silent hush' in the plane as it came into land for a second time, this time successfully. With the Munich crash only two years before, it must have been a tense moment.

The trip was hosted by FC Aims des Sports, Schifflange. Three matches were played. The first was in France, 60 miles from their Luxembourg base. On the way to play CS Blenoe, the party's coach passed the remains of the Maginot Line from World War One. The match ended in a draw, as did the other two matches on the trip, against Auden and their hosts. On the day of the last match, the party had visited a vineyard and "generously sampled the finished produce". Before the game, both teams changed in a local café, and there was a quarter-mile parade to the stadium, led by a local band. The report in the local paper concluded that "Hendon were tremendous ambassadors. They behaved themselves extremely well and were warmly welcomed wherever they went."

On tour in Luxembourg in 1960

1960–61: Champions by a point

Hendon won their third – and last – Athenian League title with a 2–0 victory at Barnet in the last match of the season. The championship was confirmed when news came through that runners-up Wealdstone had drawn their last match with Hitchin Town.

The game at Barnet had been abandoned two days earlier due to torrential rain – on Thursday 4 May. It was rescheduled for Saturday 6 May and completed one of the most dramatic Athenian League title races for many years. Hendon had faced Hitchin Town on Monday 1 May. Before that game, Hendon were a point behind Wealdstone with two games to play. Victory in both would mean the title coming to Claremont Road. Barnet were third on goal average from Hendon. But Hendon drew 1–1 with Hitchin, despite leading 1–0 at half-time. So victory at Barnet was vital. Even if Wealdstone had beaten Hitchin in their last game by five goals or less, the title still would have gone to Hendon on goal average.

Sutton United had led the league in the early part of the season, but after the turn of the year, Hendon were never outside the top two places. The defence was very tight, conceding only 38 goals, and keeping 11 clean sheets. The attack was more productive than in previous seasons, scoring 72 goals. Only two matches were lost at Claremont Road, one surprisingly against wooden spoonists Carshalton Athletic. The match was just after the FA Cup first round. Mike Candey and Miles Spector were not selected, and regular first team goalkeeper Dennis Wells was replaced by John Harwood. The pitch was a quagmire, and Hendon were 3–0 down before Jimmy Quail pulled a goal back before the end.

Players

The club had announced at the end of the previous season that all the first team players had agreed to stay with the club. John Hannam moved during the close season to become player-coach of Edgware Town, but resigned from the post in July due to business commitments.

Goalkeeper Peter Shearing turned professional with West Ham United, and Dennis Wells was signed from Barnet to take over. He had also been playing for Luton Town's reserve team. Shearing only played for one season at Upton Park, playing six first team matches. Unable to establish a regular place, he joined Portsmouth, and also played for Exeter City, Plymouth Argyle, Bristol Rovers and Gillingham.

An international signing was Swiss 'B' international Walter Louffell, who continued Hendon's reputation as a 'United Nations' club, although he never played for the first team.

Service commitments caused problems again, with full-back Ron Widdowfield, who was in the Fleet Air Arm, being posted to Scotland. In September, British Olympic and England international Roy Sleap joined Hendon from Barnet, and replaced Laurie Topp in the Hendon team. The 20-year-old Sleap had resigned from Barnet before leaving for the Rome Olympics, and it had been an open secret that he intended to join Hendon. He had been with Barnet for three years, and was also on Queens Park Rangers' books. One reporter, Harry Done, said it was "one of the biggest captures of the season". Full-back Tom Feary also moved from Underhill to Claremont Road.

In September, it looked possible that Jimmy Quail would be leaving the club, as First Division Newcastle United invited him to train with them for a week. Quail initially accepted, but then changed his mind, saying that at 25, and with a good job, he was too old to consider turning professional.

In November, winger Albert Grainger moved to Hendon, and Graham Davies, a Welsh international, joined the club from Ilford. The club programme reported that Don Kilby had moved to Finchley. In December goalkeeper Bill Farlam joined the club from Uxbridge. He was also a regular member of the Middlesex County team. Towards the end of the season, Norman Field joined the club from Dulwich Hamlet.

The 'close relationship' between Hendon and Enfield was shown on 4 March, when the Enfield line-up in the programme showed seven former Hendon players. The club programme magnanimously said "Nice to see you again at Claremont Road." Wearing the number 10 shirt for Enfield was David Hyde, who would achieve great things with Hendon in the future.

Cup campaigns

With the exception of the Middlesex Senior Cup, Hendon did not make a huge impact on the cup competitions this season. This avoided – to a certain extent – the inevitable end of season fixture congestion, although eight games were still played in April.

Winning the Amateur Cup guaranteed Hendon a place in the FA Cup first round. The draw did not produce Football League opposition for Hendon, but brought Southern League Oxford United to Claremont Road. Hendon performed creditably, drawing 2–2 with their professional opponents, who were top of the Southern League, and unbeaten at the time. They were captained by Ron Atkinson at right-half. The future West Bromwich Albion and Manchester United manager was described in the club programme as "a very strong player, signed from Aston Villa as an inside-forward and has now developed into a fine right half."

Hendon's result was even more creditable, given that they were missing Roy Sleap and Terry Howard, who were playing for the England amateur team, and Albert Grainger was cup-tied. In the replay, Hendon lost 3–2.

In the London Senior Cup, Bromley ended Hendon's challenge in the first round, winning 2–1 at Claremont Road in December.

Hendon's defence of the Amateur Cup only lasted two rounds. Carshalton were beaten after a replay, but then Walthamstow Avenue beat Hendon 2–0 in the second round. The match was originally played at Claremont Road, but had to be abandoned because of the poor state of the pitch. It was restaged the next week at the White City Stadium. Both sides were leading their leagues, and them match had two of England's most famous amateur players on opposing sides – Laurie Topp and Walthamstow's Jim Lewis. Between them they had won more than 80 caps.

Despite work being done on the pitch in the close season, it continued to cause problems. The Boxing Day clash with Wealdstone had been abandoned, and the week after the Walthamstow game, the club programme had a photo of supporters digging and forking the pitch on a Sunday morning. It looks like a ploughed field.

In the Middlesex Senior Cup, Hendon reached their 10th final, beating Hayes, Finchley and Wealdstone on the way. But in the final, after a 0–0 draw, Hounslow won the replay 3–2.

Hendon versus Carshalton Amateur Cup first round replay 1961: Graham Davies scoring for Hendon. The poor state of the pitch is very clear, and the second round match against Walthamstow Avenue was abandoned, and restaged at White City. (Courtesy Mr & Mrs Hutton)

Weight training in 1961:
Physio Don Kilby guides Jimmy Quail, Terry Howard and Mike Candey

Hendon 0 Hounslow Town 0
Middlesex Senior Cup Final

This was a dull game from all accounts. Played at Wealdstone on 29 April, one home supporter claimed it was the worst game of the season at Lower Mead, according to the *Hendon Times* report. Alan Jones was making his debut for Hendon at centre half, having just joined the club. In the first half, both centre forwards, Graham Davies for Hendon and Langton for Hounslow missed good chances. The most exciting moment came in the second half, when Hendon goalkeeper Bill Farlam saved a penalty on 78 minutes. Three young Hendon supporters ran the length of the pitch to congratulate him before being "shooed off" by the referee. A header from Jimmy Quail against the bar was Hendon's best chance in the second half. Both teams had injured players going into extra time, and Hendon's defence kept them in the game.

Hendon: W. Farlam, G. Edwards, D. Godwin, C. Murphy, A. Jones, R. Sleap, A. Grainger, D. Bell, G. Davies, J. Quail, T. Howard.

Hounslow: P. Rhodes, W. Creasey, G. Taylor, W. Digweed, K. Williams, G. Price, J. Weeks, J. Fennell, R. Langton, M. Black, R. Alder.

Hounslow 3 Hendon 2
Middlesex Senior Cup Final replay

Two weeks later, on 13 May, the replay took place at Hayes. It was Laurie Topp's final appearance for the club, in the unlikely position of right winger. Hendon fought back from being two goals down in sweltering heat, but a goal from Martin Black, completing his hat trick, four minutes from the end of extra time won the game for Hounslow.

Black gave Hounslow the lead after five minutes, beating Danny O'Leary in the Hendon goal. The 19-year-old replaced Bill Farlam, who was on holiday. Hounslow went 2–0 up on 18 minutes, when Black scored again. Reserve centre forward Ronnie Hall scored for Hendon after 26 minutes, his header bouncing gently over the line past Rhodes. Terry Howard headed Hendon's equaliser after 65 minutes from Quail's cross. Neither team could break the stalemate until Black's winner.

Hendon: D. O'Leary, W. Fisher, J. Harris, R. Sleap, A. Jones, C. Murphy, L. Topp, D. Bell, R. Hall, J. Quail, T. Howard.

Hounslow: P. Rhodes, W. Creasey, G. Taylor, W. Digweed, K. Williams, G. Price, J. Weeks, T. McHattie, M. Black, J. Fennell, R. Alder.

Wealdstone ended Hendon's interest in the Middlesex Charity Cup in the first round. In the London Charity Cup, Hendon won 3–1 at Dulwich Hamlet in October, but missed out on a first final appearance when Hayes won 3–2 in the semi-final at Claremont Road in April.

Honours

The clubs' players won a wide variety of honours. As well as Terry Howard and Roy Sleap playing in the British Olympic team, they also played for the England amateur international team, as did Jeff Harris. Jimmy Quail missed out on Olympic selection, but did play for Ireland. Quail also came close to winning a full Ireland cap. He missed out by one vote from the nine man selection panel. Graham Davies played for Wales. Sleap was still technically a Barnet player during the Olympics, and played in two matches for the Great Britain team, including an impressive 2–2 draw with hosts Italy. Terry Howard played in the final game against Taiwan. Great Britain could not qualify for the semi-finals, but beat their far-eastern opponents 3–2.

There were two notable friendly matches played during the season. Middlesex Wanderers paid their first visit to Claremont Road in August with a strong side and won 2–1. The match was for the Alaway Brothers Memorial Trophy, and Hendon as Amateur Cup holders were chosen for the fixture. In October, Hendon played a rare match under floodlights, at Maidstone United, in a match for former Claremont Road star and Kent cricketer Arthur Phebey's benefit.

156

A Hendon hero: Laurie Topp

Laurie Topp was one of the mainstays of the team during the post war period until he finished playing in 1961. He was one of the most honoured players of his generation, with two Olympic Games, 32 England caps and many other representative honours. And his period at the club saw Hendon become established as one of England's top amateur teams, culminating in the 1960 Amateur Cup final 2–1 triumph against Kingstonian.

Laurie was born in St Pancras, and moved to Edgware before starting school. Although his school was in Harrow, he played for the Hendon Borough team as Harrow did not have a team at that time.

He played for Arsenal's junior sides as a youngster, but never turned professional. "I had offers, but I turned them down", he recalled. "I wasn't sure I was quite up to it". Of course, in those days, a player who signed as a professional was disbarred from the amateur game. Also, with the maximum wage in force, there were no fortunes to be made in football.

On leaving school, Laurie's mother found him a job at Desoutters in Colindale. The firm made electrical drills, used for making aircraft during the war. Because of being in a reserved occupation, Laurie never went into the forces.

He joined Golders Green in 1942. "I played for Davis Sports, [who subsequently helped create Kingsbury Town]. There was a fellow on the committee at Golders Green, Harry Boycott, who worked at Desoutters, and he asked me to go for a trial at the club."

Training was twice a week. "We went up there on Tuesdays and Thursdays. Sometimes we would train on the pitch, but if it was too muddy, we would run in the streets, or in the park at the back of the ground." The club was well supported then. "There were big crowds during the war and at the end of the war. People wanted to get out, to have something different from the war," he remembered.

The club's first Wembley appearance, often forgotten, was at the end of the war in the Middlesex Senior Red Cross Charity Cup. Laurie and Bill Fisher were the only players from that team to play in the 1955 and 1960 Amateur Cup finals. Laurie recalled: "I played at Wembley a few times, for England amateurs as well as the cup finals. I suppose I was a bit nervous, you would worry about how you were going to play. When we played Bishop Auckland, that Bob Hardisty was a great player. And in 1960 I scored against Kingstonian."

Goals from Laurie were fairly rare. He played right half - defensive midfield in today's terms. "I was told to defend, or be more attacking, depending on who we were playing. I had to run back if someone beat me and tackle them. I didn't get many goals, the forwards told you to go back if you went up too far."

Laurie has particularly fond memories of Bill Fisher. "He was there when I joined. He looked after me, helped me out, told me what to do - he was right back and I was right half. He was my best mate at the club." He recalled Dexter Adams as a "real terror" at centre half, and Pat Lynch, who joined the club from Tufnell Park after the war as "a hard player. Not many got past him." Roy Stroud was another outstanding player: "you gave him the ball, and no one could catch him."

As well as playing for Hendon, Laurie was one of the key players in the England amateur team in the post-war period. He remembered touring the continent, playing in Holland, Belgium and Italy, "but only getting one cap for it. That was a fiddle..." He has fond memories of the 1956 Olympics in Melbourne. "They spoke English, and they took us out everywhere. The Australians supported us."

Getting time off work for football was not usually a problem. "Stan Greene [the club secretary] used to send tickets to the managing director of Desoutters for the big games. That kept them happy. I remember when we won the cup in 1960, I spoke to the managing director as I was going up the steps to the Royal Box."

Descriptions of Laurie written during his playing career show his standing in the game. The programme for a 1953 England amateur international says he was "a tenacious tackler, and great worker and one of the most popular figures in amateur football". Another England amateurs write up the same year describes him as "a great fetch-and-carry wing-half in the modern style". The 1955 Amateur Cup Final programme said he was "stylish, clean tackling, always smiling", while the 1960 Final programme described him as "a household name in amateur soccer and one of the most respected players".

After retiring from playing in 1961, Laurie coached for a short time at Enfield, but felt he "was not cut out to be a coach". He took up golf, and used to see former Hendon colleague Bob Avis at South Herts Golf Club. He worked at Desoutters until he retired at 65, showing the same loyalty he had shown in football to Hendon.

If there ever is a Hendon Football Club 'Hall of Fame', Laurie will be one of the first to be nominated...

(Photos: Laurie Topp in 2002. Shirt and blazer badges from Laurie's career. PL)

A Hendon hero: Dexter Adams

Along with Laurie Topp and Bill Fisher, Dexter Adams was one of the mainstays of Hendon in the 1950s. He joined Hendon in January 1948 from Northampton Polytechnic FC, and soon established himself at centre half, although he also played right-back on occasions. He was a strong tackler, but could also play the ball out of defence to set up attacks. He guested occasionally for professional clubs, but turned down many offers to play professionally.

He won 20 England caps, making his debut in a 6–3 win over Ireland at Coventry in February 1951. He also played for the Middlesex County team and made 10 appearances for the Athenian League side. He was also in the 1956 Great Britain Olympic squad for the Melbourne Olympics.

He captained the 1955 Amateur Cup Final team, although not fully fit. In a league match against Leyton a few days before the final, he played with 10 reserves. A crowd of 3,000 came, mainly to see if he would be fit for the final. Playing in the final presumably put behind him the memory of having a penalty saved in the 1951 semi-final at Highbury against Pegasus. He sportingly recalled: "I took the kick but Pegasus goalkeeper Ben Brown made a terrific save and Hendon went out of the Cup. My only consolation was that Ben was awarded an England cap after this match – I like to think that his save from my penalty helped him to win this."

Apart from the 1955 Amateur Cup Final, he also was in Hendon teams that won two Athenian League titles, the Middlesex Senior Cup in 1957–58, the Middlesex Charity Cup four times, and got runners-up medals twice in the London Senior Cup and once in the Middlesex Senior Cup.

Persistent knee trouble caused his retirement in 1958. He became coach at the club in 1959, and took the team to their first amateur cup success. He also coached the 1960–61 championship winning team, but left the club at the end of that season, appropriately at the same time as Laurie Topp. He was later manager of Barnet when they turned professional in 1965 and joined the Southern League.

1961–62: All change at Claremont Road

The well-trodden path from Hendon to Enfield saw several departures from Hendon's Championship-winning side, and only five players remained at the start of the new season from the team that had bought the title to Claremont Road. Jeff Harris, Alan Jones, Charlie Murphy, David Bell and Miles Spector remained loyal to the club, although in December Harris also moved to Enfield. Laurie Topp had retired – and became coach at Enfield in October, where, as the Hendon programme noted: "of course [he] has the benefit of knowing most of their first team." Bill Fisher stayed with the club, and made his 800th appearance against Sutton United at the end of the season. Another departure was coach Dexter Adams, who was replaced by Peter Rogers.

One of the prominent new recruits was Great Britain Olympic and England amateur international goalkeeper Mike Pinner. He was an RAF Flying Officer, and played as an amateur for various league clubs, including in the First Division for Sheffield Wednesday, Aston Villa and Manchester United while working as a solicitor. He had started his career at Cambridge University, then played for Pegasus, and played regularly for the England amateur team.

Right back Brian Davies joined from Kingstonian, although Maurice Williams from Hayes became the regular right-back. Right-half Roy Walker joined from Queen's Park Rangers, replacing Roy Sleap who had gone to Enfield, along with Terry Howard and Jimmy Quail. Winger Ken Aldridge came to Claremont Road from Wealdstone. Reserve centre-half Geoff Riddy also started to appear in the first team. In October, Charlie Sells joined Hendon from Wealdstone, and Eric Pattison was another recruit from Queen's Park Rangers.

Wealdstone also got drawn into the bad relations between Hendon and Enfield. Matt Farrell and John Saunders resigned from Wealdstone, intending to join Hendon, but Wealdstone blocked the move, saying that the correct procedure had not been followed.

The Athenian League said the players could only play for Wealdstone for the rest of the season, although they did not appear for the club again.

One versatile player was Dave Abrey, who made his debut in goal for the reserves towards the end of the season. He usually played for the 'A' team – either in goal or at inside-forward.

The league

Not surprisingly, Hendon dropped down the league table to seventh, with 31 points from 30 games. It was the first time since 1945–46 that they had conceded more goals than they scored – 54 compared to 56. Hendon never challenged for the title, which was won by Enfield who only dropped eight points all season. At the end of March, with five games to play, Hendon were fifth, and could have challenged for third place. But the last five league matches only produced two points, a 2–0 win at Hayes.

Hendon did manage a 2–2 draw with Enfield at Claremont Road in October, when the visitors' side had eight former Hendon players, plus Bobby Cantwell and David Hyde who would later move to Claremont Road.

Cup campaigns

There were no long cup runs to sustain supporters' interest either. In the FA Cup, a 9–1 slaughter of Leyton was followed by an exit at Corinthian League Dagenham. In the Amateur Cup, Hendon met Pegasus in the first round, bringing back memories of their heart-breaking semi-final defeat in 1951. Pegasus had declined since those heady days, and were in their penultimate season. A 1–1 draw at Iffley Road in Oxford was followed by a 6–1 win for Hendon in the replay. Hendon's victory was overshadowed by problems with the pitch – again. *The Times's* match report was headed "Pegasus upset by Pitch", described it as a "glutinous morass" and said that Pegasus had made an official protest to the FA about the conditions. However, the report did credit a "more physically powerful and experienced Hendon team" for using long passes and quick breakaways, which it said were "tactics which were the only practical ones on such a day."

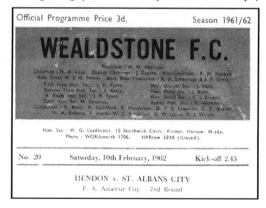

The second round tie against Isthmian League St Albans City was switched to Wealdstone, due to the state of the Claremont Road pitch, and Hendon lost 3–0.

The county cups also provided little cheer. Defeat at Enfield finished any interest in the London Senior Cup, while in the Middlesex Senior Cup, victory over Delphinian League Harrow Town was followed by a second round defeat at Hayes. In the London Charity Cup, a 7–1 win over Dulwich Hamlet was followed by a 3–0 semi-final defeat at Ilford.

As Champions, Hendon faced a Rest of the League XI in the first home match of the season, and won 5–1. Another high profile match at Claremont Road was an Athenian XI against Iceland, resulting in a 4–4 draw.

Mike Pinner won a further seven England caps, being ever-present in goal for the international team, and Jeff Harris won three England caps before his move to Enfield. They both also played for the Athenian League side, as did Roy Walker.

1962–63: Finale in the Athenian League

The 1962–63 season was probably more significant for what happened off the pitch than on it. In February, along with Sutton United, Hitchin Town and Enfield, the club was elected to the Isthmian League, around 50 years after first applying, thus bringing to an end 49 years' membership of the Athenian League. Enfield and Sutton were elected in the first round, with Hendon and Hitchin being accepted in the fourth round of the ballot. Barnet, Finchley and Wealdstone were unsuccessful. Barnet would only play another season in the amateur game before joining the Southern League in 1964.

The Athenian League also announced plans to merge with the Corinthian and Delphinian Leagues, and introduce promotion and relegation. This was an important step towards the formation of the 'non-league pyramid' that would allow clubs to rise – and fall – on merit, rather than by election. Hendon certainly justified their Isthmian League place historically. In 1961, the club had produced a table showing that of teams with more than 10 seasons membership of the Athenian League, Hendon had the highest average league position: 5.27. The next best was Tooting & Mitcham United, with 5.69, but only over 13 seasons, compared to Hendon's 36.

It is clear that the Isthmian League looked at historical records and possibly facilities rather than a club's fortunes in the 1962–63 season. Of the four clubs chosen for elevation, Enfield won the League, Sutton United finished fourth, Hitchin Town fifth and Hendon matched their performance of the previous season, finishing seventh, but with only 29 points. This was the first time since 1945–46 that the club had averaged less than a point a game.

Of course, this was also the season of the great freeze. On 22 December, Hendon lost 5–0 at Finchley. Snow, ice and frozen pitches meant their next match was on 23 February, when their interest in the Amateur Cup ended at Barking. On 2 March, regular fixtures resumed, but for the first time since the 1946–47 season, both the FA and Amateur Cup Finals were put back, to allow the fixture congestion to catch up.

Hendon's off-the-field facilities had also been greatly improved by the installation of floodlights at Claremont Road. Wolverhampton Wanderers paid the club the honour of sending their first team to open them on 25 September. Wolves won 7–1, but as they had recently won a First Division game 9–3, this was considered a very respectable result for Hendon. The Wolves team included internationals Ron Flowers and Peter Broadbent. For Hendon, Bill Fisher came on as a substitute at the age of 42.

Other floodlit friendlies were staged, with Chelsea, an International XI and Loughborough Colleges providing the opposition. At this time, Hendon were the only non-league club to have floodlights on four pylons in the corners of the ground, rather than the more common (and cheaper) system of floodlight poles along the sides of the pitch. The system cost £5,000 and was slightly smaller than one that had been installed at Crystal Palace FC. The first competitive match fully under floodlights was against Wealdstone in March, which Hendon lost 3–2.

Players

On the playing front, one significant signing was full-back David Hogwood from Wembley, who would serve Hendon for many years, and win international honours. Despite being right footed, he mainly played at left back, with Maurice Williams at right back. International forward Paul Bates joined the club from Wycombe Wanderers, and another recruit was Tony Knox. In November, centre-forward Dave Swain joined from Tooting & Mitcham United. Former reserve team player Dennis Roach, later to find fame as a football agent, left the club to join Hayes. In October, Mike Pinner left the club to return to the professional game, with Leyton Orient, still playing as an amateur, although he did turn professional and play for the east London club in their only season in the First Division. His place was taken by reserve keeper Dave Abrey.

Interviewed in 1966 by John Moynihan in his classic book *The Soccer Syndrome*, Pinner admitted that he found it difficult to adjust to playing in amateur football: "I had a season playing for Hendon... which was disastrous – I found the standard wasn't as high as I would have liked... I found I couldn't play in top class amateur football. The pace was too slow and I was anticipating what ought to have happened but did not. I was playing at a different tempo and very badly at that."

Coach Peter Rogers left the club before the end of the season, and Bill Fisher took over running the first team. In October, Hendon formed a youth team, so for the first time the club was running four teams.

A Hendon hero: Bill Fisher

Along with Dexter Adams and Laurie Topp, Bill Fisher was the third great stalwart of Hendon's post war period in the Athenian League.

He joined the club in 1941 from junior side Deerfield, at the age of 19, and soon established himself in the first team. He was ever present that season, and in 1942–43, and made his 100th consecutive appearance at Clapton in February 1944. He made 176 consecutive appearances and was presented with a gold watch by the club to mark this achievement. He played almost every defensive position, and also had a season at inside forward. Many Hendon supporters believe that his versatility cost him an England amateur cap, as he was regarded as a 'utility player'.

In all he made 823 first team appearances, including the 1955 and 1960 Amateur Cup finals, the latter at the age of 38. He also played in three London Senior Cup

HENDON FOOTBALL CLUB
Claremont Road, London N.W.2

Challenge Match

HENDON

versus

WIMBLEDON

MONDAY 4th DECEMBER, 1978   KICK OFF 7.30 pm

IN AID OF THE
BILL FISHER MEMORIAL FUND
ADMISSION BY PROGRAMME
50p

finals, five Middlesex Senior Cup finals, with one victory, four Middlesex Charity Cup finals, of which three were victorious. He was also part of two Athenian League championship sides and played in three war-time cup finals in 1945. He played for the England 'B' team against the Army in 1954, and also played for Middlesex, London, and the Athenian League. His seven appearances for the latter included a tour of the Far East.

In the 1959–60 he was made reserve team captain and coach before winning first team place back. That season he was also the Athenian League player of the year.

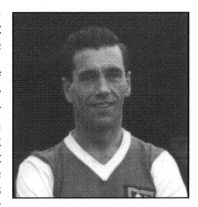

He continued to serve the club in various roles off the pitch after his retirement as a player. He took over as first team coach in 1962–63, and became manager for the 1965–66 and 1966–67 seasons, taking Hendon to an Amateur Cup final and semi-final. He then took over running the reserve team, and was also assistant manager to John Evans and Jimmy Quail. In 1974 he became first team manager again, and it was under his direction that Hendon achieved their first FA Cup victory over a Football League team with a 1–0 victory over Reading.

In 1976, when Jimmy Quail took over as manager, he went onto the club committee, and became the club's public relations officer. However, on Tuesday and Thursday nights he could still be found on the pitch helping with training. He also did some scouting for Arsenal, and was involved with a Sunday team, Sparrowhawk FC.

Bill Fisher died at the early age of 56 in 1978, The club set up a memorial fund for his family, and played a match against Wimbledon FC at Claremont Road on 4 December 1978. As the match programme said: "Bill will always be remembered, not only by those of us connected with Hendon, but by his many friends and colleagues in the game for his great sense of loyalty and warm personality, he truly was football's 'Mr Nice Guy'."

The league

Hendon never threatened the top places in the league. After being in the top five early on in the season, in early March, Hendon sank as low as 11th, albeit with games in hand on the teams above them. An improvement towards the end of the season saw a final finish of seventh, 25 points behind champions Enfield, and 18 behind runners-up Barnet. The attack did reasonably well, averaging two goals a game, but the defence also conceded two goals a game. This included two six goal defeats against Sutton United, and the 5–0 defeat at Finchley. On a more positive note, the last home match in the Athenian League was on 20 May with a 6–3 victory over Grays Athletic.

Cup competitions

There no cup runs of note to compensate for Hendon's rather average form in the league. In the FA Cup, Hendon beat Leytonstone, Ford United and Leyton – all at Claremont Road – before going out to Western League Andover in the fourth qualifying round. A 1–1 draw at home was followed by a 5–4 defeat in the replay.

In every other cup, Hendon lost in the first round. Kingstonian won at Claremont Road in the London Senior Cup, and Southall repeated this in the Middlesex Senior Cup. The Charity Cups provided no relief for supporters, with defeats at Dulwich Hamlet in the London version, and Finchley in the Middlesex competition. A new competition for Hendon was the Mithras Floodlit Cup, but that ended with two defeats against Finchley: 2–0 at Claremont Road and 2–1 in the return match.

The reserve team, after a couple of years near the bottom of the league, had a successful season, winning the Athenian League reserve section and the London Intermediate Cup. Two coach loads of supporters travelled to the Final when Wimbledon's reserve team were beaten 3–1. One of the reserve team stars was Laurie Churchill, who would soon make an impact at first team level.

Honours

Mike Pinner was once again ever-present for the England amateur team, playing the first two matches of the season while still at Claremont Road.

The future

So the club's participation in the Athenian League ended with two mid-table places. However, had promotion and relegation operated, the club would have been promoted to the Isthmian League many years earlier. The next season would offer new challenges.

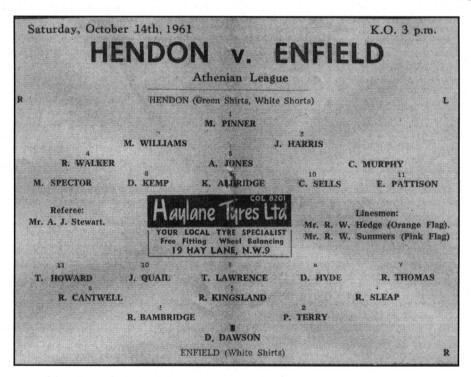

Hendon versus Enfield 14 October 1961. The Enfield team in the match programme has eight former Hendon players. Of the other three, David Hyde joined Hendon in August 1963 and Bobby Cantwell in August 1964.

7. 1963 to 1970: Wembley and much more

The club's election to the Isthmian League in February 1963 was one of the most important developments in its history. Now it would face the challenge of competing in the top league in amateur football for the first time.

The Isthmian League was set up in 1905, and established itself as the top amateur competition. However, when Hendon were elected to the league, there was no pyramid structure in amateur football. If the Isthmian league needed new clubs, it would invite suitable applicants, usually from the Athenian League, to apply.

But the lack of any relegation meant that there were a number of clubs, often with great past histories, who languished season after season at the bottom of the League. Writing in 1960, Norman Ackland wrote: "The Isthmian League can be described as the most popular competition of its kind in amateur football. Taken together, the clubs in the Athenian League are slightly stronger. There is little in it so far as the clubs at the top of the table in both competitions are concerned, but the bottom Athenian clubs appear to be stronger than the bottom Isthmian. In representative matches between the two Leagues the Athenians have the better record. Still, the fact remains that the majority of the Athenian clubs would unhesitatingly accept invitations to become members of the Isthmian League."

The Athenian League recognised the problem of stagnation that no promotion and relegation could bring, and merged with the Corinthian and Delphinian Leagues to create a three division structure for 1963–64.

If the Isthmian League had chosen its new members solely on results in the 1962–63 season, Hendon would not have been selected, having finished seventh in 1962–63 in the Athenian League. But the club's overall record was of more significance - the *FA Yearbook* for 1963–64 had Hendon as the third most successful amateur club, after Bishop Auckland and Walthamstow Avenue.

Hendon were chosen for the Isthmian League with Enfield, who were Athenian League champions, Sutton United and Hitchin Town. Runners-up Barnet stayed in the Athenian League, but within a year turned semi-professional and joined the Southern League. Wealdstone, who were third, were elected to the Isthmian League a year later, when Wimbledon turned professional and moved to the Southern League.

1963–64: A new playing squad

To face the challenge of the new League, Hendon appointed a new coach, former Tottenham Hotspur and Wales half-back Ronnie Burgess, who had previously managed Watford. He had a distinguished career with Spurs, captaining the side who won the Second Division in 1949–50 and the First Division title the next year. He played at left-half, and was a key member of that famous team and their 'push and run' style. He won 32 Welsh caps. He joined Swansea in 1954, and became player manager until 1959, before moving to Watford. He was less successful as a manger after leaving Hendon. He joined Fulham in 1965, then managed Bedford, coached Lincoln City and then did some scouting for Luton Town in the 1970s. He worked as a warehouseman and stock controller before retiring. He died in 2005, aged 87.

Two of the 'new' players were Jimmy Quail and Roy Sleap, both past stars at the club who were returning from Enfield, along with new recruit David Hyde. Quail and Sleap were both already amateur internationals, and Hyde already had a growing reputation as having one of the hardest shots in the amateur game.

Possibly the most significant signing was goalkeeper John Swannell, who joined the club from Corinthian Casuals, where he had been playing since leaving Manchester University. Other new players included forward Peter Slade from Oxford City, Gerry O'Rourke, a forward from Hayes, and Welsh international defender John Fisher from Wycombe Wanderers. However, one departure in September was long-serving forward Miles Spector. No longer assured of a regular place, he joined Wingate, fulfilling a long-standing promise to finish his career with that club. Another departure from the club was reserve player Martin Hackett, who joined Bloemfontein City in South Africa. There were also some young players coming through from the reserve team, which had won the Athenian League reserve section and the London Intermediate Cup in 1962–63.

A Hendon hero: Miles Spector

Truth is often stranger than fiction. A football novel that included a Grammar School sixth former playing truant to play for a First Division side's reserve team, missing a penalty, their famous manager arriving at half-time and on the basis of his great second-half performance selecting him for the first team would result in the author being mocked for flights of fantasy. But this happened to Miles Spector in the 1952–53 season, the school was Hendon Grammar and the manager was Ted Drake, who had previously managed Hendon. Spector was played for Chelsea in an Eastern Counties League Cup game against Tottenham Hotspur at Stamford Bridge on Monday 26 January 1953. He recalls: "We were trailing 2–0 at half-time, but improved in the second half before finally losing 5–3, although I did manage to score one of our goals."

He was called into the Headmaster's study after the game – not be punished, but to inform him that he had been chosen for the Chelsea first team: "Ted Drake telephoned my headmaster, Mr E. W. Maynard-Potts to obtain permission for me to travel with the team to West Bromwich on 4 February, which ended 0–0 after extra time. From that point onwards Mr Drake contacted the school in advance before selecting me for midweek matches." He didn't actually play on that occasion, but did play in the First Division as an 18-year-old schoolboy. He had previously played for the Chelsea reserve and youth teams.

He made his Chelsea first team debut on 7 February 1953 in a 3–2 win over Sunderland at Stamford Bridge. In all he played six first team games for Chelsea, three in the league and three in the FA Cup. In one of the FA Cup ties, a fourth round third replay against West Bromwich Albion at Highbury, his performance won all the headlines. With the score 0–0 at half time, he set up three of Chelsea's four second-half goals in a 4–0 win. His studies meant that he had to decline the invitation to tour the USA with Chelsea.

166

He turned down the opportunity to play professionally to go to university, where he got a BSc and developed a successful career in engineering. He played a couple of games for Millwall at this time, and won an England amateur cap against South Africa. He had previously played for the England youth team.

He joined Hendon in September 1955, although he had been training at the club for 18 months, while playing for Chelsea reserves, and remembers: "I was quite familiar with the Hendon players. I was living in Hendon and working at Handley Page Ltd in Cricklewood. It never occurred to me to seek another professional club after I had decided to leave Chelsea. Millwall had approached me, but after playing two games for them, I was not favourably impressed and left. I had decided that a career in engineering was right for me, after graduating in 1956 with an honours degree in Aeronautical Engineering, I started a two year post-graduate apprenticeship with Handley Page Ltd. The company was very near Hendon FC, so it was quite natural to find out whether Hendon would welcome my services."

Initially he played on the left-wing, but then switched to centre forward in 1959–60, which he preferred, and won an Amateur Cup winners medal in 1960. He says that that match was the highlight of his time with Hendon: "My one regret was that I was not 100 percent fit, having carried a cartilage injury for most of the season. Following the injury in the autumn of 1959, I was unable to train regularly, the knee swelled up after every game, and I was restricted to playing in only the most important cup matches. I am eternally grateful to our physiotherapist Len Kilby and his son, Don, without whose expert knowledge and treatment I would never have made the Final." Among players he remembers from Hendon are "Dexter Adams, who having suffered a serious knee injury himself, kept faith in me, Bill Fisher, Laurie Topp, Tommy Lawrence and Charlie Murphy, whose rise from obscurity in just one season was astonishing."

He was one of the most exciting players to play for the club, and was regularly among the top scorers. As well as two England amateur caps, he also played for the Athenian League twice, Middlesex and the FA.

Apart from the memorable Amateur Cup triumph in 1960, the first time the club had won amateur football's most prestigious trophy, he was part of two Athenian League championship sides, was a member of the team that were runners up in the London Senior Cup in 1959; in the Middlesex Senior Cup achieved two winners medals and one runners-up, and a winners medal in the Middlesex Charity Cup. In the 1957–58 Middlesex Senior Cup win he shoulder-charged the goalkeeper and the ball into the net for one of Hendon's goals.

He stayed loyal to the club in 1961, when most of the first team joined Enfield, and said that he was never tempted to leave. He left Hendon in September 1963, to finish his career with Wingate, and "spent a very pleasant six years or so helping younger players to develop. The facilities were first class, the committee most friendly and helpful and I was given the opportunity to be the player-manager for the last three years. I only resigned because of pressure of work."

As well as playing football, he was an All-England schoolboy athletics champion. At work, he left Handley Page in 1965 to be a lecturer at Hendon College of Technology – now part of Middlesex University – where he stayed until early retirement in 1986. He retired to "take full advantage of the opportunity to enjoy the relatively stress and pollution free atmosphere of the beautiful county of Cornwall", where he still lives.

League campaign

The Isthmian League campaign started with a 2–1 win at Clapton, one of the League's perennial strugglers. But a sign of things to come came with a 7–1 midweek victory at Ilford, who were to finish the season in ninth place. The first home match was against Dulwich Hamlet, another club with a great history and one of the largest grounds in amateur football, but now lacked resources and struggled at the bottom of the table.

No one could have predicted a 10–1 victory for Hendon. Hyde and O'Rourke put the Greens 2–0 up within 10 minutes, and O'Rourke made it 3–1 just before half-time. After the interval, a further seven goals followed, including O'Rourke scoring four, his second hat-trick in five days. The only forward not to score was Peter Slade, but he had created around seven of the goals, a pattern to be regularly repeated over the next two years.

The Isthmian League at this time was dominated by Wimbledon. At the beginning of November, Hendon were fifth in the League, with 18 points from 12 matches. Wimbledon were top, having played three games more, and having also dropped six points. The Greens had games in hand on all the teams above them. The attack was averaging over three goals a game, while the defence were letting in one per game.

At the turn of the year, Hendon were fourth, having lost two more games. Wimbledon were still top, and had only dropped one more point. The first two months of 1964 were dominated by cup matches, with only four league games played, although all were won. At the end of February, Hendon were top by a point from Wimbledon, who had a match in hand. However, in the last 13 matches, Hendon won just six, taking 14 points, and finished as runners-up by six points to Wimbledon. This was despite beating the 'other' Dons 3–0 at Claremont Road on 28 March, with two goals from Quail and one from O'Rourke. In the return at Plough Lane a week later, Hendon lost 2–1. Quail scored after 12 minutes, but Slade was injured, which may have cost Hendon the match.

It had still been a magnificent campaign, and showed that the club had fully justified their election to the Isthmian League. But nine defeats in 38 matches prevented the side taking the title. Lapses such as a 3–1 home defeat to Maidstone in November, and an end-of-season 1–0 defeat at Corinthian Casuals had undermined the title challenge. The club programme said on the latter match: "The boys suffered another of their unpredictable upsets at Corinthian Casuals on Saturday where they were beaten 1–0. It was something we never bargained for. We fully expected to boost our goal average."

The striking force of the team was remarkable. Even given the more open nature of football at this time, before the more defensive formations of the late 1960s, to score 124 goals in the League was incredible, averaging over three a game. This was an Isthmian League record, beating Woking's 104 (in only 30 matches) in 1956–57. Apart from the 10 against Dulwich Hamlet, who also conceded nine in the return match at Champion Hill in December, the Greens scored eight against Hitchin at home, with a further five in the return match, seven against Corinthian Casuals at Claremont Road and at Ilford, six against Woking and Walthamstow Avenue, and five on four occasions.

Cup excitement

Apart from the Isthmian League, the cup competitions were, as always, an interesting part of the season. In the FA Cup, victories against Leytonstone, Clapton (8–0) and Athenian League Dagenham led to a fourth round qualifying match at Enfield. Sadly, the cup run finished there with a 3–1 defeat.

In the Amateur Cup, Hendon's involvement in the competition ended with a first round defeat at Hampshire side Fareham Town on 11 January. Despite the support of seven coaches of supporters, Hendon went down 1–0 to a last-minute goal when goalkeeper John Swannell was knocked out by Fareham's centre forward Ray Hiron, who subsequently played for Portsmouth and for Reading against Hendon in 1975. The club programme commented on "a couple of baffling decisions" by the referee in disallowing goals for both sides, and in turning down a penalty for Hendon in the second half.

Two weeks later, the club's participation in the Middlesex Senior Cup also ended at the first hurdle, with a 3–2 defeat at Wealdstone. However, this competition did provide one of the most exciting games at Claremont Road later in the season, when Wealdstone beat Enfield 6–4 in the semi-final, after the match had been tied 3–3 at the end of 90 minutes.

The London Senior Cup was, in those days, the second most prestigious cup for amateur clubs in the capital, and was one that Hendon had never won. Wealdstone were again Hendon's first round opponents, with a 1–1 draw at Lower Mead followed by a 3–2 Hendon victory in the replay. After a 4–2 win over Corinthian Casuals in the next round at the beginning of January, the team scraped a 2–2 draw at Spartan League Croydon Amateurs. O'Rourke opened the scoring in the replay for Hendon, but soon the Greens were 2–1 down. Slade and O'Rourke scored before half-time to give Hendon a 3–2 lead, and after the tie was 3–3 at 90 minutes, ran away with the game to win 7–4, O'Rourke scoring four goals. On 14 March, Hendon beat Isthmian League rivals Kingstonian 4–2 at Hounslow in the semi-final to reach their first London Senior Cup Final since 1959. Their opponents at Wealdstone would be Enfield, who had already beaten Hendon three times, twice in the League and once in the FA Cup.

Hendon 1 Enfield 0
London Senior Cup final

The *Hendon Times* report by Fred Harris said that it was an "undistinguished final", and O'Rourke scored the vital goal that helped brighten up the almost sleepy game. He added that "[Enfield] provided little difficulty for mediocre Hendon to control." Hendon missed Sleap who had a knee injury. Riddy had an excellent game, and in goal Swannell was outstanding. Harris said his "safe handling and razor-keen interceptions played a large part in preventing Enfield getting on top."

Terry Howard hit the bar after 14 minutes, and Enfield had the better of the game early on, although Hyde and Quail had first time shots saved by Brian Goymer. The goal came in the 71st minute when the Enfield defence was stranded. Quail passed to Hyde on left wing, he gave a 'grand pass' to O'Rourke who had little difficulty in scoring. Harris said that "Hendon hung on to win amateur soccer's second most important trophy."

Hendon: J. Swannell, D. Hogwood, R. Ellison, J. Payne, G. Riddy, A. Knox, D. Hyde, G. O'Rourke, L. Churchill, J. Quail, P. Slade.

Enfield: B. Goymer, M. Neale, J. Harris, A. D'Arcy, R. Kingsland, R. Cantwell, R. Thomas, W. Broomfield, A. Edwards, R. Day, T. Howard.

The team's success had been reflected with representative honours for the club's leading players. Jimmy Quail, who had narrowly missed out on Olympic selection in 1960, played twice for Great Britain against Greece in the qualifying competition, but Great Britain were eliminated 5–3 on aggregate. Roy Sleap added to his international honours with a further England cap.

One other change during the season was the resignation of Alfred Murray as club president in February. Credited with keeping the club alive during World War Two, he had been involved with the club for over 30 years.

So, the season ended with the capture of one of amateur football's most important trophies, and a very commendable runners-up spot in the League. With Wimbledon turning professional and joining the Southern League, starting on the road that would take them to the top of the professional game, could Hendon become the dominant force in amateur football the next season?

1964–65: The Treble

Occasionally, just occasionally, a team dominate a season, play attacking, attractive football and deserve the accolade "great". In the professional ranks, the 1960–61 Tottenham Hotspur 'double' team comes to mind. In the amateur game, the 1964–65 Hendon 'treble' team are also worthy of this title. As Danny Blanchflower famously said, the game is about "glory", and for Hendon, this was truly a glorious season.

Gerry O'Rourke left the club, and turned professional with Wimbledon. Another departure was young forward Laurie Churchill to Southern League Guildford, although he returned to the club in October. New recruits included robust winger Danny Lakey, England international half-back Bobby Cantwell and George Rocknean. In October, Tony Knox moved to Wycombe Wanderers, and John Payne joined Enfield.

In the League, Hendon started with a 6–1 triumph over Dulwich Hamlet at Claremont Road. In early October, after 10 games, the Greens were third, behind Enfield and Sutton United, although with games in hand over both clubs, and were still unbeaten. The unbeaten run continued for another two games, before a 3–2 defeat at Wycombe's Loakes Park slope at the end of October. However, revenge came five weeks later, with a stunning 9–2 win over the Buckinghamshire side in the return match at Claremont Road. David Hyde and Danny Lakey both contributed hat-tricks. On 15 December, Hendon lost 6–3 at Leytonstone, but from then until the end of the season, only lost one more league match.

However, Enfield did not relent in the challenge for the League title, and after both sides had completed their programmes, both were on 63 points. Hendon had won one less game than their north London rivals, but had scored 123 goals compared to Enfield's 98. Although Enfield had the marginally better goal average, the League decided to have a play-off for the title. The programme for this game, played at Dulwich Hamlet's Champion Hill ground on 30 April 1965, explained that: "The match this evening appears to be the first time a deciding game has been played to determine the Championship, in the past on occasions when two clubs had tied for top place on points, it had not been possible for such a game to take place, owing to congestion of fixtures at the end of the season and goal average has been the deciding factor." It was agreed that if the match was a draw, Enfield's better goal average would give them the title. However, in a sparkling display, Hendon won 4–1 to secure the club's first Isthmian League title.

Hendon 4 Enfield 1
Isthmian League title play-off

Hendon's inventive forward play secured the Isthmian League title in an exciting playoff at Dulwich Hamlet's Champion Hill ground before a crowd of 4,900.

David Hyde gave Hendon the lead after 20 minutes, taking Peter Slade's pass going past Alf D'Arcy and beating Mitchell to score. Soon afterwards, Slade hit the crossbar. Hendon led 1–0 at the break. Twelve minutes after the start of the second half, Slade put Hendon 2–0 up, and a further goal from Roy Drake made the title certain. McDonnell pulled a goal back for Enfield, but a couple of minutes from the end Danny Lakey restored Hendon's three goal advantage. The *Hendon Times* report said that: "Hogwood was superb. So well did he hold England winger Terry Howard that the former Hendon star switched wings, hoping that he could get the better of Roy Sleap. Again he got little change." Wingers Danny Lakey and Roy Drake were always prominent in Hendon's win.
Hendon: J. Swannell, D. Hogwood, R. Sleap, J. Evans, G. Riddy, R. Cantwell, R. Drake, P. Slade, D. Hyde, J. Quail, D. Lakey.
Enfield: M. Mitchell, P. Terry, I. Reid, J. Payne, A. D'Arcy, A. McDonnell, R. Thomas, W. Broomfield, L. Varney, R. Day, T. Howard.

It was also an exciting season in the cup competitions. In the FA Cup, wins at Leyton and Fords Sports were followed by home victories over Athenian League Slough Town and then Leytonstone in the fourth qualifying round. The first round draw took Hendon to Third Division Port Vale, who were two places off the bottom of the table, with only two wins. Despite this, the home side won 2–1, in front of 8,039 supporters, their biggest crowd of the season so far.

Port Vale 2 Hendon 1
FA Cup first round proper

Hendon's forwards were not in form for this trip to the Potteries, but a late rally still worried Port Vale, according to the *Hendon Times*. David Hyde hardly had a worthwhile shot, and had poor support from other forwards. Hendon were saved from heavier defeat by John Swannell. Port Vale went ahead when Smith beat Hogwood after 13 minutes to score. Hendon only had two attempts at goal in first half, and on 52 minutes it was 2–0. Smith passed to Mitchell who scored. With 10 minutes left, Quail crossed for Hyde to score, but Hendon could not muster an equaliser. The report said that it was a "fine sporting game" but Hendon had a "lack of shooting power."

At one point Hendon appealed for a penalty, and the Port Vale goalkeeper put the ball on the spot, before realising that the referee had allowed play on.
Port Vale: Hancock, Alcock, Wilson, Rawlings, Nicholson, Sproson, Rowland, Machin, Mitchell, Mudie, Smith.
Hendon: J. Swannell, D. Hogwood, R. Sleap, J. Evans, G. Riddy, R. Cantwell, A. Peel, P. Slade, D. Hyde, J. Quail, D. Lakey.

Another exciting cup competition in the first half of the season was the London Challenge Cup. This was competed for by reserve strength teams of London's Football League clubs, the Southern League teams, and the two finalists from the previous season's London Senior Cup. Hendon started with a 3–1 win at home to Enfield, and the draw for the next round took them to Highbury, to face a young Arsenal team. Arsenal's first team were not doing particularly well at this time. But in the reserves were players who at the end of the 1960s and early 1970s would, under Bertie Mee's direction, lift the club to the top of English football. Among the players Hendon faced were Bob Wilson, Peter Storey, David Court, Ian Ure, John Radford and Jon Sammels.

Arsenal 3 Hendon 4
London Challenge Cup

The *Hendon Times* report headline was "Champagne night for Hendon at Highbury - Hyde hat-trick shocks Arsenal." In a remarkable season, this was surely one of Hendon's greatest victories. Playing an Arsenal team that included two full internationals, Magill and Ure, and the nucleus of the 1970–71 Arsenal double team, Hendon recovered from being 3–0 down after 18 minutes to win 4–3. Only Court and Tawse had not played in the Arsenal first team. Peter Simpson later joined Hendon for six months.

Arsenal's goals came from a hat-trick by John Radford, who scored after nine, 15 and 18 minutes. But on the half hour, a 'superb' goal by Danny Lakey, scored from acute angle, put Hendon back in the game. Future Scotland international and television presenter Bob Wilson, a £7,000 buy from Wolves, "was beaten all ends up." John Evans then hit the bar, before David Hyde scored the first of a 'superb hat trick'. Hyde was being marked by Ian Ure, who was returning from injury. At £62,500 he was the costliest centre half in English football at that time. On 34 minutes, Hyde scored with a header from a cross from Elved Price.

Arsenal were 3–2 up at the break, when John Swannell changed his studs, and was "back to his international best in the second half." On 59 minutes, Hyde was put through by a combination of Roy Sleap and Peter Slade to score the equaliser. Then with 13 minutes left, he scored the winner, cutting in from the left flank and beat Wilson. Hendon kept Arsenal out for the last few minutes to delight their supporters in the 2,352 crowd.

Interviewed in *London Football Review* 40 years later, Bob Wilson recalled the game, as the one occasion he had come very close to leaving Arsenal. He said: "...we'd lost 4–3 to Hendon despite having been 3–0 up ... I still remember it so well. I was only as bad as anyone in the side had been that day but it was me who was dropped altogether from the next game and I just totally lost it with Billy Wright."

Arsenal: Wilson, Magill, Storey, Simpson, Ure, Court, Anderson, Baldwin, Radford, Sammels, Tawse.

Hendon: J. Swannell, D. Hogwood, R. Sleap, J. Evans, G. Riddy, R. Cantwell, E. Price, P. Slade, D. Hyde, J. Quail, D. Lakey.
(Programme Courtesy Arsenal Football Club)

After that great victory, which will stay forever as one of Hendon's greatest triumphs, anti-climax followed. The London Challenge Cup run ended on a Monday afternoon a couple of weeks later at Southern League Bexley United with a 2–1 defeat. And in the London Senior Cup, holders Hendon were giant-killed by Athenian League Cheshunt, who won 3–2 at Claremont Road in the first round. David Shacklock played at right back for the Athenian League side, and joined Hendon soon after the match.

The Amateur Cup

After Christmas, attention turned to the Amateur Cup, which Hendon had not won since 1960. Fellow Isthmian Leaguers Sutton United and Leytonstone were beaten in the first two rounds, and in the third round, Athenian League Carshalton were thrashed 5–1 at Claremont Road. The quarter final draw produced a difficult match, Northern League Whitley Bay away from home. Six hundred Hendon supporters made the trip north, and were rewarded with a 3–1 win, with goals from Hyde, Drake and Slade. However, match reports credit the Hendon defence, in particular Swannell, Hogwood and centre-half Geoff Riddy for withstanding a siege in parts of the game.

Three weeks later, Hendon returned to Highbury to face local rivals Finchley in the semi-final. Two goals from David Hyde gave Hendon a convincing 4–1 win.

Hendon 4 Finchley 1
Amateur Cup semi-final

"Hendon reach Amateur Cup Final" was the triumphant headline in the *Hendon Times*, adding that "Nervous Finchley were easily outgunned".

A crowd of 9,275 watched this local derby at Highbury, paying £2,044. Although no longer in the same league, the teams had been regular opponents over the years, and were so close that they had both booked into the same hotel in Hendon for a pre-match meal. Finchley changed their booking, deciding the game was too important for the sides to have lunch together.

Fred Harris's report said Finchley's suicidal tactics gave Hendon an easier passage into the final than expected. Syd Prosser, Finchley's coach, put right-half Mick Edghill to shadow Slade, to break down Hendon's attack. But this failed miserably. David Hyde was left completely unmarked, and scored 2 goals. Hyde admitted he was "nervous" before the game, with the prize of a Wembley final awaiting the winners, but Harris wrote that the "tension was too much for some Finchley players who had never played in such an important game."

Hendon coach Ronnie Burgess said his team should have had more goals. Hendon had been thwarted by "Superb saves by one of their former goalies, Johnny Adamson, who pushed several snorters from Hyde over the bar."

After 17 minutes, Hendon took the lead. A free kick by Quail went to Hyde, who slammed the ball into the net. It was 1–0 to Hendon at the break. Hendon faced a crisis at half time, when Jimmy Quail collapsed with a dislocated shoulder. Trainer Jerry Marrable put shoulder back in joint.

But two minutes after the restart, a cross from Drake was deflected in by Dave Emson, for an own goal. On 63 minutes, Hendon made the game safe. Following a brilliant run, Slade crossed and Drake played the ball to Hyde who scored.

Six minutes later, Jimmy Cooley pulled one back for Finchley. However, with four minutes left, Peter Slade, who had scored in every round, continued his record, adding Hendon's fourth from a cross by Lakey.

Ronnie Burgess said: "Now we have reached Wembley we must concentrate on winning the Isthmian League championship." Jimmy Quail said that he "expected Finchley to provide stronger opposition."

Hendon: J. Swannell, D. Hogwood, R. Sleap, J. Evans, G. Riddy, R. Cantwell, R. Drake, P. Slade, D. Hyde, J. Quail, D. Lakey.

Finchley: J. Adamson, A. Edghill, D. Emson, M. Edghill, A. Sandell, D Neville, W Ratty, V. Lucas, J. Cooley, L. Eason, A Turley.

(Programme courtesy Arsenal FC)

In the Final, Hendon again faced Northern League opposition in Whitby Town. It was their opponents' first Amateur Cup final appearance. On the way to Wembley they had beaten Moor Green, Eastbourne, Oxford City, Harwich and Parkeston after a replay; and then in the semi-final Hendon's old rivals Enfield. None of their players had any international honours, and Hendon were clearly favourites.

Hendon 3 Whitby Town 1
Amateur Cup Final

A 45,000 crowd, 8,000 up on the previous season, enjoyed a match which *The Times* report said was "one of the finest of the post-war FA Amateur Cup finals". Tony Pawson's report said it was a "stirring match" and the *FA Yearbook* said that it was "the brightest game of the matches played at the Empire Stadium during the spring of 1965 with the exception of the European Cup-Winners Cup Final".

Hendon were pre-match favourites, and nearly took the lead in the opening minutes. Whitby's hopes were hit when left-winger Crosthwaite was injured in a tackle with John Evans after 10 minutes. It was a fair tackle, but left the winger limping for the remainder of the game.

Hendon had the better of the first half, but could not break down Whitby's defence, which used the offside tactic effectively. At half-time, Hendon's coach Ronnie Burgess told Peter Slade to pull back with the ball to avoid the offside trap. Three minutes after the break, Hendon took the lead when Hyde scored from a cross by Danny Lakey. Quail dislocated his shoulder four minutes into the second half, but managed to put it back in and continue playing. With 57 minutes gone, Hyde and Slade set up Quail to score and Hendon looked to be safe. But three minutes later, Whitby pulled a goal back through Mulvaney, and put Hendon under considerable pressure. With five minutes left, Mulvaney hit the Hendon cross bar, but Hendon then broke away for Hyde to score and make the game safe. He ran 40 yards with the ball, beat the goalkeeper and scored.

Hendon coach Ronnie Burgess said: "The boys played extremely well and I think I did the right thing when I selected Roy Drake as outside-right. It was a tremendous game with Whitby playing some excellent football."

Hendon: J. Swannell, D. Hogwood, R. Sleap, J. Evans, G. Riddy, R. Cantwell (c), R. Drake, P. Slade, D. Hyde, J. Quail, D. Lakey.

Whitby Town: N. Pybus, J. Durnall, E. Nobbs, A. Kennerley, E. Barker (c), K. Moody, B. Geldart, P. McHale, J. Mulvaney, R. Edwards, M. Crosthwaite.

Middlesex Senior Cup

The third 'leg' of Hendon's treble in the club's greatest ever season was the Middlesex Senior Cup. An 8–0 win at Athenian League Hounslow Town in the first round was followed by a 2–1 win at Enfield in February. Hendon scored eight goals again in the semi-final, against Harrow Town at Lower Mead on 15 March. The other semi-final was played at Claremont Road, and saw the return of Miles Spector, playing for Wingate against Finchley. Sadly, he could not prevent Finchley winning 3–1 to face Hendon in the last match of the season at Enfield's Southbury Road.

This game was much tighter than the Amateur Cup semi-final. "Hendon duly completed a grand treble with a 1–0 win over Athenian League neighbours Finchley at Southbury Road on Saturday. But the match proved an anti-climax to the most memorable season in their history." This was Fred Harris's conclusion in the *Hendon Times*. Finchley had learnt lessons from their Amateur Cup defeat at Highbury, and snuffed out the threat from David Hyde and Peter Slade. Barry Neame, a 17-year-old, marked David Hyde.

However, Hendon overcame their Athenian League opponents to win 1–0. The game was scoreless at half time, but four minutes after the break, a corner from David Hyde was played back into the middle by Roy Drake for Peter Slade to score. The match remained tense to the end, particularly as John Evans was injured with 25 minutes left, although he did return to play after treatment. Finchley continued to press for an equaliser, but could not break down the Hendon defence.

Hendon: J. Swannell, D. Hogwood, R. Sleap, J. Evans, G. Riddy, G. Rocknean, R. Drake, P. Slade, D. Hyde, J. Quail, D. Lakey.

Finchley: J. Adamson, D. Emson, E. Goldney, M. Edghill, A. Sandell, B. Neame, J. Cooley, D. Neville, V. Lucas, L. Eason, A. Turley.

In this remarkable season, the team scored 192 goals. David Hyde scored a staggering 59, and Peter Slade, Jimmy Quail and Danny Lakey all scored 30 or more. David Hogwood played in 57 games, followed by Peter Slade and Roy Sleap on 55 each.

Reserves

As well as the club's success at senior level, the reserves had also completed a 'treble', winning the Isthmian League reserve section, the London Intermediate Cup and the Middlesex Intermediate Cup. Players such as David Shacklock, Micky Cooper, Dave Swain, Fred Pudney and Laurie Churchill would all contribute to the club at first team level in the future. In the Middlesex Intermediate Cup, they beat Enfield Reserves 4–1 at Finchley. Their record for the season was: 36 wins, four draws, one defeat, with 146 goals scored and 41 conceded.

Port Vale versus Hendon FA Cup First Round – John Swannell in action

Representative honours

It was also a successful season for the club's players in winning representative honours. John Swannell played five times for England, David Hyde four times, including four goals against Wales on his debut, and Roy Sleap once. Roy Sleap, Jimmy Quail, Geoff Riddy, Bobby Cantwell and Danny Lakey all played for the Isthmian League side. Arthur Peel, Swannell, Sleap and Quail played for Middlesex. Swannell and Bobby Cantwell played for an FA XI. Sleap also played for the London FA team.

At the end of the season, the team had a tour to Majorca. They lost 2–1 to Mallorca, who were the island's champions, and 3–1 to Stirling Albion. These two matches were in a three team tournament. Hendon also lost 6–1 to C.D. Constancia in friendly before tournament. Hendon met the Liverpool FC players, who were having a break on the island. Liverpool had just won the FA Cup, beating Leeds United 2-1, so the FA's two cup winners were on holiday together.

Another change that occurred towards the end of the season was local government reorganisation in London, which saw the merger of Hendon Borough Council into the newly created London Borough of Barnet on 1 April 1965. The borough of Finchley and urban districts of Barnet, East Barnet and Friern Barnet were also included in the new London Borough.

The Hendon councillors had fought to keep the name Hendon, but lost, and for the first time since 1879, when the first local board was set up, the name Hendon was not part of London's local government system. However, the new borough's crest had all five towns in the borough represented, including the Paschal lamb that was Hendon's symbol, but was 'presumed to be standing on Childs Hill'. The population of the new borough was 318,000.

Non league football was well represented in the new borough, with Barnet, Hendon, Finchley and Wingate all coming within its boundaries.

The 1965 Amateur Cup win

Left: John Swannell inspects the pitch. Right: The teams come out
Below: David Hyde scores Hendon's first goal (Photos: *Hendon Times*)

Top: The lap of honour.
Bottom: The team with the cup
(Photos: *Hendon Times*)

Programme courtesy Wembley National Stadium Ltd

Triumphant return to Claremont Road (Courtesy Mike Hogan)

The Supporters Association Committee with the Cup at a reception for the club
at Hendon Town Hall. Back: Mark Rutherford (chairman), Bert Potts, Mike Hogan,
Jack Leggett (vice chairman), John Doyle, Jim Cole, Ernie Webb (treasurer),
Reg Austin, ?, George Needham (HFC assistant treasurer);
kneeling: John Scrutton, John Hutton, Les Maton.
(Courtesy Mike Hogan)

1965–66: So near...

Despite a major injury crisis, the club came very close to repeating the previous season's League and Amateur Cup double. However, the season started with two very significant changes in the club's personnel. On the pitch, Peter Slade, the previous season's 'Player of the Year' had departed. He had got married, moved further away from London, and joined Banbury Spencer. The only other departure at first team level was forward Arthur Peel, who joined Wembley as player-coach. There were no new signings, although a mysterious little item in the club programme said that Charlie Townsend had applied to join from Wealdstone, although he never played for Hendon. Reserve Bobby Ellison left the club midway through the season, and Martin Hackett returned from South Africa.

Off the pitch, coach Ronnie Burgess had returned to the professional game with Fulham. He was replaced by Hendon stalwart Bill Fisher, with former Arsenal player Johnnie Saunders as assistant coach. Another change was that the club did not run an 'A' (third) team.

The season started with two friendlies against Southern League opposition, a draw at Stevenage and 2–1 victory over Wimbledon at Claremont Road. With a bye to the first round of the FA Cup in November, and no entry into the London Challenge Cup, the club had the rare luxury of an uninterrupted League programme until November.

Clapton were Hendon's first victims in the League campaign, with a hat-trick from David Hyde and two goals from Laurie Churchill contributing to an 8–3 win at the Old Spotted Dog ground. Six further victories followed, including a 7–3 triumph over Ilford at Claremont Road on 16 September. Two days later, the team dropped their first league point, with a 1–1 draw at Wycombe, and then the following Saturday, Corinthian Casuals won 2–1 at Claremont Road. However, Hendon were missing John Swannell and David Hyde who were playing for England. Also, Casuals were having one of their better seasons, and finished 11th.

Winning ways were restored with a 6–3 victory over Sutton United at Claremont Road, and at the end of October, Hendon were top of the League, with 30 points from 17 games, four clear of second-placed Wycombe Wanderers. But a run of four consecutive League defeats, albeit interspersed with some cup matches, was to prove fatal to the club's hopes of retaining the title. To lose at Leytonstone was no disgrace, but defeats at Ilford, who were to finish 17th, and 5–1 at mid-table Woking were below the usual Hendon standards at this time. A home defeat against Enfield in November did not help.

Pride was restored with a 5–0 win at Claremont Road over Oxford City, and Wealdstone's Christmas was not a happy one when they crashed 5–2 at Claremont Road on Christmas Day. At the turn of the year, Hendon were fourth, two points behind leaders Kingstonian, with two games in hand. But Leytonstone were a point clear of Hendon in third place, having only dropped five points.

After Christmas, cup ties took over the fixture list until March. Hendon only lost one more league game, at home to Wycombe Wanderers at the beginning of April. Given the injury crisis that developed in the second half of the season, this was a remarkable achievement, but the poor run in November and early December had left the team too much ground to make up, and Hendon finished as runners-up to Leytonstone, with 59 points from 38 games, two points behind the champions.

Cup ties

After some of the high profile cup matches of the previous season, a trip to Midland League Grantham in the FA Cup first round probably did not greatly excite Hendon's supporters, who were maybe thinking about who they wanted in the second round. Sadly, it was not to be as this match came in the middle of the team's slump and Hendon went down 4–1. The club programme said that everyone was "bitterly disappointed" with the result.

The Amateur Cup run proved to be more long-lasting. Harwich and Parkeston were beaten 3–1 in the first round with a Laurie Churchill hat-trick. Athenian Leaguers Carshalton Athletic came to Claremont Road in the next round having been beaten 5–1 in the third round in 1964–65. This time the margin was the same, with the Surrey side returning home on the end of a 4–0 defeat. Leytonstone were beaten 2–1 at Claremont Road in the third round, and the next round bought another home draw, against Wycombe Wanderers.

Hendon went a goal up in the second minute through John Evans. Wycombe equalised, and then Laurie Churchill put Hendon ahead. David Hyde hit the bar with a free kick, but just before half-time, Jimmy Quail broke his leg. It was a double fracture, and meant he was out for the rest of the season. Hendon's 10 men hung on for a famous victory, and a semi-final against Northern League Whitley Bay at Sunderland's Roker Park ground, hardly a neutral venue.

Seven first-team players were receiving treatment for injuries leading up to the semi-final. Dave Bassett, later to find fame as Wimbledon's manager, was out for the season with a broken leg. He had only played three first team games before sustaining the injury playing Sunday football. Five hours before the semi-final, John Swannell slipped and hurt his back. Intensive treatment meant he played, and his heroics in the second half kept Hendon in the game. Riddy and Sleap had given Hendon a 2–0 lead, before former Hendon star Tony Knox scored a penalty to put Whitley Bay back in the game. The northerners dominated the second half, and a "sensational" save by Swannell in the closing minutes prevented an equaliser.

At Wembley, Hendon would face local rivals Wealdstone. It was Wealdstone's first Amateur Cup Final appearance, although they had played at Wembley before – in the 1942 Middlesex Red Cross Cup Final. Two of their team, Hugh Lindsay and John Ashworth, played for Kingstonian against Hendon in the 1960 final. Their other international was half-back Charlie Townsend.

Although the Greens had generally had the better of matches between the two sides in recent years, injuries took their toll, and Wealdstone won the final 3–1.

Hendon 1 Wealdstone 3
Amateur Cup Final

Despite the match being played in the middle of April, two days of snow, sleet and rain produced a heavy pitch for amateur football's showpiece match. Hendon took the lead when centre-half Geoff Riddy scored following a corner after five minutes. Hendon defended well until just before half-time, when a cross shot from Bobby Childs deceived Swannell for Wealdstone' equaliser. Hendon started the second half well, but could not create clear scoring chances. As the half went on, Wealdstone were putting the Hendon defence under more pressure. But they won the game five minutes from the end with a scrambled goal from Bremer after a corner kick with five minutes left for play. Three minutes later, Childs scored his second goal after Swannell had blocked a shot by Lindsay.

It was the first – and only – time that Wealdstone won the Amateur Cup

Hendon: J. Swannell, D. Hogwood, M. Cooper, D. Shacklock, G. Riddy, B. Cantwell (c), L. Churchill, J. Evans, D. Swain, R. Sleap, D. Hyde.

Wealdstone: B. Goymer, M. Doyle, G. Sedgley, C. Townsend, J. Ashworth (c), E. Dillsworth, B. Allen, B. Childs, J. Cooley, H. Lindsay, B. Bremer.

Wealdstone also ended Hendon's hopes in both county cups. In the Middlesex Senior Cup Hayes were beaten 3–1 at Claremont Road. The next week, in the London Senior Cup, Hendon faced Wingate in the first round at Claremont Road. However, the difference in class told as Hendon won 7–0, although the half-time score was only 1–0. Every forward scored. The draws for both cups now produced ties with Athenian League Southall. In the London Senior Cup, Hendon won 3–0 at Claremont Road, and the next week in the Middlesex Senior Cup were victorious again, this time 2–0 at Western Road.

Now Wealdstone were the opposition in both cups. In the London competition, the teams drew 2–2 at Claremont Road, and Hendon lost the replay 2–1. In the Middlesex competition, a week after their Wembley encounter, the teams drew in the semi-final 2–2 at Hayes. The replay was the seventh meeting between the two clubs this season, and at Claremont Road Wealdstone won 4–2 to face Enfield in the Final.

Friendly matches

An interesting aspect of this season was a number of high profile friendly matches. On August Bank Holiday, the Will Mather Cup was revived, with Whitley Bay beaten 4–2 at Claremont Road. In an unusual double-header, the clubs' reserve teams played a game before the main match.

In September, Hendon faced an England Amateur XI, as part of the national team's preparation for a European amateur tournament. The England side included Hendon players John Swannell and David Hogwood, and two players from Southern League Barnet, one of whom, Tony

HENDON v. ENGLAND AMATEUR XI
Monday, 13th September, 1965, k.o. 7.30 p.m.
European Amateur International Work Out

Harding, later joined Hendon. With Kingstonian's Brian Wakefield in goal, Hendon won 3–2. Inside-forward Keith Mills scored a hat-trick.

The next month, an Isthmian League XI came to Claremont Road in the traditional challenge match against the League champions. Only former Hendon star Terry Howard played against the Greens in both matches, and he put the League XI a goal up in the first minute. However, Roy Drake equalised, and a minute after half-time, Danny Lakey gave Hendon the lead. Drake scored again for Hendon before the League XI scored again near the end of the game, giving Hendon a second 3–2 win.

The 1966 Amateur Cup campaign

1966 Amateur Cup Semi Final against Whitley Bay at Sunderland:
Top: Hendon come onto the pitch
Middle: John Swannell clears as the Whitley Bay centre forward challenges for the ball.

Final programme courtesy Wembley National Stadium Ltd

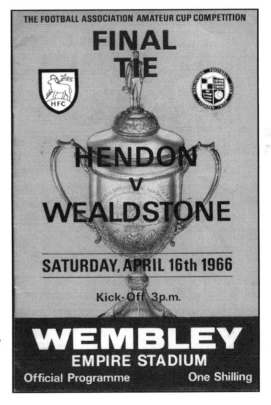

THE FOOTBALL ASSOCIATION AMATEUR CUP COMPETITION

FINAL TIE

HENDON v WEALDSTONE

SATURDAY, APRIL 16th 1966

Kick-Off 3p.m.

WEMBLEY
EMPIRE STADIUM

Official Programme   One Shilling

In November, Middlesex Wanderers came to Hendon to play the Amateur Cup holders, for the Allway Brothers Memorial Trophy. With Terry Howard again returning to Claremont Road, the Middlesex Wanderers side managed a 4–4 draw.

A less high profile friendly near the end of the season was played against Kingsbury Town, to help raise money for one of Hendon's smaller neighbours. As the programme pointed out, Laurie Topp had started his career at Davies Sports, as Kingsbury were then known.

The first team scored 168 goals. Laurie Churchill was top scorer with 39, with David Hyde, Dave Swain, Jimmy Quail and Danny Lakey all contributing double figures. Churchill's contribution in his first season as a regular first teamer was remarkable, although two seasons before he had scored 13 goals in 24 first team appearances. But only Dave Hogwood had played in every game, and despite some important contributions by reserve players, the injury problems in the second half of the season meant Hendon could not quite match the heights of the previous season, and ended without a trophy.

Hendon players were again prominent in international and representative matches. John Swannell won five England caps, and David Hyde a further two in his last season as an amateur.

At the end of the season, Hendon had a well-earned rest with a tour of Madeira. They lost 3–2 to Nacional and beat Maritimo 3–1.

Millwall winger Terry McQuade guested for Hendon, who were missing several first team players. Whitley Bay generously allowed their captain Brian Oakley and midfield player Kenny Sloan to join the tour, even though they were challenging for the Northern League title and Northumberland Senior Cup.

Bobby Cantwell exchanges
pennants on the tour.

1966–67: Semi-final agony

The 1966 season started with England as World Cup holders, with their dramatic triumph in the final against West Germany fresh in supporters' minds. Changes were also taking place throughout football that reflected the World Cup, with more defensive formations becoming common.

The major departures from Claremont Road over the summer were Laurie Churchill, who took the familiar path from Hendon to Enfield, and David Hyde, who turned professional with Wimbledon. Roy Drake, whose son briefly played for the Greens in the mid-1980s, joined Wealdstone. David Hyde had only played for Hendon for three seasons, but had a remarkable scoring record, including 59 goals in 1964–65. His powerful shooting was famous throughout the amateur game, and his power up front was not really replaced when he left. The skills of Laurie Churchill were also missed.

To replace them, Hendon recruited Tony Harding from Barnet, who had retained his amateur status, despite playing in the Southern League. Another major signing was centre-half John Ashworth, who was recruited from Wealdstone. This led to centre-half Geoff Riddy making the journey to Lower Mead, as Hendon had recruited Ashworth as the club were unsure if Riddy would recover from an ankle injury. He had completed six seasons at Hendon and was returning to his original club. A further signing was inside forward Allan Craddock. Halfway through the season, robust young defender Ray Poole joined the club from Maidstone United.

Two unusual international signings were Cypriot international Pans Charalambous, who was recommended to the club by Arsenal, and Erik Hagen, a Norwegian international. However, neither made much impact at first-team level, and Hagen moved on to Dulwich Hamlet later in the season.

Another change was the introduction of substitutes in the Isthmian League. David Shacklock was the first Hendon player to have the 'honour' of wearing the number 12 shirt. Along with Dave Swain and Mickey Cooper, he came from the reserves to establish himself as a first team player. Shacklock had made 19 appearances prior to this season, and Swain 57, but this was their first season as first team regulars.

Off the pitch, Bill Fisher continued in charge of the first team. Former Hendon star Pat Austin returned to the club as reserve team coach. And Dave Bassett left to become reserve team coach at Harrow, an inauspicious start to a successful managerial career at the top level.

Cup campaigns

The various cup campaigns provided the highlights this season. In the FA Cup, Hendon again had a bye to the first round as Amateur Cup finalists the previous season. The draw was more favourable this time, with Third Division Reading coming to Claremont Road. The supporters produced a special Hendon song, and the club tried to have one of the local bus routes diverted to run to Claremont Road for the day. But on the pitch, Reading went two goals up early on, and won comfortably 3–1, Ashworth scoring for Hendon after 49 minutes. A crowd of 4,050 watched the match. The *Hendon Times* report said that Hendon had fielded a "defensive" 4–2–4 formation, with Bobby Cantwell playing as a sweeper, and only really threatened when Cantwell moved forward in the second half.

The more realistic 'road to Wembley' in the Amateur Cup started with a comfortable 3–0 win at Ilford. The second round brought a rare trip to the West Country, to face Bristol St George from the Bristol Premier Combination. A 0–0 draw in Bristol was followed by a 5–0 win at Claremont Road, in front of a 3,000 crowd. Hendon's cause was helped by two own-goals from the Bristol centre-half, who also hit his own bar!

The third round produced one of the most exciting matches of the season. Hendon would have expected to beat mid-table Oxford City at Claremont Road, but the visitors were 2–0 up after 17 minutes. Roy Sleap pulled a goal back with a "glorious" shot, but Oxford scored again before half-time to lead 3–1. Hendon fought back, and a header from Tony Harding followed by a Danny Lakey penalty in eight minutes made the score 3–3. After Swannell had kept Hendon in the tie with a point blank save 10 minutes from time, Harding scored again to take Hendon through. The fourth round a fortnight later produced an easier victory, 3–0 at Athenian League Leatherhead.

The semi-final produced a rare match with opponents from the north-west, Skelmersdale United. The Hendon programme said that they were "up to a few weeks ago an unknown team – at least in the south", but were clearly a serious force, having beaten Bishop Auckland, cup holders Wealdstone and strong Athenian Leaguers Slough Town to reach the semi-final. In a repeat of the previous season, Hendon faced an injury crisis, with Swannell, Cooper, Ashworth, Cantwell and Harding all had serious injuries less than a week before the game. The problems facing amateur football managers were also shown by reserve goalkeeper Ron Whiteaker being abroad on business, and the club had borrowed John Daniel from neighbours Barnet as cover.

The Skelmersdale semi-final

The first game at Derby County's Baseball Ground ended as a scoreless stalemate, with Swannell keeping Hendon in the game. He was only declared fit three hours before kick-off, and admitted that he should not have played. He could only dive to one side, but recalls that "most of their shots were on that side". A crowd of 7,914 saw Hendon survive, having been outplayed for most of the game. Coach Bill Fisher accepted that Hendon were "lucky still to be interested in the competition." A last minute shot by David Hogwood which beat Skelmersdale's keeper Terry Crosbie but just went wide, but had Hendon won the *Hendon Times* report said it "would have been a great injustice."
Hendon: J. Swannell, D. Hogwood, M. Cooper, R. Sleap, J. Ashworth, R. Cantwell, D. Swain, D. Shacklock, A. Harding, J. Quail, D. Lakey.
Skelmersdale: T. Crosbie, A. Bermingham, C. Bridge, J. Unsworth, R. Wade, D. Moorcroft, N. Whitehead, M. Worswick, W. Bennett, M. Burns, A. Mansley.

The teams were unchanged for the replay at Birmingham City. Hendon went a goal down, with Jimmy Quail equalising with 15 minutes left. Hendon went 2–1 down in extra time, then Mickey Cooper scored his first goal for the first team with a 30-yard shot in the last seconds of the match. A 6,930 crowd enjoyed the drama. Cooper admitted that "the ball could have gone anywhere" and that his shots "usually end up in the stand". Skipper Roy Sleap dodged out of the way as the ball zoomed into the net. Many Hendon supporters had already left the ground, believing that Hendon had lost.

A further replay followed 10 days later at West Bromwich Albion, and this time Hendon's luck ran out, with Skelmersdale winning 3–1. For Hendon, Mickey Salter played in place of Lakey, Skelmersdale fielded the same team as in the previous two matches. Whitehead and Bennett put Skelmersdale 2–0 up at half-time before Dave Swain pulled a goal back for Hendon before Burns won the game for Skelmersdale with a goal 10 minutes from the end. The *Hendon Times* said they were "ruthlessly destroyed by a brilliant young Skelmersdale side". The match was watched by a 7,830 crowd; including Liverpool and Scotland star Ian St John, who coached the Merseyside team. They faced Enfield in the Final, and lost 3–0 in a replay.

Throughout the season there was concern that Hendon's attack was ineffective. How much this was due to changes in players and how much to more defensive play generally is debatable. However, there was no lack of goals in the London Senior Cup. Hendon's campaign opened with a 5–5 draw at Cheshunt. The Greens won the replay at Claremont Road 7–2, with four goals from Tony Harding and two from Danny Lakey.

Further victories followed at Ilford, and a convincing 4–1 win at home to League champions elect Sutton United. In the semi-final, Hendon faced Walthamstow Avenue at Claremont Road. The match took place between the two Amateur Cup semi-final replays, and Hendon lost 2–1. Three Hendon players had dashed to the game from Scotland, having been with the England Amateur team at Dundee the night before.

Hendon started their Middlesex Senior Cup campaign with a narrow victory over neighbours Wembley, who included former Hendon reserves Fred Pudney, Martin

Hackett and Bobby Ellison in their team. The next round saw an easy 7–0 win over Harrow at Claremont Road. In the semi-final, Southall were beaten 2–1 at Claremont Road on 18 February.

In the Final, almost three months later, Hendon faced old rivals Enfield, fresh from their Amateur Cup victory. In the first leg at Southbury Road, Hendon lost 2–1, with Tony Harding scoring five minutes from time. Danny Lakey scored in the second-half at Claremont Road to take the match into extra time.

A Tony Harding header won the match and the cup for Hendon. It was Enfield's only cup defeat by amateur opposition that season, and stopped them doing a treble of Amateur, London Senior and Middlesex Senior Cups.

The league

Hendon started the season with an unbeaten run of 11 matches, and at the end of September were second, a point behind Sutton United. However, Hendon had dropped four points through draws, and had only scored 21 goals, an average of less than two per game. The unbeaten run ended with a 3–0 defeat at Enfield, although the Greens' form then improved, and in the middle of December they were top of the League with 31 points from 21 games. However, Sutton United was only a point behind, with three games in hand. The next two months were dominated by cup matches, and at the beginning of March, John Swannell injured his ankle. This, combined with other injuries and a very full programme, saw Hendon lose six out of the last 14 league matches to finish fifth, with 49 points, 10 behind champions Sutton United. The defence had conceded 37 goals, less than one a game, but the attack scored 64, less than two a game and a major decline from the previous season. Tony Harding contributed 30 goals, but no one else reached 20. The Supporters Association notes in the last match programme of the season said that "Our defence has played consistently well throughout, but vastly overworked by the obvious lack of cohesion of the forward line, has conceded vital goals. The attack has been sadly at fault, showing form well below that which they are capable of." However, the same programme carried a letter criticising the selection policy, saying it was defensive.

One game which showed the difference in standards between clubs in the Isthmian League was at Dulwich. Played between the first two matches with Skelmersdale, David Shacklock, Danny Lakey and nine reserves won 3–2.

On the international scene, Hendon were again well represented. John Swannell won six England caps, Roy Sleap played twice for England and David Hogwood made his international debut, also winning two England caps.

1967–68: Olympics at Claremont Road

Two years on from the club's greatest season, only four players from that side were in the team at the start of the season - Swannell, Hogwood, Sleap and Cantwell. Danny Lakey was still with the club, although he joined Ramsgate in December. His move, with the departure of Jimmy Quail to Enfield broke the last link with the great forward line of the club's first two seasons in the Isthmian League.

Cantwell and Sleap both moved on during the season. Cantwell had joined the club in 1964, and had been captain of the successful team of the mid–1960s. He won many representative honours, but never played for England.

Other departures included Dave Swain to Wealdstone, and reserve players Micky Clay, Peter Howard and George Rocknean, all looking for first team football. Towards the end of the season, Micky Cooper joined Slough Town.

One new recruit turned out to be one of the most important players in the club's history. Midfield player Rod Haider was recruited from Kingstonian, and would be a crucial player for Hendon and the England amateur team. Already an established England international, he added class and consistency to the team. Up front, Bobby Wilson joined from Feltham, having played for Brentford as a youngster. Two new wingers were also signed: Don Whyte, from Barnet who left to join Hertford Town in January, and Paul Clements, who played as an amateur for West Ham United and had already won England amateur honours. However, he was about to go to Leeds University, which restricted his appearances in Hendon's colours. Another young forward signing was John Barnard, who was recommended to the club by Plymouth Argyle. In September another forward recruit was Peter Drabwell from Walthamstow Avenue. Towards the end of the season, diminutive midfielder John Wilson joined from Chelsea.

An interesting recruit off the pitch was Doctor Alan Bass, who had been team doctor for the 1966 England World Cup winning team.

The Olympics

The highlight of the season did not involve Hendon, but was the staging of a Great Britain Olympic qualifying match against West Germany at Claremont Road. Hendon were represented with Swannell, Sleap, Hogwood and Haider playing, but despite this, West Germany won 1–0. Great Britain had won the first leg 2–0, and thus qualified for the next round.

However, at a time when such matches were often staged on Football League grounds, or venues such as Wembley Stadium and White City, being able to successfully stage such a match was a great credit to the club. The club had also had to overcome fire damage to the main stand in the close season, just four weeks before the start of the season.

The league campaign

Once again, Hendon spoiled Dulwich Hamlet's start to the season, with a 5–0 win at Champion Hill on the opening day, including two goals from Tony Harding and debut goals for Bobby Wilson and Don Whyte. By the end of September, Hendon were third, with 15 points from 11 games, six behind leaders Enfield. However, Hendon's three defeats included away matches at Clapton and Corinthian Casuals. Although the latter were in mid-table, these matches were ones any team with championship aspirations would expect to win.

The team's inconsistency continued, with easy victories being combined with the odd defeat against the top sides, and other points dropped through draws. At the end of December, Hendon were fourth, 12 points behind leaders Enfield, albeit with two games in hand. In the final 16 league matches, Hendon won 11, but a final record of nine defeats in 38 games resulted in third place, 12 points behind champions Enfield. The defence was still very solid, letting in less than a goal a game, and the attack improved on the previous season with 90 goals. Towards the end of the season, Maidstone United turned up at Claremont Road with only 10 players, and borrowed a player from a team playing in Clitterhouse Playing Fields next door to the ground. He came onto the pitch 10 minutes into the match, and all Maidstone officials knew about him was that his name was Malcolm. The *Hendon Times* report christened him 'Malcolm X' and he nearly scored near the end, Swannell blocking his shot. Two Maidstone players had not arrived due to a car accident, and another had to take his pregnant wife to hospital.

The reserve team were more successful, winning the Isthmian League reserve section with 43 points from 30 games. They also held the England Amateur XI to a 1–1 draw in a private practice game.

Cup campaigns

The previous season's London Senior Cup semi-final meant that Hendon again entered the London Challenge Cup. A 1–0 win at Walthamstow Avenue took the Greens to Upton Park to face West Ham United. It was Hendon's third visit to Upton Park in this competition, having played twice in the 1950s, with a victory to each side. This time, a young Hammers' team including future England internationals and Hammers' stalwarts Trevor Brooking and Frank Lampard won 1–0. Seven of the Hammers' side had first team experience, but it was 18-year-old Tim Clements, younger brother of Hendon's Paul, who made the late winner for Doug Eadie.

In the FA Cup, having played in the first round proper for the past two seasons, Hendon were given a bye to the fourth qualifying round. However, Southern League Romford won 2–1 at Claremont Road to end Hendon's chances of facing Football League opposition in the first round. Reports said that Hendon had been unlucky not to get a draw, as Bobby Cantwell hit the inside of the post with a few minutes left.

The first two weeks of January saw Hendon's interest in the Amateur Cup and London Senior Cup end. In the Amateur Cup, Hendon lost 1–0 at Barking, where former stalwart John Evans was player-coach. In the London Senior Cup, Hendon had won 3–2 at Southall in December. The next round bought Wembley to Claremont Road, and the Athenian Leaguers avenged their previous season's defeat, winning 2–1. The result was more embarrassing because the visitors including three former Hendon reserves: Ellison, Hackett and Brian Woozley. The Supporters Association's notes in the club programme said the result was "humiliating", and the club's notes spoke of "the absence of punch in our forward line" and "a lack of enthusiasm and urgency" in the Barking game. Ken Ellis played in goal for Hendon, at the age of 16, one of the youngest ever to play at that level, although Barry Mitchell had played in goal for the first team aged 14 in a 3–2 win at Woking in 1964–65. Reports said Ellis was not to blame for the defeat.

The draw for the first round of the Middlesex Senior Cup could not have been tougher: Enfield away. 2–1 down in extra time, two goals in the last three minutes gave Hendon a 3–2 win, with goals from Drabwell, Harding and Sleap. It was Enfield's first defeat of the season.

In the next round, Hendon won 4–1 at Feltham, but then in semi-final lost 1–0 at Wealdstone. On August Bank Holiday Monday, Hendon had renewed friendly rivalry with Whitley Bay in the Will Mather Cup, this time in the north east, and lost 2–0. So the season ended with any trophies or final appearances for the first time since the club had joined the Isthmian League.

The club's lack of success was analysed by *Evening Standard* journalist Peter Blackman. He said that the club's 4–2–4 system was not working and that despite all the talent available to the club, they were "bouncing awkwardly through the season". He felt that the club were using a "jack-of-all-trades" policy and that too many players were being "given dual roles instead of being allowed to master one job." He also pointed out that players who had left the club were successful, mentioning Danny Lakey and Dave Swain. However, with another point of view, supporter Jeffrey Fox wrote to the club programme pointing out the club's overall record of success, and that they could field two complete teams of internationals from players over the past 20 years.

It was maybe not a great surprise when the club announced the appointment of a new first-team coach at the end of the season, with former Northampton Town player Ron Patterson taking over for 1968–69. Patterson had played against Hendon for Northampton in 1952, and was working in London.

Another change at the end of the season was Supporters' Association chairman Mark Rutherford announcing his retirement from a post he had held since the Association's formation in 1933. He was 82, and was standing down for health reasons, although he hoped to continue attending matches. He was elected as the Association's president in recognition of his outstanding service, having first seen the club play in 1919.

On the international scene, representative honours had continued for the club's leading players. Apart from appearances in the Olympic team, John Swannell, Rod Haider, David Hogwood and Roy Sleap all won England honours.

1968–69: London Senior Cup victory

Third place in 1967–68 was something to build on. To strengthen the squad, Hendon recruited winger Peter Anderson from Southern League neighbours Barnet and Micky Cannon from Barking. Anderson was one of the most skilful forwards the club had signed for sometime, and gave the attack a new dimension. Cannon was a ball-playing central defender, and also played in attack on occasions. Derek Gamblin, an England international full-back joined from Sutton United, and Mickey Cooper returned to the club from Slough. Gamblin's international colleague Larry Pritchard was listed in the match programme on 7 September at centre-forward, but did not actually play for the club, saying he "changed his mind" about joining. A month later, striker Paul Collett joined from Walthamstow Avenue. In the spring, centre-half Chris Joy was signed from Corinthian Casuals. John Ashworth left, joining Hitchin Town. In August Peter Drabwell went to Dagenham. On the coaching side, with Ron Patterson taking over the first-team, Bill Fisher became the reserve team coach. At the end of September, Charles Geary resigned as secretary, Jack Orlog took over temporarily until Harry Cartwright took the post permanently in October. In April, George Needham celebrated 50 years as an official with the club.

London Senior Cup

After failing to reach a cup final for the first time in five years the previous season, Hendon succeeded in winning the London Senior Cup for only the second time in the club's history. This was particularly commendable as the draw gave Hendon away ties in every round. In the first, Hendon won 4–0 at Hounslow. Two trips to Hertfordshire followed, a 4–0 win at Hitchin at the beginning of January, and a tremendous 3–0 win at St Albans in March. The semi-final saw a visit to Barking, managed by former Hendon star John Evans. Goals from Haider, Jameson and Allen gave Hendon a narrow 3–2 victory, with Frankie Allen's winner coming eight minutes from the end of the match.

190

Hendon 1 Dagenham 0
London Senior Cup Final

The Final was against the cup-holders, Dagenham, at Barnet's Underhill ground. Dagenham included two former Hendon players: Fred Pudney and Roy Drake. They had beaten Isthmian Leaguers Leytonstone in the semi-final after a replay.

A 1,200 crowd had seen Hendon win at Barking, but only 1,014 were at Underhill to see Hendon's 1–0 victory. The first-half was scoreless, but 10 minutes into the second half, Rod Haider put Hendon ahead following a corner. Hendon's goalkeeper John Swannell had gone into the game with a thigh injury from playing cricket, but Dagenham never managed to take advantage of this to threaten Hendon's lead. The *Hendon Times* said that the cup was a "magnificent trophy" but the game was "drab", and lacked "colour or excitement". To date, this is the last time the club has won this trophy.

Hendon: J. Swannell, D. Hogwood, R. Poole, D. Shacklock, M. Cannon, R. Haider, P. Anderson, M. Cooper, P. Collett, R. Wilson, E. Devlin. Sub: G. Rocknean.

Dagenham: I. Huttley, D. Robertson, G. Dudley, M. Smith, J. Willingham, D. Moore, F. Pudney, R. Drake, J. Smith, D. Morris, G. Brooks. Sub: B. Smith

Cup disappointments

In the FA Cup, the Greens beat Athenian League Hertford Town 1–0 in the first qualifying round, following a scoreless draw at Hertford. However, any hopes of a glamour tie later in the competition ended when Hendon lost 2–1 at Slough Town.

The Amateur Cup campaign started in December, with a 2–0 win at Claremont Road over Hornchurch. The second round saw another 2–0 win, this time at St Albans. The third round draw produced a more distant - and difficult - away tie, at North Shields. Coaches of supporters left Claremont Road at midnight for the trip north, and some of the younger ones had a kick about in the park next to Newcastle United's ground on Saturday morning before travelling onto North Shields for the match in the afternoon.

Hendon got a commendable 1–1 draw, but the day was marred by the death of four supporters in a car crash on their way to the game. Another supporter was seriously injured. Later in the season, the club played a match against the Frigidaire works team, where two of the supporters had worked, to raise money for their dependants.

A minute's silence in memory of the four supporters who had died was held before the replay at Claremont Road. The northerners proved too strong for Hendon, won 2–0, and went on to win the Cup for the first time.

In the Middlesex Senior Cup, Hendon beat Hayes in the first round, and then had a short trip to Willesden, for a rare match against their Greater London League neighbours. Despite Swannell and Haider missing the match through playing for England, Hendon won comfortably 2–0.

The semi-final saw Wembley visit Claremont Road. The previous year, the Athenian League side had won 2–1 at Claremont Road in the London Senior Cup, so the Greens should have been forewarned of their potential. Despite this, Wembley won again, 2–0, to end Hendon's hopes of capturing the Cup. The report in the club programme said it was a "rather inglorious" exit, and Wembley deserved to win.

The league

The league campaign started with a disappointing 2–1 defeat against Walthamstow Avenue at Claremont Road. Seven wins in the next nine matches followed, and in mid-October, Hendon were seventh, with 18 points from 13 games. But November was a poor month for Hendon, with a defeat at lowly Clapton followed by Ilford winning at Claremont Road, a 2–2 draw with Barking and defeat at Walthamstow Avenue. Things picked up with wins at home to Sutton United and at Maidstone, and by early December, Hendon were fourth, with 31 points from 23 games. But in the highly competitive top reaches of the Isthmian League, seven defeats at this stage of the season ruled out any realistic hopes of a title challenge.

The league took second place to cup matches over the next couple of months, although one noticeable result was a 2–1 win at Wealdstone on Christmas Day in one of the last matches ever played on that day. Only four league matches were lost in the second-half of the season, but four more draws saw Hendon finish sixth with 49 points. Most clubs would be satisfied, but this was Hendon's lowest finish at that time in the Isthmian League. The attack had again scored less than two goals a game, not a good return given the disparity in standards in the Isthmian League. In the league, Hendon's highest score in a match was four goals, and single goal victories were common.

One victory that augured well for the future was the reserves winning the Isthmian League Reserve Section championship, with 42 points from 28 games, five points clear of runners-up Wealdstone.

Bobby Wilson was top scorer with 25 goals, and Peter Anderson finished with 17. Anderson had added skill to the forward line, but there had not been an adequate replacement for Tony Harding.

The Isthmian League was in need of new blood at this time, and Hendon recognised this, calling for promotion and relegation with the Athenian League during the season. Their idea was not taken up at this time.

Towards the end of the season, the club staged an unusual friendly. The current first XI faced the all-conquering 1965 team. Only two current players were eligible for the 1965 team - John Swannell and David Hogwood. Of the other nine, one was playing in the Southern League (David Hyde at Brentwood), four for other Isthmian League clubs (Danny Lakey and Geoff Riddy at Maidstone, John Evans at Barking and Jimmy Quail at Enfield), three in the Athenian League (Roy Drake and Bobby Cantwell at Dagenham and Roy Sleap at Slough) and Peter Slade was with Thame in the Hellenic League.

Representative honours

John Swannell and Rod Haider continued to represent the club for England regularly, and David Hogwood also won two international caps.

Hendon players also appeared regularly for the Middlesex County team. Seven Enfield players withdrew from the County side against Hertfordshire in the autumn, resulting in the team fielding seven Hendon players, including reserve team skipper George Rocknean. In November, five Hendon players were selected for the County side to play Essex at Wealdstone. Bobby Wilson toured the Far East at the end of the season with Middlesex Wanderers.

The Scotland international team trained at Claremont Road at the end of the season before playing England at Wembley.

At the end of the season, the club toured Majorca. Two matches were played, a 1–0 defeat against Manacor, and a 4–1 win over Collerence. Two goals from Peter Anderson helped Hendon achieve their first victory on the island.

1969–70

This was another season that promised much, but did not deliver. The playing squad was largely unchanged from the previous season. One new recruit was 19-year-old centre-forward Johnny Baker. He was signed from Kingstonian, and had also been playing for Brentford. Another signing was Newton Ashman, who had been playing junior Sunday football the previous season. He signed amateur forms for Arsenal early on in the season, and was one of the first West Indian players to play for the club at first-team level. The 17-year-old had been born in Jamaica and had lived in Hendon for seven years. Another recruit was Len McKendry, a defender from Walthamstow Avenue.

Some of the club's reserve team players moved on, seeking first team football. George Rocknean, Eddie Devlin, Fred Hilling and Johnny Culverwell went to Hounslow, Frank Allen and Johnny Brooks joined Walthamstow, and Chris Joy went to Woking, having failed to win a regular first team place at Claremont Road. John Swannell joined Fulham as an amateur, but on the understanding that Hendon had first call on his services. Also on the goalkeeping front, Philip Bonetti, younger brother of Chelsea and England goalkeeper Peter, played regularly for the club's reserve team.

In October, Ron Patterson resigned as coach for business reasons. He said he expected to leave in a month's time, but in fact stayed until the spring. Bill Fisher was acting first team coach for a few weeks before supporters welcomed the appointment of former player John Evans, who took charge on Easter Monday. He had previously been coach at Barking.

Cup ties

The cup campaigns provided many of the season's highlights. In the FA Cup, the team faced three away draws in the qualifying competition. A 2–1 win at Bishop's Stortford was followed by a 1–1 draw at Rainham, with a 7–2 victory in the replay. A Peter Anderson hat-trick and two goals from Bobby Wilson overwhelmed the Essex side. More Athenian League opposition was beaten next, with a 4–2 win at Hertford.

The fourth qualifying round draw saw Southern League Cambridge City, including former Hendon hero David Hyde at Claremont Road. Nine of the Cambridge team had Football League experience, but a Johnny Baker goal 15 minutes from time gave Hendon a 1–0 win and a place in the first round for the first time since 1966. Instead of a Football League team coming to Claremont Road, Hendon faced more Athenian League opposition, Carshalton Athletic. A 5–3 win saw Hendon safely into the second round. This time, Southern League Brentwood Town came to Claremont Road, and won 2–0. Hendon had chances to win the game in the first-half, but did not take them, and the chance of a third round place for the first time was lost.

The following week, the Amateur Cup campaign started, with the rare visit of a Cornish club to Claremont Road. South-Western League champions St Austell had a 242 mile trip to London. It must have felt longer on the way back after a 5–0 defeat. In the second round, it was Hendon who would face a long journey, as the draw served up a tie at Northern League Evenwood, a mining village in County Durham.

The first tie, on 10 January, was abandoned at half-time due to fog, with Hendon leading 2–1. A week later, the match was postponed. So on 24 January, the team and supporters headed north again. One player got off the coach and said "Are you sure we've been here before" as the fog had gone. This time, a 1–1 draw resulted, with a replay the following week at Claremont Road. Hendon finally won 4–2 after extra time, with some supporters finding it hard to remember when Hendon were not playing Evenwood. The third round brought Athenians Walton & Hersham to Claremont Road. A 1–1 draw meant a replay, and a 1–0 defeat ended hopes of Wembley for that year.

A London Challenge

The previous season's London Senior Cup victory meant the club entered the London Challenge Cup again. For the preliminary round, Hendon travelled to Barnet. Having played their Underhill neighbours regularly throughout the club's Athenian League membership, now clashes with their Southern League neighbours were fairly rare, and eagerly anticipated by Hendon's supporters.

Barnet started well, but Bobby Wilson gave Hendon the lead after 16 minutes. Hendon controlled the match, and a couple of minutes from time, according to the Hendon programme, Peter Anderson "cut in from the right touchline and, leaving four or five bewildered defenders in his wake, flashed the ball home with his left foot." It was a triumphant return for Anderson to his former club at Underhill.

A 2–2 draw with Millwall at Claremont Road was a commendable result. For the replay at The Den, Hendon had to play without Swannell, Hogwood and Haider due to international commitments. With Cannon and Cooper also unfit, Hendon did well to lose 2–0 with a side including four reserves and midfielder Keith Jameson at right-back.

Interest in the county cups ended in a disastrous seven day period. In the London Senior Cup, Barking and Kingstonian were both beaten 3–2 at Claremont Road. A 1–1 draw at Hitchin in the third round was followed by the Hertfordshire side winning 2–1 at Claremont Road on 28 February. David Hogwood missed a penalty, and Hitchin's winner came seven minutes from time.

In the Middlesex Senior Cup, Hendon started with a 5–0 win at Middlesex League Harefield United. The second round saw 2-1 defeat at Spartan League Staines Town, despite Hendon taking the lead. This was surely one of the worst results in many years.

The league

The league campaign started with a 7–0 massacre of Walthamstow Avenue at Claremont Road - ample revenge for defeat in the same fixture the previous season. Paul Collett scored a hat-trick against his old club, and Bobby Wilson and Johnny Baker contributed two goals apiece. This was followed by a 4–1 defeat at St Albans and a 5–1 win at strugglers Corinthian Casuals. This erratic form continued with three consecutive draws and a 4–0 win at Claremont Road over Oxford City.

By the end of October, Hendon were fourteenth, with 16 points from 14 games. Only three games had been lost, but a further six points had been dropped through draws.

Cup matches meant that Hendon had matches in hand over most of the teams above them. St Albans in second place had played 21 games, seven more than Hendon.

In November, Enfield won both local derbies, 3–0 at Southbury Road and 1–0 in the return three weeks later. Christmas was cheerful for Hendon, with a 2–1 win over Wealdstone at home on Christmas Day, and a 1–0 victory in the return at Lower Mead.

The defeats in the county cups were followed by a 3–2 defeat at home to Woking. But after that the team's form improved, with nine wins, five draws and only one defeat. Hendon finished a respectable fifth, with 50 points, one place and one point better than the previous season. The attack had improved, with 77 goals, but 12 points had been dropped through draws, and that was the margin between Hendon and champions Enfield. Home points dropped through draws against opposition from the bottom half of the table, such as Ilford, Kingstonian and Dulwich Hamlet were costly.

Honours

Once again Hendon were well represented at international level. Rod Haider and John Swannell both toured the Caribbean with England in the summer, playing in exotic locations including the Bahamas, Trinidad and Guyana – different from a cold, muddy day at Claremont Road. David Hogwood also won two further England caps. Johnny Wilson and Paul Collett represented the London FA against the Birmingham FA.

Hooliganism

A sign of the times was comments in the Supporters' Association notes in the programme about hooliganism faced by Hendon supporters on their travels to some grounds. While this never reached the scale of the problems in the Football League, some away midweek matches were difficult for Hendon supporters, with individuals and coaches being attacked on occasions. It was a sad change from the good spirit that had been a tradition of amateur football. At Walton & Hersham, a 'Hendon for the Cup' banner was stolen and set on fire. On the other hand, a call to police said there was a riot at Hendon's home game against Corinthian Casuals. Just as it finished, 20 police arrived, to find supporters leaving quietly after a dull game – it had been a hoax call.

It was now five years since the glory days of 1965, and four years since a Wembley appearance. By the high standards the club had set, they had slipped a little. Change was needed for to challenge again to be at the very top of amateur football.

Hendon's four players in the Great Britain team:
David Hogwood, John Swannell, Roy Sleap and Rod Haider. (HT)

8. 1970 to 1974: Italy and Newcastle

1970–71: John Evans in charge

This season promised much, but again failed to deliver trophies to Claremont Road. From John Evans' former club Barking came England international defender Peter Deadman and forward Neville Fox, although he returned to Barking in December, having failed to win a regular place. In September, Derek Baker was signed from Barking, but the move was not completed and he did not play for the club at this time.

Roy Sleap briefly returned at the start of the season, but then left to join Slough Town. Mike Doyle made the reverse trip, coming to Claremont Road after leaving Slough. Paul Collett moved on to St Albans. In December, John Wilson returned to the club from Wealdstone, and Tony Slade joined from Dulwich Hamlet. Keith Jameson became established as a first team player. Ray Poole left to join Eastbourne. However, the club had kept most of the previous season's squad. The programme for the first home league match paid credit to John Evans for this, and said it had been achieved "despite all the close-season rumours". One departure that hit the club hard, but was not entirely unexpected was that of Peter Anderson, who signed for Third Division Luton Town in February.

A Hendon hero: Roy Sleap

Roy Sleap first joined Hendon in September 1960, at the age of 20. He came from Barnet, where he had already made an Amateur Cup final appearance in 1959, and played for the Great Britain Olympic team at the 1960 Rome Olympics. He played in defence or in midfield, and according to a profile in the club's fanzine written many years later was the "hardest and most powerful tackler to play for the Greens since the War", although he was "pleasant and polite" off the pitch.

He won an Athenian League championship medal with Hendon in 1960–61, and then joined Enfield with most of the first team, winning two more championships. He then returned to Hendon in 1963 and was a key member of the great Hendon team of the mid–1960s before joining Slough Town in 1968. He briefly returned to Hendon in 1971, but, unable to claim a regular first team place returned to Slough, and subsequently played for Guildford in the Southern League.

As well as playing for Great Britain, he won 16 England amateur caps, and played for the London and Middlesex teams. He was one of four Hendon players in the Great Britain team that faced West Germany at Claremont Road in 1967. He died on 3 October 2005, at the age of 65. John Swannell was one of the speakers at his funeral.

On the administrative side, Charles Geary became the club's general manager. In October, former club chairman and president Alfred Murray died. He had served the club for many years, and ensured the club's survival during the Second World War. In the close season, committee members Roy Ambrose and Harry Infield had also died.

Middlesex Senior Cup

The season did produce another cup final appearance, albeit in the Middlesex Senior Cup, which offered less prestigious opposition than the other cups that Hendon entered. In the first round, Hendon won 3–0 at Staines, revenge for the embarrassing defeat the previous season. This was followed by a 1–0 win at Hayes, and a further triumph by the same score in the semi-final at Wembley. Old foes Enfield were Hendon's final opponents. The Greens lost the first match at Southbury Road 1–0 on Easter Monday. Johnny Wilson hit the bar near the end of the match, but otherwise Hendon's attack did not threaten to score.

Enfield: I. Taylor, A. Gibson, L. Pryor, J. Payne, P. Betson, M. Smith, C. Duggan, R. Richards, J. Brooks, K. Gray, T. Turley. Sub: R. Hill
Hendon: J. Swannell, D. Hogwood, M. Cooper, P. Deadman, M. Cannon, R. Haider, R. Wilson, M. Doyle, J. Baker, N. Ashman, K. Jameson. Sub: J. Wilson.

The return leg was a month later, and was the club's final game of the season. Two goals in the first 10 minutes of the second half gave Enfield a 2–0 win and 3–0 victory on aggregate. In the second leg, full-back Mickey Cooper was critical of the referee's decision to give a free kick from which Enfield scored. Former Hendon player Johnny Brooks scored Enfield's second goal. He had also won England amateur international honours since leaving Claremont Road at the start of the previous season.

Hendon: J. Swannell, D. Hogwood, M. Cooper, P. Deadman, M. Cannon, R. Haider, R. Wilson, J. Wilson, J. Baker, A. Randall, K. Jameson. Sub: N. Windsor.
Enfield: I. Taylor, L. Tilley, L. Pryor, J. Payne, P. Betson, M. Smith, T. Gibson, R. Richards, J. Brooks, C. Duggan, T. Turley. Sub: R. Hill

Other cup campaigns

In the FA Cup, Hendon had a bye to the fourth qualifying round. The draw brought high-flying fellow Isthmian Leaguers St Albans to Claremont Road. After a goalless draw, Hendon won the replay at Clarence Park 2–1. In the first round proper, Fourth Division Aldershot came to Claremont Road, with former England international Jimmy Melia as their player-manager. They proved too strong for Hendon, winning 2–0.

The Amateur Cup first round saw a rare trip to Hampshire, to face Hampshire League Alton Town. A minute's silence for the victims of the Ibrox disaster was held before the game. Sixty six supporters had died when crush barriers collapsed at the end of a Rangers versus Celtic match. The clash with Alton resulted in a 1–1 draw. Hendon won the replay 6–0, with Johnny Baker scoring a hat-trick.

After a 4–1 win over Barking at Claremont Road in the next round, when FIFA president Sir Stanley Rous was a guest of the club, Hendon faced Slough Town in the third round.

Coached by former Hendon centre-forward Tommy Lawrence, assisted by former Hendon winger Laurie Churchill, included in Slough's squad were former Hendon forward Dave Swain, and eight former Enfield players. A 1–1 draw at Claremont Road was followed by a 3–1 defeat in the replay.

Hendon's interest in the London Senior Cup was even briefer. A 3–0 win at Dulwich Hamlet was followed by a 1–0 defeat at Athenian League Boreham Wood.

Hendon versus Aldershot in the FA Cup first round – John Swannell in action. (HT)

Sixth in the League

Hendon slipped a place from the 1969–70 season, finishing sixth. The attack improved slightly, with 81 goals, and the defence conceded less than a goal a game. But 11 draws and five defeats at Claremont Road meant that Hendon were never really challenging for the title, and finished 15 points behind leaders Wycombe.

The biggest win was 8–0 at Corinthian Casuals, and the Greens scored six at Clapton and at home to Hitchin Town. Johnny Baker was top scorer with 21 goals, Bobby Wilson and Peter Anderson contributed 18 each.

In October, the club programme reported that Hendon's proposal for an Isthmian League of two divisions, with promotion and relegation had been rejected. But the disparity between the top and bottom of the League meant that change was inevitable, and this was to come about over the next couple of seasons.

In December, club officials had attended a meeting to discuss joining the semi-professional Southern League, but the committee rejected the idea, and it was not pursued any further.

International honours

The recruitment of Peter Deadman meant that the club now had three players who appeared regularly for the England amateur team. John Swannell and Rod Haider won a further five caps each, and Peter Deadman appeared three times.

Currency change

One sign of the times was on 19 December, the match programme was priced at 3NP, reflecting that decimalisation of the currency was coming in February 1971.

199

1971–2: Cup triumphs

The work done by John Evans the previous season, combined with some new recruits gave Hendon supporters great optimism for the forthcoming season. New recruits included Tony Bass from Dagenham and John Connell from Slough. Bass was a 6 feet 4 inches tall centre forward, and Connell was a regular goal scorer, who had often been a thorn in Hendon's side when playing for Enfield. To strengthen the defence, Welsh international centre half Alan Phillips was recruited, and replaced Mickey Cannon at the back. Two other new recruits were full-backs Tony Jennings (from Leytonstone) and Gary Hand (after a short period at Wealdstone, returning to Hendon in December), who were to become the regular full-backs, replacing long-serving Hendon stalwarts David Hogwood and Mickey Cooper. The latter had knee injuries during the season. Hogwood felt that his 10 years service with the club was not recognised when he was released early in the season. He moved to St Albans City, but did return to Hendon a couple of years later. Two other first team regulars from past seasons to leave were David Shacklock and Bobby Wilson, who both joined Kingstonian.

Bobby Childs joined from St Albans, providing attacking options from the right. During the season, Ted Moore joined from Dagenham. In October, Ken Ellis moved to Edmonton, frustrated at the lack of first team chances. His place as reserve team goalkeeper was taken by Arthur Paisley, who joined the club from Wealdstone.

One change at Claremont Road was the installation of new floodlights. This meant a couple of pre-season friendlies kicking off at 7.00 p.m., and the first two midweek League home matches were switched to 'away' fixtures to avoid having to kick off at 6.00 p.m. or 6.30 p.m. The new floodlights were 'officially' opened with a match against Luton Town, including Peter Anderson, on 4 October. Hendon drew 1–1 with a strong Luton side.

Amateur Cup again

At the start of the Amateur Cup, Athenian League Horsham was beaten in the first round at Claremont Road. The second round draw saw Hendon visit Midland League Highgate United, who had played six games in the competition to reach this round, having started in the qualifying rounds. Four years before, a tragedy had seen Highgate making the national news, when one of their players, Tony Aveyard, was killed by lightning during an Amateur Cup match against Enfield. Peter Deadman gave Hendon the lead before Highgate scored to force a replay. Hendon then won 2–0. Hendon also needed a replay to reach the fourth round, winning 1–0 at Maidenhead after a goalless draw at Claremont Road. Hitchin Town were the next visitors to Claremont Road, and a 2–0 victory saw Hendon into the semi-final for the first time since 1967. The other semi-finalists were Enfield, Wycombe and Northern League Blyth Spartans, all very strong sides. The draw produced a Hendon versus Wycombe Wanderers clash at Brentford's Griffin Park. Wycombe were Isthmian League champions, and were heading towards a further title win. But at least a clash with old rivals Enfield or a trip north to face Blyth had been avoided.

Hendon's supporters were heavily outnumbered by Wycombe's followers in a crowd of 9,210. Johnny Baker put Hendon ahead with a header from a Bobby Childs corner after 14 minutes. Wycombe equalised early in the second-half, but with 16 minutes left, a spectacular long range shot from Peter Deadman soared into the Wycombe net, and

Hendon held on to win 2–1. Hendon had defended well against strong opponents, who were leading the Isthmian League. Skipper Rod Haider said the win was "bloody marvellous", and Wycombe's manager Brian Lee acknowledged that the winning goal was scored by the game's finest player.

Hendon: J. Swannell, A. Jennings, G. Hand, P. Deadman, A. Phillips, R. Haider, B. Childs, J. Connell, A. Bass, J. Baker, K. Jameson. Sub: T. Moore
Wycombe Wanderers: J. Maskell, I. Rundle, D. Bullock, E. Powell, J. Delaney, R. Williams, M. Mellows, D. Gamblin, K. Searle, A. Horseman, J. Hutchinson. Sub: T. Waughman.

In the other semi-final, Enfield had beaten Blyth Spartans 2–0 at Newcastle, so the scene was set for a north London derby in the final. It was Enfield's fourth appearance in the final in the last nine years. One of their stars was Ken Gray, who had nearly 40 England caps. John Payne and John Brooks had previously played for Hendon.

Hendon 2 Enfield 0
Amateur Cup Final

Hendon's cup preparations included a visit to a training session from the members of the Royal Ballet, who were appearing at the Golders Green Odeon. The longstanding and sometimes bitter rivalry between the two clubs was highlighted by Hendon secretary John Doyle who said to the *Hendon Times*: "I have never forgiven them following the migration of some of our star players to Southbury Road which began in 1959… Friction between the two clubs, on and off the field, lasted for four years." He recognised that the situation had calmed, but that he could not forget it all. And, of course, former Enfield star John Connell was now playing for Hendon. For Enfield, John Payne and Johnny Brooks were former Hendon players.

It was not an outstanding match for the 38,000 crowd. Fred Harris in the *Hendon Times* said that Hendon were "super efficient" and that Hendon's "industry and efficiency outshone the short-comings of an ultra cautious Enfield."

Hendon took the lead after 33 minutes. John Baker shot, and the ball hit the Enfield defender Mick Smith and spun over keeper Andy Williams's head. Swannell kept Hendon ahead with saves from Butterfield and Turley. Hendon led 1–0 at half-time, and their defence kept control. With 11 minutes left, Tony Bass scored with a diving header from Rod Haider's free kick to make the score 2–0, and take the cup back to Claremont Road for the first time since 1965.

John Evans paid credit to his midfield, saying "Cup finals are won and lost in the middle of the park and there was no doubting that we were the more efficient in that department." In the *Sunday Express*, Danny Blanchflower said that Hendon "were worthy enough winners, although they definitely had a touch of fortune."

Hendon: J. Swannell, A. Jennings, G. Hand, P. Deadman, A. Phillips, R. Haider (c), B. Childs, J. Connell, A. Bass, J. Baker, K. Jameson. Sub: T. Moore
Enfield: A. Williams, T. Gibson, S. Hill, J. Payne (c), P. Betson, M. Smith, J. Albon, J. Adams, J. Butterfield, K. Gray, T. Turley. Sub: J. Brooks.

The 1972 Amateur Cup Final

Top: The pre-match presentation.

Middle: John Swannell and Tony Bass clear the ball as Peter Deadman and Alan Phillips watch. (*Hendon Times*)

Bottom: Rod Haider receives the Cup

Programme: Courtesy Wembley National Stadium Ltd

Top: Celebrating with the Cup.

Middle: Training for the final with a group of ballet dancers

Bottom: The Hendon team after the Middlesex Senior Cup Final win.

(Photos: *Hendon Times*)

Further Cup success

In the FA Cup, the fourth qualifying round draw brought Barnet to Claremont Road, looking for revenge for Hendon's victory at Underhill the previous season. They got it, with a 2–0 replay victory after a 2–2 draw at Claremont Road.

The county cups bought more success. In the London Senior Cup, Hendon needed replays to overcome relatively humble opposition, Croydon Amateurs and Erith & Belvedere in the first two rounds. In the third round, St Albans were beaten 4–0 at Claremont Road, and in the semi final, another Hertfordshire team, Bishop's Stortford lost at Claremont Road, this time 1–0. In the final, Hendon faced Enfield at Wealdstone in a repeat of the Amateur Cup final, but this time Enfield were successful 2–0.

Hendon 0 Enfield 2
London Senior Cup Final

Enfield took revenge for Wembley and defeat by Hendon in the Middlesex Senior Cup by reversing the Wembley result to win the London Senior Cup. The match was played at Wealdstone's Lower Mead ground, and attracted a crowd of 1,341. Tony Bass missed the game with an ankle injury. Ted Moore came into midfield, with Bobby Childs moving up front.

Kenny Gray gave Enfield the lead after 37 minutes, and Rod Haider came close to equalising minutes later, a brilliant save from Andy Williams thwarting him. Hendon had further chances in the second half, with Baker coming close twice, but on 86 minutes, Butterfield won the cup for Enfield. Hendon coach John Evans recognised that "Enfield were the better side this time."

Enfield: A. Williams, J. Albon, F. Gibson, J. Payne, S. Hill, M. Smith, R. Richards, J. Adams, J. Butterfield, K. Gray, T. Turley. Sub: J. Brooks.
Hendon: J. Swannell, A. Jennings, G. Hand, P. Deadman, A. Phillips, R. Haider, T. Moore, J. Connell, B. Childs, J. Baker, K. Jameson. Sub: R. Butler.

In the Middlesex Senior Cup, Hendon were drawn at Staines Town for the third season running. A 3–0 victory was followed by a 6–0 win over Borough Road College at Claremont Road. In the semi-final, Enfield came to Claremont Road. A rare goal from Tony Jennings put Hendon one up. A 2–0 victory was secured when Rod Haider volleyed a drop-kick from Andy Williams back over his head into the net. Haider was on the half-way line, and the Hendon programme said the goal was "truly amusing". That probably was not Williams' reaction.

In the Final, Hendon faced Athenian League Hampton, who were contesting their first Middlesex Senior Cup Final. Hendon won 2–1 at Hampton in the first leg. Connell and Baker scored for Hendon, but Connell was then sent off after a clash with former Hendon goalkeeper Ron Whiteaker. Connell was angry about the incident, feeling that the goalkeeper had overreacted.

Hampton: R. Whiteaker, A. Earl, P. Minor, K. Reed, S. Markham, I. Wenlock, P. Farren, M. Roach, P. Allen, P. Sperling, J. Sillett. Sub: H. Lindsay.
Hendon: J. Swannell, A. Jennings, G. Hand, P. Deadman, A. Phillips, R. Haider, B. Childs, J. Connell, A. Bass, J. Baker, K. Jameson. Sub: T. Moore.

In the return leg, Hendon won 3–0, goals from Bass, Haider and Childs giving Hendon a comfortable victory over the two matches.

The League: fourth place

Had it not been for end of season fixture congestion and the demands on the players from the England amateur team, Hendon could have repeated the 'double' the club had achieved in 1964–65. The league had a new look this season, with Wealdstone and Maidstone United having turned professional and joined the Southern League. They had been replaced by Walton & Hersham (who finished the season in third place), Bishop's Stortford (who finished fifth) and Hayes from the Athenian League. The recruitment of these clubs made the League more competitive. There were also two more fixtures, 40 instead of 38.

The season started with one point from two games - difficult away matches at Sutton and Wycombe. But after the 1–0 defeat at Wycombe, Hendon did not lose to an amateur team again until a home League match against St Albans on 25 March, a staggering 38 games. At the beginning of November, Hendon were in second place, two points behind Wycombe, with 36 points from 21 matches.

At the turn of the year, Hendon were still second, with 44 points from 26 games, six points behind Wycombe, but with three games in hand. But then, with the heavy cup programme, not helped by four replays, Hendon only played one more league game until 21 March. In April, Hendon played nine matches, including the Amateur Cup Final and two county cup semi-finals. A further five League matches had to be completed in May, combined with three matches in the county cups (the Middlesex Senior Cup Final was over two legs). An example of the problems the club faced was playing in the League at Hayes without Swannell, Haider, Deadman and Bass who were on England duty. In the end, the team finished in a respectable fourth place, with 56 points, nine behind champions Wycombe.

More professional opponents

Hendon had a further Wembley appearance when the club were invited to play in the *Evening Standard* London Five-a-Side competition at the Wembley Pool. Hendon replaced Arsenal, who were otherwise engaged in the FA Cup Final. This was the first time an amateur club had taken part in the competition. Hendon beat Watford 1–0 in the first round, but then lost by the same score to Queens Park Rangers, who went on to win the tournament.

In September, Hendon played a practice game against Torino's first team, who were in London to play Tottenham Hotspur. Hendon lost 3–1, but were 1–0 up at half-time, which suddenly made the game a little more serious for their famous visitors.

International honours

The team's success on the pitch was reflected in further representative honours for the players. Mickey Cooper won three caps for England on a summer tour to Scandinavia. As well as John Swannell, Rod Haider and Peter Deadman appearing for England, Tony Bass won two caps. Alan Phillips played for the Welsh international side.

An unusual honour, and almost certainly a first for the club, was the selection of David Hogwood by the Great Britain Post Office team, who were competing in the European Post Office championship for the first time.

1972–73: The League Championship

It was now seven seasons since Hendon's last league title. Maybe helped by a relative lack of success in the various cup competitions, and subsequently less fixture congestion than the previous season, the team could concentrate on the league. The previous season had shown that Hendon could again challenge for the title. However, with an unprecedented run, the title was won at Leatherhead on 24 March, with the team still unbeaten in the league.

The bulk of the playing squad remained with the club. However, new recruits were Derek Baker and Phil Fry from Dagenham, and Jimmy Wilsonham from Barking. Former players George Rocknean and Fred Pudney returned to the club. Pudney's return was slightly controversial as a group of players had walked out at Hornchurch, his former club, and he trained with the club before he signed.

An early season recruit was 18 year-old centre half Graham Thompson from Edgware Town. In October, Scottish amateur international Ian Denholm joined the club from Queens Park and in December, Keith Searle was signed from Wycombe Wanderers. There were also departures. At the start of the season, Keith Jameson joined Hayes and Mickey Cooper went to Walton & Hersham, having been injured for most of the previous season. In September, John Connell went to Wealdstone.

An important change on the coaching side came halfway through the season. John Evans announced in November that he was emigrating to South America to take a coaching position, and the club decided he would be replaced by Jimmy Quail, who took over in January.

On the administrative side, long-serving club chairman Freddie Debenham stood down at the end of the season. John Doyle also resigned as club secretary.

The league campaign

Leatherhead had been elected to the League, adding another two matches to the League programme. A 2–2 draw at Clapton was not a promising start to the club's most successful ever League campaign. But nine consecutive wins followed, before Bishop's Stortford forced a goal-less draw at Claremont Road on 19 September. Another point was dropped in the next league match at Hitchin, but a further run of 10 wins followed. At the end of October, Hendon were top of the table with 41 points, a staggering 12 points clear of Enfield in second place. Two points were dropped in November, as lowly Leytonstone drew twice with the Greens. But a further run of 10 consecutive wins meant that Hendon won the League on 24 March with a 1–0 win at Leatherhead. It was the club's second Isthmian League title. The unbeaten run continued until 17 April, when Walton & Hersham won 2–1 at Claremont Road. The only other defeat in the league was at Bishop's Stortford on 1 May. Hendon finished with 74 points (out of 84), 13 clear of runners up Walton & Hersham.

The team were not particularly prolific scorers, with 88 goals, an average of just over two per game, although maybe this reflects rising standards in the league, as they were top scorers by 12 goals. Hendon's highest score in the league was five, against Bromley and Barking. But the defence was incredible, with only 18 goals conceded, six in the first four games, overall an average of less than half a goal per game. Six were conceded after the league title was won. There were 30 clean sheets in 42 games, a remarkable achievement, six games with only one goal was conceded, and six with two.

Into Europe

Although the club had a rich history of touring, the Barassi Cup was the first time it participated in an official match against European opposition. The tournament put the Amateur Cup winners against the Italian Amateur Cup winners. It started in 1968, when Leytonstone won it. The next year it was shared. In 1970, Enfield won it and in 1971 Skelmersdale continued England's record of never losing the trophy. The cup was named after Dr Ottorino Barassi, a former president of the Italian Amateur Football League.

Hendon's opponents were Unione Calcistioa Valdinievole from Monsummano Terme. The club were backed by a wealthy businessman, and had recently achieved promotion as well as winning the cup. Their ground had staged a match between an Isthmian League XI and an Italian representative side.

Hendon won the first leg at Claremont Road 2–0, and managed a 1–1 draw in Italy three weeks later. Thirty four supporters went by coach to support the team, a memorable trip for all involved. It took two days to get to there, they stayed one night, and then headed home. It was a very happy group which arrived at Dover early in the morning. Supporters club stalwart Malcolm Graves organised the trip.

Hendon 2 Unione CV 0 (First leg)

Goals from Rod Haider and Bobby Childs gave Hendon a clear lead to take to Italy. Unione's team included former Inter Milan goalkeeper Giuliano Sarti, and two amateur internationals. However, Sarti went off injured after letting in the first goal, and spent the rest of the game signing autographs. Hendon's manager John Evans complained that the Italian side had been shirt-tugging and body checking his players, and that the referee had not controlled the game strictly enough.

Hendon took the lead after 10 minutes, Haider scoring with a header from a Bobby Childs free-kick. Then Childs scored from 35 yards early in the second half to give Hendon a two goal lead for the second leg.

Hendon: J. Swannell, A. Jennings, G. Hand, P. Deadman, P. Fry, R. Haider, B. Childs, J. Connell, J. Baker, J. Wilsonham, W. Koller. Subs: A. Paisley, G. Thompson, D. Poole.
Unione CV: G. Sarti, P. Ramgini, G. Liggia, M. Magli, F. Mazzacane, V. Batini, E. Guerra, R. Farradini, E. Gattelli, L. Lombardi, M. Rossi. Subs: G. Papini, A. Dezio, U. Rabussi.

Unione CV 1 Hendon 1 (Second leg)

The concern that Hendon had about the refereeing in the first game was shown to be justified in the return match. John Baker and Unione's Mazzacane were both sent off in the first half, and other players were cautioned in a tense match.

The game was goalless until three minutes from time, when Tony Bass scored with a header from a cross by left back Gary Hand. Unione's substitute Rossi scored a minute later, but by then it was too late for the Italian side to make a comeback. Club chairman Freddy Debenham said "Hendon came out of it with dignity and deserved to win. There was more tension in the game than I have ever known before."

Unione CV: G. Papini, P. Ramgini, G. Liggia, M. Magli, F. Mazzacane, V. Batini, E. Guerra, L. Lombardi, R. Farradini, E. Gattelli, Tacgota. Subs: Rossi, Fortania.
Hendon: J. Swannell, A. Jennings, G. Hand, P. Deadman, A. Phillips, R. Haider, F. Pudney, J. Wilsonham, A. Bass, J. Baker, P. Fry. Subs: B. Childs, A. Paisley, W. Koller.

The Barassi Cup

Left: The team for the away leg. Back: Arthur Paisley, Johnny Baker, Phil Fry, Gary Hand, John Swannell, Tony Jennings, Peter Deadman, Jimmy Wilsonham, Tony Bass; front: Walter Koller, Rod Haider, Fred Pudney, Bobby Childs, Alan Phillips.

Right: The players in front of the leaning tower of Pisa

Bottom: The teams from the programme for the match at Claremont Road

THE LINE UP

HENDON		UNIONE C.V.
(Green and White)		(Maroon and White)
John SWANNELL	1	SARTI
Tony JENNINGS	2	RAMAGINI
Gary HAND	3	LIGGIA
Peter DEADMAN	4	MAGLI
Alan PHILLIPS	5	MAZZACANE
Rod HAIDER	6	BATINI
Bobby CHILDS	7	GUERRA
John CONNELL	8	FERRADINI
Tony BASS	9	GATTELLI
John BAKER	10	LOMBARDI
Phil FRY	11	ROSSI

Substitutes
A. Paisley
J. Wilsonham
G. Rocknean

Substitutes
Papini
Dezio
Rabussi

Referee: K. Walker (Ashford)
Linesmen: M. F. Stimpson, A. H. Baker

Professional opposition

As Amateur Cup holders, Hendon again had a bye to the first round of the FA Cup. The draw produced a long trip to Third Division Plymouth Argyle, one of the few other teams to also play in green. A 5,697 crowd watched Hendon come close to achieving a goal-less draw and replay at Claremont Road until Plymouth scored a couple of minutes from time. Plymouth manager Tony Waiters said that Hendon had done well, but that he had always been confident of going through.

Plymouth Argyle: Furnell, Provan, Sullivan, Hore, Saxton, Hague, Reed, Rickard, Hinch, Welsh, Latcham. Sub: King.
Hendon: J. Swannell, A. Jennings, G. Hand, P. Deadman, A. Phillips, R. Haider, B. Childs, J. Wilsonham, A. Bass, J. Baker, P. Fry. Sub: F. Pudney.

In the London Challenge Cup, Barnet came to Claremont Road in the preliminary round, and won 2–0.

Amateur Cup

In the Amateur Cup, Sussex County League Chichester City came to Claremont Road in the first round. Hendon won 7–0, with four goals from Fred Pudney. The second round draw produced more difficult opposition, with a trip to Northern League Blyth Spartans, who had reached the semi-final the previous season. A Tony Bass goal gave Hendon a 1–1 draw at Blyth, but the northerners won 1–0 at Claremont Road in the replay the following week to end Hendon's attempt to defend the trophy.

County cups

In the London Senior Cup, a hat-trick from Rod Haider saw off Athenian League Southall in the first round at Claremont Road. Dulwich Hamlet were beaten in the second round before Enfield came to Claremont Road in the third round. A 3–3 draw was followed by a 1–1 draw in the replay. The teams met for the third time in 10 days at Claremont Road, and Enfield won 1–0.

Hendon found more success in the Middlesex Senior Cup. Feltham and Hampton were beaten in the first two rounds, and Southall followed up their London Senior Cup defeat at Claremont Road with another defeat in the Middlesex Senior Cup semi-final. The final saw another clash with Enfield. The first leg of the final was a 1–1 draw at Claremont Road. The match was a 'tale of two penalties'. Fred Pudney gave Hendon the lead after half-time, Joe Adams equalised for Enfield 18 minutes from time. Peter Deadman was unhappy about the penalty award, saying he was only two yards from Turley's shot which hit him on the hand.

Hendon: J. Swannell, A. Jennings, G. Hand, P. Deadman, A. Phillips, R. Haider, F. Pudney, J. Wilsonham, A. Bass, J. Baker, P. Fry. Sub: D. Baker.
Enfield: A. Williams, L. Stonebridge, R. Grant, J. Payne, A. Gibson, P. Wood, J. Butterfield, J. Adams, J. Brooks, T. Turl, A. Turley. Sub: G. Beale.

At Southbury Road, the second leg ended in a 2–2 draw after extra time. For Hendon, Bobby Childs replaced Wilsonham; Kenny Gray replaced Stonebridge for Enfield, who was on the bench. Bass gave Hendon the lead before half-time with a header, but Turley equalised. Brooks gave Enfield the lead six minutes after the break, and Childs equalised for Hendon five minutes later. Enfield's goalkeeper Andy Williams broke his arm with three minutes left. Defender Tony Turl took over, but only had to make one real save.

So the teams met again at Finchley the next week. Hendon were unchanged from the second leg, and for Enfield, Taylor was in goal, Stonebridge played in place of Wood, with Cochrane on the bench. This time goals from Bass, Childs and Pudney gave Hendon a 3–0 win in front of 977 fans. In the first half Hendon had faced a strong wind, but despite this took the lead. Manager Jimmy Quail said they had done "particularly well to contain Enfield in the first half." The teams had met eight times during the season, Hendon had won three matches, Enfield one, and four had been drawn.

Champion of Champions

The season was completed when Blyth Spartans came to Claremont Road as Northern League champions to challenge Hendon for the Champion of Champions title. Hendon took revenge for the Amateur Cup defeat to win 2–0.

At Easter, Whitley Bay had come south for the Will Mather Cup match, and been beaten 3–0. The following week, Swiss First Division side FC St Gallen came to Claremont Road for a friendly, and were beaten 2–0. Further success came for the club at reserve team level, where Hendon won the Middlesex Border League by six points.

Representative honours

As well as the usual spread of representative honours, the club achieved a rare feat in the England versus Wales amateur international in December, when both captains were Hendon players - Rod Haider for England and Alan Phillips for Wales.

The club had a close season tour of Iran, followed by a week's rest in Greece. Missing Swannell, Haider and Deadman who were on tour with England, Hendon drew 2–2 with TAJ, 1–1 with Iran Youth, who were the Asian Youth champions, but lost 3–0 to Persepolis, Iran's top professional side, in front of a 21,528 crowd.

Change on the horizon

The end of the differentiation between 'amateur' and 'professional' footballers was now on the horizon. In October1972, the Isthmian League decided to have two divisions for 1973–74, and dropped the word "amateur" from its rules. From the 1974–75 season, the FA was proposing that football should go open. The issue of 'shamateurism' and illicit payment of players had been a problem for many years. An article in the *1973–74 FA Yearbook* said: "The only reason why some clubs and players *pretend* to be amateur is that there is an advantage to be gained: that of dominating the amateur world and in particular the Amateur Cup, and by doing so, build prosperous 'amateur' clubs. At the same time, a relative handful of players, say a few hundred, make a nice tax-free income."

This had major implications for Hendon, who would now face competition from the semi-professional clubs, with greater resources and support. However, it would also open the possibility of recruiting both young professional players with a couple of years Football League experience, and older players at the end of their careers. But there was still one more season of amateur football to come before the 'brave new world' loomed.

210

1973–74: FA Cup Glory

On the wall at the top of the stairs leading to the club offices at Claremont Road was a huge black and white photo. It is Rod Haider scoring Hendon's equaliser at St James's Park, to earn a 1–1 draw with First Division Newcastle United in the third round of the FA Cup. Hendon lost the replay 4–0 four days later at Watford's Vicarage Road ground, in front of 15,385 supporters, an incredible crowd for a Wednesday afternoon, as floodlights were out of use due to government restrictions on the use of power during the miners' strike.

Hendon had received a bye to the fourth qualifying round of the Cup, and there were given a tough draw away to local Southern League rivals Barnet. A 2–2 draw at Underhill was followed by a 3–0 victory at Claremont Road, with a Roger Connell hat-trick. In the first round proper, fellow Isthmian Leaguers Leytonstone came to Claremont Road and were beaten 3–0. The second round draw took Hendon to another Southern League club, Merthyr Tydfil in the depths of the valleys of South Wales. Playing for Merthyr was one of the legends of Welsh football, John Charles, formerly of Swansea, Leeds United and Juventus, finishing playing days in more humble surroundings as player-manager.

This was Hendon's first competitive match in Wales since an Amateur Cup tie in Cardiff in the early 1920s, and Merthyr's Pennydarren Park had a near capacity crowd. A John Baker goal put Hendon 1–0 up after three minutes, and although the home side put the Greens under pressure at times, two second half goals from Alan Phillips and Keiron Somers, both from corners, saw Hendon safely into the third round proper for the first time in the club's history.

The players were enthusiastic about the draw – Bobby Childs said it would be nice to go home as his parents came from Northumberland, and Mickey Cooper optimistically said that Hendon had just beaten a club that play in black and white stripes. Only Gary Hand was disappointed – he had wanted Watford!

Newcastle United 1 Hendon 1
FA Cup third round proper

"Hendon are already the moral victors," wrote Brian James. "Hendon's finest hour," added John Dougray. "A deserved draw by the fighting amateurs," said another report. Just some of the reactions to a result which reverberated throughout football, as Hendon drew with a team pressing for the top of the First Division.

Hendon were the last amateur side in the cup. But Brian James quoted Rod Haider saying that "...Everyone in this team had a chance to become a pro at one time; the money offered wasn't good enough to turn down a life of playing football and working. Essentially we feel we are their equals."

Over 600 Hendon supporters made the trip north. Many regard this match as Hendon's finest hour. The crowd was 31,606, the largest ever for a Hendon game not at Wembley. Craig hit the bar for Newcastle early on, but then Philip Fry forced McFaul to make a brilliant save. Three minutes before half-time, Pat Howard gave Newcastle the lead, heading in Malcolm Macdonald's long throw.

Newcastle were on top in the second half, although Hendon continued to press. A Tony Jennings free kick on 68 minutes was headed on by John Baker, and Rod Haider scored an equaliser from the edge of the six yard box. Hendon held out to achieve a

Newcastle United versus Hendon

Pat Howard's goal at St James's Park. Below: The Newcastle United programme (courtesy NUFC), a replay match ticket and the teams from the replay at Watford FC

remarkable result. It was truly one of the club's greatest days. Manager Jimmy Quail said: "We have a good team, as everybody must now realise, and they sweated blood to prove it." Quail had gone to watch Newcastle at Arsenal on New Year's Day and "was not very impressed with their back four."

Rod Haider remembers "Bobby Childs giving Kennedy the run around" and that Hendon should have prevented Newcastle's goal. Hendon's goal was a planned move, and he recalls Derek Baker forcing McFaul to make an' excellent' save in the second half although Rod feels that he could have scored had the ball come to him.

Newcastle United: McFaul, Craig, Kennedy, McDermott, Howard, Clark, Gibb, Smith, Macdonald, Tudor, Hibbitt. Sub: Barrowclough.
Hendon: J. Swannell, A. Jennings, G. Hand, P. Deadman, A. Phillips, R. Haider, D. Baker, R. Childs, J. Baker, K. Somers, P. Fry. Sub: M. Cooper.

Hendon 0 Newcastle United 4
FA Cup third round proper replay

Four days later, Hendon faced Newcastle again. A goal behind after 14 minutes, Hendon only succumbed in the final stages of the match.

Malcolm Macdonald put Newcastle ahead on 14 minutes with the Hendon defence appealing for offside. The half-time score was 1–0 to the First Division giants. On 58 minutes, Somers came close to equalising with a header from a Bobby Childs corner. Donald Saunders wrote that "Had Hendon drawn level then they might well have gone on to wear down their unimpressive opponents with the neat progressive football that, for so long, had threatened to give them control."

Instead, Newcastle scored twice in five minutes, Hibbitt making it 2–0 in the 64th minute, and McDermott adding the third from the penalty spot. John Tudor made it 4–0 on 78 minutes. Hendon's achievement was shown as Newcastle went on to reach Wembley, being beaten there 3–0 by Liverpool.

Rod Haider believes that Cassidy made a big difference for Newcastle at Vicarage Road, but that Hendon still had some chances in the match.

Hendon: J. Swannell, A. Jennings, G. Hand, P. Deadman, A. Phillips, R. Haider, D. Baker, R. Childs, J. Baker, K. Somers, P. Fry. Sub: R. Connell.
Newcastle United: McFaul, Craig, Kennedy, McDermott, Howard, Clark, Gibb, Cassidy, Macdonald, Tudor, Hibbitt. Sub: Barrowclough

The club had started the season with the squad from 1972–73 intact, and Jimmy Quail continued as coach, although he was to resign at the end of the season due to business commitments. However, after a couple of games, Tony Bass decided to move to Bishops Stortford. The loss of the club's leading scorer for the past two seasons left Hendon short of scoring power, and this was remedied towards the end of September when Roger Connell and Kieron Somers were recruited from Walton & Hersham, having helped the Surrey side win the Amateur Cup in 1973. Connell was an England international. At the same time, diminutive midfielder John Wilson returned to the club. Another player now pushing for a first team place was Paul Currie, brother of Sheffield United star Tony Currie. Mickey Cooper had returned to the club. In September, Johnny Wilson returned to the club, having played for Hitchin and Bishop's Stortford since leaving. However, a major blow came in March, when Philip Fry, Derek Baker and Tony Jennings all left to join Enfield – the latest group of players to go round the North Circular to Join Hendon's biggest rivals. Two weeks later, David Hogwood returned to the club from St Albans.

One player who had stayed loyal to the club for over 10 years was John Swannell, who played his 500th game for the club in October.

A Hendon Hero: David Hogwood

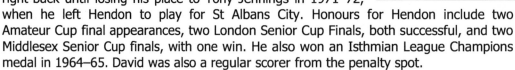

David Hogwood was near the end of his playing career when he returned to the club towards the end of the 1973-74 season. David started his career at Wembley FC, and he joined Hendon at the start of the 1962–63 season at the age of 18, having played for Wembley's first team at the age of 16 and had also appeared 12 times for the Middlesex youth team. He had also played for Arsenal's junior teams.

David played initially at left-back, but was Hendon's regular right-back until losing his place to Tony Jennings in 1971–72, when he left Hendon to play for St Albans City. Honours for Hendon include two Amateur Cup final appearances, two London Senior Cup Finals, both successful, and two Middlesex Senior Cup finals, with one win. He also won an Isthmian League Champions medal in 1964–65. David was also a regular scorer from the penalty spot.

Another achievement was to be one of four Hendon players to represent Great Britain in the Olympic qualifying match at Claremont Road in 1967, and to win seven England amateur caps. He also played for Middlesex and the Isthmian League. He worked for the Post Office as a telephone engineer, and represented the Post Office at an international tournament. David was also a good cricketer.

After retiring as a player, he became Hendon's assistant manager in 1974–75 until Christmas 1977. He then managed the first team, but did not have as much success as he had enjoyed as a player, and left the club less than a year later.

A sign of the change in non league football was the sponsorship by Rothman's of the Isthmian League. The next season, football was to go 'open', and in anticipation of this, the League allowed two permit players (former professionals) to play for each club. Three points were given for a win, to encourage attaching play. Also, prize money was paid to the champions, runners up and third placed team of each division, and to teams winning by three clear goals, who received £40 for each such a win. However, clubs would lose their cash prizes if they had too many players cautioned or sent off.

This was also the first season where clubs could be relegated, as the League now had two divisions.

The League campaign

The season opened with two friendlies – at home to Slough Town, managed by Roy Sleap, and then against a Rothmans Isthmian League XI, the traditional challenge match for the champions. In 1965, Hendon had beaten the League XI 3–2, but this time, despite taking the lead with a rare goal from Peter Deadman after 30 minutes, the League XI scored twice just before half-time to secure a 2–1 victory.

Despite starting the season with a 1–1 draw at home to an improving Dulwich Hamlet, after 11 games, Hendon were top of the League, with 22 points, level on points with Wycombe Wanderers, who had a game in hand. Although the defence had conceded only 4 goals, Hendon had only scored 13, although the arrival of Connell and Somers improved the team's goal scoring dramatically.

After 20 games, Hendon still topped the League, with 47 points, after a run of eight consecutive victories in October, including a 7–0 win at Clapton, and 2–1 triumph over Wycombe Wanderers at Claremont Road. That run ended with a defeat at Leytonstone on 10 November. Then cup ties took over, combined with the miners' strike which restricted midweek matches, and a couple of postponements, so only four more league games were played by the end of February. On 19 March, when Hendon faced Walton & Hersham at Claremont Road, there were still 17 league matches to play. Inevitably, this fixture congestion caught up with the team, and although only 4 league matches were lost, 13 points dropped through draws, particularly punitive with the new three points for a win system, saw Hendon finish as runners up to Wycombe Wanderers by two points. Under the old two points for a win system, both teams would have had 63 points, but – to be fair – Wycombe had a far better goal difference. The team had conceded less than half a goal a game, with just 20, but only averaged 1.5 goals a game scored, with 63, far below Wycombe's 96. The defence was again resolute, with 26 clean sheets in 42 matches. In two seasons, Hendon had conceded 38 goals in 84 league matches, an average of less than half a goal a game.

The cup competitions

Three days after facing Newcastle at Vicarage Road, Hendon faced more humble opposition in the Amateur Cup when Harwich and Parkeston visited Claremont Road. A 0–0 draw was followed by a 1–1 draw at Harwich, and a 2–2 draw at Colchester United's Layer Road in the second replay. These matches had been on consecutive Saturdays; Hendon finally got past Harwich, after 420 minutes of football in the third replay at Claremont Road with goals from Haider and Connell.

Roger Connell on the attack against Tilbury, Amateur Cup at Claremont Road, February 1974 (HT)

Victory over Harwich took Hendon east again, to Tilbury. A 0–0 draw was followed by a 2–0 win in the replay, and the third round bought fellow Isthmian League first division Leatherhead to Claremont Road. This was Hendon's seventh consecutive match in the Amateur Cup – enough games to reach the final and more. A 1–1 draw at Claremont

Road was followed by the same result at Leatherhead. The second replay, at Loakes Park, Wycombe, was Hendon's last match in the competition, a 2–0 defeat.

The programme for the match against Tilbury had outlined that the rule changes to end 'amateur' status would not come in until 1975–76, but that the Isthmian League would go open anyway in 1974–75, and that the Amateur Cup would be replaced by the FA Trophy, which would now be open to teams outside the Football League, and a new, junior national competition, the FA Vase, would also be launched. Hendon was invited to compete in the FA Trophy, but facing clubs with greater resources in the 'open' era, would never – to date – find the success that the Amateur Cup had produced.

In the London Senior Cup, Hendon beat Staines, Hitchin Town and Leytonstone to reach the semi-final, where Bishop's Stortford came to Claremont Road on 6 April. The fixture congestion was not helped by some players being selected for the England amateur team and other representative fixtures. Swannell, Deadman and Haider all played for England in Coventry the night before this key cup semi-final, and the latter two turned out for Hendon the next day. Hendon lost 2–0.

However, the club did win the Middlesex Senior Cup, making it a hat-trick of victories in this competition. Wins at Harrow Borough and Finchley produced a semi-final with Ruislip Manor. After a 1–1 draw in Ruislip, a 1–0 victory in the replay at Claremont Road produced a final against Edgware. A 3–1 victory in the first leg at Claremont Road put Hendon in a strong position, and a 1–0 win at the White Lion Ground in the second leg meant that one of senior football's oldest cups was Hendon's only trophy in their final season in the amateur game. The teams in the first leg were:

Hendon: J. Swannell, D. Poole, G. Owen, P. Deadman, A. Phillips, R. Haider, E. Devlin,
J. Wilsonham, J. Baker, R. Connell, M. Cooper. Sub: J. Quail.
Edgware: M. Gavigan, J. Rowland, B. Cook, D. Finn, J. Maclean, B. Elliott, G. Mackenzie,
T. Higgins, A. Simmons, P. Gaze, E. Ford.

On the representative front, Hendon continued to be well represented in the last season of the England amateur team. Rod Haider and Peter Deadman both made eight international appearances, and John Swannell won another seven caps. Deadman was also selected for England non-league side, but decided to play for Hendon instead.

A Hendon hero: Jimmy Quail

Jimmy Quail was one of Hendon's best players for a 10 year spell from the mid–1950s to the mid–1960s, with a short break at Enfield in the middle. He was the classic inside forward of that era, both creating for goals for others, and scoring a lot himself.

He was born in Banbridge in Northern Ireland in 1935, but came to England with his family just before the war, to live in Harlesden. He recalls: "I passed the 11 plus exam and went to St Clement Dane's Grammar School in 1947. I played football and cricket at school; one of my teachers thought I was better at cricket. I didn't play for any representative teams, just enjoyed playing." He left school at 16, played for a local church side, Presbyterian FC, and was selected for the Middlesex Youth team. His father wrote to Hendon to ask them to give Jimmy a trial: "Teddy Owen, who was a former player, looked after the Strollers side [third team] came to see me, and I joined Hendon in 1953. I remember the first team won the League for the first time that season." He played in the third team, but when he was 18, in 1954, did National Service for two years. He joined the RAF and after his initial training was based in Weston Super Mare for a year, but then moved to Henlow, near Hitchin, and could come home at weekends to resume his football career.

After a short time in the reserves, Jimmy established himself in the first team in 1956. He recalls training at Claremont Road: "We did a lot of training on asphalt where the car park is now. On the main stand there were two or three lights so we could play five-a-side. It wasn't very strict, we used to train on Tuesdays and Thursdays, and then play on a Saturday. We always looked forward to the matches against Wealdstone at Christmas – one on Christmas Day and the return on Boxing Day."

He never had any contact with professional clubs when he was younger, but there were clubs interested in signing him as he became more prominent with Hendon: "Every boy wanted to play professionally, but the pay was poor. I earned as much as a footballer working in the advertising industry. Dexter Adams had played for Tottenham's reserve team as well as Hendon, and he put me in touch with Arthur Rowe at Crystal Palace, and I played some midweek reserve games for them, although I never played for the first team. Soon after I joined Crystal Palace, Ron Greenwood from West Ham rung me, and later on Charlie Mitten from Newcastle wanted me to sign for them, but nothing came of that, and he got sacked soon afterwards. I preferred to keep my job and play as an amateur."

One of the highlights of his time at Hendon was the 1960 Amateur Cup win: "I remember the semi-final against Enfield at Brentford. We kicked off, Miles Spector gave me the ball, and Tommy Lawrence flew into a tackle and flattened me. I had played with Tommy when he was at Hendon, and we are friends to this day! We won 2–0 and I set up our second goal for Brian Figg." Jimmy also hit the bar early in the game. In the Final "I remember Hughie Lindsay was playing for Kingstonian – he was a friend of mine from school. After we took the lead in the last couple of minutes, they still had time to hit the post."

Jimmy's part in Hendon's successes at this time brought him to the attention of the international selectors: "I went to Brescia with the Olympic party, but wasn't chosen for the final squad for the Games. I didn't get a chance to play, and was very disappointed at the time." However, two caps for Northern Ireland came the following season: "I had never played football in Northern Ireland. But when we won the Cup, people there got to know about me. I played against England at Wycombe, and scored twice, although we lost 3–2. I was up against Les Brown and Laurie Brown, who I knew well, and got a fat lip from both of them, but fortunately Roy Sleap, who was a fearsome tackler and in the England defence, didn't get me. I played against Wales and we lost, and was never selected again. I think they were very insular, and stuck to home grown players."

Jimmy also came very close to selection for the full Northern Ireland team: "We played Oxford United in the FA Cup first round, and drew 2–2. Ron Atkinson was playing for them. The replay was on a Tuesday night, and I was told later that if I hadn't been involved in that match, I would have been picked for the full side to play Scotland at Hampden." For an amateur player to even be considered to play in a full international at this time is remarkable, but Jimmy points out that: "I had the skill and awareness to play." He feels that a lot of amateur players could have played professionally, but it wasn't worth it financially at this time. In 1964, he did play for the Great Britain team against Greece in the Olympic Games qualifying tournament. He won many other representative honours, including playing for Middlesex Wanderers, the Isthmian League and the Middlesex FA.

After another successful season with Hendon, which included winning the Athenian League again, Jimmy and a number of other players moved round the North Circular to Enfield. There he joined former Hendon colleagues already at Southbury Road: "Tommy Lawrence, Derek Dawson and Ray Kingsland were already there. There was some upheaval in the committee at Hendon, so a group of us left to join Enfield." Two Athenian League championships for Enfield followed.

When Hendon joined the Isthmian League in 1963, Freddie Debenham bought Jimmy back to Claremont Road: "It was better playing in the Isthmian League – there were better clubs and bigger grounds. David Hyde, Bobby Cantwell and Roy Sleap came with me from Enfield, and we had a very settled side. Ron Burgess was the manager, but he never really gave us any direction, just let us play. We didn't really have any tactics, just a freewheeling attack, and some very strong characters in the side." In 1964, Jimmy played in the London Challenge Cup win at Arsenal, and recalls Peter Storey "giving me a few scars".

In today's terms, Jimmy was an attacking midfield player: "A bit like Paul Scholes – starting moves and finishing them. We played 4–2–4, with me and John Evans in the middle. John was a more aggressive and defensive player, I just wanted him to give me the ball so we could attack."

As outlined elsewhere in this book, the League and Cup were won in 1965. Jimmy recalls the Isthmian League championship play-off as his most memorable game for Hendon: "Enfield thought they should have won the league. I enjoyed that one. We took them to the cleaners that night."

The following season, Jimmy broke his leg playing against Wycombe Wanderers in the Amateur Cup fourth round at Claremont Road: "It was a nasty break, a double fracture, from a high tackle." Although he recovered from the injury to play the following season, he feels he was never the same player again: "We made it to the Amateur Cup semi-final, but lost to Skelmersdale, who were a good side. But I was struggling at Hendon. Alf D'Arcy rang me. He said Enfield needed an experienced player. Tommy Lawrence was the manager so I moved there in the summer of 1967. But I was in and out of the side. I then played at Walton & Hersham for a season, with Allan Batsford, but he played a long ball style that didn't suit me. That was the end of my playing career."

Jimmy then had a spell as manager of Hornchurch, to help out a mate who was involved at the club, and then managed Cheshunt. Then in November 1972, he was contacted by John Evans, who asked if he could help out at Hendon, where he was manager. "John was going to Bogota, and wanted me to take over. My first game was in the FA Cup at Plymouth, and John left soon afterwards. We won the league easily. I used to talk to Rod Haider a lot. I wanted us to play a more relaxed style, John's way was very well organised; I wanted to enhance their skills. I brought Keiron Somers and Roger Connell to the club, getting my own back on Allan Batsford!"

The next season Hendon faced Newcastle United in the FA Cup: "In the second round we were drawn at Merthyr. I went to watch them the week before, and noted certain things about them. After we won the draw took place straight away, and I knew we would be going to Newcastle. I was interviewed on the radio. I went to watch Newcastle play at Highbury just after Christmas. I took my daughter Jane with me, and she became an Arsenal supporter! We just wanted a good crowd and to bring some money into the club. I thought the real threat would come from John Tudor, not Malcolm MacDonald." Before the game there was some drama: "Keiron Somers had broken a contact lens, and he and Roger Connell were late for the coach to take us to the station to get the train. Then I had to persuade Peter Deadman he was fit to play as he was injured." Jimmy did not prepare specially for the match: "They were fitter than us, that was the only difference. We had nothing to lose; I wanted the players to show how they could play. We had good players in every position. We had to concentrate on keeping possession, especially against a professional team. Tudor was a handful in the air. Maybe Newcastle did take us a bit lightly."

For the replay "I said to the board we couldn't play it at Hendon. So we played at Watford on a Wednesday afternoon. They were fitter and I knew they would be up for it. I think they'd had a rocket from their manager. I knew we wouldn't win. Then a few weeks later, Derek Baker, Tony Jennings and Phil Fry left to join Enfield, and that team broke up. I had a lot on at work, so I left the club at the end of the season."

Jimmy returned to manage the club for 18 months in 1976, leaving at Christmas 1977, and then again in 1982, when he worked with Gary Hand: "Gary was the manager and asked me to help out. I found it very different, it was a new generation, there were different attitudes and less of a social life around the club. When I played it was a whole day out with our families." Jimmy and Gary left at the end of the season, and he has not had any involvement with football since then.

For most of his working life, Jimmy was involved in advertising. In sport, when his football days finished, he took up golf and plays regularly. He joined Mill Hill Golf Club in 1976, and plays with former football colleagues at the Middlesex Wanderers Golf Day each year and on other occasions. He is now retired and lives with his wife Maureen in Kenton. He pops into Hendon games occasionally and keeps in contact with many of his former playing colleagues.

Along with Roy Sleap, Jimmy was the link between the first two Hendon teams to win the Amateur Cup. Undoubtedly one of the great amateur players of his generation, he won every honour in the game, but is remembered as much for the skill and excitement he bought to the game as for the medals he won.

The future

It was the end of an era. The 'amateur' would be no more. The 1974–75 *FA Yearbook* said that: "Unhappily, the Amateur Cup did not die a natural death; it committed suicide. The players themselves – especially those attached to our leading amateur clubs – have made a mockery of their status, until the FA has been compelled to yield and admit that the amateur game was no more." That is as may be, but there had been some wonderful times for the club in 56 years participation in senior amateur football.

From August 1974, the club would face new challenges and new opportunities. Already there was talk – again – of the need to unify the structure of 'non-league' football, and create a pyramid structure for the leagues, so that clubs could work their way up towards Football League status. Whether Hendon would be able to take advantage of this new era would remain to be seen.

Hendon Football Club 1973–74 – the last season of the 'amateur' era

Finchley versus Hendon, Middlesex Senior Cup in March 1974 (HT)

9. 1974 to 1992: Into the open era

Hendon's recent history – stretching back over more than three decades – has one theme running through it: a failure to take chances to advance when they have arisen. The club completed its centenary season in level three of non league football; in 1974 it was not only in level one, but also was one of the most highly respected clubs outside the Football League, albeit one of the 'amateur' ones who did not aspire towards Football League status. However, since the game went 'open', the 1974–75 season was the one which saw the greatest turmoil.

The Football Association's decision to end the amateur-professional divide and make football 'open' from 1974 was embraced wholeheartedly by a number of Isthmian clubs, Enfield, Wycombe Wanderers, Dagenham and Tooting & Mitcham United to name but four. Hendon shied away. In fact the committee appeared to have a death wish by its insistence that they would not be signing players for money.

It meant the summer of 1974 saw a revolving door at Claremont Road, with stars leaving and mainly inferior replacements arriving. Manager Jimmy Quail had stepped down and his replacement, the ever-willing Bill Fisher, was too nice a person to be a very successful manager. Thus, from the 13 players Hendon named for the two matches against Newcastle United in January 1974, only two remained for the opening matches of the 1974–75 campaign.

John Swannell had moved to Leatherhead, although not for financial reasons, where he would enjoy more FA Cup glory with another third round appearance. Tony Jennings, Phil Fry and Derek Baker had all left to join Enfield in the spring. Gary Hand was now at Wycombe Wanderers, along with Alan Phillips – they too enjoyed more FA Cup glory, this time against Middlesbrough. Peter Deadman resumed his career under the guidance of John Evans, who was now in charge at Ilford, who had been runners-up in the last-ever FA Amateur Cup. Bobby Childs was, briefly, at St Albans City, but returned to Claremont Road during the season. John Baker was with Swannell at Leatherhead. Finally the two strikers who arrived from Walton & Hersham in 1973, Keiron Somers and Roger Connell, had joined Wimbledon, where their careers would include further high profile FA Cup ties and, a couple of years later, brief spells in the Football League. Only Mickey Cooper and Rod Haider remained, Cooper's injury against Woking a few weeks from the end of the season probably being the straw that broke the camel's back in terms of the 1973–74 Rothman's Isthmian League championship campaign.

The new arrivals – or those stepping up from the reserves – were Arthur Paisley, who finally got his chance to be Hendon's first choice goalkeeper. That experiment lasted only a few weeks. Peter Smith, from Hitchin Town, who had played in the last-ever England amateur international in May arrived, but he had an unhappy season, especially in matches played under floodlights. Cooper, David Hogwood, John Field – a former Tottenham junior – and David Poole filled the full-back positions in the early games until Ray Coombes arrived from Sutton and took over the left-back spot. Alan Randall, who would become coach, reserve team manager, assistant manager and, ultimately, manager at Hendon was centre-half for the opening game, partnered by Brian Stevens, the first former professional at the club in the new era. He joined from Stevenage Town. Another defensive arrival early in the season was Barrie Davies, a Welsh international whose brother was in midfield. In that midfield, there was Rod Haider, partnered by Roy Davies, and Jimmy Wilsonham. Davies joined from Slough, but would return to the

Rebels during the season and, within a couple of years started a successful Football League career. Southam came from Corinthian Casuals while Wilsonham, who had been in the reserves, had come from Leytonstone. This group was soon augmented by Tony Field, released by Fulham after he was shot in the leg outside Putney rail station – the rumour at the time was it was a case of mistaken identity. Up front, Eggie James, a tall, awkward central striker from Staines, led the line. Another striking option was Steve Jefferies, a City of London policeman with great pace. He was a devastating substitute, using his speed to unsettle tired defences. A young Mike Gatting also made four first team appearances. After playing at Hendon for a couple of seasons, he concentrated on his main sport, cricket, and achieved great success with Middlesex and England.

For all the limitations of this squad, it was far too good to struggle in the Rothman's Isthmian League. That said, the final finishing position of 13th was by far the worst in Hendon's dozen seasons in the Isthmian League, and the 20 defeats was also a new low. A couple of heavy defeats – notably 5–0 at Enfield and Wycombe were offset by some big victories – 4–1 at home to Woking and a 4–2 trouncing of Walton & Hersham, who had just suffered a second mass walkout in 18 months.

There was no glory in the FA Cup, a 2–0 defeat at home to Maidstone in the fourth qualifying round was Hendon's only match. In the FA Trophy, Hendon overcame Cambridge City at Milton Road in their first ever match in this competition, but Hillingdon Borough won a second round replay 3–1 at Yiewsley after a 2–2 draw at Claremont Road. There was some success in the Middlesex Senior Cup, with a fifth consecutive Final reached, this time a neutral venue one-off game at Wealdstone. A 1–1 draw was followed by a 1–0 defeat in the replay. A 3–0 defeat of North London Polytechnic and a 6–1 surprise drubbing of Kingstonian – followed three days later by a 2–1 home reverse in the league against the same opponents – were the high spots of an all too brief London Senior Cup run. Eggie James was top scorer with 19 goals.

Hendon 1 Staines Town 1 after extra time (90 mins: 0–0)
Hendon 0 Staines Town 1
Middlesex Senior Cup Final and Replay

Hendon set a new Middlesex Senior Cup record by becoming the first team to contest five consecutive finals, but they eventually came up just short in their bid to make it a County-best four straight wins. Staines Town, who had won promotion from Rothmans Isthmian League Division Two to the First Division, Hendon's level, proved tough and uncompromising opposition over the two games at Wealdstone, the first on 5 April.

The Greens' cause was certainly not helped by the arcane regulations of the time that meant that both Tony Field and Bobby Childs, key attacking and creative components of the team, were ineligible. The upshot was that Johnny Wilson became possibly the shortest player ever to wear Hendon's No. 9 shirt. Without Field and Childs, it was of little surprise that Staines enjoyed the better chances in both games

Peter Smith made three good first half saves, the pick being one from Tim Soutar, while Hendon failed to get any notable efforts on target. David Poole was just wide with a header from a Rod Haider cross, while Eggie James narrowly failed to get a touch to Brian Stevens' flick-on of Dave Yerby's free-kick.

In the second half, Staines had a loud appeal for a penalty turned down. Soutar appeared to have been fouled inside the penalty area but the referee saw nothing wrong with the challenge. With 10 minutes remaining, former Hendon favourite Gerry O'Rourke fired just wide from an acute angle.

Two minutes into extra-time Hendon took the lead. John Field started the flowing move, which was continued by Haider and Steve Jefferies before the ball was sent out wide to Bobby Southam. His cross was inch-perfect and James applied the final touch.

Staines's equaliser came from man-of-the-match Arthur Rowlands, who went on a long, mazy run off the right wing, past Ray Coombes and his low shot went through the crowded penalty area and past the unsighted Smith on its way into the net. Hendon finished extra time the stronger, but could not take advantage of the unconvincing handling by Staines goalkeeper Graham Yates.

In the replay, played on 6 May, veteran Mickey Cooper replaced Wilson – as he had done during the first match when the substitute – and 17-year-old Mike Gatting took over from Steve Jefferies, further weakening Hendon's attacking options.

Staines were unchanged and kicked-off with a strong wind at their backs. They failed to use it well and it was Hendon who created the better chances. Yates fumbled a looping ball from Cooper and was grateful to grab it at the second attempt. Then Rob Williams rescued the beaten Yates by heading off the goal line from an effort by Gatting and Yates made a fine save from Southam. The Swans' best effort was a header by Soutar from a Richard Brown cross, but Smith was equal to it.

In the second half, most of the chances continued to go Hendon's way, but they could not work out how to beat Yates and the Swans defence. A corner from Southam was headed over the crossbar by James and the goalkeeper then produced a brilliant save to deny Southam after Cooper and John Field had set him up.

Almost inevitably, Staines would snatch a breakaway winning goal and it came in the 81st minute. There wasn't much danger as Yerby went to pass back to Smith, who moved away from his goal to receive the ball. However, Yerby was dispossessed by Rowlands, who wasted no time in firing a cross-shot past Smith, who never had a chance to regain his ground. Hendon tried valiantly to get back on terms but time ran out on them.

Hendon: Smith, Poole, Coombes, Yerby, Stevens, Haider, Jefferies, J. Field, Wilson (Cooper, 70), Southam, James.
Replay: Smith, Poole, Coombes, (Wilson), Yerby, Stevens, Haider, Southam, J. Field, Gatting, Cooper, James.
Staines Town: Yates, Talbot, Brown, Williams, McCready, Bax, Beasant, Salkeld, Soutar, O'Rourke (Coulton, 90), Rowlands.
Replay: Yates, Talbot, Brown, Williams, McCready, Bax, Beasant, Salkeld, Soutar, O'Rourke, Rowlands. Sub: Coulton.

1975–76: FA Cup triumph

A distinct turnaround in fortunes occurred in 1975–76, highlighted by Hendon's first ever defeat of a Football League club in the FA Cup. Among the players coming in at the start of the season were goalkeeper Malcolm Dalrymple, midfielder Dave Metchick, a former professional at Arsenal and Peterborough and striker Tony Amos, although the latter's career was ended by a serious ankle injury in mid-November. More heartening was the return of both Johnny Baker and Alan Phillips.

The strength of the team was the midfield where the diverse talents of Tony Field, Rod Haider and Metchick, provided strength, boundless energy, great touch and control. Metchick's smart thinking was never better displayed than an own goal he created against Ilford at Claremont Road in August. Awarded an indirect free-kick inside the

Ilford penalty area, in a central position, Metchick drilled the ball against the shoulder of George Brooks, one from the end of the wall. Brooks could not get out of the way as the ball struck his shoulder and flew into the net. The only shame is that Metchick didn't get the credit for the goal.

The FA Cup run

A 1–0 win over Canterbury in the fourth qualifying round gave Hendon a home draw against Reading, who had won 3–1 at Claremont Road in the same round in 1966.

Hendon 1 Reading 0
FA Cup 1st round proper

Hendon finally managed to beat a Football League team for the first time when Division Four high-flyers Reading were sent crashing at a soggy Claremont Road on 22 November. Reading suffered a couple of blows before the match when Robin Friday and Eamon Dunphy were ruled out. Adding spice to the occasion was the inclusion in Hendon's line-up of Dave Yerby, who had been in Reading's reserves a season earlier. Replacing Friday – who had played against Hendon for Enfield and Hayes – was another former opponent, Ray Hiron, who had played for Fareham when they knocked Hendon out of the Amateur Cup in 1964.

And it was Hiron who had the first real chance of the match. In the 17th minute Jack Witham, set up Hiron, but the striker missed from close range. Eleven minutes later, Hendon's former Arsenal midfielder Dave Metchick had a one-on-one with Reading goalkeeper Steve Death, and the latter did enough to put off Metchick.

Hendon began to take over and, in the 35th minute, Death made a fine save to deny Bobby Childs. It delayed what proved to be the only goal by a mere eight minutes.

Childs was fouled by Dave Moreline a few yards inside the Reading half, near to the right touchline. Metchick took the free-kick and aimed it at the edge of the penalty area, where Johnny Baker had lost his marker. Baker flicked the ball with his head into the penalty area and Alan Phillips, who had played against Newcastle in 1974 and for Wycombe Wanderers against Middlesbrough in January 1975, enjoyed more FA Cup glory with a header that beat Death.

A minor pitch invasion celebrating the goal wasn't the story it would be today and Hendon were able to go into half-time with a deserved lead. The second half wasn't quite one-way traffic, but it was the Hendon defence which had to answer most of the questions. Less than a minute after the restart, John Murray had the ball in the Hendon net, but referee Malcolm Sinclair disallowed it because of a foul on Yerby. Nine minutes later, Hiron and Bryan Carnaby set up Witham with a great chance, but he shot wide.

In the final quarter, the Hendon hero was goalkeeper Malcolm Dalrymple, who made three superb saves. After 70 minutes he denied Hiron and, three minutes later, kept out an effort from Tommy Youlden. With seven minutes to go, he produced a double save, blocking a shot from Youlden and keeping out the follow-up from Gordon Cumming.

After the match, manager Bill Fisher said, "What a tremendous team performance. We did not have any stars today, but they were all heroes." He also admitted "Our players weren't on a win bonus today, though the club could get a donation or two from well-wishers."

Hendon: Dalrymple, J. Field, Hand, Yerby, Phillips, Haider, A. Field, Metchick, Childs, Baker,

Jefferies. Sub: Coombes.
Reading: Death, Lenarduzzi, Moreline, Cumming, Barker, Youlden, Murray, Hiron, Witham (Peters). Carnaby, Stuckey.

The second round draw gave Hendon another home tie, and more Football League opposition. This time Third Division Swindon Town came to Claremont Road on 18 December.

Hendon 0 Swindon Town 1
FA Cup 2nd round proper

Hendon's hopes of a second FA Cup third round proper appearance in three seasons were dashed by Division Three strugglers Swindon Town at Claremont Road on 18 December. The crowd, smaller than the Reading match, witnessed a dour encounter in which the luck certainly went the Robins' way.

Bill Fisher named the same 12 players who had seen off Reading for the match and they made a bright start. Baker made a break down the wing in the opening minute and sent over a teasing cross that needed a touch to send it goalwards. Unfortunately was no Hendon forward was on hand and Swindon breathed a sigh of relief.

Their defending continued to be less than secure and they were very fortunate not to concede a penalty when Alan Phillips was bundled off the ball by a defender, but the referee ruled there was no foul. A few minutes later, Baker was taken out by a combination of Frank Burrows and John Emmanuel inside the penalty area. As Hendon fans and players appealed for a penalty, the referee awarded only an indirect free-kick and Metchick's effort came to nothing.

Midway through the second half, Emmanuel did well to head a curling Metchick shot clear from the goal line with Jim Barron well beaten. Five minutes later, Swindon got the all-important goal. A corner was curled into the Hendon penalty area and Malcolm Dalrymple was knocked out of the way as he went for it. Dave Syrett sent in a shot that was going into the top corner, until Dave Yerby made a flying save – one that would have earned him a red card in today's football.

Despite Hendon protestations about the foul in the build-up, the referee would have none of it, so it was a penalty to Swindon and a caution for the flame-haired defender. David Moss stepped up and coolly struck the ball past Dalrymple.

With 14 minutes left, Hendon tried desperately to save the situation and, with six minutes to go, Barron saved a Tony Field effort by sticking out a leg in desperation. Two minutes later, Bobby Childs struck a shot that Barron would probably not have reached, but a defender's leg deflected the ball to safety.

Swindon manager Danny Williams admitted: "We were lucky to win." Their reward was a tie against another Isthmian League team, Tooting & Mitcham United and the Terrors knocked them out in a third round replay.

Hendon: Dalrymple, J. Field, Hand, Yerby, Phillips, Haider, A. Field, Metchick, Childs, Baker, Jefferies. Sub: Coombes.
Swindon: Barron, Taylor, Trollope, Emmanuel, Burrows, Stroud, Moss, Dixon, Eastoe, Syrett, Anderson. Sub: Butler

FA Cup action

Hendon versus Reading – Metchick and Jefferies attack (*Hendon Times* – Peter Beal)

Hendon versus Reading – Baker, John Field, Phillips, Childs, Haider and Jefferies celebrate taking the lead (*Hendon Times* – Peter Beal)

Hendon versus Swindon – Hendon on the attack.

A final sixth place finish was fine reward for a much improved season, indeed only seven goals difference separated the Greens in sixth and Dulwich Hamlet in fifth, Hamlet ending 67–41 and Hendon 60–41 in goals with both teams on 71 points.

There was no glory in the FA Trophy, although the Greens did hammer Basingstoke Town 6–1 in an early round. Hendon failed to make it six consecutive Middlesex Senior Cup Finals, losing 3–0 to Enfield in a replayed semi-final and the London Senior Cup again proved a disappointment with a 2–0 loss at Leatherhead. Hendon had more success in the Middlesex Charity Cup, beating Wembley in the Final on 9 March.

Hendon 1 Wembley 0 after extra time
Middlesex Charity Cup Final

Hendon won the Middlesex Charity Cup for the 10th time in the club's history with a hard-fought victory over Wembley at Claremont Road on 9 March. Unfortunately, the hard-fought part was mirrored on the terraces and the Police, with dogs, had to calm things down just before the end of the goalless 90 minutes.

Hendon were on top for large parts of the game, but their finishing was not of the highest standards and although Steve Redwood was much busier than Malcolm Dalrymple, the Lions' goalkeeper was not overworked.

The only goal came midway through the first period of extra time. Full-back John Field was released by a superb pass from Bobby Childs. He burst through the midfield and suddenly had a clear run at goal – until he was stopped illegally by Redwood, a foul that in the modern game would have resulted in a straight red card, but in those days was just a free-kick without sanction on the offender.

Rod Haider took the free-kick, rolling it into the path of Tony Field, whose drive flew past Redwood into the top corner. Wembley tried to get back into the game with the wily Keith Cassells and Dennis Gill working hard, but there was no way past the combination of John Field and Alan Phillips.

Hendon: Dalrymple, J. Field, Hand, Cooper, Phillips, Haider, A. Field, Hutchinson, Childs, Baker, Jefferies (Yerby). Sub: Gatting.
Scorer: A. Field (97).
Wembley: Redwood, Joughin, Witham, Watts, Devlin, Tottman, Taylor, Read, Cassells, Gill, Green. Subs: McGonigle, Chivers.

1976–77: The League Cup

Peter Deadman returned from Ilford for the new season, joined by Peter Anderson – not the winger, who was still enjoying his career in the Football League, but a full-back or centre-half – and midfielder David Holden, the latter two both north-easterners. Also returning was full-back Gary Hand. Two top strikers also joined Hendon, Irishman George Brooks and former England amateur international John Butterfield. Another new signing for the new season, originally on a month's trial from Finchley, was teenager central defender Alan Campbell, who would give the club great service in three spells as well as becoming a cult hero with the fans.

This squad was significantly stronger than in the past two seasons and the results reflected this. It would be stretching credibility to say that Hendon challenged for the title, because they finished 12 points adrift of third-placed Dagenham and 19 behind champions Enfield, but fourth place was still something to celebrate – especially as it would not be matched for another 10 years. Strangely, the Greens collected four more points in 1975–76 – 71 – than they did in 1976–77. Butterfield enjoyed a pretty good season, his highlight undoubtedly being a 20-minute cameo against Sutton United on New Year's Day at Claremont Road. A groin injury ended his participation before the match had reached the quarter mark, but he had already completed his hat-trick – in fact it was 3–0 after nine minutes, and 90 as well. There was also a rather strange encounter at Woking, which ended with Hendon winning 4–2, converting two out the three penalties they were awarded in the match.

The FA Cup was a huge disappointment. Entering in the fourth qualifying round, Campbell scored after just 50 seconds at Waterlooville, but John Robson grabbed a hat-trick for the Ville as they ran out 4–1 winners at Jubilee Park. At 3–1 Butterfield hit a post when he should have scored and that was the end of the Greens' dreams of FA Cup glory. It was a different story in the FA Trophy, where Hendon reached a best-ever last 16, which has not been bettered since. A win at Bishop's Stortford was followed by another trip to Waterlooville. Jimmy Quail, back in the managerial hot seat, found himself sitting in the same train carriage as the Waterlooville team travelled to a match a week before the Trophy tie and he took careful notes of the tactics that were discussed. The Ville also left Robson on the bench as a substitute and Hendon won 2–0, a Tony Field penalty, after Brooks had been brought down, making the game safe. It set up a tie at Weymouth and it needed a last-minute equaliser from the Greens to force a replay. In thick fog, Weymouth scored twice in the opening 10 minutes and won 5–1.

For the first time, Hendon entered the League Cup competition and, as a very congested season came to an end, they were the last men standing. Rod Haider's ninth minute goal was all it took for the silverware to come to Claremont Road for what remains the only time. There was nearly a cup treble, too, because Hendon met Enfield at Finchley in the Middlesex Senior Cup, but lost 2–0. The other competition won was the Middlesex Charity Cup, Uxbridge being beaten in the Final at Claremont Road.

Hendon 2 Uxbridge 0
Middlesex Charity Cup Final

Hendon retained the Middlesex Charity Cup on 8 March in what could not be called bloodless style because of the injury sustained by Peter Anderson that saw him enter and leave the pitch on numerous occasions. The incident was after eight minutes, when Anderson jumped with Steve Church to contest a cross. The Hendon full-back won the challenge, but a sickening clash of heads opened up a gash above his eyebrow. Unwilling to leave the game and go to hospital, Anderson had the cut bandaged.

Of course, it did not stop him heading the ball, with the result that both it and the bandage soon took on the same hue as the Uxbridge shirts. The referee ordered Anderson to get his bandage replaced and while he was off the field, Malcolm Robinson should have given the visitors the lead. Phil Duff had a shot blocked by a Hendon defender, and Robinson lifted the rebound over the bar with most of the goal to aim at.

A minute before half-time, Hendon took the lead. The Greens – in their midweek white – won a free-kick near the edge of the Uxbridge penalty area. Rod Haider curled in the ball and Alan Campbell thumped home a header. Early in the second half, Hendon suffered a further blow when goalscorer Campbell went down with a knee injury, but he could not continue, so Steve Jefferies, a striker, had to replace him. Campbell's obvious centre-back replacement was Anderson, who had been advised not to head the ball if possible. The lead was doubled just past the hour mark, again from a set-piece. This time it was a corner, taken by George Brooks. John Butterfield headed on the ball and, as he did so often, Haider arrived unmarked to knock home the loose ball.

After 82 minutes, with Anderson's shirt more red than white, manager Jimmy Quail withdrew him, sending on winger Ray O'Callaghan and forcing Roy Butler into an emergency defensive role. It worked well enough and Hendon were able to see out time to claim the Charity Cup for the 11th time.

Hendon: Dalrymple, Anderson (O'Callaghan, 82), Hand, Deadman, Campbell (Jefferies, 65), Haider, Field, Southam, Butterfield, Butler, Brooks.

Uxbridge: Nicholls, Pickett, Stewart, Robinson, Spoard, Smith, Heggarte, Pashouros, Church, Duff, Howard. Subs: Boulter, Williamson

Barking 0 Hendon 1
Isthmian League Cup Final

At the end of a very congested season, Hendon and Barking met on Thursday 19 May at Harrow Borough. The Blues had finished 13th in the table, nine places below Hendon, but they would be league champions just two years later and the team that played on this evening provided the majority of Eddie McCluskey's title-winners in 1979.

The Isthmian League Cup was so new that no sponsor was in place, but that did not detract from the magnificent rearguard action that brought the trophy to Claremont Road. One goal decided the match and it came after just nine minutes.

Tony Field passed to George Brooks, who sent the ball on to John Butterfield. The former England international slipped a short diagonal pass into space and Rod Haider, as he did so often over the years, was quickly onto it. Nicky Markwick sprinted off his line, but Haider lifted the ball over him and into the net.

It was a rare Hendon attack on an evening when Barking did everything but score on countless occasions. The whole of the Hendon defence – Peter Anderson, Gary Hand, Peter Deadman and Alan Campbell – was heroic as was goalkeeper Malcolm Dalrymple, who produced a number of excellent saves and gave an exemplary display of handling.

Barking went into half-time unsure how they had not got the game already in the bag and, in the second half, they upped the tempo and dominated even more. Peter Burton was magnificent leading the attack and he was ably supported by Laurie Abrahams, who had already agreed to join Charlton Athletic in the summer.

After 68 minutes, Haider fouled Abrahams to concede a penalty, but Dalrymple saved his skipper's blushes with a magnificent save from Abrahams' spot-kick. Five minutes later, Abrahams did have the ball in the net but a linesman's flag was up for offside.

As the Barking attack grew more frantic, Chris Ballard hit the crossbar with a header and, from their next raid, Abrahams saw a shot cannon off the inside of a post and bounce to a Hendon defender, who was able to clear.

With two minutes to go, Hendon launched their second attack of the second half and Brooks suddenly found himself in the clear. The Irishman, normally a clinical finisher, failed to score and it meant that Hendon's fans had another few minutes of anxiety before the final whistle went and they could celebrate a thoroughly undeserved victory.

Barking: Markwick, G Anderson, Makin, Barrett, Twidell, Haley, Ballard, Brothers, Burton, Ford, Abrahams. Sub: Weights.

Hendon: Dalrymple, P. Anderson, Hand, Deadman, Campbell, Haider, Field, Southam, Butler, Butterfield, Brooks. Sub: Swaby

1977–78

The slippery slope towards Isthmian League mediocrity began from the start of this season. Off the field, a lack of leadership in the committee room was a problem with a number of posts being unfilled. There was a distinct lack of a "money man" to take the club forward. Monty Hyams – who refused to take on the mantle of chairman preferring, instead the title of joint president, along with Bobby Butlin – was the main benefactor, but he did not or could not match the wage bills at clubs such as Enfield, Wycombe Wanderers and Dagenham, who completed a fourth consecutive season as the top three. At least on the field there was success in both FA competitions. Watford, managed by Graham Taylor and on their way to the Fourth Division title, won a first round tie 2–0 at Vicarage Road, while in the Trophy, Hendon again reached the last 16, this time going out 2–1 to Barry Fry's Bedford Town in a replay, after beating Romford and Falmouth Town.

Watford 2 Hendon 0
FA Cup 1st round proper

Hendon could hardly have been given a more difficult FA Cup first round proper tie than their trip to Vicarage Road on 26 November. Watford, under the management of Graham Taylor, were just beginning their rise to the upper echelons of English football and they were running away with the Fourth Division championship. The Greens had struggled to overcome Essex Senior League Billericay Town to get past the fourth qualifying round. The Hornets were too strong for Hendon and if it hadn't been for a heroic performance from Gary Steel in the Hendon goal, it could have been embarrassing.

From just about Hendon's first attack, they almost took a shock lead. Peter Anderson fed John Butterfield, who passed to Tony Field. His shot was brilliantly saved by Steve Sherwood to keep the game goalless. It served as a wake-up call for Watford who took the lead just three minutes later. Watford forced a corner which Keith Pritchett delivered to the head of Ross Jenkins. The 6 feet 4 inches tall striker, who towered above every other player on the pitch, headed the ball against the crossbar and Alan Garner knocked home the rebound.

Hendon had little answer to the pace and guile of Watford's wide men Bobby Downes and Luther Blissett, Downes, in particular, giving Anderson a torrid afternoon, while Hand was kept more than busy by the future England international on the other flank.

Blissett picked up a slight knock in the first half and was replaced at half-time by Allan Mayes, who continued where Blissett had left off. After 48 minutes, Denis Booth had a goal disallowed and the same fate befell Jenkins just past the hour mark. It was really only a matter of time before the second goal arrived and it came in the 69th minute when Mayes set up Keith Mercer, who made no mistake.

Taylor said of the game: "There was only one team in it. Our crosses were not put to good use and should have produced more goals."

Jimmy Quail admitted "We did as well as expected and did not disgrace ourselves. In all, it was a good day out and we earned the club a few bob."

Watford: Sherwood, Joslyn, Pritchett, Booth, Ellis, Garner, Downes, Mercer, Jenkins, Bolton, Blissett (Mayes).
Hendon: Steel, Anderson, Hand, Deadman, Campbell, Haider, Field, Southam, Jefferies (Butler), Butterfield, Brooks.

Hendon FC 1977–78, with the League Cup and Middlesex Charity Cup. Back: Tony Williams, Jimmy Quail, fitness co-ordinator, Peter Deadman, Arthur Paisley, Roy Butler, Alan Campbell, Gary Steel, Glenn Swaby, David Hogwood, John Muir; front: Dave Holden, George Brooks, Bobby Southam, Gary Hand, Rod Haider, Tony Field, Denis Holder, Ray O'Callaghan.

Managers continued to come and go. Jimmy Quail left at Christmas, and David Hogwood took over as caretaker, and was appointed permanently at the end of March. One highlight was Rod Haider's testimonial, a well deserved reward for one of the club's outstanding players. In the league, Hendon finished 13th, with 55 points from 42 games. There was some success in Middlesex – Hendon reached both county cup finals, losing the senior final to Enfield and the charity one to Hillingdon Borough. George Brookes was the top scorer with 19 goals.

Hendon 0 Enfield 2
Middlesex Senior Cup Final

Enfield were far too strong for Hendon in a disappointing Middlesex Senior Cup Final at Finchley on 27 March. Any hopes the Greens had of forcing extra time disappeared in the 82nd minute when substitute Bobby Southam – who had been on the pitch for less than five minutes – was dismissed for kicking out at Micky O'Sullivan. Five years after the Amateur Cup Final, only Tony Gibson was still in the Enfield team, while Hendon had Gary Hand, Peter Deadman and Rod Haider. Tony Jennings had switched sides!

The opening goal came in the 34th minute when John Bishop fired in a shot which Gary Steel did well to save. The ball rebounded to Keith Searle and he made no mistake from close range. Hendon's best chance of getting back into the game came midway through the second half, but George Brooks missed an excellent opportunity. With 12 minutes to go, Southam replaced the tiring Dave Holden, but his involvement was over after 81 minutes when referee Philip Don saw him kicking out and Southam's dismissal was inevitable. In the final couple of minutes, Enfield put the game beyond Hendon's reach with a second goal scored by John Knapman.

Enfield: Moore, Wright, Tone, Jennings, Elley, Knapman, O'Sullivan, Gibson, Searle, Glover, Bishop. Subs: Bass, Howell.
Hendon: Steel, Anderson, Hand, Deadman, Campbell, Haider, Field, Swaby, Butler, Holden (Southam, 78), Brooks. Sub: Martin.

Hillingdon Borough 1 Hendon 0
Middlesex Charity Cup Final

Hendon finished their campaign without a trophy after Hillingdon Borough deservedly won the Middlesex Charity Cup on 3 May. The final took place more than four months after Hendon had won a stormy semi-final at Southall on New Year's Day.

The Greens' best chance of the game came after just five minutes, when a pass from George Brooks put Rod Haider in the clear. Unusually the skipper was unable to control the ball properly and the opportunity went begging.

After 19 minutes Hillingdon scored what proved to be the winner. Robin Wainwright played a one-two with Alan Davies, who was tackled late by Alan Campbell. Referee Terry Maber played an excellent advantage, allowing Wainwright to find Chris Hullett and he drilled a low shot past Gary Steel. Five minutes before half-time, Eddie Reeve should have doubled Borough's advantage when he was set up by Ian Osborne. However, from close range, directly in front of goal, he fired wildly over the crossbar.

Hullett limped off during the second half, to be replaced by Chris Low, but the substitute survived for only five minutes before he too succumbed to injury and was replaced by Andy Budd. Borough were in complete control and should, again, have extended their lead in the final five minutes. This time Wainwright was denied by a superb save from Steel.

The final whistle was greeted enthusiastically by Hillingdon fans, who celebrated their ever trophy in their 14 years as Hillingdon Borough.

Hillingdon Borough: Phillips, Davies, Pearce, Millett, Goelson, Hullett (Low 65 [Budd 70]), Wainwright, Reeve, Osborne, Milsom, Cleary.
Hendon: Steel, Anderson, Hand, Deadman, Campbell, Haider, Field, Swaby, Butler, Holden (Southam, 78), Brooks. Sub: Martin.

1978–79: Loss of a legend

The 1978–79 season was marred by the tragic death of assistant manager Bill Fisher, who collapsed and died from a heart attack driving back from training a couple of days before an FA Cup 4th qualifying round tie at home to Hitchin. The match went ahead but a disconsolate Hendon went down 3–1. In the FA Trophy Witney Town won 2–1 at Claremont Road. On the day of Fisher's funeral, Hendon travelled to Granleigh Road to take on Ilford for the last time. The home team, near the bottom of Division One, won this League Cup tie 2–1, but most of the Hendon team's minds were elsewhere. In the Isthmian League, Hendon won more games than they lost, 16 to 12, but the 14 draws resulted in a ninth-place finish. If five of those draws had been turned into victories, Hendon would have been fifth. Enfield knocked Hendon out of the London Senior and Middlesex Senior cups. In the Middlesex Charity Cup, Hendon played Harrow Borough in the Final and won 3–1. Mick Garrini was the top scorer with 19 goals.

Harrow Borough 1 Hendon 3
Middlesex Charity Cup Final

Hendon didn't encounter much in the way of charity as they contested a fourth consecutive Middlesex Charity Cup Final, this time against Isthmian League Division One runners-up Harrow Borough at Earlsmead on 14 May. They won the game comfortably enough, but had to endure a tough physical encounter.

It took just 10 minutes for Hendon to open the scoring. Mick Garrini found Graeme Sewell out wide and the youngster delivered a teasing cross which should been dealt with by Roy Thomas. The defender, however, managed only to knock the ball into the path of player-manager Rod Haider, and he wasted no time is dispatching the ball past Les Currell.

Jimmy Hendrick should have made it 2–0 a few minutes later, but he missed a great chance. At the other end, 45-goal Peter Sharratt was given a chance for number 46 when he rose well at the far post. His header narrowly missed the target and Hendon breathed a sigh of relief.

The second goal arrived two minutes into the second half. Sewell was once again involved, this time firing in a shot which Currell saved well, but could not hold. The ball bounced up and Graham Stewart – like Sewell a product of the Reserves, although not a local resident – nodded home the rebound.

Stewart scored only three goals in the season, but in every game he did notch one, Roy Butler scored too. It looked as if this statistical nicety might not survive this game, until the 87th minute, when a long clearance released the centre forward. Currell came off his line, but Butler shot the ball low past him and into the bottom corner.

In the final minute of normal time a left-wing cross found Borough substitute Alan Clarke unmarked and he converted the chance to give Harrow a consolation goal.

In stoppage time, Borough's other substitute. Bobby Bennett got involved in an incident involving Butler and Harry Manoe. The Harrow defender made a bad challenge on Butler, who got up angrily and confronted the former Southall man – who had been dismissed against Hendon in the 1978 Charity Cup semi-final.

Bennett ran in and threw a punch, an offence for which the referee had no hesitation in producing a red card. It was an unfortunate end to the game, but the referee really didn't have any alternative but to send off the Harrow player.

Harrow Borough: Currell, Metz (Clarke), Thomas, Forrest, Brown, Manoe, Schools, (Bennett), Stein, Sharratt, Steward, Caines.

Hendon: Thomas, Deadman, Hand, Roughan, Campbell, Haider, Hendrick, Stewart, Butler, Garrini, Sewell.

1979–80: Non league changes

In 1979–80, the football map of England changed again. Although the pyramid *per se* had yet to appear, the advent of the Alliance Premier League gave non-league football a very clear apex. Unfortunately, the Isthmian League was not a part of the set up in the inaugural season, 12 teams from the Southern League joining eight from the Northern Premier League. At a stroke, the Isthmian League lost its place as one of the country's top leagues – although the losses in terms of clubs to the Southern and Northern Premier were more keenly felt.

There was a lack of uniform support for the APL, with many clubs and supporters questioning the viability of a national division in non-league football. What has become clear over the past 25 years is that for all the extra travelling involved, what is now the Blue Square National League is far and away the best outside of the Football League, with chasms separating it from the North and South divisions and equally large gaps between them and the Isthmian, Southern and Northern Premier top divisions.

This lack of support was keenly felt at Hendon because, in 1980, Hendon, along with Oxford City, Dagenham and Enfield were invited to join the APL. The latter two jumped at the chance, Oxford City – under the management of Bobby Moore – turned it down, as did Hendon, another example of the club missing an opportunity to progress. On the pitch, the season was another huge disappointment, with 13th place in the league. In the FA Cup, a last second goal saved goalkeeper Alan Thomas's blushes. He misread a cross to put Hendon 2–1 down at Maidenhead United, but the equaliser forced a replay. It was in vain because the Magpies ran out 3–0 winners at Claremont Road in a surprising and disappointing early exit. In the FA Trophy, Barnet won a replay at Underhill in round one to end Hendon's interest.

In the spring of 1979, Hendon had appointed Rod Haider as player-manager, a difficult role at the best of times. Rod was determined not to resign. So, when the committee felt a change was needed in the autumn of 1979, and decided to bring back John Evans, Rod informed them he would have to be sacked – a move they made with huge regret. This was felt even more keenly because Rod also felt he could not continue only as a player at the club and left to join Harrow Borough. Thus ended one of the most distinguished Hendon careers.

A Hendon hero: Rod Haider

The defeat by Skelmersdale in the 1967 Amateur Cup semi-final marked the end of an era. The team that had been a leading force in amateur football from 1963 had broken up. A period of rebuilding was necessary. The key recruit in the summer of 1967, who would make the number 6 shirt his own for the next 12 years, was half-back – central midfielder in today's language – Rod Haider.

Rod was born in Kingsbury, and lived there until he was 11, when his family moved to Bracknell. His father was a football fan, and Rod recalls watching Laurie Topp and Bill Fisher play for Hendon, along with trips to Edgware and Arsenal. He played football at Oliver Goldsmith Primary school, and was selected for the Wembley Schools side.

In Bracknell, he went to Ranelagh Grammar School. But the school did not have a strong football side, and Rod remembers heavy defeats against far bigger schools: "We had 200 boys to choose from, they had 1,200" he ruefully reflected. The headmaster was a keen rugby man, which did not help. So Rod never played for representative teams, but played for Wokingham Town's 'A' team from the age of 12: "It was supposed to be under–19, but became the third team. I did alright, but there were older guys trying to kick lumps out of us." Rod would play for the school on a Saturday morning and Wokingham in the afternoon. He was playing for the reserves when he was 15 and the first team at 16.

In 1960, he moved to Woking, then a force in the Isthmian League, and two years later signed for Kingstonian. As with many leading amateur players at this time, he played some reserve team football for a professional club, in Rod's case Charlton Athletic: "Charlton wanted me to turn pro when I was 21, and offered me terms. Eddie Firmani was the manager, and I remember Mike Bailey, Keith Peacock and Ray Harford were playing there. But I found some of the players were cynical, especially in the reserves. If their contract was up for renewal, they would try, but others would just go through the motions. At least amateurs gave their best in every game." Rod also had a secure job, as an insurance surveyor, and had he not made it, the only alternative was the Southern League. Another factor was the foreign travel available to leading amateur players, something that was not common to Second Division professionals at that time.

Rod recalls Kingstonian as "A good footballing side, but I felt I would never win anything there. Hendon was a more business-like set up, and wanted to win trophies."

So, despite a difficult journey from his home in Wokingham, Rod moved to Claremont Road in 1967. He had played for Surrey while at Kingstonian, and had become established in the England amateur team, making his debut in 1966.

Bill Fisher was the manager at Hendon when Rod arrived: "He was a nice guy, very straightforward, not forceful. He was very loyal to Hendon — maybe he was 'used' a bit by the club."

Success did not come immediately at Hendon, although Rod continued to play regularly for England, and was part of the Great Britain team in the Olympic qualifying tournament in 1967–68. Rod ended up as the record holder for appearances for the England amateur team with 65 caps: "I enjoyed playing for my country". One particularly memorable tour was to the West Indies: "One match had to be delayed because of a monsoon. In Trinidad we played on the test match ground, the Trinidad Oval. We also played at the test match ground in Guyana. I made my debut against the Republic of Ireland in March 1966 at Brentford. Jimmy Conway was playing for them — he later joined Fulham. One of their wingers played wearing glasses. I remember beating Scotland 5–0 at Celtic Park. Most of their players came from Queens Park FC." Rod also played for Middlesex Wanderers, and recalls playing on a pitch of packed sand in Bahrain.

At Hendon, the arrival of John Evans as coach in 1971 heralded a new era. By now Rod was club captain, and has many memories of this period. A key match was the 1972 Amateur Cup semi-final at Brentford: "There were lots of Wycombe fans there, and that inspired us. They were favourites, but we had some great competitors in our team, such as John Swannell and Peter Deadman." He recalls Peter Deadman's great winner: "When we had a corner, I would be on the goal line. If it went out of the box I would go wide, as Peter usually couldn't shoot straight and I would head the ball back into the middle. But that shot of his flew into the net."

Rod had played at Wembley for Great Britain against Bulgaria in 1971, but found the Amateur Cup final a different experience: "It was very quiet for the Great Britain game, but against Enfield the crowd gave us a lift. We could have been 1–0 down in the first five minutes. Kenny Gray was through but fluffed his shot. Our first goal — John Baker's shot — looped up in the air, and then Tony Bass scored from a free-kick on the left. Tony was a wonderful header of the ball. Tony Jennings would take free kicks, Tony would head the ball back into the middle and I would have a chance to score. The Amateur Cup Final wasn't a great game of football, but it was well supported."

Winning the Amateur Cup led to the matches against Unione: "Some of their players were former professionals, and it was a kicking match. We did quite well, and didn't get provoked when they were trying to wind us up. Derek Baker went on the trip, despite having a broken leg, and when we visited the Leaning Tower of Pisa, we took photos of him 'holding up' the tower with his crutch." That season Hendon also won the Isthmian League, with a long unbeaten run: "We beat Leatherhead 1-0, I scored, and the results that day meant that we couldn't be caught. So we were celebrating. We explained why to the Leatherhead players, who replied 'We'd all given up the League at Christmas' [such had been Hendon's domination]".

The Newcastle match, and Rod's equalising goal, is another cherished memory, although he says that for the underdogs to win, they only get one chance.

Rod remembers John Evans as "an efficient player who knew about football. He was a good motivator. On one occasion we'd played abysmally in the first half. He sat us down, and said 'you can only do better' that took the pressure off us and we won the game." Rod also regards Jimmy Quail as "a very good player and smashing guy."

Being captain of a team of strong minded players bought its own problems: "If a player wasn't playing well, I would aim to bring him into the game, and get him playing. John Swannell and Alan Phillips would shout at me, but I wouldn't shout at the players." Rod remembers Tony Harding and Bobby Cantwell as "great characters" and felt that it was important that the players socialised together.

Rod was only booked once in his career, when he was alleged to have moved out of the wall when a free kick was being taken. Fortunately, a supporter had taken a photo showing the referee was wrong, and the booking was overturned on appeal.

After the game went 'open' in the summer of 1974, Rod stayed at Hendon. His loyalty to Bill Fisher was an important factor in this decision. In 1975, Hendon beat a Football League team in the FA Cup for the first time, beating Reading 1–0 at Claremont Road. Rod recalls: "That was a good performance. Gary Peters, who lived near me, played well for them, otherwise they didn't turn up."

The club gave Rod a testimonial season in 1977–78, which he appreciated. However, problems were on the horizon. He became player manager in the spring of 1979, taking the post reluctantly permanently before the 1979–80 season. But after three months, the club decided to bring John Evans back, and Rod refused to resign, so was sacked: "I had made promises to people, and did not want to continue as a player after being player manager." It was a sad end to 12 years at Claremont Road. John Evans found it difficult to get a player to wear the number 6 shirt in the first match after Rod's departure.

A few weeks off followed, then Rod went training with Harrow Borough, played initially for their reserves, and then for a season and a half in the first team, including against Hendon, which must have seemed strange. By then he was 38, and went to Slough to manage their reserve team, although he played a few first team games. Some coaching at Hayes followed: "I enjoyed coaching if you had players who wanted to listen and learn, then you can show them things. But I didn't want to be a manager."

At the age of 43, he decided to return to playing, for Corinthian Casuals veterans: "I played until I was 57, and then I was dropped for being too old!" He does not have any involvement in the game today, but still enjoys playing golf. He made over 600 appearances for Hendon, and led the team to some of their most memorable triumphs in the League and the cup competitions.

1980–81

With Enfield and Dagenham now in the Alliance Premier League, Hendon took advantage of a weakened Isthmian competition to finish sixth, recording 18 victories. In the FA Cup, Hendon went out in a third qualifying round replay to Aylesbury United at Turnfurlong Lane, a late own goal sealing their fate. The Dons drew each in each of the three qualifying rounds, winning replays against Hillingdon Borough and Woking, before losing to the Ducks.

The FA Trophy showed what might have been. Hendon went out to the eventual winners, Isthmian League Division One Bishop's Stortford in the final qualifying round. The Middlesex Senior Cup semi-final defeat against Hayes was notable if only because a player – Kevin Folan – missed the match because he went to the wrong ground. From Derbyshire, Folan had recently moved into north London and signed for Hendon. He made his debut at Bromley, whose ground is at Hayes Lane. He soon played at Church Road, Hayes, but mixed up the two when it came to the county cup semi-final and was severely disciplined for travelling to Kent for the match against Hayes.

Another new arrival at Claremont Road that season would give Hendon fine service in two spells. Dermot Drummy, a London-born Irish youth international was sent by Arsenal on loan to Blackpool, where he made five Football League appearances. He was a fine ball player who would have been an out-and-out winger in the old days, but was more a wide midfielder in his time.

Hendon made a significant change by hiring a new manager with no previous links with the club, the first since Ron Patterson in 1967. Former Wealdstone manager Ken Payne arrived, with his assistant, former Swindon Town full-back, Alan Fursdon. They recruited aggressively and signed some expensive and experienced players, including two from the Birmingham area, attacking midfielder Trevor Dark and striker Bobby Gough, a prolific goalscorer in the Football League, former Barnet striker Martin Sperrin and a couple of youngsters from Wealdstone, Anthony Bennett and Tom Murphy.

1981–82

The quality of the team could be seen during this season as Abingdon Town, Ampthill Town, Banbury United – in a spectacular pair of games featuring a 55-yard strike from Paul Currie in the first game and miraculous double comeback in a 4–3 extra time win in the replay – Tring Town and Harrow Borough were seen off in the FA Cup to set up a first round proper tie against Wycombe Wanderers on 21 November.

Hendon 1 Wycombe Wanderers 1
Wycombe Wanderers 2 Hendon 0
FA Cup 1st round proper and replay

Hendon's FA Cup run to the competition proper was a rather long and tortuous one. Their reward after seeing off, Abingdon Town, Ampthill (both very unconvincingly), Banbury United (in a heart-stopping replay described elsewhere), Chesham and Tring (quite comfortably), drew fellow Isthmians Wycombe Wanderers in the first round.

The match ball was sponsored by long-time supporter Adrian Warren, who had just emigrated to Australia and it burst during the match. This was a game Hendon should have won but had to settle for a replay.

After eight minutes, a cross from Dermot Drummy was headed goalwards by Kevin Folan, but Gary Lester made a good save. Midway through the first half, Wycombe attacked and Steve Long was denied by a brilliant save from Fred Smart. From Bobby Dell's corner Anton Vircavs headed home to give Wycombe an undeserved lead.

Although Hendon were on top, chances were few and far between. The closest the Greens came to an equaliser was in the 64th minute when Peter Deadman, who had scored spectacularly against the Chairboys in the 1972 Amateur Cup semi-final, almost repeated the dose with another pile-driver. This time Wycombe were saved by the crossbar. Two minutes later, Deadman set up Anthony Bennett for Hendon's equaliser, flicking on a Drummy corner. Bennett's diving header from close range gave Lester no chance. With 15 minutes left, Hendon should have won the tie when Paul Currie found an unmarked Folan a few yards out. Sadly for Hendon, his header was off target.

Three days later, the replay at Loakes Park was a one-sided affair with Wycombe controlling for long periods. Hendon had two chances in the first half. After 20 minutes, Drummy had a run and shot that flew inches wide of the target with Lester beaten. Then, just before half-time, the goalkeeper made a good save to keep out a Bobby Gough effort. Ten minutes into the second half, Hendon forced a trio of corners, but the Wycombe defence held firm and the spell of pressure fizzled out.

After 65 minutes, Ken Wilson, who had replaced Mark West seven minutes earlier, attacked down the wing. His cross was back-heeled by Terry Glynn right into the path of Howard Kennedy, who fired past Smart. Ten minutes later, with the Loakes Park faithful baying for blood, Wycombe made the game safe. Former Hendon player Terry Glynn applied the final touch and Hendon's FA Cup dreams were over.

Hendon: Smart, Bennett, Hand, Deadman, Anderson (Sperrin, 30), Murphy, Drummy, Gough, Folan, Currie, Brannagan.
Replay: Smart, Bennett, Hand, Deadman, Sylvester, Murphy, Drummy, Gough, Folan, Currie, Brannagan (Simpson 73).
Wycombe: Lester, Birdseye, Borg, Toll, Vircavs, West (Wilson, 62), Dell, Kennedy, Glynn, Long, Jacobs.
Replay: Lester, Birdseye, Borg, Toll, Vircavs, West (Wilson, 58), Dell, Kennedy, Glynn, Long, Jacobs.

Hendon on the attack against Wycombe in the FA Cup (Photo: HT – Peter Beal)

The FA Trophy run was also remarkable. It started on a snow and ice-covered Claremont Road, where Hendon scored in the last minute to beat Barnet 2–1, Sperrin looping a tame header over Gary Phillips. A long cold winter left Claremont Road – and most other grounds in the south-east – unplayable, but Hendon got around this. Somehow the Greens were able to hire Loftus Road, the home of Queens Park Rangers, where Tony Currie was a player on the newly-installed Astroturf pitch. Taunton Town came up from Somerset on a Sunday afternoon for the FA Trophy first round tie, which followed an Alliance Premier League scoreless bore-draw between Barnet and AP Leamington. Hendon, with Paul Currie in fine form, appeared to have the right footwear for the surface, something none of the other three teams playing at Loftus Road that day could boast – maybe the Currie brothers were able to get the right footwear from Rangers – and they ran out easy 4–1 winners. The season and club's future, however, was about to lurch into uncertainty.

The next round involved a trip to Cheshire and Witton Albion of Stalybridge. Albion had former Walton & Hersham striker Russ Perkins as their player-manager, and he played a key role in their free kick move which led to the only goal of the game. It was a long and unhappy journey back to London, but that was nothing compared to the shock which followed: before the next game on the Tuesday night, Dark, Gough, Sperrin, Currie, Peter Deadman and Peter Anderson were all released on financial grounds.

Payne and Fursden not surprisingly left soon after and the management role was given to youth team manager Dave Mawson, a local club cricketer, but a man with neither knowledge nor experience of non league football at this level. The team plummeted down the Isthmian League, finishing 13th after being in a challenging position in February. A Middlesex Charity Cup Final defeat at Uxbridge, a flattering 2–1, ended a season which had started with high hopes and ended with worries on all fronts.

Uxbridge 2 Hendon 1
Middlesex Charity Cup Final

Hendon had confirmed Dave Mawson's appointment as permanent manager a week before the Final, which was on 11 May at Uxbridge, resulting in the immediate departure of influential midfielder Pat Morrissey, who had been interested in the role himself. With everything else going on, it was no surprised that the Greens were more than a bit disjointed and were there for the taking by the Spartan League club.

Uxbridge scored after 10 minutes, Steve Williamson scoring from close range following a throw-in by Mike Pickett. Two minutes into the second half, Ali Sylvester brought down Ian Howard in the penalty area and Gordon Stewart made no mistake from the spot to make it 2–0. The home were in complete control, with goalkeeper Roger Nicholls (the father of future Hendon player Mark Nicholls and no relation to Hendon sub Alex Nicholls) rarely tested.

Hendon did give themselves a glimmer of hope with a couple of minutes to go when Dencell Green (who would later briefly open the bowling for both Somerset and England 'A' before injuries ended both his football and cricket careers) headed home a cross from Phil Brown. It was too little too late.

Uxbridge: R. Nicholls, Pickett, Stewart, Hegarty, Spoard, Turner, C. Williamson, S. Williamson, Church, Duff, Howard. Subs: Everley, Weller (not used)
Hendon: Taylor, Wiltshire, Hand, Sylvester, O'Brien, Bennett, Drummy, Green, Brown, Bhatia, Sewell (Simpson, 55). Sub: A. Nicholls

A Hendon hero: Peter Deadman

Peter Deadman was one of the key players in Hendon's great period in the early 1970s. He played around 550 games for the club in two spells, part of a playing career that lasted over 25 years. As an article in the *Daily Telegraph* pointed out on 1986, he was the last England amateur international still playing – amateur status having been abolished 12 years earlier.

Peter lives in Upminster now, and went to school in that area. He first played organised football at primary school, and then went to Hornchurch Grammar School for seven years. While there he played for the District team, the Essex Grammar Schools team and attended the FA Schools Week.

One of his school friends was Barry Chapman, whose father was Eddie Chapman, the West Ham United club secretary. Eddie Chapman asked West Ham's chief scout, Wally St Pier to go and watch his son play. Peter was playing in the match, and he was invited to Upton Park for training. He had always been a West Ham supporter, and remembers taking his wife Sue to watch them when he was 11 years old!

Peter went to Upton Park on Tuesday and Thursday evenings for training: "I took the bus to Hornchurch, then the tube to Upton Park. I had to do my homework as well, and walked home from the bus on my own after training." Peter made his debut for the youth team at Stamford Bridge on 6 January 1962 in a South East Counties League match. Dennis Burnett, Peter Bennett and Bobby Howe were in the West Ham team; John Hollins and Ron Harris were playing for Chelsea. However, school matches took priority for Peter, and "after training with West Ham for two years, Ron Greenwood wanted me to turn professional, but I decided to go to university. My dad had played football at club level, and encouraged me to play, but also to look after my education. I thought I could turn professional later if I wanted to."

Peter went to study chemistry at Loughborough, and played for the Loughborough Colleges team. His first appearance in the Amateur Cup was for Loughborough Colleges, at Bishop Auckland: "John Evans was in his final year, and Dario Gradi was there as well. John was the captain and very tough. He told us how we'd been good players for our counties, but now we had to start from scratch, as everyone had played at county level. Loughborough ran six teams, and I played for the first team in a friendly at Wealdstone before playing in the Amateur Cup."

The third year of Peter's course was spent on placement in industry, and he returned to London to play for West Ham again. He had been invited to pre-season training, and played for Clapton in the Isthmian League, when West Ham were asked to help their neighbours out when they were short of players. But Clapton refused to release him from the Isthmian League forms he had signed, much to Ron Greenwood's annoyance, so he spent a year playing for West Ham's 'A' team in the Metropolitan League.

Peter has many fond memories of the players at West Ham at this time. Frank Lampard (senior) was a colleague in the 'A' team: "he was very focussed on the game, and very serious. He did a proper warm up which was unusual then." Peter also remembers Harry Redknapp, Eddie Bovington and, of course, Bobby Moore. Some of the players would go to see Bill Jenkins, the West Ham physio, in his surgery across the road from the ground: "If Bobby Moore was there he would take his place in the queue like everyone else" Peter recalls.

Another team mate in the 'A' team was Alan Sealy, who had scored the two goals that won West Ham the European Cup Winners Cup in 1965, but then broken his leg in a pre-season training accident.

When Peter returned to university, he could only play for Loughborough University, not the stronger Colleges team. He would have preferred to play for Barking, but was told he should represent the university. However, a bonus was playing for – and captaining - the England Universities team, including a memorable trip to Iran: "I was interviewed on Iranian television. The place was a culture shock, we played on sand in very hot conditions, and got dysentery from the water."

When he finished university, Peter returned to London and joined Barking where John Evans was player-coach and building a successful team. In 1970, he went with John to Hendon, playing his part in one of the best defences in amateur football.

One particularly fond memory for Peter is the Amateur Cup win in 1972, and his winning goal in the semi-final at Griffin Park: "There was a huge crowd there, and the Wycombe supporters hated me. We never thought about losing. I was so mad when they equalised that I went up field and scored." The goal, a 25 yard shot following a corner, was truly memorable, and took Hendon to Wembley: "I was certain we would win at Wembley. It was everyone's dream to play there." Peter says that Alan Phillips was the best centre half he played with, although Alan Campbell and John Delaney were also very good.

The next season, Peter played a key role in Hendon winning the league - "we hardly let in any goals" - and he believes Hendon would have won the league in 1973–74 if three players hadn't left to join Enfield.

Another great memory from this period is the FA Cup run in 1973–74. Peter was injured playing for England before the first match against Barnet: "I got a gash on my ankle and it had to be stitched. I made a pad to fit around my ankle so I could play. But I could hardly walk, let alone run. I did a bad back pass and they scored, so I was relieved when we equalised to earn a replay. At Merthyr, the crowd was very hostile, it was a very competitive game and was one of our best wins. For the Newcastle match, I had dislocated my shoulder on the Wednesday before the game. Jimmy Quail said have a fitness test, and I don't know how I got through the game. We could have won up there, but for the replay they knew what to expect from us."

Peter left Hendon in the summer of 1974, linking up again with John Evans for two years at Ilford before returning to Claremont Road in 1976. He played a further six years for Hendon, but it was a not a good time for the club, with a high turnover in managers and players. In February 1982, he and Peter Anderson were released following an FA Trophy defeat, as they were not on contracts. A short spell with Dagenham and Redbridge in the Conference followed. But although Peter enjoyed playing for Ted Hardy, he found the travelling too much, and in August 1982 signed for Grays Athletic.

Peter enjoyed his time at Grays, who were going up the pyramid, winning three promotions and two cups in his spell there. He played until he was around 42, then coached the reserves for a couple of years. One special memory is playing for Grays reserves with his two sons, John and Steve. John went on to play for Hendon before retiring through injury. "I enjoyed running the team, I did everything from taking the kit home to wash it to making the sandwiches. We produced some good players for the first team." The Grays Athletic history, published in 1990, includes Peter in the team of the decade for the 1980s, and top of the list of special club players of the decade.

Changes at the club saw Peter leave Grays, and he now enjoys cross country running to keep fit. He took early retirement from his printing job at the Bank of England in 1995, and now teaches sport at a special needs school. Having always wanted to work with children, he finds the job very rewarding.

As well as playing football at club level, Peter also made over 40 appearances for the England team, and was part of the Great Britain squad that played in the Olympic qualifying competition. Charles Hughes, the England amateur international manager, was a major influence on Peter and someone he greatly respected: "He was very disciplined, we were scared of him". Peter remembers that once they were with the full England team on tour, and Bobby Moore, Peter Shilton and Alan Ball were drinking Champagne and "wished us the best for our match. Charles Hughes told us: 'Don't you behave like that'". Another memorable occasion was a practice match against the full England team and having the chance to talk to Bobby Charlton at half-time.

Peter feels that some of the England amateur team's best performances were away from home, often in front of large hostile crowds, whereas at home the crowds were – inevitably – smaller. One memorable trip was to the West Indies, where he broke his cheekbone, and was operated on by the same surgeon who had done Geoffrey Boycott's fracture. Trips to Bahrain, Scandinavia and Iceland were also successful. The 1973 European tour, when the team were unbeaten and played Italy before the full England team faced Italy was very special. However, training for the Olympics was very demanding, with trips to Bisham Abbey for Sunday training and then a trip to the north or the midlands for a friendly against a professional club.

The best players Peter played with were John Swannell – "so enthusiastic and fearless" – Rod Haider – "a tremendous player" – and Roger Day – "incredible and brave". Hendon fans would say that Peter was one of the club's best defenders since the war, helping bring the Amateur Cup and Isthmian League title to Claremont Road.

1982–83

The team Mr Mawson had for the 1982–83 season was, to be kind, callow. Teenagers filled many positions and they were ill-equipped for the challenge. Tony Jennings returned to the club in a coaching capacity, but it was a brief appointment and John Drabwell – brother of former amateur international Peter – replaced him. The Isthmian League found a new sponsor, Servowarm, and Hendon celebrated this deal by recording back-to-back four-goal victories at home to relegation-bound Woking and Leatherhead.

Within a couple of weeks, a new broom was sweeping out the cobwebs of the old committee. Charles Geary, club secretary during the 1960s, returned as chairman and he immediately replaced the incumbent secretary Eric Abrey and treasurer Mick Scott with Dave Barrett and Tony Williams – the latter not being the publisher of the *Non League Directory*. Soon it was the turn of Mawson and Drabwell to move on and Gary Hand and Jimmy Quail took charge until the end of the season. At the end of a season of such turmoil, 12th place was not a bad finish. Neither the FA Cup, nor the FA Trophy had brought any success with early exits suffered against Wealdstone and, embarrassingly, Tilbury, 3–0 at home. There was also little progress in any of the county cups. Dermot Drummy was top scorer with 14 goals.

Monty Hyams presents John Evans with life membership of the club in 1983

1983–84

Gary Hand could not continue as manager for the new season, and Jimmy Quail also left. Another outsider was brought in. He was Roy Ruffell, who had enjoyed success at both Hayes and Hounslow, and was unfortunate to be sacked from both clubs with them sitting in second place in the League at the time. He had a young team and made them competitive.

A shock home defeat to Addlestone & Weybridge in the FA Cup was compensated for by an excellent couple of FA Trophy results, including a 3–2 win at Weymouth.

The season ended with Hendon in ninth place in the league and they also reached the Middlesex Senior Cup Final. This match at Harrow Borough, however, was a disaster because Wembley routed the Greens. Ruffell lost his temper with the players in the dressing room after the game, the reason given by Charles Geary for dismissing him and replacing him for the 1984–85 season with Eddie Presland, who had been hugely successful at both Dagenham and Dulwich Hamlet. Steve Wilkins and Gary Allen were joint top scorers, with 10 goals each. It was the club's 75th season, and to mark this, friendly games were played against an Isthmian League XI and Middlesex Wanderers.

Hendon 1 Wembley 5
Middlesex Senior Cup Final

Hendon were torn apart at Earlsmead on 23 April by an inspired performance from Wembley striker Richard Cadette, who was soon to embark on a long and successful

Football League career. The Lions finally turned their superiority into goals only in the final nine minutes and they struck four times in that period.

For the Greens, chairman Charles Geary revealed that manager Roy Ruffell's post-match dressing-room tantrum was the reason for his dismissal a few weeks later.

Wembley took the lead after just 12 minutes when a cross-shot from Steve Jackson flew past Clive Kemplen. The Lions continued to set the pace and the Hendon defence was at full stretch to keep the lead at one.

Amazingly, out of nothing, Hendon drew level after 36 minutes, Awarded a free-kick just beyond the angle of the penalty area, Steve Wilkins lined up the ball for a shot. His brother Ray could not have struck the ball better and Fred Smart could do little more than pick the ball out of the back of the net.

Kemplen produced a magnificent save to deny Cadette after 72 minutes and, two minutes later, Hendon had a lucky escape when Andy O'Brien conceded a penalty, fouling the rampant Cadette. Ian Whitehead took the spot kick but he fired wide.

Nine minutes from time, O'Brien was again penalised inside his own penalty area, this time for handball and Whitehead made no mistake with his second spot-kick to give Wembley the lead again. Three minutes later Jackson was on hand to finish of a move orchestrated by Cadette.

It got worse for Hendon in the 87th minute when Don Lucas fired in a long-range shot to make it 4–1 one. Then, in the final minute, having teased and tormented Hendon to destruction Cadette got the goal he thoroughly deserved.

Wembley: Smart, Whitehead, I. Lucas, Murphy, Shields, Simpson, Jackson, Schools, McGonigle (D. Lucas, 75), Cadette, O' Doherty. Subs: Bhatia.

Hendon: Kemplen, Waddock, Hand, Bradford, O'Brien, Stapleton, Drummy, Hudson (Mitchell, 65), Allen, Adrian Smith, Wilkins. Sub: Holland

Hendon FC 1984–85: Back: Dave Barrett, Ray Cochrane, ?, Gary Hand, Steve Ringrose, Robbie Holland, Bobby Knock, Tony Baldwin, Stuart Mitchell, Steve Wilkins, Eddie Presland, Martin Binks; front: Andy O'Brien, Gary Allen, Gary Waddock, Derek Williams, Neil Norman, Gary Hewitt, Adrian Smith, Alan Roughan.

1984–85

It would be something of an understatement to say that Eddie Presland's magic didn't work at Claremont Road. First hurdle FA Cup and Trophy exits – at home to Dunstable and at Harlow Town, respectively, were no more than Hendon deserved and a season of struggle ensued.

Eddie Presland was relieved of his duties in February, with Gary Hand again taking over, this time being able to continue into the following campaign. Relegation was avoided but only just as Hendon ended up in 17th position with just 46 points, three points clear of Leytonstone/Ilford who finished 21st.

The Middlesex Charity Cup provided some relief, with a 5–1 win over Feltham in the Final at Claremont Road on 7 May. George Duck was the top scorer with 20 goals.

Hendon 5 Feltham 1
Middlesex Charity Cup Final

Hendon ended five barren seasons with the victory in the Middlesex Charity Cup Final, beating an ill-disciplined Feltham team which had done well to even reach this stage. Apart from Hendon's victory, the match was notable for Phil Gridelet's senior debut. He was the third member of John Newing's all-conquering under–18 squad to make it to the first team, joining Steve Newing and Danny Worley.

Gridelet was named as a substitute but was called into action after just 21 minutes when centre-back John Palmer caught an elbow in the face and suffered a very messy broken nose. It seemed a deliberate offence, but the aggressor received no sanction from the referee.

It took until the 40th minute for Hendon to break the deadlock, but having taken the lead, they quickly doubled it. First George Duck played a ball into space and Martin Coates ran to slip the ball into the net. Three minutes later, the predatory Gary Allen lost his marker and guided home a header from a corner.

After 62 minutes, the violence reached its peak as Kelvin McDonagh delivered a vicious elbow to the face of left-back Paul Robinson. The referee didn't see the incident, but the Hendon bench did, as well as the linesman and after a very brief consultation between the two officials, McDonagh was dismissed. This galvanised Feltham and they actually pulled a goal back with 15 minutes to go, Mike Strzadala netting.

However, the effort of playing a man short for half an hour proved too much for Feltham and Hendon added three goals in the final dozen or so minutes. Two minutes after conceding the goal to Strzadala, Duck restored the two-goal lead with a close-range header.

With four minutes to go, Coates grabbed his second of the evening, again arriving late in the penalty area to finish off a flowing move. Two minutes later, substitute Bob O'Leary, who had replaced the groggy Robinson, rounded off a successful evening's work with the fifth.

Hendon: Broughton, Langley, Curren, Palmer (Gridelet, 21), O'Brien, Hewitt, Coates, Robinson (O'Leary, 71), Allen, Duck, Wilkins.
Feltham: Bones, Noad, Hyatt, McDonagh, Girvan, Wainwright, Clarke, Woodard, Strzadala, Reynolds, Beach. Subs: Fionda, Edwards (both played)

1985–86

The off-season recruitment didn't go well and Hendon looked awfully weak in pre-season. Quite how bad things were became clear in the first week of September when Ruislip Manor easily won an FA Cup first qualifying round game at Grosvenor Vale, albeit only 1–0. The previous week, Hendon had travelled to Epsom & Ewell, strolled into a 2–0 lead and appeared to be coasting. It ended 5–3 to the hosts as the Hendon defence disintegrated in the second half. The FA Trophy campaign also lasted a solitary outing, Wokingham Town winning 1–0 at Claremont Road. Even the arrival of Tony Currie for a handful of games couldn't turn things around. It needed something far more than the fading brilliance of a former England international. Hendon hit rock-bottom with a defeat at Barking in early November and they were still there when Gary Hand was dismissed.

Desperate measures were needed and they arrived in the shape of non league legend Ted Hardy. A championship winner at almost every club he managed, his task at Claremont Road was significantly tougher: to take a team hopelessly out of its depth and take it to the promised land of safety in 20th position. It wasn't easy and things looked bleak indeed on a March night in Farnborough as the Greens slumped to a 5–0 defeat. Their position was parlous to say the least: after 31 matches, Hendon had 20 points, and were nine points behind Epsom & Ewell, who had a mere eight games in hand. In what must rank as one of the greatest runs in non league football history, Hendon didn't lose another match all season, playing 11 League fixtures and two cup ties. They won their way through the Middlesex Senior Cup Final and eventually saw off Isthmian League Division Two Southall – FA Vase finalists a year earlier – at Southbury Road on 31 March. There was also a good run in the London Senior Cup, which ended with a 2–0 defeat at Finchley in the semi-final.

Hendon 2 Southall 0 after extra time
Middlesex Senior Cup Final

Hendon won a trophy for a second successive season when they overcame a stern examination from 1985 FA Vase finalists Southall in an afternoon of ever-changing weather at Enfield. During the match, there was sunshine, rain, hail, thunder and even snow. Midway through the first period of extra time, there was the distinctly odd sight of the giant floodlights with the big "E" formation shining futilely at full blast as there was a spell of bright sunshine.

The game didn't match the weather for its variety. Hendon who were in the middle of a desperate relegation battle, and probably would have preferred a League match, while Southall were determined to show they could match a team two divisions above them.

At the back, Southall had the clear man of the match in Mick McGovern. The former QPR central defender did not dirty his kit until the 115th minute, while both teammates and opponents wore similar all-brown uniforms, courtesy of the slippery, muddy conditions. Chances at both ends were rare, with Andy O'Brien and Roger Wade doing well to keep Bruce Rowe and future full England international Les Ferdinand quiet.

Southall, who had the better of the second 45 minutes, thought they had made the breakthrough with 11 minutes remaining when Rowe bundled the ball home. The referee, however, had spotted a foul on Greens' goalkeeper Mark Broughton so the effort was disallowed.

It took until the first period of extra time for Southall to have a lucky escape. Steve

246

Newing, who had replaced Danny Worley, tried a drive from 25 yards. The ball crashed against the crossbar but the rebound favoured Southall.

Newing's strength made a big difference and as Southall tired in the difficult conditions, he took control of the game. After 110 minutes, he delivered an inch-perfect pass into the path of Colin Tate, who fired Hendon into the lead.

Five minutes later, McGovern finally got his shorts dirty. Mick Kiely and Tate launched a joint attack. The former's strike was blocked but it fell to Tate who played almost a one-two with McGovern before knocking in the second chance from five yards. In his effort to keep out the second Tate shot, McGovern fell backwards and ended up sitting on the grass in the back of the net, probably the least muddy part of the playing area.

There was no way back for Southall and Hendon could not only celebrate some silverware, but look forward to an eventually successful battle against relegation.

Hendon: Broughton, Smart, Derek Brown, Wade, O'Brien, Gridelet, Gibson, Harding, Kiely, Tate, Worley (Newing, 71). Sub: Shirt.

Southall: Bridges, James, Holland, McGovern, Croad, Powell, Rowe, Sweales, Ferdinand, Cordery, Pierre. Sub: Richmond (played).

Ted Hardy brought in his style of player, veterans who knew not only how to look after themselves, but also the dark arts and how to win from difficult positions. Much-decorated players such as John Knapman, Roger Wade and Tony Gibson righted the ship, joined by the amazing Steve Parsons, a player of incredible confidence, but a gambler of the worst kind; his pro career had ended when he made a veteran defender look bad once too often and the retaliatory tackle snapped his leg, leaving it an inch shorter than the other one.

Somehow, the final 11 League fixtures brought six victories and five draws, 23 priceless points. So many games in this run stand out in the memory: a 4–1 drubbing of Billericay at New Lodge and two equalisers in the last five minutes of a game at Wokingham. The Greens' final game of the season was on Tuesday 29 April 1986, at Slough. Wade scored inside the first five minutes; looking yards offside, he lobbed the goalkeeper from 25 yards. The defence, with goalkeeper Mark Broughton pulling off one 'Gordon Banks-type' save, held out under extreme pressure until the interval. Early in the second half, Mick Kiely and Andy O'Brien added goals, then Slough pulled one back. The nerves were jangling until the 88th minute when a break out of defence ended with Gibson scoring from five yards. The elation of safety lasted – in the author's case – for days after.

1986–87: Two cup finals

The next two seasons were different – Hendon were distinctly successful. In 1986–87, the Greens played an incredible club record 76 competitive matches, including one which was void. Neither the FA Cup, nor the FA Trophy saw significant progress, Welling United in the third qualifying round and Tooting & Mitcham United, surprisingly, in the second qualifying round, beating Hendon in the FA Cup and Trophy, respectively. However, the new Premier Inter-League Cup, sponsored by General Motors Acceptance Corporation (GMAC) and Isthmian League Cup (sponsored by Hitachi) were much more to the Greens' liking.

The GMAC Cup involved the 22 teams of the Alliance Premier League and the top divisions of each of the Isthmian, Southern and Northern Premier Leagues. For non-league teams it could be considered second in prestige or difficulty to win behind the FA Trophy. Hendon started with a narrow victory at Hayes before stepping up through several gears. Superb performances against Conference clubs Fisher Athletic at home, Sutton United away – a bogey ground for more than a decade – and Dagenham at home and away, saw Hendon reach the semi-final. A Sunday trip to FA Trophy finalists Burton Albion ended in a violent 1–1 draw; the replay was won 3–1 after extra time. The organisers had promised the finalists a trip to a First Division club for the Final and both Maine Road (Manchester City) and Villa Park (Aston Villa) were mooted as possible venues. In the end, the competition ran later than hoped, the invitations were rescinded and Hendon lost a coin toss held by telephone for home rights with Kettering Town.

In the AC Delco (Isthmian League) Cup, Hendon's progress was serene and relatively unmemorable until the semi-final. Yeovil Town were undoubtedly the 'big boys' of the Isthmian League and they had home advantage in the first leg. It took less than 60 seconds for the home fans to be raging at the referee as a handball by Phil Gridelet went unpunished. Two goals in three late first-half minutes, from Mick Kiely and Dermot Drummy – the second caused by goalkeeper Dave Walter stumbling on the slope and dropping the ball behind him as he tried to gather a lob – put Hendon on top and a magnificent second half rearguard action preserved the 2–0 first leg victory. Everything went against the Glovers in the second leg: the match was postponed 30 minutes before kick-off after an afternoon storm flooded Claremont Road; goalkeeper Walter told his manager that – as a farmer in lambing season – he wouldn't and couldn't make the same trip 24 hours later; their coach broke down at Staples Corner on the way back to Somerset; then, when the game was played 24 hours later on a very heavy pitch, Hendon won 2–1 to reach the Final against Bognor Regis Town at Windsor & Eton.

There was equal drama in the quarter-final of the Middlesex Senior Cup against Harrow Borough. The first match, at Claremont Road, was drawn, the replay at Earlsmead went Harrow's way... except they played two men who had not been registered in time to play in the first game. They asked the Middlesex FA for permission to play them and, against the competition rules, were told to go ahead. Hendon appealed and won but the County FA ordered a new match, voiding the replay. Four days before the semi-final, the replay of the quarter-final replay was postponed because of a waterlogged pitch, despite no rain having fallen for a couple of days. The match finally went ahead on the Thursday night. Harrow raced into a 3–0 half-time lead and also missed a penalty. As the Hendon players returned to the pitch for the second half, the supporters cheered them long and loudly and left-back Alan Roughan said to striker Colin Tate, "Come on, let's give this a real go for the boys behind the goal."

It took 22 seconds for Roughan to send in Tate for Hendon's first goal. By the 63rd minute, it was 3–3, when a floodlight pylon failed. The lights were still good enough, in referee David Ellery's opinion, to continue so the match went on. At 90 minutes it was still 3–3. After 105 minutes the score had still not advanced. This time it took 37 seconds for Hendon to start a half and score. A fifth goal sealed a truly incredible night. Forty hours later an exhausted Hendon were beaten 3–0 at Hayes - with Harrow fans cheering on Hayes - in the semi-final.

The league season ended with Hendon in a very respectable fourth place, though it would almost certainly have been higher but for the fixture congestion at the end of the season. The team had 73 points from 42 games, but were 28 behind champions Wycombe Wanderers. Fourteen out of 22 wins came away from Claremont Road. Iain

Dowie was top scorer with 23 goals. Hendon's two cup finals took place in the last week of the season.

Bognor Regis Town 3 Hendon 2
AC Delco (Isthmian League) Cup Final

Hendon lost a controversial Isthmian League Cup Final to Bognor Regis Town on 6 May after an entertaining match at Stag Meadow, Windsor. Ted Hardy's men were playing their 74th match of the season and they made a bad start, considering a goal after just 10 minutes when Kevin Clements headed home a Gary Poole corner.

The Greens equaliser, after 33 minutes, was somewhat fortunate. A Dermot Drummy free-kick struck the Bognor wall, set inside the penalty area, but Mick Windsor stuck out an arm and the ball hit. Referee Andy Williams was perfectly placed to see the outstretched arm of the striker deflect the ball away and he had no hesitation in pointing to the penalty spot. Drummy made no mistake from 12 yards and the teams were level. But, two minutes before half-time, another Bognor corner, this one from Geoff Cooper, was headed home by centre-half Graham Marriner.

Despite their exhaustion, Hendon took control in the second half. Drummy grabbed his second equaliser with a powerful drive after 55 minutes. With 15 minutes to go a Drummy cross was met by Alan Campbell, but the header was cleared off the goal line.

The real controversy came four minutes later when a Drummy shot was deflected by Billy Gill and clawed away by the brilliant Alistair Sperring. It was clear to those standing behind the goal Hendon were attacking that the ball was a good foot behind the goal line when Sperring reached it, but the linesman was very slow to get into position and did not award the goal. It is almost inconceivable that Hendon would have lost the match if the goal had been given.

It got even worse for Hendon after 83 minutes when Neil Wolstenholme shot goalwards. The ball beat Sperring but a defender was able to clear it not only off the line, but to straight to Cooper, who launched an attack that was finished by Russell Burtenshaw for what proved to be Bognor's winner.

Bognor Regis Town: Sperring, P. Pullen, M. Pullen, Burtenshaw, Gill, Marriner, Clements, Poole, Windsor, Guille, Cooper. Subs: Price, Grey.

Hendon: Root, Smart, Roughan, Wade, Campbell, Gridelet, Gibson, Drummy, Kiely, Tate, Wolstenholme. Subs: Bickles, Harding.

Kettering Town 3 Hendon 1
GMAC (Premier Inter-League) Cup Final

Hendon lost their second cup final of the season, just six days later, falling to Alliance Premier League Kettering Town, who were unable to field future Greens boss Frank Murphy because he was ineligible.

In truth, Hendon were distinctly second best for much of the game and were a little fortunate to be ahead at half time when Dermot Drummy got around Arthur Mann and saw his shot deflect off Phil Wood and into the net for an own goal.

Kettering were level two minutes into the second half when a foul by Alan Campbell on Paul Richardson led to a

free-kick. Steve Daley, Britain's most expensive footballer only eight years earlier, curled in the free-kick and Billy Kellock scored.

The Poppies took the lead midway through the second half when a cross from Phil Caverner was turned into the net by the prolific Dougie Keast. And, 13 minutes later, the match was over as a contest when Mark Smith struck a magnificent third goal for Kettering. In the end 75 competitive matches (including the void Middlesex Cup tie with Harrow Borough) were just too many for Hendon.

Kettering Town: Harrison, Ward, Mann, Caverner, Lewis, Wood, Keast, Richardson, Kellock, Smith, Daley. Subs: Birch, Crawley.

Hendon: Root, Smart, Roughan (Keen, 65), Wade, Campbell, Gridelet, Gibson, Drummy, Dowie, Kiely, Wolstenholme. Subs: Tate.

1987–88: Another Wembley final

Pre-season, Hendon were tipped to go all the way to Wembley in the FA Trophy. It wasn't to be, largely because the club allowed Ted Hardy to go after losing 2–1 in the second qualifying round of the FA Cup at home to Hertford Town. Mickey Janes, Hardy's assistant, didn't leave with him, and took over as manager, his first such role. In the FA Trophy, Hendon made it to the competition proper and beat Fareham 2–0. The second round tie against Barrow, ended in a 1–1 draw at Claremont Road, but a 2–1 defeat at Holker Street. Goalkeeper Dave Root, who would go on to give almost 10 years' service to the Greens, was dropped at the start of the season, with John Jacobs, surely the only Jew to be nicknamed the 'Flying Pig', taking over. It was not a successful gamble and, by the end of 1987, Root was back between the posts.

The league form suffered as a result of the management change and Hendon finished 10th with 60 points. The highlight of the season was the Greens' final official visit to the old Wembley Stadium. Russell Grant, the television astrologer and celebrity, decided to sponsor the Middlesex Charity Cup and persuaded Wembley Stadium to stage the Final. With a Wembley appearance on the cards, Brentford and Chelsea both entered, but the latter got careless in an early round, while the Bees slipped up 2–1 at home to Wembley in the semi-final. Hendon opened with a 3–1 victory over Haringey Borough, won 1-0 at Hayes and then saw off Finchley in the semi-final. Hendon's league season ended in early May 1988, the Charity Cup Final was on 2 June; in between, the Greens played a friendly against Aylesbury United at the Met Police ground in Hendon – Aylesbury's season was extended because they had a friendly against the full England squad at their new Buckingham Road ground before England flew out to be embarrassed at Euro 88. Hendon versus Aylesbury was abandoned 10 minutes from the end, because the referee could see a serious injury about to happen.

Iain Dowie was again top scorer with 27 goals. Only two other players reached double figures.

Hendon 2 Wembley 0
Middlesex Charity Cup Final

TV personality Russell Grant took on the sponsorship of the Middlesex Charity Cup and hired Wembley Stadium for the Final, it being the last of a few County youth cup finals staged at the famous arena that day.

The Hendon team at Wembley. Back: Phil Gridelet, Mark Furneaux, Neil Wolstenholme, Mick Keily, Erskine Smart, Dave Robotham, Colin Tate, Dave Root, Iain Dowie, Bill Fenlon, Robert Tenkorang; front: Neil Henry, Roger Wade, Alan Roughan, Andy Smith, Dermot Drummy, Alan Campbell.

Hendon had worked their way to the Final without encountering much serious opposition, while Wembley overcame a strengthened Brentford reserve squad at Griffin Park in the semi-final. The date of the final, 2 June, was the latest Hendon had played a fixture since 1947 and it was the same day as England's first cricket test match of the 1988 summer against the West Indies.

Wembley manager Tony Waugh surprisingly omitted Sylvester Williams and Henry Pacquette from the Lions starting line-up, preferring Dereck Browne, whose rise to non-league football stardom was still some years away. The only selection query for Hendon boss Micky Janes was whether to give the returning Colin Tate a starting role or to stick with Mick Kiely, who had been with the Greens all season. Tate got the nod.

In front of a crowd of 3,715, mainly supporting Hendon, the game began. The Greens' fans had a new chant at the much-quieter Wembley faithful, "You're supposed to be at home."

Hendon started very confidently and soon had the Wembley defence at sixes and sevens. Four corners were forced in the first six minutes, but Wembley held on. In fact, they had a good chance to open the scoring after 19 minutes, but Dave Root was equal to Browne's powerful effort.

At the other end, Jeff Fanner made an equally good stop to deny Iain Dowie, who had been set up by Dermot Drummy. Five minutes later, however, he was beaten. The move started with Phil Gridelet, who released Drummy into space. He attacked the edge of the penalty area and drilled in a low cross which Dowie turned into the net.

The Greens' lead was nearly doubled after 32 minutes when Dowie headed past Fanner, but Charlie Flaherty made a goal line clearance. Seven minutes later, former Don Adrian Smith made an excellent block of a shot from Gridelet.

Although Hendon were mainly in control, they did let their concentration slip on a couple of occasions. Both Lance Cadogan and Browne, again, had chances to equalise,

251

but they were spurned, while both Tate and Dowie saw attempts saved by Fanner.

The game was made safe with just four minutes remaining. Drummy collected a ball in midfield and ran straight at the heart of the Wembley defence. No one came out to make a tackle and when Drummy got to the edge of the penalty area, he fired a superb low shot past Fanner into the bottom corner. Wembley introduced Williams and Pacquette, but it was too late from them to have an impact and Hendon claimed their 14th Middlesex Charity Cup win.

Hendon manager Micky Janes said, "I am delighted for all our lads, but especially for Alan Campbell. He has never given less than 100 percent for me and has twice been on the losing side in FA Trophy semi-finals with Dagenham, but now he has a Wembley winner's medal.

Hendon: Root, Smart, Furneaux, Wade (Andy Smith, 75), Campbell, Gridelet, Drummy, Henry, Dowie, Tate, Wolstenholme. Subs: Robotham, Kiely, Roughan.

Wembley: Fanner, Flaherty, Simpson, Murphy, January, Adrian Smith, Bhatia, Browne (Williams, 86), Dolling (Pacquette, 86), Cadogan, O'Connor. Subs: Ray, McGrath.

1988–89

Following the victory in the Middlesex Charity Cup, Hendon changed chairmen, Charles Geary moving to chief executive and former Haringey Borough chairman Tony Beatty taking on the same role at Claremont Road. It was to be a short-lived arrangement, with the unwell Beatty relinquishing his post after less than a season.

That was not the only change, however. Iain Dowie, scorer of one of the goals in the win over Wembley, worked hard on his game during the summer under the strict eye of coach Ronnie Duke. Duke – who died not long after – must take huge credit for turning Dowie into the most sought-after striker in non-league football. He had scored 27 goals by time he was transferred to Luton Town for £30,000 in December 1988. He still finished as top scorer at the club. His departure came at the end of an FA Cup run which was terminated at Elm Park by Division Four leaders Reading 4–2.

Reading 4 Hendon 2
FA Cup 1st round proper

Almost 13 years to the day after being embarrassed by Hendon at Claremont Road, Reading gained revenge at Elm Park. It was far from plain sailing for the Royals, who saw two-goal half-time lead disappear in the opening 11 minutes of the second half.

Reading made a great start and took the lead after just six minutes when Les Taylor, an FA Cup finalist with Watford four years earlier, scored from a Stuart Beavon cross. Seven minutes later, Date Root made a fine save to keep out an attempt from Karl Elsey. The Greens were in danger of being over-run, but they kept their nerve and gradually started contributing more than just desperate defence.

Nevertheless it was a huge blow when, in first-half stoppage time, Steve Moran flicked on a through ball and Elsey drilled home a great shot. Whatever Micky Janes said in the dressing room during the interval must have had the desired effect because, within 60 seconds of the restart, Hendon had clawed a goal back.

Dermot Drummy started the move out on the wing and a little bit of magic took him past two defenders and gave him room to cross. His delivery towards Iain Dowie was perfect and the striker's flick-on invited Gary Keen to drill the ball home from eight yards out. With the bit between their teeth Hendon began to play with the confidence that had seen them rise to near the top of the Isthmian League table. In the 57th minute, the Greens forced a corner which Drummy curled into the penalty area. The ball was not completely cleared by Reading and Martin Duffield fired a shot past Gary Phillips, which Elsey cleared off the line. The ball rolled only a few yards and Dowie pounced, knocking it home from just inside the six-yard box. Could history repeat itself?

Sadly, the answer was no. After Root had made a brilliant save to keep out a shot from Moran in the 64th minute, Royals substitute Keith Knight – later to play for rivals Harrow Borough – delivered a perfect cross for Taylor to bag his second goal.

There were still 15 minutes to go and Hendon committed themselves to grabbing another equaliser. They paid the penalty, albeit controversially, with five minutes to go, when Moran – looking yards offside – ran clear and fed Trevor Senior, who made no mistake. Two Hendon players were booked for their protests, complaints Reading manager Ian Branfoot could sympathise with. He said, "Two of our goals were debatable, but I won't complain about them as they went in our favour. Our attitude was never right – we were never aggressive enough."

Reading: Phillips, Richardson, Gernon, Beavon (Knight, 73), Hicks, Tait, Elsey, Senior, Taylor, Moran, Gilkes. Sub: Conroy

Hendon: Root, Smart, Furneaux, Duffield, Campbell (Hardy, 33), Gridelet, Drummy, Scott, Dowie, Tate (Smith, 81), Keen

The FA Trophy was nothing if not eventful. A third qualifying round tie against Hayes was put in the charge of local Middlesex referee Doug Douglas, who was utterly unaware of the war brewing, especially between Hendon's Duncan Hardy and Reg Leather of Hayes. The first foul by Leather on Hardy came after 30 seconds. That foul, in 2008, would have resulted in a straight red card, but Mr Douglas satisfied himself with a lecture. Three more fouls followed before Hardy retaliated and both players were booked. Ninety seconds later – with less than 30 minutes on the clock – a mini war broke out. Hardy was about to retaliate to another Leather foul, but could not get in a blow as Leather knocked him unconscious before Hardy could swing. Every other player, except for Iain Dowie and Hayes's Derek Payne got involved. Leather and Hayes goalkeeper Paul Hyde were dismissed; Hendon lost Hardy, Alan Campbell and Steve Scott, whose only offence, by most accounts, was to be standing in the way of a kick from Hyde which apparently left stud marks on his hairline. The match, oh yes, it was a thriller which ended 3–3. The replay, in front of 820 fans hoping to see round two, ended in a tame 2–0 win for Hendon.

The next round saw Hendon travel to Enfield and this game ended nine-a-side with both teams losing two players, all four going in separate incidents. The match was won 4–1 by the hosts. In the league, the team finished 12th with 56 points.

Off-field turmoil came to head when Micky Janes took a brief leave of absence. With Tony Beatty also departing, permanently, things were beginning to go wrong at Claremont Road. The new chairman was not Mr Geary, who remained in his chief executive's role – his wife was the bar manageress – but Fred Philpin, formerly on the board at Barnet FC.

A colourful character, Philpin worked in demolition and, like Geary, relied on his ability to attract investors. At around the same time, it was decided to make the secretary's role a full-time position and David Stanley took the job.

This was Dermot Drummy's last season with the club. He was one of the most exciting players to play for Hendon in the 1980s, and is fondly remembered by many supporters.

A Hendon hero: Dermot Drummy

Dermot Drummy was born in Hackney, East London, on 16 January 1961, to Irish parents, giving him dual nationality and played for the Republic of Ireland at youth and under–21 levels while at Arsenal and, briefly, on loan at Blackpool, where he made five Football League appearances.

Thought to be the successor to Liam Brady, it didn't quite work out for Dermot, so he dropped into the semi-professional game with Hendon. Watched loyally by his parents and later his wife and children, Dermot was an old-fashioned winger, but described as a wide midfielder. Clever on the ball, his party trick was to stop, drop his hands as if going to pick up the ball, then stand up and spring past the invariably bemused defender.

Dermot's first spell at Hendon last for four seasons, during which time he scored 30 goals for teams that finished inside the top eight of the Isthmian League Premier Division only once and also only once averaged better than 1.5 goals per League game.

The subject of a four-figure transfer to Enfield, Dermot won a Conference champions winners medal in 1986 and twice suffered the heartbreak of losing FA Trophy semi-finals. In the summer of 1986, Hendon took on their supporters in an end-of-season behind closed doors friendly. The supporters team was boosted by the appearance of Drummy, who left a deep impression on the author as he spent 25 minutes polishing his boots before putting them on – mine had never enjoyed that privilege and indeed had probably not even seen the light of day since the previous season's fixture.

Later that year, Dermot left Enfield and members of the Hendon FC Committee put their hands in the pockets – a move suggested and led by Malcolm Graves – and they raised the transfer fee to bring him back. With a top-class goalscorer for company up front, Dermot had his most prolific season in the almost interminable 1986–87 campaign, finding the target 17 times in just 47 appearances – an impressive strike rate for the leader of the attack rather than a playmaker.

One honour that will always remain with Dermot is that of being the last Hendon player ever to score at the old Wembley Stadium. Four minutes from the end of the Russell Grant Middlesex Charity Cup Final at the famous old venue, he slipped the ball past Jeff Fanner to make it 2–0 to the Greens.

After leaving Hendon, Dermot, along with teammate Alan Roughan, were briefly joint-managers at Finchley and Dermot, on his own, was also in charge of Ware. Having passed the 'The Knowledge' while at Claremont Road,

Dermot gave up driving taxis to move into coaching full-time and spent a number of years working for Liam Brady at Arsenal. However, in the summer of 2007, he moved across London to work at Chelsea where, in July 2008, his title was assistant academy manager.

In 2000, in a ballot of Hendon FC supporters for the all-time best Hendon players, Dermot came 10th overall. He played 349 games for the club, scoring 61 goals.

1989–90

The 12th place finish was repeated in 1990, with Hendon finishing with 55 points. The season lit up by the arrival of a teenager from the youth team, Uche Egbe. Sadly, he was never realised his full potential, but did finish as top scorer this season with 17. Hendon did play six matches in the FA Cup, but needed three games to see off Barking and eventually fell in the final qualifying round, 4–1 at Aylesbury. FA Trophy dreams ended at Wivenhoe in round one. There was also little progress in the county cups. Phil Gridelet left the club at the start of the season. In 1988-89 he had won two caps for the England Non League XI, in Italy and against Wales at Kidderminster.

1990–91

The end of the decade was not a happy time at Claremont Road. The club was still run by a committee of well-meaning people, but there was no one backing the club financially to ensure it could afford to play at the level to which it had become accustomed. In the dugout, Janes had been replaced by Alan Randall, a former player and highly regarded coach, with Steve Ringrose as his assistant. Sadly for Randall, a local man with a passion for football, all his success came when he was either an assistant manager or club coach; when he was the manager, things didn't go so well. This was especially true at Hendon, where an embarrassing FA Cup exit at Ruislip Manor was followed by a dire 3–0 FA Trophy defeat at Gravesend & Northfleet. It became clear that Randall and Ringrose – both fine coaches – had lost the support of the players. Hendon finished the season in 15th place with 46 points. In the Middlesex Senior Cup, Enfield won 3–2 at Claremont Road in the semi-final, and Aylesbury United ended a run in the Full Members Cup in the fourth round with a 4–1 victory. Colin Tate was top scorer with 14 goals.

During the following season, Randall was replaced by Gwyn Walters, but Randall's career turned for the better. In 1992–93, he was coach at Chesham, who won the Isthmian League title.

1991–92

Walters had not been in charge for long when all hell broke loose – the Greens had gone out of the FA Cup at home to a poor Baldock team and lost in the FA Trophy to Wealdstone, who were playing their home games at Watford's Vicarage Road. Hendon thus have had the unique experience of losing at Vicarage Road to three different clubs: Newcastle United, Watford and Wealdstone. The club had failed to provide accounts for the previous year – a broken leg had left Dave Stanley unable to work for many weeks at the end of 1990 and start of 1991 – and finances were very difficult. A new committee member was Harold Nass, who had experience of impecunious sports clubs after being involved with Fulham / London Crusaders Rugby League Club.

Committee meetings became a matter of the members advising Philpin and Stanley which bills should be paid each month, while Philpin was begging and borrowing funds to keep other creditors at bay. When it came to Barnet Council, in November 1991, Philpin gambled, and lost, a game of chicken. Despite advice to the contrary, he decided not to pay Barnet outstanding rent, despite warnings that the ground would be closed. A committee meeting on Monday 11 November was interrupted by the arrival of bailiffs, who were sent by Barnet Council to close down the ground. A check of the notice, however, showed that the bailiffs had actually arrived a day early.

When the bailiffs left, Philpin told the committee that he didn't have the money to pay the council. With the exception of Supporters Association chairman Len Burt none of the other committee members could commit to putting in money. Len said to Fred, "I will give you £4,000 tomorrow morning." It was an amazing gesture, but part of the reason the Supporters Association chairman had been given a position on the Football Club committee was so the Supporters Association could know how difficult things were for the main club. This money, however, would not have been Supporters Association money, this would have been from Len's personal account. Before the meeting closed, Harold Nass recommended to the committee that they take out from the dressing rooms everything that they could, just in case the council refused to accept the payment and the bailiffs took over the ground.

It was a vital decision. Reserve team secretary Graham Etchell, who had been at the club since June 1990, but who would play such vital role in the club over the next almost 20 years, went home with the reserve team kit, Walters with that of the first team – all except for one sock. The following day, Tuesday 12 November 1991, Hendon were due to play an Isthmian League Cup tie at Tilbury. By a happy coincidence, both first team and reserves were scheduled to be away on 16 November.

On the morning of 12 November, when it became clear that Hendon FC's payment to the London Borough of Barnet would not be accepted, the bailiffs took over the ground, padlocking it, the clubhouse, Supporters Association shop, tea bar, car park and dressing rooms. Late in that afternoon, the players – who had been notified of the situation and were told to come to the ground rather than making their own way to St Chad's Road – arrived outside the bleak, rainswept and very dark clubhouse at Claremont Road. They set off in a convoy to Tilbury where, in the still pouring rain, a disconsolate team were beaten 3–0 in the League Cup by the Dockers. Hendon regrouped on the Saturday and fought out a 0–0 draw at Chesham, but the Greens' most valuable playing asset, Martin Duffield was sold to Sutton United within days. The club was still alive, but only just. Had they not played at Tilbury – possibly at Chesham – the problems could have been much greater. Harold Nass's advice undoubtedly saved the club significant embarrassment.

A couple of weeks later, after long negotiations with two parties looking to take over and save Hendon Football Club, Victor Green was announced as the new Hendon FC chairman. The first thing to happen was that the club was dissolved and a company was formed, thus saving the members from the very real possibility of bankruptcy if Hendon Football Club had folded. Mr Green, his wife and son David, held all the shares and, as he informed members, he "spent around £1million" wiping out debts and setting up the company. Things would never be the same at Claremont Road again.

Victor Green was a hard-nosed businessman and he blew through Hendon like a hurricane. Football is built on passion, and popularity is important. It helps if the main personnel – chairman, secretary, management and playing staff – are liked (it is taken as read that they are respected), but the chairman appeared not to care about popularity: he only wanted results. He did not seem to appreciate that supporters took a bad defeat for their team personally; it ruined their weekend. Committed football fans, the ones who brave all weathers and travel huge distances to watch their team play, have no equivalents in business. It took him to some time to grasp that.

What he did understand was the need to produce results and that he addressed very quickly. The team was in grave danger of being relegated, so a team of highly-experienced and expensive players were signed and the club's premier division status was saved relatively comfortably, with a 17th place finish with 48 points, 15 clear of relegated Bishop's Stortford. Dave Stanley was not so fortunate; he left the club within a couple of months of Green's takeover. In his place came Michael Cox, a longstanding supporter and qualified company secretary who had written to Victor thanking him for saving the club and offering his services if they were required.

It was not a successful move, not really through anyone's fault. Because Michael did not drive and had a 90-minute commute by Underground and bus, he simply could not do some of the tasks normally expected of a club secretary. Also, he had a limited knowledge of football administration. Cox was secretary for around a year before he left and Graham Etchell was promoted from reserve team secretary to club secretary.

A Hendon hero: Alan Campbell

Alan Campbell arrived at Hendon on trial from Finchley in the summer of 1976. The epitome of a young raw centre-half, Campbell was very fortunate to be partnered by one of the wiliest and most clever central defenders in non-league football, Peter Deadman. They were different as players: Campbell: strong, good in the air, hard tackler and rough around the edges; Deadman: cool, calm, collected, good positional sense, always playing within his – albeit wide – limitations. They made a superb defensive duo.

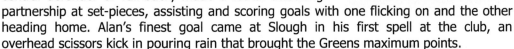

In his first season, Alan and Peter Anderson, the central defender or full-back, made a lethal attacking partnership at set-pieces, assisting and scoring goals with one flicking on and the other heading home. Alan's finest goal came at Slough in his first spell at the club, an overhead scissors kick in pouring rain that brought the Greens maximum points.

After four seasons at Claremont Road, Alan was lured up the road to Barnet, where he gave the Bees three good seasons. He then moved to Dagenham, where he enhanced his reputation. At both clubs, he enjoyed success in the FA Cup and only his relative age, late 20s, stopped two or three Football League clubs from signing him.

When Ted Hardy took over as manager, he persuaded Alan to return to Claremont Road and he was there for three more seasons, although the last two were somewhat injury hit. The older more mature AC was a much better defender, but his goals dried up. In fact, in three seasons, he managed just two goals. Nevertheless, for all of his cup successes at Underhill and Victoria Road, it was not until Alan was in the second season of his second spell at Claremont Road that finally he got to play at Wembley Stadium. He was a member of the team which won the Russell Grant Middlesex Charity Cup in 1988.

After leaving Hendon for the second time, Alan came back for a third, briefer spell, in 1991–92, making 19 appearances. Then in the summer of 1992, he was appointed assistant manager to Barrie Williams. It was a strange appointment by chairman Victor Green as Alan had not been in coaching before. He stayed for only seven months, leaving in February 1993. Overall, Alan played 394 games, scoring 29 goals. A tube train driver, Alan remains close friends with former teammate Roger Wade. Interested in life at Claremont Road, Alan has been back to watch some games in recent seasons.

Hendon FC 1992: Alan Campbell, Ronnie Duke, Paul Shirt, Andy Beattie, ?, Robbie Garvey, Dave Root, Lawrence Holmes, ?, Jude Monteith, Malcolm Stewart, Michael Cox, Gwyn Walters; front: ?, Gary Keen, Dermot Drummy, Colin Sowerby, ?, Tony Hopkins, Marc Xavier, Simon Clark.

Guitarist Hank Marvin, Ivor Arbiter and Victor Green at Claremont Road. Ivor Arbiter's Fender Guitars company were club sponsors before he took over from Victor Green as chairman.

10. 1992 to 2000: FA Cup excitement

Gwyn Walters' reign ended during the summer of 1992. He was replaced by a manager with a huge reputation: Barrie Williams, the man who had guided Sutton United to FA Cup glory against Coventry City. His assistant was long-time Hendon favourite Alan Campbell, who had enjoyed two long and successful spells as a player at Claremont Road. He had not been in a high profile management or coaching position before his appointment at Hendon.

Having been out of football for around 18 months, it soon became clear that Williams's style of management needed years, as opposed to weeks, to come to fruition, especially with a squad of players that he had not recruited. Time was one thing that was not on his side. What was essentially a collection of high-priced experienced players went along with him for the ride, taking home comfortable money, but not always earning it. Short of sacking the players and swallowing the financial burden of the contracts, Victor Green made the players available for transfer, but many on the gravy train refused to get off. Those seen as 'troublemakers' were given short shrift and effectively frozen out.

In the summer of 1992, Green also decided that supporters had enjoyed too many benefits of membership – especially those who had become life members. At a stroke he cancelled all the life memberships, including those that had been given to former players, managers, committee members and helpers, many of whom had given hundreds of hours to the club without recompense. In the letter to the members, Green used an unfortunate piece of phrasing which suggested that he didn't need supporters: what he meant was that the club now had sufficient funds that supporters' donations would no longer be the lifeblood of Hendon FC. It created a firestorm of dissatisfaction – as did the decision to change the club's badge.

Green felt the lamb and flag – similar to Preston North End and also the Middlesex Wanderers Football Club – was not unique, so he brought in a design that made it clear what the club was, but the shape was more appropriate for a baseball club than an association football one. He was probably unaware that the flag was actually that of the former borough of Hendon and still the emblem of the parish of Hendon. What is incontrovertible, however, is that Hendon Football Club's lamb and flag badge did not have a consistent design – the lamb was standing or resting, the flag was at different angles as well as varying in shape and the ground was sloping or flat.

There is no question that Victor Green wanted success for Hendon and he was determined that it would happen. He carried a notebook around with him and if he thought of something or received a good idea he would note it down. He created plans for redeveloping the Claremont Road site, building a new stand and dressing rooms and making the whole place better. Barnet Council looked at the plans and considered them, but took it no further for quite a while. Meanwhile, his wife, Elaine effectively became the bar manageress, a role she took on with relish.

Hendon opened the season against Chesham United and won. It would be Chesham's only league defeat for almost five months as they ran away with the title. The Greens could not keep up the good start, despite plenty of goals from Gary Donnellan and the front two of Kurt Davidson and Colin Sowerby – the latter in his second spell with the club; his first had been as a teenager, totally out of his depth in Hendon's struggling sides of 1982 to 1984. An embarrassing FA Cup exit at Wembley in October 1992 was horrible to watch. In the FA Trophy, Hendon were very unlucky to lose Roy Parkyn – one of the first signings of the Green era – but who dislocated his shoulder in the last of the pre-season friendlies. Parkyn made his comeback against Grays, dislocated the same shoulder and never played for the club again.

In early February 1993, with the players certainly not giving the effort expected of their income, Alan Campbell left the club – he and Michael Cox left on the same day. Replacing Campbell was Bobby Makin, a former professional player with Orient, who then enjoyed a long and successful time at Barking. The Williams-Makin partnership lasted barely a month before Williams departed. Makin stepped up to become manager, and appointed former Hayes defender and Enfield coach Alan Carrington as his assistant. The pair worked well and while the results didn't necessarily match all of the talent, at least all the players looked as if they cared more.

With one game left of the 1992–93 season, Makin was sacked by Victor Green, who told him and Carrington that they need not travel to Carshalton for that match and he would "put on a tracksuit and sit in the dugout if necessary". It is to Makin's eternal credit that he not only went to the match and managed the team, but after a dismal 3–1 defeat, he spent a good amount of time in the dressing room going over what had been done wrongly. Hendon finished 11th, with 54 points, 13 clear of Staines who were relegated. Barry Blackman was top scorer with 16 goals, the only player to reach double figures.

Once again, however, it was all change at Hendon Football Club.

1993–94: League Cup victory

The man who took over as manager was Peter Taylor, a former England international who had enjoyed a long professional career at Southend United, Crystal Palace and Tottenham Hotspur before he turned to management. He worked at Dartford and Enfield before becoming Steve Perryman's assistant at Watford. Peter left Watford to take over at Hendon, and then turned down the chance to be Glenn Hoddle's number two at Chelsea. Hoddle contacted Hendon twice and twice Taylor said no to the Blues, saying that he had just taken over at Hendon and couldn't simply leave them.

There is no doubt that Taylor's professionalism was top-class. With a new squad, playing a different, very attractive and efficient style, Grays were thumped 3–0 on the opening day. The new front two were Richard Cherry and Gary Crawshaw, the midfield contained Jon Daly and Barry Blackman, with Taylor himself on the wing. The defence was superb with Lee Hunter and Tommy Mason at full-back and Simon Clark and Bob Dowie as centre-backs, all playing front of long-serving Dave Root, who had joined the club when Ted Hardy was the manager and played almost 400 matches for the Greens. The demolitions of Basingstoke and Hertford Town – the latter in the League Cup – had Hendon fans dreaming realistically of a championship come May.

Hendon went top of the table for the first time since 1988 when they won 3–2 at Aylesbury United, Daly scoring in the final minute, but the FA Cup proved to be Hendon's downfall. A trip to Great Yarmouth meant Hendon escaped with a 2–2 draw and the replay was won by a less than convincing 4–2. An injury to Dave Root meant that, after Heybridge Swifts had been despatched, Christian Davies was in goal for third qualifying round tie against Chelmsford City. The reserve goalkeeper – on the bench – was now Richard Cherry and his ability in attack was sorely missed as the Clarets won 1–0.

Dowie was sent off in a top-of-the-table clash with Stevenage Borough – he conceded an 88th minute penalty for punching Dave Venables. The converted spot-kick gave Stevenage a 2–1 win. Suddenly things weren't so rosy. Cherry's apparent lack of enthusiasm wore out Taylor's patience and when in early December Enfield asked about his availability for transfer, he took the familiar route round the North Circular to Southbury Road. Three days later he scored the only goal of the game for the Es against Hendon at Southbury Road – a scenario that modern transfers would not allow.

At the same time, in Southend, Barry Fry was leaving the club to become Birmingham City manager. The Shrimpers approached Hendon and Taylor decided to take the job. "There is no other club I would have left Hendon for," he said. "They are my hometown team and it is where my heart is."

Peter's departure upset Victor Green, who was suddenly dealing with his fifth manager in less than two years. The new man in charge was Terry Harris, but his stay lasted only four games, three defeats and a draw. Just after Christmas, Victor Green told Terry that the budget for players had to be slashed and Terry, after looking at the figures, decided he could not work under those circumstances and resigned. Paul Brush, the former West Ham United defender, was offered and accepted the job, only to change his mind and he resigned after being in charge for around 45 minutes.

Green now turned to the senior professional player, Bob Dowie and so he became player-manager. At the same time, Green was being courted by Stevenage Borough to become an investor there. Barnet Council had still not approved his plans for the renovation of Claremont Road and advancement for Hendon was looking more and more remote. The two best players, Clark and Crawshaw, were made free agents. Crawshaw left immediately but Clark, who had been with the club for three seasons, not only did another training session – the match that day was postponed because of bad weather – but made a point of saying goodbye to all his team-mates, other staff and supporters who were around. Both players signed new contracts at Stevenage Borough. This was a move that enraged Hendon fans because both players would have commanded significant transfer fees. Of course, as these fees would have gone directly or indirectly to the chairman, the club would not have seen any of it.

The next move came a couple of days later. Green decided to resign as Hendon chairman and he sold his interest in the company to his wife Elaine. As it happened, it was the best thing that could have happened to the club, because Elaine almost seemed as if she wanted to prove her husband wrong and make the club successful. Sadly, Blackman and Daly left in a few weeks and a weaker squad faced the rest of the season.

Somehow Dowie turned things around. The club avoided an abyss of mediocrity and enjoyed a great run in the Full Members Cup, reaching the Final. It was played at Marlow against Wokingham Town on 3 May. A 2–1 victory meant that Mrs Green had achieved in three months, with a massively reduced squad, something her husband had failed to do – win a trophy. In the league, Hendon finished 11th, mid table safety with 63 points. Gary Crawshaw was top scorer with 14 goals.

Hendon 2 Wokingham Town 1
Carlsberg (Isthmian Full Members) Cup Final

Hendon ended a season which had started with so much promise with some silverware, albeit the Carlsberg (Isthmian League Full Members) Cup after deservedly beating Wokingham Town at picturesque Marlow.

The 1994 Carlsberg Cup Final

Top: Paul Kelly on the attack

Middle: Hendon supporters

Bottom: The team celebrates a memorable win. Back: Duncan Hardy, Andy Polston, Scott Ashenden, Dave Root, Dennis Rodway, Mark Hill, Ian Rutherford, Mark Kane, Bobby Bourne, Bob Dowie, Peter Lawrence; front: Paul Kelly, Lee Hunter, Curtis Warmington, Tommy Mason, Steve Heffer.

Player-manager Bob Dowie had to miss out on the Final – on the pitch at least – as he was starting a three-match suspension. It meant quite a reshuffle, with striker Duncan Hardy dropping back to partner Curtis Warmington and Mark Hill at the heart of the three-man defence. Wokingham had the effective partnership of former Chelsea star Tommy Langley partnering young Elliot Pearce for whom a bright future was predicted – tragically he died in a car crash six months later.

It was an excellent cup final, with the result in doubt until Graham Barber blew the final whistle at the end of eight minutes stoppage time. Andy Polston's surging runs from midfield caused consternation in the Wokingham defence and following one of these, after 25 minutes, Russell Meara made a magnificent save to keep out an effort from Paul Kelly. At the other end, Dave Root had to show off his safe handling skills, catching a number of teasing crosses, mainly from Freddie Hyatt.

Hendon made the breakthrough in the 40th minute. Tommy Mason attacked down the left wing and played a one-two with Scott Ashenden. He cut into the penalty area, but was upended by Barry Miller. Ashenden celebrated as if a goal had already been scored, but Mason said: "Don't celebrate too soon. We've still got to score the penalty."

Mason it was who had the responsibility and the eight-time New Zealand international made no mistake driving the ball past Meara's dive. A fans' favourite, Mason ran to celebrate the goal with the fans behind the goal.

Wokingham stepped up the pace in the second half and, after 55 minutes, Root made a brilliant save to keep out an effort from Langley. When he was beaten, seven minutes later, Lee Hunter was perfectly positioned on the goal line to head clear.

Hendon's second goal came from a most unlikely source: Mark Hill, a defender who rarely ventured deep into opposition territory. Nevertheless when a cross from the right wing was deflected across the face of goal after 71 minutes, there was Hill sliding in to score his only goal for the club. Three minutes later, Wokingham were back in the game when Hunter brought down Pearce and the young striker converted the spot-kick.

The reason for the extraordinary length of stoppage time was an 80th-minute injury to Ashenden. A clash of heads left the youngster with a badly broken nose and he was replaced by Robert Bourne. As is often the case after a bad or messy injury, some of the passion went out of the match, and that suited Hendon down to the ground.

Bob Dowie said after the game: "It was a tremendous team performance tonight. And it has been a remarkable achievement for the club to win a trophy this season."
Hendon: Root, Hunter, Mason, Hill, Hardy, Warmington, Polston, P. Kelly, Ashenden (Bourne, 80), Rutherford, Heffer. Sub: Rodway.
Wokingham Town: Meara, Miller (Aseh, 72), Leather, Smith, Line, Devereux, Hyatt, Duncan, Pearce, Langley, Hurdwell. Sub: Bradley.

At the season's end the squad was disbanded and now Hendon's troubles reached their nadir. Victor Green, now on the board of Isthmian League champions Stevenage Borough, decided to end his interest in Hendon Football Club, as did Elaine. The club was put up for sale and Wealdstone showed great interest. If they had been successful, Hendon Football Club would have died in 1994.

Wealdstone's plans appeared to be along the lines of: move into Claremont Road for 1994–95; merge the two clubs as Wealdstone & Hendon (taking Hendon's top-flight status over theirs in Southern League Division One) – only keeping the Hendon name to grab the many sponsors brought in by commercial manager Denis Pobjoy; then, in 1995–96, dropping the Hendon name. When a new ground could be found Wealdstone would move out of Claremont Road and football in NW2 would be no more. However, the Wealdstone board could not agree to take over Hendon and the deal fell through.

Hendon heroes: Iain and Bob Dowie

In terms of service to Hendon Football Club, Iain and Bob Dowie fall far short of the Burgess twins, Mark and James. In terms of contribution to football, there is no comparison, with Iain earning 59 caps for Northern Ireland, scoring 12 goals, before becoming a manager in the Football League. Bob didn't quite reach that level, but he has been director of football and non league scout for Iain – and Peter Taylor – after spells managing a number of clubs, including Hendon.

Iain was studying at Hatfield University, while working at the large BAE plant in the town. He moved from Hatfield to Cheshunt to Hertford Town, then St Albans City, before Ted Hardy brought him to Claremont Road in November 1986. The big bustling striker was very raw, but he had pace and an eye for goal.

Bob, the older brother and a central defender, was already working full-time, in oil exploration, and was often away in the Middle East. However, Hardy brought him to Hendon too and they played a few games together. Their contribution was important in 1986–87, when Hendon played 75 matches and every available player was used.

Bob disappeared from the scene on business, but Iain continued to knock in the goals, including one in the Middlesex Charity Cup Final at Wembley in June 1988. That summer, Iain worked hard with coach Ronnie Duke and it had an incredible effect on him. A few pounds lighter, a yard or so quicker and suddenly, Iain could not stop scoring. Against Bishops Stortford in the FA Cup, he scored a hat-trick and he scored against Reading in one of his last games before a £30,000 move to Luton Town.

Unfortunately, a mix-up in the transfer contract resulted in the sell-on clause being omitted and when he moved to Southampton for £450,000, Hendon lost out on more than £40,000 – an injudicious word early in the transfer negotiations had rapidly taken international appearances out of the equation. Including internationals, Iain played more than 400 games as a full-time professional and scored close on 100 goals.

Since retiring, Iain has been manager of Oldham Athletic, Crystal Palace, Charlton Athletic and Coventry City – plotting Manchester United's League Cup downfall in 2007. He left the Sky Blues later in the season and was appointed boss of QPR – he had two games as caretaker player-manager in 1998 – in the spring of 2008.

Bob was a no-nonsense centre-half, who could have gone far if he had been prepared to take a massive drop in pay by going professional. Hendon manager Micky Janes once named Bob in a programme for a match against Ted Hardy managed Dagenham & Redbridge, purely to put the wind up Ted's sails. Hardy admitted the ruse had worked. In the summer of 1993, Peter Taylor made Bob his first signing and, alongside Simon Clark or Curtis Warmington, they formed a solid defensive barrier.

Peter's stay at Hendon was all too brief and when the club lurched into crisis at the very end of 1993, Bob took over as player-manager for the remainder of the 1993–94 season, finishing up with victory in the Loctite (Isthmian League Full Members) Cup. Bob left at the end of the season and went on to manage at Harrow Borough, Chesham United, Aylesbury United and St Albans City, before taking up a full-time post as director of football at Crystal Palace. He still regularly visited Claremont Road, as a close friend of Dave Anderson, and he would often assist or even take Thursday night training sessions.

When Iain left Crystal Palace, Bob remained in place, leaving his replacement Peter Taylor in the interesting position of now reporting to a man he had once signed as a player. After a match-losing red card and penalty-conceding foul by Bob against Stevenage Borough at Claremont Road in October 1993, Peter stormed, "I don't want to even talk to Bob ever again, I want to sack him." Asked about that – and their relationship 14 years later, Peter just laughed and admitted he got on well with Bob.

Another player who left Hendon at the end of the 1993–94 season was goalkeeper Dave Root, who had the rare honour of a testimonial from the club.

A Hendon hero: Dave Root

Dave Root gave Hendon eight seasons of loyal service between the posts from 1986 to 1994, making 442 appearances for the Greens between 1986 and 1994. Born and raised in East London, his parents moved to Cornwall and Dave played for, among others, Launceston. Back in the south-east, Dave joined Barking where first-team opportunities were limited by Kevin Hitchcock. Dave's first appearance against Hendon was a 3–1 defeat at Mayesbrook Park when he was beaten from 45 yards by Jimmy Richardson.

When Mark Broughton moved on at the end of the 1985–86 season, Ted Hardy brought in Root to replace him and he played 70 matches in the memorable 1986–87 campaign, despite suffering a bad knee injury in March. Hendon reached two cup finals that season and Root had a bad time in the defeat against Bognor in the Hitachi (League) Cup final. Hardy held Dave responsible for the loss and brought in John Jacobs for the start of the following season.

Dave joined Enfield, but wasn't a regular in the first team and, when Hardy surprisingly left Hendon in the early autumn of 1987, new manager Micky Janes brought Root back to Claremont Road. He remained first choice for the rest of his time at Hendon, though he nearly left to join Leytonstone-Ilford as they looked to build a championship winning team. A transfer tribunal set the fee at £1,500, a figure they considered too high, and Root was flattered by. It meant, happily for Hendon, that Dave stayed where he was. Dave played for a few years after leaving Hendon, first for Kingstonian, then Boreham Wood among others. He was close to 40 when he retired.

Dave Root with his testimonial committee: Mike Hogan, Graham Etchell, Janet Hamlyn, Tim O'Connor and Len Burt.

1994–95: The Arbiter Group

As the summer went on, new manager Micky Browne, from Malden Vale – hired on the advice of Stevenage boss Paul Fairclough – tried to put together a squad that had no certainty of playing Isthmian League football come August. Pre-season training started, friendlies were played, including a match against a very young Chelsea team. The match was nearly abandoned at half-time as the Blues resented Hendon's tactics; there was nothing sinister about Browne's style; it was simply a matter of competing as best they could. Hendon won the game, but in the programme was the ominous sentence, "This may be the last match played on the ground by Hendon FC."

However, there was another suitor. Hendon's main sponsor for the previous two years had been the Arbiter Group, chaired by Ivor Arbiter at their offices in Wilberforce Road, Hendon. They were the suppliers of Fender guitars and, for the previous two seasons, the Fender logo had adorned the Hendon shirts.

Ivor was prepared to buy the club, but the group financial director John Wheeldon was less certain, to the extent his advice was, "Don't touch it with a bargepole!" The timing was now critical. Less than a week before the start of the season, the club had no budget, officially no playing staff and no backing. Graham Etchell went through the process of getting the players, who had done the pre-season training for no payment, to sign registration forms, effectively stopping them from joining another club in the shortest of terms.

It was now Friday 12 August 1994, and Hendon had signed no players. The Isthmian League officers were aware of the situation and were ready, if no players were signed on, to postpone the match the following day. It was agreed by the parties involved in the Club sale that the forms would be sent by fax over to the League's offices by noon on the Friday. At 11.30, Graham sat with John Wheeldon in the latter's office awaiting the call to say that the deal had gone through.

Nothing happened. Noon came and went and still there was no phone call. Hendon's often glorious 86-year existence was on the point of coming to an end. John Wheeldon then asked Graham what the company's commitments to the players would be if the registrations went through and the deal could not be completed. Graham said that there would be no more than one week's wages to pay, but as the company would not be in charge, technically probably nothing.

"Go ahead," John said. "Start faxing the forms." Graham did as he was bid and Hendon Football Club would at least play their opening day fixture against Slough Town at Wexham Park.

However bad the situation was on 11 November 1991, when the ground was closed, and whatever will happen when the sale of Hendon Football Club by the Arbiter Group goes through – to the Supporters Trust as is expected at the time of writing - the club will not be as close to going out of business as it was at lunchtime on 12 August 1994.

The Hendon team which took the field against Slough Town was: Dave Hudson, Lee Smart, Greg Sadler, Mick Dalton, Nick Chilvers, Dave Stephenson, Rodney Richards, Tony Matthias, Stan Blair, Uche Egbe, Steve McKimm. On the bench were Bradley Anderson, Carl Procopi and Andre Nolan. Of that 14, only Egbe had played for Hendon before 1994 and Anderson joined towards the end of the 1993–94 season; of the others, Lee Smart had enjoyed a few games in the Premier Division with Kingstonian, while Anderson had also played for St Albans City; Hudson, Smart, Dalton, Stephenson, Blair and McKimm were from Malden Vale, Chilvers had been at Barton Rovers, Matthias at

Croydon, Richards and Sadler at other clubs of a similar or lower level. Slough scored in the opening two minutes, Egbe equalised after 19 minutes and McKimm put Hendon in front two minutes later. Slough equalised later in the first half and the second half was goalless. This must stand as one of Hendon Football Club's finest ever results.

The takeover of the Hendon Football Club Limited by the Arbiter Group plc was completed during Monday 15 August 1994. The Football Club became a wholly owned subsidiary of the group, with Ivor Arbiter as chairman, his son-in-law Andrew Landesberg, vice-chairman, John Wheeldon as chief executive and Joanne Landesberg (Ivor's daughter, Andrew's wife) a fourth director. Graham Etchell – who had helped to keep the club alive administratively during the summer – remained as club secretary. The management, Micky Browne and his assistant Ged Murphy, remained in place, as did the players. Thankfully for this story, most of the remainder of the club's 100 years will focus on on-field events and not those in the boardroom.

The 1994–95 season was a memorable one. Ivor and Andrew were clearly smitten with the club and went out of their way to let the supporters know this. The team was undoubtedly the poorest – in terms of experience and depth – in the division, but they were a very tight unit. Arbiter used his show business and media links to get some great publicity which saw not only the players appearing naked on breakfast television – with footballs covering the vital parts (except for striker Dave Flint, a veteran brought in to bolster an inexperienced team; he was in his business as opposed to his birthday suit) – and also a women's magazine. *Penthouse* sent two female models and one male model to the ground for a photo story before a match against Purfleet. The two girls who had done all sorts of things with "Kev Weeks" in the dressing rooms, then – more attired – led out the two teams, with both captains looking rather sheepish, carrying huge bouquets of flowers for the models.

This was the season of experimental use of the kick-in and, in first Lee Flynn and then Graham McVie, Hendon had two players expert at this replacement for a throw-in. Up the road at Clarence Park, Martin Duffield and Alan Cockram – joint managers at St Albans – threatened to sack any players not throwing the ball in. On the field, there was no expectation of success and that was clearly the case from early on. The FA Cup run ended at home to Chelmsford City in the third qualifying round and the FA Trophy in a home replay against the rapidly rising Rushden & Diamonds.

Many of the team that played against Slough were not quite up to the necessary standard and, among those who joined the club during the season, were Lee Flynn, Nick Sweetman, Flint, Martin Gittings, and the McVie brothers, Graham and Gary.

Tragically, Hendon's hold on the Full Members Cup came to end just a couple of hours after Len Burt had died. He was visiting Ellie Peck, the wife of kit-man Ted, when he was taken ill and died almost immediately. News reached the club just before kick-off and, for most fans, what happened that night really didn't matter. Len Burt had been Hendon through and through. Although it appeared that Len had little influence on the Football Club committee, he – as Supporters Association chairman – in fact, literally supported the club, in whatever decision it took. It is almost certain that things were said and done that Len personally did not agree with, but as Supporters Association chairman, he supported the club's words and deeds. At the next Supporters Association committee meeting, the vice-chairman, Mike Hogan – who had been running the tea bar for a decade or so, to say nothing of the hundreds of jobs he did around the ground as a carpenter – was promoted to chairman.

The kick-in saved Hendon from relegation. Numerous games were saved because vital goals came from kick-ins. Many games stand out that season, but one of the oddest was at home to Grays Athletic. It ended in a 3–3 draw, with goalkeeper Dave Hudson scoring with a drop-kick in first-half stoppage time, then palming a kick-in into his own net barely a minute into the second. How often has a goalkeeper scored for both sides into the same net and the two goals being separated by barely a minute's playing time?

Relegation was avoided in the penultimate match, when Nicky Sweetman scored in the final couple of minutes at Hayes. Victory over relegated Wokingham Town in the final match saw Hendon rise to 17th in the table with 50 points, five clear of the relegation places. Uche Egbe, Philip Gallagher and Nick Sweetman were joint top scorers with 10 goals apiece.

Incredibly despite this amazingly inexperienced squad Hendon were in the relegation zone of the Premier Division for just one match – and that was in October. Micky Browne should have been the manager of the year in the Isthmian League because his performance was undoubtedly the most impressive of the season – far more than even the manager of the League champions.

Off the field, the Arbiters were determined to improve the facilities and work started on the magnificent Brent Cross Banqueting Centre. It was also agreed to run reserve and youth teams in 1995–96, and the first reserve team manager was Ray Brandon – who had been a coach under Ken Payne a dozen years earlier. Three youth teams were set up, at under–16, under–14 and under–13 levels.

1995–96

This season was not one which Hendon will look back on with any fondness. It started with a 3–0 hammering in a friendly at Baldock Town and pre-season results did not improve thereafter. One new signing of note was John Deadman, Peter's son, but he left in November. Micky Browne had a disastrous time and was dismissed in early November; Ray Brandon took charge of two cup games – an FA Trophy defeat at Cambridge City and Full Members Cup exit at home to St Albans when a young lad called Keith Dowson scored a hat-trick on what proved to be his last appearance for the club. In the FA Cup, Hayes enjoyed a 3–0 stroll at Claremont Road in the third qualifying round after the Greens had bashed Flackwell Heath 8–0 in the first qualifying round, including a hat trick from Junior Haynes – this result coming four days after a magnificent League Cup win at Yeovil. The new manager was Neil Price – a member of Watford's 1984 FA Cup Final side – assisted by Richard Parkin.

The dressing room door became little more than a turnstile as players came and went at an alarming rate. No less than seven different players had at least part of one game in goal and 62 players appeared in matches during the campaign. Price brought in Micky Banton, Mark Dawber and Josh Price (Neil's brother) for what proved a vital 2–0 win over Molesey on 2 December, but it would be Hendon's only victory for three months. A late rally brought the club up to safety, but it had been a close run thing. The final league position was 14th, 10 points clear of the relegation places. Remarkably, Hendon were knocked out of every cup the club had entered by the end of November. Banton was top scorer with 12 goals.

At the end of the season, the new Banqueting Centre was opened and the two guests of honour were contemporaries from Whitefields School – one a former Hendon player, the other a supporter: Tony Currie and David Bedford, respectively.

Hendon FC 1993–94: Back: Alan Gemmill (Asst Mgr), ?, Jon Daly, Curtis Warmington, Richard Cherry, Christian Davies, Barry Blackman, Dave Root, Bob Dowie, Mark Hill, Antony Sibanda, Simon Clark, Jude Monteith; front: Marc Salmon, Gary Crawshaw, Scott Ashenden, Mark Kane, Malcolm Stewart, Peter Taylor, Lee Hunter, Tommy Mason, Dennis Rodway, Gary Keen, Mark Xavier, Andy Polston.

Hendon FC April 1996: Back: Duncan Kennedy, Graham Etchell, Dean Murphy, Tony Lynch, Ted Peck, Darren Brodrick, Paul Hobbs, Scott Ashcroft, ?, Mark Dawber, Simon Clarke, Andy O'Brien, Darren Powell, Martin Duffield, Sam Old; front: Richard Parkin, Micky Banton, Andrew Landsberg, Ivor Arbiter, Neil Price, Steve Smart, Tony Kelly.

Left: Len Burt presents Bob Dowie with the Player of the year trophy in 1994 (Courtesy Mike Hogan).
Right: Frank Murphy and Steve Bateman with the FA Cup.

1996–97

Neil Price started the new season almost as badly as Micky Browne had opened the previous one. His big-name signing was David Speedie, who finished the opening game of the season in goal after brilliant young prospect Scott Ashcroft had suffered what proved, effectively, to be a career-ending injury. Speedie played in five matches, was cautioned in four of them, but he was also dismissed because of a second booking in the fifth game, and was released by the club that evening.

The goalkeeping situation was not easy; with Ashcroft out, Tony Wells took over until Jan-Gert Wagenaar joined. A Dutchman with top-level experience in his homeland, he was studying in England and proved to be a top keeper. His performance in Hendon's FA Cup third qualifying round win at Conference club Dover Athletic was genuinely outstanding as the Greens sneaked a 1–0 victory through a controversial Paul Kelly goal. Another new signing Junior Lewis, from Dover, proved very useful, as did a team-mate from the Crabble, Jermaine Darlington. Darlington scored the goal at Hastings in the fourth qualifying round that secured a draw and added another in a 2–0 replay win that took Hendon into the first round proper, where Cardiff City won easily 2–0.

Cardiff City 2 Hendon 0
FA Cup 1st round proper

After a wait of eight years, Hendon finally made it back into the FA Cup proper, but an away tie against Cardiff City would have been tough for a team in good form – let alone one propping up the Isthmian League Premier Division table, as Hendon were.

The Bluebirds had just changed managers so also were not in the best of form, but they had too much firepower for Hendon. Cardiff were determined to keep it simple and play long balls out of defence, while Neil Price had the Hendon team trying to pass their way down the pitch.

Little of note happened in the first half hour and then, out of almost nothing, Cardiff struck. Ian Rodgerson crossed, Scott Young knocked the ball back and Steve White timed his run well to meet the ball and head it past Jan-Gert Wagenaar.

On the stroke of half-time, Josh Price drilled a free-kick against the Cardiff crossbar, though whether the goal would have been allowed is debatable as the assistant referee had his flagged raised for offside. The game was more open in the second half and Dean Murphy had a chance to shoot an equaliser two minutes into the period. He didn't hit the ball cleanly and Elliott made a comfortable save. Four minutes later, Wagenaar produced a great save to deny Carl Dale, then Tony Philliskirk fired over from a good position.

Hendon felt they might have had a man advantage for the final 25 minutes when Jimmy Bolton – on for Jermaine Darlington – was pushed over by Scott Young. The defender, who had already been booked, was very close to being the last man and if he had received a second yellow card, there might well have been a different conclusion. As it was, the referee awarded Hendon a free-kick and nothing more

Just how important that decision was became clear with five minutes to go. John Richardson delivered a cross almost perfectly into the patch of Bolton, until Young deflected the ball out of harm's way. Cardiff clinched the tie in the final two minutes when Craig Middleton drilled home a long-range shot that cannoned off the underside of the crossbar and bounced into the net.

Hendon manager Neil Price said, "The team gave their all and, for long periods, we played better football than they did. We are disappointed to have lost because we thought we could bring them back to our place."

Cardiff City: Elliott, Jarman, Philliskirk, Eckhardt, Young, Fowler, Rodgerson, Middleton, White, Dale, Bennett. Subs Fleming, Lloyd, Perry.

Hendon: Wagenaar, White, Clarke, Murphy, Warmington, P. Kelly, Adams (T. Kelly), Price (Smart), Darlington (Bolton), Richardson, Lewis.

In the league Hendon struggled, not helped by a terrible facial injury suffered by Micky Banton. In his comeback game, he broke his arm. Neil Price received some very unpleasant threatening calls as results didn't improve and in late January he was relieved of his position. Amazingly, Price ended his Hendon management career with an identical league record to that of his predecessor. Andy O'Brien, a stalwart of an earlier era, was promoted from reserve team manager to take over the first team but he lasted only two games before Frank Murphy came in.

Murphy had been a hero at Kettering Town and Barnet – helping the latter to achieve Football League status – before becoming player-manager at Dulwich Hamlet. His relaxed demeanour certainly helped the club – as did the signing of Richard Nugent at the heart of the defence. Murphy's last signing of the season was a goalkeeper, Gary McCann, whose debut was a 3–0 defeat at home to Aylesbury United at the end of March. But it was a different story when the two teams met for the rearranged return match. The Ducks destroyed Hendon in the first half at Buckingham Road, but had only one goal to show for it. Aylesbury manager Gary Phillips withdrew two midfielders who had run the show, inserting a pair of youngsters unprepared for the battle and two goals in the last seven minutes, from Simon Clarke and Dean Murphy brought Hendon maximum points. Hendon eventually avoided the drop with 13 points in hand, finishing 16th with 51 points. Junior Lewis was top scorer with 18.

1997–98: Win at Leyton Orient

Frank Murphy had an almost unlimited bankroll to rebuild the squad. Among the new arrivals were Steve Bateman, a title winner with Chesham in 1993, Tony Lynch, who had been with Murphy as Barnet entered the Football League, Steve Heard and Nas Bashir. On opening day another player arrived: Freddie Hyatt, a midfield artist with a penchant for the spectacular. Other players came during the season, including Matt Howard and, more expensively, Paul Whitmarsh, who signed for the club the day after the Greens beat Leyton Orient.

The new players took a while to settle in, but the club was fortunate to receive a bye to the fourth qualifying round of the FA Cup on the back of the appearance at Cardiff a year before. Normally clubs needed two or three good runs in four or five seasons to earn a bye to that stage, but someone in the FA was smiling at Hendon. The FA Trophy run was short; a replay victory over Havant Town was followed by a 2–1 exit at Bromley.

In the FA Cup, the Greens were drawn to play at St Albans, who were near the top of the Ryman League and hot favourites to advance. But, kicking down the hill in the first half, Hendon snatched two goals from Colin Simpson, a journeyman striker who had just joined the club. The Saints launched everything at Hendon as they tried to get back into the game. One goal was pulled back, but not another and Hendon were into the first round proper for the second consecutive year. St Albans have rarely reached the fourth qualifying round, but only one club has ever beaten them at that stage at Clarence Park – Hendon and this was the second time the Greens had done it.

Hendon 2 Leyton Orient 2
Leyton Orient 0 Hendon 1
FA Cup 1st round proper and replay

When the draw was made, Leyton Orient chairman Barry Hearn invited Hendon to cede home advantage, promising a crowd in excess of 5,000. As it was, less than 3,355 turned up at the Matchroom Stadium (Brisbane Road) for the replay on 25 November, 2,241 having seen the first match at Claremont Road on 15 November.

In games against Football League opposition, it is always vital that the non-league team doesn't concede an early goal, but Hendon made light of doing just that. There were only four minutes on the clock when Martin Ling curled in a corner. The Hendon defence failed to deal with the ball and when it fell to Carl Griffiths, he put it in the net.

Rocked by this early goal, Hendon struggled to make an impression on the Os, but Griffiths was guilty of squandering a couple of chances he would normally have snapped up and by the time the game was 20 minutes old, it was more of a contest. Hendon's equaliser, in the 25th minute, came out of the blue and was missed by many fans. There seemed no danger when Mark Warren rolled a pass back to Paul Hyde. This time the goalkeeper was to suffer the indignity of seeing his clearance blocked by the thigh of the chasing Colin Simpson and could only watch as the ball looped over him and into the net. Credit must go to Simpson, but it was a moment of outrageous fortune for Hendon.

The Greens failed to capitalise on their good fortune and, within eight minutes, were again trailing. Once again the route was a corner, but this time the Hendon midfield did not close down Mark Smith on the edge of the penalty area when the ball was cleared to him. Smith's shot flew through a crowd of players and Gary McCann, who had made some good saves earlier, was unable to do much about this one.

It was hard to know which club was the one from the Football League and the one from the Ryman Premier in the second half. Hendon certainly gave as good as they got and equalised 10 minutes after the restart. John-Simon White delivered a cross which Simpson reached before former Hendon defender Simon Clark. Simpson's header was not perfectly placed, but Hyde missed it and it was 2–2.

Both teams made a couple of changes, Hendon being forced to replace Tony Kelly with Matt Howard and Tony Lynch taking over for the exhausted Simpson. Orient introduced Roger Joseph and the mercurial Joe Baker, who gave Hendon a few problems with his ball control. The Os' finishing, however, was poor.

In the final couple of minutes, Hendon almost snatched a winner. Lynch easily got past two defenders. He picked out Junior Lewis with a teasing cross. Lewis rose well and headed the ball past Hyde and the far post too. When the final whistle was blown by referee Graham Poll it was the visitors who appeared the more relieved to have a second chance, proof if ever it was needed that Hendon had been more than a match for them.

The Os did their best to disrupt Hendon's replay plans by putting in a bid to sign Simpson, publicising the offer a few days before the return. Simpson, desperate to return to the Football League, was obviously interested, but would not make a move while Hendon were in the FA Cup.

For the replay, both teams made a solitary change, Hendon's Howard coming in for Richard Nugent, while Leyton Orient dropped Dave Hanson to the subs bench and brought in Alex Inglethorpe. The match was chosen by BBC Radio 5Live for live second-half commentary with John Murray behind the microphone, assisted by John McGovern.

Once again the Os started well, but didn't take their chances. After two minutes, Griffiths missed from eight yards out and Hendon fans breathed a sigh of relief. Midway through the half, Simpson lifted the ball over Stuart Hicks and ran onto it towards goal. Hyde came off his line and did enough to force Simpson to shoot wide.

McCann was by far the busier goalkeeper, and was in inspired form. He made three or four top saves, mainly low down, denying Griffiths, Ling and Jason Harris. A drive from Orient's Simon Clark narrowly missed. At half-time Os boss sent on Paul Linger for Inglethorpe and he set up Griffiths with an excellent chance, but it was wasted.

Orient, frustrated at not being able to break down the Hendon defence which had been forced to send on Curtis Warmington for the injured Tony Kelly, introduced Baker and Hanson for Harris and Justin Channing, respectively, After 71 minutes, an Orient through ball was over hit and McCann came towards the edge of his box to gather it. He threw the ball out to Simon Clarke, who passed to Hyatt. A piece of outrageous skill saw him flick the ball over the covering Baker. Bringing the ball down quickly, Hyatt sent the ball out to the right wing, where John-Simon White was making a determined run.

Hyatt's pass was perfect. White's cross was inch-perfect for Junior Lewis, who left Clark trailing in his wake as he launched a powerful diving header giving Hyde no chance. With 18 minutes left, Hendon had a lead to defend.

Within three minutes, McCann made another fine save, denying Hicks, who had been pushed forward. Time seemed to stand still for Hendon's fans as wave after wave of Orient attack were launched and failed. Then, with two minutes to go, Griffiths had another chance. He poked the ball goalwards only to see McCann fly across the goal to block the ball out for a corner.

After many minutes of stoppage time, referee Martin Bodenham blew the final whistle to signal a massive Hendon celebration, on the pitch and in the stands. Disgruntled Orient fans called for the head of manager Tommy Taylor.

Hendon boss Frank Murphy said, "We have battled hard and will do the same at Ninian Park. We won't fear Cardiff City, just as we didn't fear Leyton Orient.

Hendon: McCann, White, Clarke, P. Kelly, Nugent, Bateman, Heard, Hyatt, Simpson (Lynch, 81), T. Kelly (Howard, 60), Lewis. Subs: Bashir, Tello, Lomas.
Replay: McCann, White, Clarke, P. Kelly, Howard, Bateman, Heard, Hyatt, Simpson (Banton, 85), T. Kelly (Warmington, 67), Lewis. Subs: Gallagher, Lynch, Lomas.
Leyton Orient: Hyde, Channing, Naylor, Warren, Hicks, Clark, Smith (Joseph, 65), Ling, Griffiths, Hanson, Harris (Baker), 60). Subs: Linger, Inglethorpe, Mackenzie.
Replay: Hyde, Warren, Naylor, Smith, Hicks, Clark, Ling, Inglethorpe (Linger, 46), Griffiths, Harris (Hanson, 74), Channing (Baker, 74). Subs: Joseph, Mackenzie.

Hendon's historic victory at Brisbane Road was followed by a trip to Wales, to face Cardiff City who had beaten the Greens 2–0 in 1996.

Cardiff City 3 Hendon 1
FA Cup 2nd round proper

Hendon's hopes of making the third round of the FA Cup for the second time in their history were dashed at Ninian Park on 6 December. Tony Kelly's knee injury kept him out of the tie, but Richard Nugent was able to return. Only three players were in the Bluebirds' starting line-up in 1997 which had kicked off against the Greens in 1996: Craig

Middleton, Scott Young and Carl Dale.

Cardiff took control of the game from the opening minutes and Hendon struggled to make any sort of impact. Gary McCann was busy dealing with crosses and making saves, albeit routine ones in the opening 20 minutes, while Steve Bateman, Nugent and Howard were kept fully occupied down the middle, with John-Simon White and Simon Clarke struggling to stem the flow of crosses from Anthony Carss and Scott Partridge.

Cardiff took the lead in the 21st minute. A Partridge corner was headed goalwards by Carss but was blocked by a defender. The ball fell to Dale, who slammed the ball home.

If Hendon had been able to go into the break trailing by a solitary goal, they might have had a chance of getting back into the match in the second half. As it was two goals in three minutes sealed the tie in favour of the Welshmen. After 41 minutes, Dave Penney made good ground and got past Paul Kelly. He rolled the ball into the patch of Andy Saville, who shot home. Two minutes later, the Hendon defence was breached again. A cross by Partridge was met by Dale and his header found the bottom corner.

Frank Murphy made a brave substitution at the interval, bringing on the more attacking Greg Tello in place of Howard. But Cardiff, having got a three-goal cushion, were comfortable and confident without needing to inflict more misery on Hendon. Their defence was pretty solid all afternoon, though they did allow the Greens a couple of chances in the first 25 minutes of the second half.

Junior Lewis was in the clear after 55 minutes, but was not able to get much power on his shot, allowing Hallworth to make an easy save. Then midway through the period, Colin Simpson, on what was going to be his final appearance of his first Hendon spell, found himself in some space. His shot beat Hallworth but was off-target. By this time Naseem Bashir had replaced Steve Heard in midfield and it was he who would give Hendon their moment of glory late on.

Jim Rollo, Lee Jarman and Gareth Stoker were all sent on by Cardiff for the final 10 or so minutes, with Chris Beech, Mark Harris and Penney, respectively, given late rests. Murphy had one more change up his sleeve, with Micky Banton and Tony Lynch available – Andy Lomas was the substitute goalkeeper. Banton took over from Paul Kelly for the final five minutes. With four minutes remaining, Freddie Hyatt found Tello, who beat a couple of Bluebirds. His diagonal pass to Bashir was perfect and the substitute made no mistake, lifting the ball over Hallworth into the net.

Cardiff City: Hallworth, Middleton, Beech (Rollo, 80), Young, Harris (Jarman, 80), Partridge, O'Sullivan, Penney (Stoker, 85), Saville, Dale, Carss. Subs: White, Elliott.

Hendon: McCann, White, Clarke, P. Kelly (Banton, 85), Nugent, Bateman, Heard (Bashir, 64), Hyatt, Simpson, Howard (Tello, 46), Subs: Lynch, Lomas

In the league, inconsistency was a byword for Hendon's performances through the first threequarters of the season, but thereafter, the Greens were flying. On 7 March, Hendon were trounced 4–1 at Chesham, Paul Towler unfortunately scoring two own goals. A week later, against Sutton at Claremont Road, Hyatt scored with a 55-yard volley off a goalkeeper's clearance and Hendon won 4–2.

It was not until 21 April, more than seven league matches later, that Gary McCann conceded another goal. Hendon finished the season with nine wins and two draws from their last 11 matches to climb to fifth in the table with 73 points, behind Dagenham & Redbridge on goal difference, but 14 points behind champions Kingstonian.

In the Puma (Full Members) Cup, Hendon did not play lower division opposition until the semi-final, seeing off Purfleet, St Albans City, Gravesend & Northfleet and Dagenham

& Redbridge, before struggling to overcome Maidenhead United 2–1 at home. The final, at Chesham on 29 April, was against Basingstoke Town – the only Premier Division opponents who were lower in the table than Hendon when the match was played.

Basingstoke Town 1 Hendon 4
Puma (Isthmian Full Members) Cup Final

The Frank Murphy era at Hendon was epitomised by fine cup runs and great success in knock-out competitions. This Puma Cup victory was, apart from the one at Leyton Orient, probably the best win of his reign, because Basingstoke, the only team who could match the Greens in terms of recent form, were blown away. To give an indication of what a good team performance it was can be seen by the fact that only Simon Clarke and Steve Heard did not score or assist directly with any of the four goals.

Basingstoke opened the scoring after 14 minutes with a header from Ian Mancey at the far post from a cross by Richard Skelly. The goal knocked back Hendon's confidence for a brief while and Basingstoke looked likely to add to their advantage in the opening 30 minutes. Gary McCann, however, was in fine form and he made a couple of good saves. As the half came to an end, the balance of power shifted the Greens' way and, even without ineligible Paul Whitmarsh, they looked more likely to score.

Tony Kelly put a header from a corner just wide and Steve Bateman blazed over from 12 yards. Junior Lewis could have scored a couple of times, Dean Beale making one good save while he was inches away from connecting with a diagonal ball from Freddie Hyatt which almost shaved the far post.

Six minutes into the second half, the Basingstoke defence had another let-off as Steve Bateman saw his goal-bound header cleared off the line with the now shaky Beale beaten. It delayed the inevitable for about five minutes. Hendon were awarded a free-kick a couple of yards inside their own half. With defenders committed to attack, McCann took the free-kick and sent into the penalty area, where Bateman won a header and set up Tony Kelly, who finished in clinical fashion.

After 57 minutes, Heard was fouled 15 yards outside the Basingstoke penalty area, near to the touchline. Hyatt took the free-kick and Matt Howard headed on the ball. This time it was Lewis who timed his run to perfection and he slotted the ball home.

Basingstoke were struggling to withstand Hendon's attack. A succession of corners and free-kicks were repelled. In the 70th minute, Hyatt curled in a corner and Curtis Warmington, stormed into the penalty area and smashed a header past Beale.

With eight minutes left, Hendon finally scored from open play. Paul Kelly threaded a pass between two Basingstoke defenders into the path of Micky Banton. He controlled the ball, looked up, lobbed the ball over Beale and celebrated with the fans.

After a second half performance like that, there was much to celebrate. As skipper Bateman said, "We showed strong discipline in battling away after falling behind to an early goal. We kept on playing football and 4–1 reflected our superiority.
Basingstoke: Beale, Asker, Emsden (Line, 58), Marshall, Huxford (Coombs, 73), Barker, Wilkinson, Skelly, Mancey, Carey, Tydeman. Sub: Ferrett
Hendon: McCann, T. Kelly, Clarke, P. Kelly, Bateman, Warmington, Heard (Bashir, 84), Hyatt, Banton (Lynch, 86), Howard, Lewis (Nugent, 88).

After winning the Cup, Hendon enjoyed an end-of-season romp against Carshalton Athletic, winning 4–0. Junior Lewis was top-scorer, with 22, followed by Whitmarsh on

15. Third was centre-half Richard Nugent, who contributed eight of his 11 goals in cup ties – four of which came as an emergency centre-forward during an 8–1 romp at Chertsey, when Frank Murphy scored not only on his debut, but with his first significant touch. Simpson, the FA Cup hero, signed for Leyton Orient once the Cup run was over. Half of his eight Hendon goals came in his first two FA Cup ties.

1998–99: Full Members Cup win

Entering the new season, Hendon were made favourites for the league title, based on the great run at the end of 1997–98. An opening day 3–1 defeat at newly promoted Hampton was not in the script, but it was a sign of things to come. In Ryman League matches, Hendon were frequently second-best and finished a disappointing 13th.

Cup competitions were entirely different. The Football Association's decision to make FA Cup entry points based entirely on league status was disappointing, not because Hendon would have benefited, but because as an independent competition, previous success therein should decide the entry point. It nearly all went wrong in the first match – a second qualifying round tie against Southern League Division One Chelmsford. The Clarets, homeless and playing at Billericay, led at Claremont Road until Tony Kelly grabbed a late equaliser. At New Lodge it was 2–0 to Chelmsford before the Greens rallied to win 3–2. Harlow Town were despatched 4–2 and, in the fourth qualifying round, on a dreadful pitch, Bath City made two trips to London and lost on the Tuesday night 4–0. Their captain, and most influential player, was unavailable and Bath thought a fast one had been pulled with the Saturday postponement until they squelched onto the pitch. In the first round proper Hendon faced Notts County at Claremont Road.

Hendon 0 Notts County 0
Notts County 3 Hendon 0
FA Cup 1st round proper and replay

Hendon really should have celebrated a second consecutive season of beating Football League opposition, but settled for a replay against Notts County at Claremont Road. The match was on Sunday 25 November, at lunchtime and drew more home fans than the previous season's Leyton Orient match. However as County brought fewer fans, the overall attendance was lower, 1,627.

The conditions were not to County's liking and if Hendon had scored early in the game – as they should have – the Magpies could have suffered a serious beating.

In the opening minute, Mark Pye set up Paul Whitmarsh, but his shot failed to beat Darren Ward. Seconds later, the goalkeeper made a good save from a Freddie Hyatt free-kick and was nearly caught out by the same player's corner, tipping it over the bar. The next corner was met by Andy Cox, but he put his header over the bar. After nine minutes, Ward was beaten, but Whitmarsh's effort hit the inside of the post.

Having weathered the early storm, County began to get into the match and McCann made a good save to deny Sean Farrell. Hendon's stopper was again at the forefront of the action as he was quickly off his line to deny Farrell again.

Just before half-time, Ward was hurried into a clearance of a Matty Redmile back-pass. The ball fell to Junior Lewis, who tried his luck from 40 yards. Ward sprinted back and was relieved to see the ball bounce just outside the post.

In the second half, the visitors, with the strong, bitingly cold wind at their backs, were more comfortable, without putting the Hendon defence under too much pressure. Gary Jones did have one good chance but Steve Bateman got back well to clear the danger with McCann beaten. In the dying moments, Hendon substitute Matt Maran nearly snatched a winner, but his drive beat Ward and just cleared the crossbar.

The two managers were happy with the result. Frank Murphy said "I am happy with the result. We will have to do it the hard way like we did last year." He also admitted to erring on the side of caution when not sending up his big defenders to attack a last-minute free-kick, which came to nothing. "We had done all the hard work, and it would have been a shame to ruin it all with some Kamikaze tactics at the death," he said.

Sam Allardyce was more circumspect: "We've only got half the job done. We must make sure we don't take Hendon for granted in the replay and we finish the job off."

Ten days later, Hendon set off in bright sunshine for Meadow Lane. As they drove up the M1 the weather closed in. After a brief stop in a local hotel everyone was shocked to find the area blanketed in thick fog. Arriving at the ground, on the banks of the River Trent, it was clear – or not clear actually – that the match was in doubt. And it was no surprise when referee Eddie Wolstenholme called off the game at 7.15pm. Five miles outside of Nottingham it was completely clear. The delay in the replay, now on 1 December, allowed Paul Whitmarsh to complete a three-match suspension.

Hendon again started brightly and, after five minutes, Junior Lewis was sent into the clear by Matt Howard. Darren Ward was quickly off his line and forced Lewis wide. He passed inside to Freddie Hyatt, whose shot was well saved by the recovering Ward. A minute later and Lewis was again clear. This time he could not even get off a shot because Ian Richardson made a magnificent defensive tackle.

Almost immediately, Notts County made a substitution when Hughes limped off and Richard Liburd replaced him. County were soon probing dangerously. After 26 minutes, McCann made a brilliant save to keep out an effort from Liburd, meeting a cross from County skipper Ian Hendon – probably the first time Hendon have played against Hendon (the former Spurs junior did admit to looking for the club's results).

After 33 minutes, Gary Jones burst through, but McCann stopped him. Having weathered late first half pressure, Hendon were grateful to go in at half-time all square.

Notts County started the second half like the first ended – completely on top and it took only two minutes for McCann to be beaten, Gary Fitzgerald, however, making a goal line clearance to keep out an effort from Matty Redmile.

It was no surprise when the Magpies took the lead on the hour mark. A cross from Liburd was met by Shaun Murray, who set up Jones. The ball was half cleared, but Gary Owers drilled it back past McCann for a fine goal.

After 70 minutes, Hendon's best chance of the second half fell to Whitmarsh, but he shot wide. It was a crucial miss because, five minutes later, County effectively sealed the tie. Liburd set up Jones who made no mistake.

With eight minutes to go, Jones got his second of the evening and – on the balance of the two ties – an undeserved third, when he converted a cross from Richard Garcia.

Hendon: McCann, Howard, Clarke, Daly, Bateman, Cox, Pye (Heard, 80), Hyatt, Whitmarsh (Maran, 88), Fitzgerald, Lewis, Subs: T. Kelly, Warmington, Gill.
Replay: McCann, Howard, Clarke, Daly, Bateman, Cox (T. Kelly, 80), Pye (Heard, 80), Hyatt, Whitmarsh, Fitzgerald (Brady, 80), Lewis, Subs: Maran, Gill.
Notts County: Ward, Hendon, Pearce, Fairclough, Redmile, Richardson, Owers, Murray, Jones, Farrell (Liburd, 81), Jackson. Subs: Beattie, Garcia, Quayle.
Replay: Ward, Hendon, Pearce, Redmile, Jackson (Quayle, 87), Richardson, Owers, Garcia, Hughes (Liburd, 6), Jones, Murray. Subs: Beattie, Fairclough

The FA Trophy run also started slowly with a late goal forcing extra time in a replay at Rothwell Town. Hendon had been reduced to 10 men with Simon Clarke's first half dismissal, but the reliable duo of Whitmarsh and Lewis bailed them out. Trips to Worthing and Chesham were successful but the reward was a trip to holders and favourites for the Conference title, Cheltenham Town. An injury-hit Hendon fell 3–0 at Whaddon Road, but Cheltenham didn't do the double, enjoying promotion to the Football League as Conference champions being great solace for a Trophy exit.

Hendon did retain the Puma Full Members Cup and won the Middlesex Senior Cup, playing 25 cup ties in all. With the Claremont Road pitch in a terrible condition, it was just as well the Greens played only four home cup-ties after Christmas. In their 67 matches, Hendon scored 115 goals, with 70 coming from Whitmarsh with 42 and Lewis with 28, but the next highest contributors were Steve Heard, eight, and youngster Matthew Maran, seven, including the winner in a dull Full Members Cup Final. In the Middlesex Senior Cup Final, it needed a penalty shoot-out for Hendon to see off Wembley, for whom Davis Haule was so outstanding Hendon signed him later in 1999.

Hendon 1 Worthing 0
Puma (Isthmian Full Members) Cup Final

Hendon became the first club to retain the Full Members Trophy with a tired victory over Worthing at Sutton United's ground on 6 May.

Freddie Hyatt almost gave Hendon the lead after five minutes. He struck a free-kick which Phil Read should easily have dealt with, but instead fumbled it just over the crossbar. The only goal of the game – after 20 minutes – was certainly deserving of winning a cup-tie and it was out of keeping with most of the match. Matt Maran picked up a ball on the left wing just inside his own half. He carried the ball forward and, with a change of pace, ghosted past Mark Smith. After cutting into the penalty Maran fired a low shot across Read and the ball ended up in the bottom corner.

After 35 minutes, Hendon were awarded a free-kick just outside the Worthing penalty area. John-Simon White slipped the ball to Hyatt, who shot. Read made a brilliant save.

Worthing had much the better of the second half, but they found McCann in inspired form. The goalkeeper produced two magnificent saves, denying Paul Kennett and Ben Carrington. He was ably assisted by both White and Hyatt who made clearances when McCann was beaten.

Hendon: McCann, White, Clarke, Daly, Warmington, Fitzgerald, McKoy (Watson, 85), Hyatt, Whitmarsh, Maran, Lewis. Subs: Howard, T. Kelly.
Worthing: Read, Smith, Knee, Burt, Webber, Kennett, Rutherford, Cox (Robinson, 57), Weston (Simmons, 46), Holden, Carrington. Sub: Craven.

Hendon 2 Wembley 2
Hendon won 4–2 on penalties, after extra time (90mins: 2–2)
Middlesex Senior Cup Final

Hendon were somewhat fortunate to see off a spirited Wembley side that twice led in a stormy Middlesex Senior Cup Final on 5 April.

After failing to take a number of first-half chances, Wembley made the breakthrough after 53 minutes. Danny Norris started and finished the move, albeit following a corner. He instigated a Wembley break with a superb challenge to stop Junior Lewis and, when

278

the ball was played into the opposite box, Matt Howard conceded a corner. The ball, crossed by Ian Bates, was headed home powerfully by Norris.

Hendon's equaliser came from a similar set piece, eight minutes later. Freddie Hyatt delivered the corner, Kelly got the first touch and Jon Daly the second to leave the ball around the penalty spot. What should have been an easy clearance for Wayne Walters suddenly wasn't as Paul Whitmarsh displayed cat-quick reflexes to get in front of the defender and knock the ball past Keita Karamoko.

In the last minute of normal time, Curtis Warmington was cautioned for a foul and Kelly added a comment on the decision. The referee immediately produced a red card, so Hendon faced the extra 30 minutes a man down.

Things should have got significantly worse for the Greens seven minutes into the first period of extra time. Warmington was penalised for handball in his own box. The penalty decision was obvious, the decision not to issue a second yellow card – and thus a red one – not so. Davis Haule made no mistake with the spot-kick.

Whitmarsh's speed around the penalty six-hard box led to Hendon's equaliser after 103 minutes. He sprinted onto a loose ball and was stopped only by Carl Levene's illegal intervention. Whitmarsh picked himself up and made no mistake with the spot-kick.

This led to a penalty shoot-out. Hendon went first. White, Bates and Lewis were all successful. The score stayed at 2–1 when Christie shot wide with Wembley's second penalty before Whitmarsh converted his. Leon Callender made it 3–2. Hendon's next taker was McCann and his effort ended up outside the ground. He atoned by producing a brilliant save to keep out Avi Schwarz's shot. This set up Hyatt who chipped the ball over the diving Karamoke. The ball hit the net behind the crossbar and bounced back into the field of play. Those close by knew it was a goal; everyone else thought it was a miss, until they saw the Hendon celebrations.

Hendon: McCann, Howard (White, 85), Clarke, Daly, Warmington (Brady, 100), Kelly, Fitzgerald, Hyatt, Whitmarsh, Heard (Watson, 53), Lewis.
Wembley: Karamoko, Christie, Mitchell (Schwarz), Walters, Norris, Levene, Bates, McCarthy, Thompson (Callender), Haule, Woodruffe. Sub: Whall.

McCann made 63 appearances out of 67 – Hendon's second straight 67-game campaign – with Simon Clarke, Jon Daly, Matt Howard, Gary Fitzgerald, Hyatt, Lewis and Whitmarsh passing 50 and Steve Bateman, Heard, Maran and Jon-Simon White all topping 45. A dozen players appearing in two-thirds of a team's fixtures suggests a settled side, but 36 appeared in competitive fixtures, showing what a mixed bag the season was.

Off the field, apart from chief executive John Wheeldon's departure after three seasons and Terry Neill's absence, since the Arbiter Group's takeover, the club had run smoothly. However, it became clear that too much money was being spent on the football side and cutbacks, albeit small ones were made. Eventually, in the light of the poor league finish in 1999, a decision had been made to cut the budget significantly.

A Hendon hero: Junior Lewis

Junior Lewis and Peter Taylor can count seven clubs at which the former has been a player and the latter a manager. Whereas they were together at Dover Athletic, Gillingham, Leicester City, Brighton & Hove Albion (Junior on loan), Hull City and Stevenage Borough, at Hendon Taylor pre-dated Lewis by three seasons. Junior's three-season Hendon career will always be remembered for his match-winning goal against Leyton Orient in the FA Cup first round on 25 November 1997. Almost uniquely, he has played at eight of the top nine levels of English football, from the Premiership to the Spartan South Midlands League – only Level 2 of non league football, Conference North and South, has eluded him.

The Wembley-born midfielder's career began at Fulham, but he was released by the Cottagers and joined Dover Athletic, where Taylor became manager in 1995. Junior – not his real name, but woe betide anyone who calls him by anything else – left Dover at the end of the 1995–96 season and signed for Hayes, but left them after a couple of games, signing for Neil Price at Hendon. Nominally a midfielder, Junior played in a far more advanced role at Hendon, where he was a prolific goalscorer, averaging around a goal every other game. One of his best performances in that first season was back at The Crabble, where Conference club Dover were knocked out of the FA Cup by the Greens. Junior was the leading goalscorer in his first two seasons at Hendon, but his most prolific campaign was his last, in 1998–99, when he was partnered by Paul Whitmarsh for the duration. Between them, they scored 70 goals, with Lewis contributing 28 in 55 appearances. Unfortunately, the success in cup competitions affected the league form and Hendon were never really contenders during Junior's time at Claremont Road. He scored 68 goals from 141+5 games for Hendon.

Although, Junior's demeanour on the pitch was often laid back, he possessed an intense desire to succeed. After leaving Hendon, Junior seemed set to join neighbours St Albans City, but just before he signed a contract at Clarence Park, Taylor got the Gillingham manager's job and he invited Junior to join him. Lewis helped Taylor to win promotion to what is now the Championship and stayed with the Gills when Taylor went to Leicester. Junior's last game for Gillingham was an embarrassing 4–0 FA Cup defeat against Chelsea, when Andy Hessenthaler played him at left-back and he was roasted by a rampaging Mikkel Forssel.

Depressed after that performance – he was taken off at half-time – the call to go to Leicester, in the Premiership, even on loan, was a pleasant surprise. Junior's first start, six days after FA Cup debacle, was against Chelsea. The match contained players of the calibre of Gianfranco Zola and Roberto Mancini, but Junior picked up the man-of-the-match award in the Foxes' 2–1 victory. He earned a similar accolade after a win against Manchester United shortly after. The loan deal was quickly made permanent, but things quickly went sour after Taylor moved on. Junior made only 25 league appearances for Leicester in three seasons and went on loan to Brighton, Swindon Town and Hull City. Lewis and Taylor enjoyed promotions on both the south and east coasts.

After leaving Hull in 2005, Junior played briefly at Brentford before joining MK Dons, assisting Martin Allen in the Dons' youth set-up. In this role, Junior sent a few players to Hendon on loan to get playing experience. When Taylor took over at Stevenage Borough during the 2007–08 season, Junior left Edgware Town and went to Broadhall Way, but was released soon after Taylor left in May 2008. Later in the summer, Wycombe Wanderers boss Peter Taylor added Junior to his management team as first team coach.

1999–2000: Bontcho Guentchev arrives

Before the season started, however, the club announced plans to radically redevelop Claremont Road, something that had been necessary for more than a quarter of a century. In simple terms, the ground was falling apart and needed massive work, not just the simple tarting-up of the post-amateur days.

A variety of fund-raising ideas were promoted, from a weekly result prediction game and sponsoring a brick in the new stand for fans to larger more grandiose suggestions for the corporate side. Sadly, but unsurprisingly, given the low level of support for the club, they did not come close to reaching the target. How different things would have been had Blackpool been beaten in the FA Cup in November. The Tangerines' reward for their victory over Hendon was a trip to Highbury; if Hendon had made the trip, the ground rebuilding might have been funded on the back of that match – though quite how many the Gunners would have scored is another matter. John-Simon White admitted that, although heart-broken not to have the opportunity to play at Highbury, he was equally relieved he didn't have to face the speedy Marc Overmars.

Nevertheless, Hendon's feat of reaching the FA Cup proper for the fourth consecutive season in 1999 equalled the club's previous best record set in the 1960s – and for the third straight year made it into the second round draw. Junior Lewis's departure to Gillingham was offset – in terms of goals – by Dominic Gentle, who passed the 20 mark, but got only two in the final third of the season. An injury to Paul Whitmarsh meant he missed a third of the campaign and his goals dried up too – he scored 13 in 35 starts.

Also joining the club was Bulgarian Bontcho Guentchev who, just five years earlier, had replaced World Footballer of the Year Hristo Stoichkov in a World Cup semi-final against Italy. Guentchev had joined Ipswich Town from Sporting Lisbon following the 1994 World Cup and then had a spell at Luton Town. With two boys, Lubomir and Iavor, growing up and part of the Chelsea FC Academy, Bontcho moved into a house on Claremont Road, an easy commute up the M1 to Luton. Released in 1998, Bontcho went home to Sofia to play for CSKA and scored in a UEFA Cup defeat against Atletico Madrid. Nine months later, with a stunning overhead scissors kick volley, he opened his Hendon account against Canvey Island. A Hendon legend was born.

Bath City 0 Hendon 2
FA Cup 1st round proper

Twelve months after Hendon had beaten Bath City at sodden Claremont Road in a fourth qualifying round tie, the two teams were drawn against each other, this time at equally wet Twerton Park on 30 October.

Hendon had only six players left from the team which had won convincingly 12 months earlier and manager Frank Murphy gave the captain's armband to Paul Towler, so he could lead the team out alongside his older brother Colin. Many modern referees would have shown cards to both as they kissed when meeting in the centre circle.

The game kicked off in torrential rain and strong winds (Bath officials kindly allowed Hendon fans – standing in the open – to sit under cover for no extra charge). Hendon sat back for the first 25 minutes, soaking up pressure and playing the ball quickly to the front pairing of Whitmarsh and Gentle. Although Bath had more possession, Hendon's outstanding back four of John-Simon White, Simon Clarke, Towler and Gary Fitzgerald were rarely stretched.

Midway through the first half Mike Davis hit the post. This seemed to wake Hendon up enabling Jon Daly and Freddie Hyatt to prompt from midfield, though with little success as both back fours dominated.

Hendon began the second half in determined fashion as Dale Binns and Marvyn

Watson started running at the Bath full backs. Watson, however, was up against former Welsh international and Bath player-manager Paul Bodin, who had the better of most of the exchanges. Whitmarsh and Gentle were beginning to acquire the service on which they thrive but at the same time, Bath still appeared dangerous on the counter attack.

Neither team could fashion a clear-cut opening, with McCann making three or four excellent claims from dangerous crosses. Elliot Jackson in the Bath goal looked less secure on balls entering his box but he – like McCann – had no direct shot to save.

The deadlock was eventually broken after 88 minutes when substitute Jason McKoy pulled the ball back for Gentle to score with a diving header from 10 yards out.

From the kick off, Bath dangerman Davis went on a mazy run and appeared to be upended in the penalty area. The referee Mr Castle ruled that there was no infringement much to the amazement of both sets of supporters.

Whitmarsh was replaced by Bontcho Guentchev in the first minute of injury time and in the 94th minute Gentle laid a perfect ball through for the Bulgarian who confidently stroked the ball past Jackson into the bottom corner from 15 yards out.

That goal turned out to be effectively the last kick of the match. As Bath trudged off having lost their unbeaten record in all competitions this season, Hendon were celebrating reaching the 2nd round proper for the second time in three years.

Bath City: Jackson, Clode (Tisdale, 46), Bodin, Harrington (Walker, 82), C. Towler, Lloyd, Davis, James, Colbourne, Paul (Fraser, 77), Holloway. Subs: Skidmore, Richards.

Hendon: McCann, White, Clarke, Daly, P. Towler, Fitzgerald, Binns, Hyatt, Whitmarsh (Guentchev, 90+1), Watson (McKoy, 75), Gentle. Subs: Waller, Howard, O'Carroll.

Blackpool 2 Hendon 0
FA Cup 2nd round proper

Blackpool may not have been the draw of 40 years earlier, when Matthews and Mortensen were the Tangerines' stars, but the Greens' fans relished their trip to Bloomfield Road on 20 November where those legends had plied their trade. Struggling in the lower reaches of Division Two, they were not entirely confident of progressing to the next round, especially as their top scorer was out with a broken leg.

Hendon started the game with Jason McKoy attacking on the right and Bontcho Guentchev on the left. The first half was a closely fought affair, but Blackpool had the first chance after nine minutes when Phil Clarkson blazed a shot over the bar. Hendon soaked up the pressure in the opening period, and began to gain more possession.

Guentchev caused Blackpool problems on the left, and McKoy got in a couple of good crosses from the other wing. Gentle and Whitmarsh were proving a handful for the home defence and Whitmarsh came close late in the half. At half-time it was Hendon who went in the happier team. Blackpool realised they had a match on their hands.

In the second half Hendon took the game to Blackpool, who seemed worried as they made a double substitution early in the half. Soon afterwards, Guentchev received a pass on the edge of the area and hit the ball first time. The ball beat Tony Caig, but hit the crossbar and bounced away to safety.

McKoy sent a good cross from the right which Gentle just failed to turn into the net. Blackpool found it more and more difficult to get possession, and were stunned a few minutes later when Guentchev received the ball on his chest with his back to goal, and launched an overhead kick which Caig did extremely well to turn over the bar.

The strong wind, at Blackpool's backs in the second half proved to be the Tangerines' saviour. A long clearance from Caig deceived Paul Towler, who headed the ball back towards his own goal, and Gary McCann had to turn the ball over the bar for a corner.

The corner was scuffed into the penalty area and cleared for another one. This time, from another mis-hit, the ball fell to Simon Clarke, who could only clear it back to the taker. This time the cross found Phil Clarkson who gave Blackpool an undeserved lead.

Four minutes later, a ball from the Hendon left bounced between McKoy and John-Simon White, with neither able to reach it. Instead, Blackpool took possession and, when the ball was delivered into the penalty area, John Durnin was able to score.

At 2–0 it looked as if it was all over, but the Hendon supporters stayed behind their team, and substitutes Matthew Maran and Mavuto Sakala both caused trouble for Blackpool. In a magnificent gesture at the end of the match, hundreds of Blackpool supporters stayed to give the Hendon players a standing ovation.

Blackpool: Caig, Hills, Carlisle, Hughes, Clarkson, Bushell, Bryan, Lee, (Bent, 54), Coid (Forsyth, 54), Murphy, Durnin (Nowland, 89). Subs: Beesley, Lambert.
Goals: Clarkson (72), Durnin (76).
Hendon: McCann, White, Clarke, Daly, Towler, Fitzgerald, Guentchev, Hyatt, Whitmarsh (Sakala, 82), McKoy (Maran, 75), Gentle. Subs: Howard, Baker, Watson.

In the Ryman League, the opening game of the season saw Aldershot Town attract a crowd of 1,005, the Green's biggest home league attendance for many years, an indication of how support for non-league football in London had fallen since the 'amateur' days, when an attendance for a home first team game below 1,000 was rare. Hendon were a little more consistent than in the previous season and ended in eighth place, though their 62 points left them closer to relegation than to second-placed Aldershot Town. The champions – Dagenham & Redbridge – were 39 points clear of the Greens. Frank Murphy's budget was again cut for the season as bad weather continued to hamper the club. Gary McCann suffered what would prove to be a career-ending knee injury at Harrow Borough.

In early September, Hendon made a significant signing. Nathan Edwards, aged 17, was put on contract, the first member of the Sunday youth set-up to be signed. Other players had made a few first-team appearances, notably Jerrel Ifil, who – if he had not been snapped up by Watford – would certainly have preceded him. In the 14 seasons of the Hendon youth teams, no player has been a regular in the first team, though a few have played League football - Chris Moore, Ifil and Leon Constantine to name three.

Apart from the FA Cup run, which nearly changed the club's history for ever, there was little to celebrate in knock-out competitions. Hendon played only 15 cup ties, including the George Ruffell Memorial Shield (Middlesex's version of the FA Charity Shield, for the County Cup and Charity Cup winners), five of which were in the FA Cup. Hendon lost the Memorial Shield 4-2 to Hampton and Richmond Borough. In the Full Members Cup, a 2-2 draw after extra time at Claremont Road against Wealdstone was settled by a penalty shoot out, which Hendon lost 7-6.

Hendon's last match of the 20th century was a 3–2 victory at Aylesbury United on 18 December, Paul Whitmarsh scoring the third goal. The first match of the new Millennium, on 3 January 2000, was a dreary 1–0 defeat at Dulwich Hamlet. The Greens' first goal of the 21st century was by Dominic Gentle in a 2–2 draw at home to Enfield.

Claremont Road

HENDON F. C.

Photos taken in 2004 and 2005 by Peter Lush

11. 2000 to 2008: Into the new century

With another budget cut set for the 2000–01 season, it was surprising that Frank Murphy agreed to stay. He had replaced his long-time assistant Barry Simmons with Dave Anderson – a passionate Ulsterman. They made for a strange couple: Murphy a Catholic and rabid Celtic fan; Anderson, Protestant and equally keen Rangers supporter. They put their religious and philosophical differences behind them and worked well as a team. On the bench, long-time physio Caroline Brouwer moved jobs and was replaced by Gary Anderson, who had been at Barnet when Murphy played there.

The squad contained a number of new faces, but the biggest concern was in goal, where McCann was injured. Andy Iga was out of the country for the pre-season friendlies and former youth-team goalkeeper Farai Jackson played. For all his agility he was simply too slight for Hendon's level, and Iga's return days before the season started was welcomed. He lost form and Richard Wilmot came in on loan from Hitchin Town.

The team did not reach the FA Cup first round proper this season. In the fourth qualifying round, after six postponements, Dagenham & Redbridge triumphed 3–1, Ross Pickett scoring. The game should not have been played because the Claremont Road pitch was terrible. It was nine weeks before Hendon could host another fixture.

The resulting fixture congestion was a real problem – it was not confined to the Greens, but Hendon were the worst hit – and as a result of a League vote in March, the season could not be extended and a number of clubs finished the season without playing a full 42-game schedule. On 1 March 2001, Hendon had played 21 League matches; on 1 April, it was 25, leaving 17 matches to be played in 35 days.

In the end, the weather won, because Hendon finished the season having played just 40 League matches. On the final day, an FA ruling meant the Greens' fixture at Sutton United, having been postponed three times, including twice in the final week, was scheduled for 8am, the match against Dulwich Hamlet for 3pm and then back to Claremont Road for a game with Harrow Borough at 8pm. All this was after meeting Aldershot 24 hours and Gravesend three days earlier. Sutton could not stage their game because they could not arrange security, and the Harrow match did not need to be played because Borough were safe from relegation as a result of other matches kicking-off at 3pm. To add to the problems of the final day, Dulwich's captain suffered a serious injury, which resulted in a 45-minute delay in the first half. Every other match in the Ryman League had been completed before Hendon kicked off for the second half at Champion Hill. Hendon won 3–0 to finish the season in 12th place.

It could be considered fortunate that Hendon were not bothered by cup competitions, Tiverton Town having surprised the Greens at Claremont Road in January with a 2–1 win in the FA Trophy, while the Full Members Cup tie, played on the last Saturday of 2000 was an 11-goal thriller which Hendon lost in extra-time despite leading 4–1 after 45 minutes. The pitch at Heybridge was unplayable, especially at one end and the referee admitted after the match that he would not have allowed a penalty shoot-out had Guentchev taken a chance to equalise in the 120th minute.

Guentchev was also involved in one of Hendon's more remarkable matches of recent times. In November, on the day of the FA Cup first round, the Greens travelled to Carshalton. It was Wilmot's last match on loan and after 30 minutes, he broke his arm. However, he didn't come off and kept goal for the final 15 minutes in agony. At half-time it was clear he could not continue, but Hendon having already made one defensive substitution in the first half were considering putting full-back Simon Clarke in goal. Guentchev told Frank Murphy he had kept goal in Bulgaria. Hendon fans were shocked to see the veteran World Cup star coming out in a goalkeeper's shirt.

Trailing 1–0 at half-time, Hendon drew level with a goal from Pickett, while Guentchev caught a couple of crosses. The one save he had to make was in vain, because the referee had already blown for a foul, but it was a decent one. When the ball came along the ground to Guentchev, the Bulgarian controlled it, dribbled past a bemused attacker and passed the ball 30 yards to a team-mate. In the Hendon dug-out Frank Murphy and Dave Anderson could not believe their eyes.

In the last two minutes, skipper Gary Fitzgerald was sent off for a second bookable offence. But Hendon dealt with the danger from the free-kick which resulted and David Adekola set up Dale Binns for Hendon's winner. Although Binns joined Hendon from the youth set-up, it was in the midweek under–18 team where he first showed his talents and not the Sunday sides. Nevertheless he became a long-standing member of the squad, scoring more than 40 goals in just over 200 appearances, and was this season's top scorer with 18.

2001–02: Middlesex Senior Cup victory

At the end of the previous season, another budget cut was forced on the manager and, this time, Murphy resigned. Curtis Warmington, by now player-coach, and Dave Anderson, were interviewed for the post, with the latter chosen – and it proved to be an inspired choice by Ivor Arbiter and Andrew Landesberg. Dave brought in Jon Turner as his assistant and Warren Kelly became player-coach, though his playing days ended in a pre-season friendly at Hillingdon Borough.

It took a while for the new-look team to come together. In the FA Cup, Hitchin Town won a second qualifying round replay 3–1 after extra time, having equalised in the last minute of the second game. The FA Trophy was different. Entering in the first round proper, Hendon saw off Sutton United, Maidenhead United and Cambridge City, before falling 2–1 to Gravesend & Northfleet at Stonebridge Road in the fourth round. The third round tie was dramatic. In the game at Milton Road, Dale Binns was dismissed. A brilliant free kick by Byron Bubb hit the angle of crossbar and post for Ofori to score. But a couple of minutes later Cambridge equalised from a free kick to set up a replay.

The game at Claremont Road was called off half an hour before kick-off after the referee discovered glass on the pitch. A pile of sand heaped against the outside wall of the ground near the car park, to be used on the pitch when necessary, had been tainted with some broken bottles or glasses. The fixture was moved to St Albans' Clarence Park on the day of the fourth round, where Hendon won 2–0. Three days later Gravesend & Northfleet won 2–1 to end Hendon's run.

The last game of 2001 was undoubtedly the best one, a 6–4 League victory at Billericay Town, Hendon scored three times at the wrong end and six at the correct one. Trailing 3–1 at half-time, the Greens produced an incredible 45 minutes of thrilling, football. A third six-goal haul away from home came in March when Heybridge Swifts were demolished 6–1. In November relegation bound Enfield had succumbed 6–0 at Boreham Wood.

Eight wins and a draw from the last 10 league fixtures – starting with the game at Heybridge and followed by a 5–0 crushing of Bedford Town away – resulted in a finishing position of eighth, a superb result. Martin Randall and Ricci Crace finished as joint top scorers with 13, but both Binns and Eugene Ofori reached double figures. Overall Hendon netted 100 goals in 57 matches. There was silverware, too, to be celebrated as the Greens won the Middlesex Senior Cup Final against Northwood at Hayes. In five County Cup ties, Hendon scored 20 goals, including five each against Kingsbury Town, Staines Town and Conference club Hayes.

Part of the turnaround must be attributed to the centre-back pairing of Steve Butler – the son of former player Roy – and Mark Cooper. Three matches apart from the Middlesex Senior Cup Final were played on either neutral or the opponent's ground: the FA Trophy tie at St Albans; Hendon ceded home advantage to Aldershot Town in the League Cup and lost 2–0; Staines did likewise in the County Cup and Hendon won 5–0.

Hendon 4 Northwood 2 after extra time (90 mins 1–1)
Middlesex Senior Cup Final

Hendon won the Middlesex Senior Cup for the 13th time with a hard-fought 4–2 victory over Northwood at Hayes on 1 April. In the 21st minute, a drilled cross from Binns was met by Martin Randall at the near post, but Riordan produced a spectacular save. After this, Northwood began to get into the match, but Steve Butler and Mark Cooper dealt with everything thrown at them.

Photo: Hendon celebrate (PL)

Ten minutes after the break, Ofori took a quick corner to Binns, who crossed the ball first time. First to react was Randall, and his header was parried by Riordan into the net.

Midway through the second half, Scott Fitzgerald replaced Gavin Hart who had struggled to make an impression. In the 75th minute, Micky Woolner was booked for fouling Yaku. Three minutes later, Woolner committed another foul, and it cost Hendon dear. The kick was taken quickly and short. Chris Gell buried a header past Hook.

In the 103rd minute, however, Riordan was beaten as Hendon got a stroke of luck. A shot from Binns, following a cleared corner, fell to Steve Butler. He helped the ball on to Randall, who scored. And, less than a minute later, Randall was denied a hat-trick when a fine shot cannoned off the base of a post. The goal of the game came seconds before the end of the first period of extra time. Substitute Ricci Crace picked up the ball just outside the Northwood box and beat three defenders before shooting low past Riordan.

With five minutes left, Yaku scored with a chip over Hook. Suddenly Northwood were back in the game, although time was against them. In the last minute, with Northwood over-committed to attack, Randall passed to Binns, who waited for Riordan to commit himself before scoring. "I have never lost a cup final," said Hendon manager Dave Anderson. "But I had also never won against Northwood, so something had to give."

Hendon: Hook, Towler, M. Burgess, Forbes (Bates, 89), Butler, Cooper, Bubb (Crace, 90), Woolner, Randall, Ofori, Binns. Subs: Clarke, Yates, McCann (gk).
Northwood: Riordan, Nolan, Sargeant, D. Butler, Hamlet, Williams, Cook, Gell, Hart (sub Fitzgerald, 66), Yaku, Ashe. Subs: Carter, McIntosh, Felton.

A Hendon hero: Simon Clarke

Simon Clarke is almost uniquely qualified to become a football coach or manager as he has played in almost every position. He began his career as a striker at West Ham United, making three substitute appearances for the Hammers. After leaving them, he joined Kettering Town then, in the summer of 1995, Hendon, now as central or left-sided midfielder. By the time he left Claremont Road in 2002, having played 341+12 games and scored 16 goals, he was a left-back and emergency goalkeeper, having donned the gloves around 10 times. Simon's final appearance at Claremont Road was playing for Maldon Town, by which time he was a central defender.

It would be fair to say that he took a while to become the managers' favourite because Micky Browne, Neil Price and Frank Murphy all transfer-listed him, but there were no takers. In Simon's seven seasons, he played under four managers.

Simon struggled to fit in with Browne's style, his midfield skills being too intricate for the coach's preferred high-tempo, high-pressure system. He was being frozen out when Neil Price replaced Browne and the former Watford player tried him at left-back, a move that worked well. Early in 1996–97, Clarke fell out of favour with Price and was again put on the transfer list. A near ever-present in cup-ties, Simon missed a third of the league campaign with Price leaving him out and he suffered an injury late in the season.

Price's reign ended in the winter of 1997 and Frank Murphy replaced him, keeping Clarke in the team at left-back. In a rare game in midfield, late in the 1996–97 campaign, Simon scored one of the most important goals of that season, the last-minute winner at Aylesbury. His left-footed drive fairly flew into the top corner of the net at Buckingham Road.

When the team started slowly in the 1997–98 season, Simon was one of four players made available for transfer, though all kept their places in the team. It was a spur that seemed to work because Simon's form improved dramatically and he was a key part of the great FA Cup run that season. Simon picked up winners' medals in both the Middlesex Senior Cup and the Full Members Cup.

He took over the gloves for Hendon at Enfield in 1999 when Gary McCann was injured with a knee strain.

The weather-affected 2000–01 season was not Simon's best as he was restricted to only 44 appearances, missing six League games in a frantic end to the season. It was the only time in his final five campaigns that he failed to break the 50 mark.

Commuting from Chelmsford became too much for Simon, so although he won the 2001–02 Supporters Association Player of the Year Award, he decided to leave the club, joining Chelmsford City. He played 341+12 games for Hendon, scoring 16 goals. Unfortunately a broken leg curtailed his first season, but he was the Clarets player of the year in his second campaign. A move to Boston followed, but he then returned to Essex playing for Maldon Town.

A fine left-back, with a sweet left foot, Simon will be remembered as a loyal servant to Hendon and a thoroughly nice person to boot.

2002–03: Middlesex Senior Cup retained

For the new season, Hendon had the unusual experience of playing 46 League matches as the Ryman League expanded to 24 clubs. It was a two season experiment and it did not work for the Greens who collected just four points from the extra eight games, costing them a runners-up berth in 2004.

This season was remarkably successful. Hendon finished third in the table with 79 points, which left them 27 clear of relegation, but 26 behind champions Aldershot Town, who themselves had a 13-point cushion on perennial runners-up Canvey Island. Canvey and the Greens met four times with the two matches at Park Lane providing 14 goals. In the League in September, the 4–4 draw was remarkable. Hendon led 2–0, were pegged back to 2–2, only to go 3–2 up. Canvey went down to 10 men when Lee Protheroe saw red just before the break but, in the second half, Hendon keeper David Hook, in his second season as first choice keeper, was completely overworked as the hosts laid siege on the Greens' goal. They equalised, but Hendon went 4–3 up after 81 minutes. Canvey won a penalty in the final minutes. Both teams finished as disappointed not to have won and grateful not have lost. The management teams hated the game; the fans loved it.

In the Bryco (League) Cup semi-final, the Gulls were slightly fortunate to take a two-goal lead from the game at Park Lane, winning 4–2, but they stifled the return and having jumped to a 2–0 lead, were not concerned as Hendon pulled back two of their four-goal deficit. The Ryman League fixture at Claremont Road was uneventful, Ricci Crace scoring the only goal.

Summer signing Keiron Gallagher proved a little disappointing. He was outstanding when at Aylesbury, playing under Anderson, who was Bob Dowie's assistant at Buckingham Road, but a terrible leg injury meant he was never the same player.

The FA Cup was again a disappointment with a third qualifying round exit to Hastings United. However, their goalkeeper, Dave King, would join Hendon for 2003–04 and spend three seasons at Claremont Road. The FA Trophy was more entertaining, but again the Greens were unable to advance too far. Victories over Bognor Regis Town and Heybridge Swifts set up a fourth-round tie at Wakefield & Emley, played at Wakefield Trinity Wildcats rugby league club. The 15,000 capacity stadium had 519 fans watching a 0–0 draw. The referee dismissed three players in the first half: Paul Yates of Hendon and Ryan Crossley and Mark Wilson of Wakefield & Emley. Wilson had the last laugh in the replay, scoring in extra time after Gallagher had a first half penalty saved.

The Trophy run may have been over but the Middlesex Senior Cup was won again, for the 15th time, equalling the County record. Hillingdon Borough, Wealdstone (after the first match was abandoned at half-time) and Hampton & Richmond Borough were beaten before Enfield Town – formed by disillusioned former Enfield FC officials and supporters – provided the Final opposition on 21 April.

Enfield Town 0 Hendon 2
Middlesex Senior Cup Final

Hendon became the first team in 22 seasons to retain the Middlesex Senior Cup when they overcame Enfield Town 2–0 at Northwood FC. If the Greens had taken their chances, the game could have been over in the opening four minutes. After barely a minute, Eugene Ofori put Ricci Crace clear. His strike beat Andy Hall, but flew wide.

In the fourth minute, Paul Yates and Crace linked on the edge of the penalty area and when the former crossed towards the near post, Ofori got in front of his marker, but at full stretch he diverted the ball inches wide of the near post.

Enfield Town had their best spell of the match between Hendon's two misses and the first goal, barely 15 minutes. David Hook was forced into making a couple of saves and

Daniel Clarke shot wide. Apart from that, Steve Butler and Mark Cooper totally dominated Enfield Town's front two and Jamie Burgess and Rob Hollingdale ensured little danger came from the flanks.

The opening goal arrived in the 19th minute, much to the dismay of Enfield Town's defenders, who were convinced that Crace was offside. The ball from Dale Binns was perfect and Crace was alone as he headed home.

Jon-Barrie Bates and Paul Towler exerted a tight grip on the midfield, with Bates making a number of incursions towards the Enfield penalty area. Crace and Ofori both had half-chances before Hendon scored a second goal 10 minutes before the interval.

The move started with Ofori, who passed to Bates, who quickly fed Yates. He was closed down by Mathew Negus, so passed back to Burgess, who delivered a cross right into the path of Ofori, who buried a header beyond Andy Hall. With 55 minutes remaining the game was decided. If Hendon's finishing had been more clinical, the previous County record of 5–0 would have been blown away.

Enfield brought on Tommy Morgan and Steve Baldwin for veteran Paul Turner and Graeme Hall, respectively, while Iain Duncan replaced Burgess for Hendon. The two newcomers could do little for Enfield, while Duncan slotted smoothly at right back.

The second half was a litany of chances for Hendon, none of which were taken.

"We were always in control," said manager Dave Anderson. "But we had to be professional and keep our discipline. I am delighted that we have retained the cup."

Enfield Town: A. Hall, Allen, Negus, Gant (Riley, 65), G. Hall (Baldwin, HT), Quinn, Brotherton, Ridout, Clarke, Turner (Morgan, HT), St. Hilaire. Subs: Alleyne, Carr.

Hendon: Hook, J. Burgess (Duncan, HT), Hollingdale, Towler, Cooper, Butler, Ofori, Bates, Crace (Randall, 59), Yates, Binns. Subs: Alves, Endersby, McCann (gk).

Hendon triumphant after retaining the Cup (PL)

Off the field things were far from rosy; indeed it would not be an exaggeration to say that fans had no idea how parlous the situation had become. For financial reasons, the Arbiter Group planned to disinvest in the club as soon as Claremont Road was sold. The Council was happy for Hendon FC to take over at Barnet Copthall Stadium, a desolate running track stadium – the Borough Sports Ground – but totally unsuited to football both in terms of its location and accommodation. Plans were put in place for the development of the stadium but, unfortunately, Ivor Arbiter was unaware of the true cost of the project. Nevertheless things started moving forward, albeit at a glacial pace.

2003–04: Middlesex Senior Cup hat-trick

Andrew Landesberg's final match watching Hendon was the first game of the 2003–04 season, a 1–0 defeat of newly-promoted Hornchurch. Another team new to the division were Kettering Town, relegated from the Conference, who decided the Ryman League was an easier option – or so their chairman claimed in print.

Another team with a big payroll was Grays Athletic and Hendon had no answer to their star striker Freddie Eastwood, whose hat-trick ended the Greens' FA Cup interest in the third qualifying round. The FA Trophy run was even briefer, a single tie against Kettering which ended in a penalty shoot-out defeat in a replay. The Bryco (League) Cup was a huge disappointment, with a 4–3 defeat at Bracknell Town on 3 January 2004, although the Greens felt aggrieved at their exit. Four penalty appeals were turned down and Bracknell's first goal was a 25-yard shot which struck a divot and flew seven feet in the air, over the diving Dave King, who was made to look bad by the capricious bounce.

At least there was the Middlesex Senior Cup to enjoy as Dave Anderson completed a hat-trick of wins. Potters Bar, Northwood and Southall were dispatched before the final.

Hendon 3 Uxbridge 1 after extra time (90 min: 1–1)
Middlesex Senior Cup Final

Hendon won their third consecutive Middlesex Senior Cup for the first time in 30 years with a 3–1 extra-time victory over Uxbridge. It was hard work, though, especially after Dale Binns had been sent off following a 58th minute clash with John Swift.

Hendon dominated the first half, but failed to turn their advantage into goals. In the 17th minute, Ricci Crace curled a shot just wide of Ray Francis' right post and it signalled a period of dominance from Hendon. In the 27th minute, Francis parried away a shot from Andy Cook. In the 39th minute, Binns volleyed just over the bar.

As the half wound down, Hendon upped the pressure and Cousins struck a 22-yard free kick just wide. Then Forbes beat three defenders but Francis blocked a low shot.

The first 15 minutes of the second half ensured that passion would be to the fore for the rest of the game. It started in the 50th minute, when Crace got in front of Stuart Bamford, crossed and joined in the celebrations after Eugene Ofori scored.

Five minutes later, Binns conceded a free-kick just outside the Hendon penalty area. The ball was crossed in and Mark Weedon smacked it home for the equaliser.

In the 58th minute, Binns and Swift contested a ball 15 yards from the Uxbridge goal line and a throw-in was awarded Hendon's way. Binns stepped back towards Swift, who raised his hands to stop his opponent trampling on him. Binns responded by lowering his head towards Swift. He didn't make contact, but the referee sent him off.

With a man advantage, Uxbridge took control, but Steve Butler, Mark Cooper and

Mark Burgess were in commanding form and limited their chances. Dave King produced a magnificent save to keep out a shot from Jamie Cleary. Then, in the fourth minute of stoppage time, a low cross was parried by the goalkeeper into the path of Mark Royal eight yards out with the goal gaping. To Uxbridge's horror, he shot tamely over the bar.

And as the first extra period went into added time, the Greens struck. The goal was almost identical to the first. Ofori took the ball off Chris O'Leary and rolled the ball to substitute Dave Hunt, who gleefully found the back of the net.

There was still enough time before the period ended for to score again. This time it was Scott Cousins down the left who crossed. Ofori had a shot blocked, but when the ball fell to substitute Martin Randall, he despatched it with aplomb. Uxbridge were broken by this quick fire double strike and the Hendon defence held on comfortably. "I am delighted to win the Cup again," said a happy Dave Anderson. "You never win a cup easily, and Uxbridge made us work very hard tonight."

Hendon: Dave King, Cousins, M. Burgess, Howard, Cooper (Hunt, 100), Butler, Crace (Randall, 102), Cook, Ofori (Gavin, 113), Forbes, Binns. Subs: McLeish, J. Burgess.

Uxbridge; Francis, Swift, O'Leary, Weedon, S. Bamford, G. Bamford, Cleary, Walters (Rundell, 81), Tunnell (Jones, 90), Royal, Howell. Subs: Poulter, Daryl King, Swift.

Action from the match, and the Hendon team with the Cup. (PL)

Among the new signings for the season were former Chelsea youngster Scott Cousins, whose father – also Scott – had played for Hendon's reserves in his younger days, and Dave Hunt, yet another former Ware player, like Crace and goalkeeper Luke Thornton. During the season striker John Frendo also signed, played in the County Cup at Northwood and was then loaned back to Ware for the rest of the season.

But it was the Ryman League Premier Division where Hendon really excelled. Eugene Ofori, now in his third season a respected and feared striker at this level, averaged a goal every other game, scoring 27 times, including 20 in the league, while Crace, in another injury-ravaged campaign scored 12 times in 43 games of which only 29 were starts. Martin Randall's goals dried up, not for the want of trying, with only six in 34 appearances. A sign of stability in Anderson's squad was that by the end of the season, Dale Binns had made 210 appearances, seven others – Jon-Barrie Bates, Steve Butler, Mark Cooper, Crace, Iain Duncan, Steve Forbes and Ofori – had passed the 100 mark, while Randall was on 99. This list excludes Gary McCann, who made a one game comeback to lift his career total to 195, James and Mark Burgess and Dave King, all of whom would reach three figures later in their Hendon careers.

A 15-game unbeaten run from the end of January 2004 took Hendon to second in the table, a position they held until to the final weekend of the season, albeit a long way behind leaders and eventual champions Canvey Island. This was the second and last season of the 24-team division and was also the end of the Isthmian League at the second level of non league football. The FA bowed to pressure and created the Conference South and North Divisions, feeding into the Conference Premier or National.

This had a major effect on not only the Ryman League, but also the Southern and Northern Premier Leagues, who lost 40 clubs between them to this new level, and effectively became more minor leagues. To fill the two new divisions, each of the three feeder leagues, after years of bickering, gave up 14 clubs, to form the new division, plus their champions who moved straight to Conference Premier. Teams from second to 13th automatically went up, while all the others not in a relegation position played off (together with the two Division One champions). The upshot of the playoffs was the Lewes – Division One South champions – and St Albans rose to Conference South.

Dave Anderson (PL)

Hendon finished fourth in the table, and a point a game from matches 43 to 46 would have brought a runners-up berth. While club officials were debating the future, Dave Anderson had already been interviewed twice by AFC Wimbledon – the latest in the trend of clubs run by their fans – who were about to take their place in the reconstituted Ryman League Division One South. It was a job opportunity he could not turn down.

It was a difficult time for the chairman and the holding company. Ivor Arbiter – who had ceased to be an executive of the company bearing his name a year earlier – fell seriously ill having, in the last few years lost his 96-year-old mother and his son and watched his wife battle cancer. The Arbiter Group were not prepared to finance Hendon FC to the level they had over the previous decade. They had downsized significantly, selling their headquarters and making some staff redundant. The former employees looked at Hendon and asked why the company financed football and sacrificed them.

Back at Claremont Road, the financial situation was simple: if Hendon went up to Conference South, the club would almost certainly go broke. However, Dave Bedford agreed, through various sponsorships he had found, to provide funds exclusively for players' wages, provided they were put in a 'ring-fenced account'. On the Friday before the scheduled Monday announcement of the make-up of the two new divisions, a painful meeting took place involving Hendon. Arbiter contacted Ryman League chairman Alan Turvey from the meeting, to inform him of the gravity of Hendon's situation. Turvey said that Hendon could remain in the Ryman League if they wished. Immediately a fax was sent to the FA and the Ryman League that Hendon Football Club would not be taking their place at level 2 of non-league football, effectively relegating themselves, although without the stigma of being in a relegation place. The club was accepting demotion to a lower level than their performances on the pitch had merited.

The club website and message board almost melted down in a sea of vitriol from angry fans. Other clubs, however, complained to Hendon that their decision had come too late for them to make the same one which they wanted to take but didn't wish to be the first to be seen to refuse promotion. It was a very brave decision by the club and if it really meant its survival, then it was correct. From a purely football standpoint, however, it was another example of a chance for Hendon to advance being missed.

2004–05

Ivor Arbiter, with his new vice-chairman, Dave Bedford – the former world record-holding athlete was a long-time fan of the club – and Graham Etchell set about finding a new manager. There were almost 20 applicants, with four of a high quality. They were invited for an interviews and one stood out. He was offered the job and accepted.

The choice was Tony Choules, who had worked minor miracles at Northwood, overseeing their rise from the lower divisions of the Isthmian League to the Premier, and had left just before the season ended. He brought with him as his assistant Gary Farrell. A few pre-season friendlies were arranged, but with almost all of the 2003–04 squad no longer under contract, there were few players left. When pre-season training started, Hendon had eight players in attendance. Choules and Farrell worked very hard and put together a squad that should have been competitive in this new, lower level division.

However, all the promise of pre-season disappeared as Yeading, newly-promoted from Division One North, beat the Greens 3–2. Hendon's goals came in the final few minutes after DJ Campbell – who would end the season at Brentford – had missed many chances and still scored twice. Central defenders Danny Butler and René Street, back for his second spell at Claremont Road, were not quick and the midfield was similar with neither Richard McDonagh nor Wayne Carter blessed with much pace.

For goals, Hendon looked to John Frendo, Eugene Ofori and Mark Nicholls, the latter who had been in Chelsea's 16 when they won the 1998 European Cup Winners Cup. Sadly, there were few games when Nicholls was outstanding. Nevertheless he scored 24 goals in two-thirds of the season.

Hendon actually were more than competitive and were in the top two when they travelled to Stevenage for an FA Cup fourth qualifying round. Holmer Green, Bedford Town and Leyton, after a replay, had been beaten in the first three qualifying rounds. In an embarrassing afternoon, Borough won 5–0, but Hendon finished with eight players, the Burgess twins, Mark and James, and McDonagh all dismissed. Mark Burgess's red card was overturned on appeal, but his gesture to a fan got a two-game ban.

It was the end of Choules's brief reign. He resigned following the game, partly because of the performance, but mainly because he felt he had misled the players when he agreed terms with them. At his previous clubs, what the players agreed to receive in payment was what they got in their pay packets. At Hendon, since the days of Victor Green and what was now common practice in most senior clubs, the players were taxed at source. This meant that players did not have worry about paying tax, but the money they received was net rather than gross, i.e. around threequarters of what they were expecting. Many players initially were upset at this payment but once it was explained to them, they understood; Choules, however, felt he was responsible and quit.

Gary Farrell was appointed manager and his first game was against Dave Anderson's AFC Wimbledon at Claremont Road in the FA Trophy. There were 13 former Hendon people at Kingsmeadow, including assistant manager Jon Turner, coach Warren Kelly, physio Mike Rayner, reserve team manager John Morris and two reserve team players. The new Hendon was too strong for old Hendon, crushing AFC Dons 3–0 in front of 1,184 fans. The Trophy run continued into the new year after another fine performance – and same scoreline – saw a win at Taunton Town.

In the Ryman League, things started going wrong. A couple of awful decisions and some bad luck led to some defeats, but things spiralled out of control in December. It started just before Christmas with a 5–2 hammering at Heybridge Swifts. On Boxing Day, goalkeeper Dave King was sent off after three minutes against Wealdstone. Full back Dave Nolan, who made his first team debut 15 years after he left the club as a youth team player, took over, conceded a goal from the free-kick, and Hendon lost 4–1.

There was respite on New Years' Day, as a Nicholls penalty was too good for relegation-bound Dover Athletic. The next seven matches – four league, three cup – saw 32 goals conceded, including seven at Eastleigh. At Slough, in the FA Trophy, Hendon were lucky only to lose 4–3, despite nearly snatching a replay. Three days later Division One Leatherhead scored four times in 10 minutes to first force extra time and then run away with a Bryco (League) Cup tie, taking it 6–3.

Yeading and Fisher Athletic both won County Cup ties scoring four times, the former needing extra time after a rare cohesive Hendon performance. But at Fisher, when James Parker made his debut, it could have been six or eight at half-time. Fisher eased up in the second half and nearly let their advantage slip.

The Fisher defeat was the last straw. Hendon had a 10-day gap until the next fixture and Ivor Arbiter was back from a period of overseas recuperation following surgery to make the obvious decision. Mr Farrell and his assistant Colin Payne were dismissed.

In came an old face, but actually quite a young one. Gary McCann's playing career had been ended by a serious knee injury before his 30th birthday and he now wanted to get into management – commitments to his business having prevented him from applying when Dave Anderson had resigned. He took over, bringing with him Andy Pape and physio Gary Anderson. Sadly the latter two had left the club within 12 months. But the trio set about rebuilding the team, many of whom walked out when Farrell left, including Nicholls – promoted to player-coach by Farrell – but whose performances at Eastleigh, Slough and Fisher had been poor. Another to leave was Dave Sargent, but he stayed for McCann's first match in charge, a relegation clash with Cheshunt. Sargent scored twice, including a stoppage-time winner, but left after the game.

The football played under McCann in those first few weeks was uninspiring, but effective. One goal victories against Cheshunt, Windsor & Eton, Folkestone, Kingstonian and Harrow Borough were enough to lift Hendon clear of relegation and they finished the season in 11th place, with one more defeat, 18, than victories.

2005–06: Relegation escape

Before the new season started, the club was shocked by the death of Ivor Arbiter, the man who had rescued the club from the brink of oblivion in the summer of 1994. Eleven years later, he succumbed to cancer, leaving the club without a chairman. As Andrew and Joanne Landesberg were no longer visitors to Claremont Road, the day-to-day organisation of the club fell to Graham Etchell who became, in effect, chief executive, although he prefers the title of club secretary. Without his expertise since February 1993, Hendon would probably not have survived to enjoy their 100th season in 2008.

This season was one of the most forgettable in Hendon's history. Apart from an appearance in the London Senior Cup Final for the first time since 1972, it was a season of unremitting struggle. Non-league's football's 'Brave New World' meant that relegation would be for the bottom three teams in each of the Northern Premier, Southern and Isthmian (Ryman) Leagues, plus the team in 19th place with the worst playing record – all three divisions had 22 teams so they all played 42 matches.

Hendon lost their first three matches, then won 5–4 at Wealdstone, Danny Murphy drilling in a 30-yard shot with a minute to go seal a great comeback. The Greens won the next match, 2–1 at home to Bromley, but then went two months without a win.

During this spell, Hendon's interest in the FA Cup ended against the Metropolitan Police after a replay and at the hands of Fisher Athletic in the FA Trophy. In the Middlesex Senior Cup Wealdstone were again beaten 5–4, while AFC Wimbledon were shocked in the Westview League Cup. The next matches in both competitions proved a step too far, Northwood and Fisher – again – ending Hendon interest.

Four wins in five matches suggested the corner might have been turned with 23 points from 19 games. But it was a false dawn. There was one win in January – a shock 1–0 defeat of Fisher Athletic – and one in February – over almost doomed Redbridge; that apart a few draws saw Hendon slip inexorably towards to brink of relegation. In the other two leagues, the 19th-placed teams had similar records, so there was still hope. A 4–0 defeat of Leyton on Easter Monday ended a 12 match winless run, but going into the final day control of their future was out of Hendon's hands. Before the visit to Margate, 1,444 supporters had seen Wimbledon win 1–0 at Claremont Road.

Before the Margate match, there was the London Senior Cup Final. Seven goals against Redbridge – John Frendo scored four – was the highlight of the cup run. The opponents were Fisher Athletic, for the fifth time this season and sixth in 15 months.

Fisher Athletic 3 Hendon 2
London Senior Cup Final

Hendon gave Fisher Athletic a huge fright at the start and finish of the London Senior Cup Final at Tooting & Mitcham's Imperial Fields, but were on the wrong end of a 3–2 final score. It was Hendon's first cup final defeat for 19 years.

In the 13th minute, Hendon should have taken the lead. A pass from Jeff Campbell found Blaise O'Brien, whose dink into the box caused chaos. Crace and Deen both missed the ball, but impeded Will Packham, who could only push it towards the edge of the box, where Andy Cook was waiting, but he lashed a shot high over the bar.

Fisher skipper Chris Piper then scored 11 minutes later. A flowing move ripped apart the Hendon defence and Piper's shot, a powerful, low drive, arrowed past King. That was the only goal of the half, but Hendon were unlucky not to get a penalty 10 minutes after going behind. The referee blew his whistle but gave a free-kick to Fisher instead.

Ninety seconds into the second half, Fisher doubled their lead. The Hendon defence failed to deal with the Fisher forwards and Lenny Piper emulated his brother by scoring in the Final. Things got worse for the Greens just before the hour mark. A clumsy challenge on Steve Watts resulted in him going down in the penalty area and the referee had no hesitation, this time, in pointing to the spot. Hamid Barr confidently converted.

At 3–0 down, and with barely half an hour to go, the game was pretty much over as a contest. Except that Fisher lost concentration. In the 65th minute, Hendon got a lifeline. Campbell's free-kick aimed for Marc Leach, whose delicate header found the net.

On 85 minutes, substitute Charlie Mapes delivered a free-kick into the Fisher penalty area, where Dave Hunt rose well and sent a powerful header against the underside of the crossbar. The ball bounced down on the line and spun away from the goal. But Cooper was there to score; 3–2. In the final five minutes, Hunt, Mapes and Leach all came close to forcing extra time with powerful shots. But they all narrowly missed.

Gary McCann said, "I am proud of the way we fought back from 3–0 down. We couldn't take advantage of the chances that came our way and we left ourselves with too much to do."

Fisher: Packham, C. Piper, Deen, Davis, West, Hearn (Scannell, 74), Riviere, Clancy, Barr (Taylor, 80), West (Richards, 83), Piper. Subs: Duku, Pullen (gk).

Hendon: King, J. Burgess, Murphy, Cook, Cooper, Leach, Busby, Hunt, Crace (Edwards, 64). O'Brien (Pickett, 60), Campbell (Mapes 75). Subs: Street, Banks (gk).

Left: action from the match

Below: The Hendon players waiting for their runners-up medals. (PL)

A victory at Margate would, almost certainly, ensure safety and goals from Jeff Campbell, a New Zealand full international who lived in Cricklewood, and Ricci Crace offered hope. In the 51st minute, Blaise O'Brien had the ball at his feet, 10 yards out, level with the edge of the six-yard box, but he missed by two yards. The chance of an insurmountable 3–0 lead was lost. Two minutes later it was 2–1; two minutes after that 2–2; and after another three minutes, 3–2 to Margate. Campbell had an equaliser ruled offside. Margate added a fourth in the last minute. Hendon were relegated. There were tears on the pitch and on the terraces as the enormity of the situation dawned.

There had been a number of unfortunate events during 2005–06 that contributed to the situation. Both Gary Anderson and Andy Pape left the club in the first half of the season. However, a gain was that Freddie Hyatt – Gary McCann's closest friend in football – became assistant manager. On the field, Eugene Ofori joined Braintree Town three weeks into the season, new recruit Belal Aiteouakrim broke down after three starts and missed the next 14 months and Ricci Crace was also injured for the second half of the season. But in reality the team simply had not functioned. Nine wins from 42 matches tells its' own story, and players with good reputations did not fulfil expectations.

During this disastrous campaign, a few Hendon supporters, led by long-time fans Simon Lawrence and Mike Harte, looked into the possibility of forming a supporters trust, to take control of the club. This was how Enfield Town had successfully broken away from Enfield FC and how AFC Wimbledon operated. There was plenty of interest – relatively, given Hendon's low support numbers – and a working party committee of around half a dozen was formed. They received plenty of help and advice from experts in the field and it was decided to put it to a vote of Hendon supporters that a trust should be formed. At a meeting in November it was made clear that the move to Barnet Copthall would not take place. Apart from having a running track, making it awful for football fans, so much work was required that it became financially impossible.

Instead, it was agreed to find a local club at which to enter into a ground sharing arrangement. The decision was to go to Kingsbury Town, probably closest to Claremont Road, but they had problems and were taken over by a new owner, who did not want a ground share. In the end the choice was Wembley FC, not in the Borough of Barnet either, but a stable club with an acceptable – or nearly acceptable – ground grading.

Just before the end of the season, some 60 Hendon supporters attended a second meeting, at which it was agreed that a supporters' trust would be formed. Annual membership fees were agreed and some supporters made further donations as well. A monthly snowball draw was set up, and its membership quickly passed the 100 mark.

With the covenant on Hendon's ground finally lifted, which had prevented building development on the site, it was thought that the AFC Wimbledon match at Claremont Road on 22 April 2006 would be the final fixture at the ground. It was billed by the Supporters Association as such – though not confirmed by the club –and some former players, Jimmy Quail, Rod Haider, Dermot Drummy and Alan Campbell among them, turned up to watch the south London Dons win with a solitary goal.

Two weeks after the season ended, the make-up of the various divisions were announced with Hendon set to play in Ryman League Division One North, level four of the national game – as the FA had re-branded non-league football. Then, on 15 May 2006, Canvey Island resigned as members of the Nationwide Conference because their manager and main backer Jeff King had pulled out. They were originally reassigned to the Ryman Premier Division – the two-division drop being the FA's punishment for reformation – but they had to go down one more level to the Ryman League Division

One North. As the only 19th placed team to be relegated, the FA and Ryman League offered Hendon the chance to keep their Premier Division place. Gary McCann was consulted and was happy to try his luck there. Hendon were reprieved.

The deal to move to Wembley FC was minutes from being signed when the Arbiter Group suddenly decided not to sign, a move that caused Dave Bedford to resign as the club's vice-chairman. He remained a strong supporter of the club and continued to work with the Supporters Trust, but no longer held a position at Hendon FC.

2006–07

With the move to a new ground suspended, Hendon started the 2006–07 season still at Claremont Road, though with no idea of how long the situation would last. The Arbiter Group, in an act of great kindness, agreed to fund the football side of the club until they relinquished control, meaning that the Supporters Trust's funds could grow until they were needed. Nobody could have imagined that, two years after what many thought was the last ever game at Claremont Road the club would complete its Centenary season at the stadium that was now more than 80 years old.

Some of the younger players from 2005–06 were retained, most notably Lee O'Leary, James Parker and Jamie Busby, while James Burgess, the loyal defender or midfielder, also returned. Among the new faces were Wayne O'Sullivan, an Irish winger or full-back with great ball control and pace. Coming back was Richard Wilmot the goalkeeper who had been so brave playing under Frank Murphy in 2000–01.

The squad were out of their depth in the early games, losing nine out of 11 League matches, and drawing the other two 0–0. A little composure and luck in front of goal might have brought some reward, but many of the teams won games comfortably. The most heartbreaking loss of this run was at home to Ramsgate, when the visitors scored three times in the final five minutes to win, most undeservedly, 4–2.

Things came to a head with the FA Trophy exit against the same opposition, a late goal being little more than a consolation in a 2–1 defeat. Lewes, from Conference South, had ended Hendon's interest in the FA Cup, while Staines Town had done likewise in the League Cup. Gary McCann decided to resign; it was not a decision he wanted to take, but he felt it almost a matter of honour. It was agreed that he would be given a few days to reconsider, before the next match against fellow strugglers Walton & Hersham.

By Sunday morning, McCann had rescinded his resignation and it proved a wise decision. The match at Stompond Lane signalled the first brief turnaround. Ross Pickett scored twice as Hendon won 2–0. A week later East Thurrock were beaten 2–1 at Claremont Road and, suddenly, not everything was doom and gloom.

McCann had a simple plan: win the games against the bottom third teams, try to get as much as possible against the middle third and, the top third would probably be too good anyway. Only two of the first 11 opponents Hendon faced finished in the bottom six, and the Greens managed a draw against Ashford Town (Middlesex) but lost unluckily at Folkestone. How well did the plan work? Against the bottom three teams, Hendon collected 18 points; against the bottom seven, 32 points; against the middle seven, 15; and from 14 games against the top seven, only seven points were won.

Hendon got 54 points and finished 14th. It was a magnificent performance, especially as 52 of those points came from 31 games, almost play-off form. In the second half the season, only Hampton & Richmond Borough and Bromley had better records than Hendon. Hendon were nine points clear of Harrow who were 19th.

The return of Belal Aiteouakrim, Marc Leach, Brian and Davis Haule, plus the arrival of Dean Green and Darragh Duffy played a huge part in the turnaround, because goal-scoring improved, even if Aiteouakrim finished as top-scorer with just 13 goals.

O'Leary had a magnificent season as the fulcrum in midfield and captain. However, after a match-winning performance against AFC Wimbledon, the Kingsmeadow club made him an offer he could not refuse. The Supporters Association player of the year was goalkeeper Richard Wilmot, who was beyond exceptional in the early part of the season, which included saving two penalties in a minute during a 3–1 defeat at champions-to-be Hampton in the second game.

Top: Lee O'Leary scoring against AFC Wimbledon at Claremont Road (PL)

Left: Richard Wilmot – 2007 Player of the Year (PL)

2007–08: Two County Cup Finals

For the 2007–08 season, Hendon's centenary season, McCann set a target he only told a few people: if the squad stayed intact, he felt the team could make the play-offs. The bookies thought otherwise. They believed the turnaround was a fluke and relegation was more likely. They were wrong. For most Hendon fans, even reaching the centenary season was something to be celebrated. Many had doubted that the landmark would have been reached, and that it was going to start at Claremont Road was even better.

The squad remained pretty much intact. Bontcho Guentchev, who had returned to the club in a player-coach role during 2006–07, remained and he brought along his two sons Iavor – who played for three minutes in the finale of the previous season (and almost set up his father for a goal) – and older sibling Lubomir, who had spent the previous season playing in Bulgaria's national Second Division.

An opening day draw 0–0 at Heybridge Swifts was preserved by Richard Wilmot penalty save and a late Davis Haule goal brought a first win in the next game, at home to Leyton. A reasonable start, but what happened on the second Saturday gave fans an inkling that the centenary season might be special. The Greens entertained Tonbridge Angels and fell behind to goal from Jon Main. A second goal came with 18 minutes to go and when Brian Haule missed a penalty with eight minutes left, some fans departed.

In the final minute of normal time, Hendon were awarded a free-kick just outside the Angels penalty area. Marc Leach drove it by the wall and past the unsighted goalkeeper into the bottom corner. In the third minute of stoppage time, Brian Haule scored with a header to equalise. Then, after a stoppage for treatment to an injured defender, the Greens nearly conceded a goal, cleared and Wayne O'Sullivan slammed home the winner. Three goals in five minutes, starting from the 90th, is surely the greatest comeback in the club's illustrious history.

A 2–1 victory at Harrow Borough, thanks to another very late goal, this time from Rakatahr Hudson, was followed by a 3–2 defeat at East Thurrock United. However, three days later, after AFC Hornchurch were beaten 3–1 at Claremont Road, Hendon went top of the table. The FA Cup proved slightly problematic as the Greens played four matches, but only two rounds, going out at Hornchurch, but not without controversy as the referee's final whistle blew just as Craig Vargas was shooting from inside the penalty area. The goal did not stand and Vargas was dismissed, post-whistle, for his dissent.

An amazing 4–4 draw at Ashford Town (Middlesex) followed, but Wilmot picked up an injury in the game and missed a few weeks. His replacement, Luke Blackmore was unavailable for the FA Trophy tie at AFC Wimbledon and a hobbling Wilmot had to play. The Greens were far from disgraced, going out 2–1. The FA Cup and Trophy exits came during the first blip in the season, as Hendon collected only 10 points from eight League matches, as well bowing out of the League Cup.

But a 2–0 defeat of Horsham on 17 November righted the ship, and this was followed by a 4–2 revenge win over East Thurrock and a comprehensive 4–0 demolition of Folkestone Invicta. Two weeks later, on Saturday 15 December, Hendon – who had ceded top spot when losing 5–1 at Chelmsford on 15 October – returned, albeit briefly, to the top of the pile with a League record victory at Leyton. The final score was 11–1, with O'Sullivan bagging four. In 1987, Hendon had suffered a League worst 9–1 mauling on the same ground, so the Greens fans were pleased when the ninth goal went in.

That was the high point of the season. The Greens' home form was undoubtedly the reason Hendon didn't make it to the play-offs. Eight draws and four defeats in 21 matches meant 28 out of 63 home points were dropped, eight against the bottom five teams. From the beginning of December to the second week of March, Hendon failed to win a Ryman League match at home, and picked up only two points from the eight games following a Boxing Day victory at Boreham Wood. Such had been Hendon's fine form up to Christmas, combined with the inconsistency of the chasing pack, it was not until February that Hendon dropped out of the top two.

Despite the second dip, the play-offs were still attainable and a magnificent 2–0 defeat of runners-up-to-be Staines Town in the penultimate match of the season saw the Greens back in the last of the play-off spots. All that was needed was a victory over Wealdstone at Claremont Road. Sadly, it wasn't to be as the small squad was affected by too many injuries and Hendon finished the season seventh, the best finish since 2004.

On the county cup front, there were two excellent runs. Hendon strolled into the finals of both the London and Middlesex Senior Cups, recording superb victories at Bromley and Staines, respectively. In the Middlesex Senior Cup Final Hendon faced Hampton & Richmond Borough. In the London competition, the defence had an off night and lost 3–2 to Tooting & Mitcham United,

Hampton & Richmond Borough 3 Hendon 0
Middlesex Senior Cup Final

Hendon went into the 2008 Middlesex Senior Cup Final as underdogs against Blue Square Conference South Hampton & Richmond Borough. Hendon gave a good account of themselves and, in deservedly runners-up, certainly not meriting a three-goal defeat.

A beautiful pitch certainly helped both sides and the first half was an open affair, although neither team had looked like making a breakthrough in the opening 25 minutes. A Jamie Busby shot being easily saved by Matt Lovett after 19 minutes was Hendon's best effort, while Lawrence Yaku shot over the bar for Hampton.

In the 26th minute, nobody shut down Shaun McAuley and his 25-yard angled drive gave Luke Blackmore no chance. In response, both Lee O'Leary and Lubo Guentchev had shots, but neither really troubled Lovett.

In the second half Hendon rarely had a clear glimpse of the Beavers' goal. The Greens' best chance came on 78 minutes, but Guentchev could not control and shoot a loose ball in the Hampton penalty area before Lovett was out to block his effort.

Four minutes later, another long-range effort from McAuley made it 2–0. Substitutes Graham Harper and Kelvin McIntosh combined to give the former a third goal in the fourth minute of stoppage time. After the match, both managers agreed that not only was the outcome the right one, but that the scoreline had flattered Hampton.
Hampton & Richmond Borough: Lovett, Fernandes, Tanner, Jeffrey, S. Lake, Matthews, Inns, McAuley (R. Lake, 90), Hodges (McIntosh, 67), Yaku (Harper, 88), Quarm. Subs: Godfrey, Wells.
Hendon: Blackmore, Parker, Maclaren (Dyer, 86), Leach, S. Page, Busby, L. Guentchev, O'Leary, B. Haule, Aiteouakrim, D. Haule (Hudson, 86). Subs: Burgess, I. Guentchev, Hudell.

Hendon 2 Tooting & Mitcham United 3
London Senior Cup Final

Hendon ended their Centenary season without a trophy after a strong Tooting team had deservedly won the Final of the London Senior Cup at the Metropolitan Police FC's Imber Court ground. However much the Terrors deserved the trophy – and that is indisputable

– a refereeing decision with 10 or so minutes to go was crucial.

Tooting started very brightly and Hendon had no answer to the threat posed by Paul Vines and Jon Henry-Hayden. Henry-Hayden should have scored twice in the opening 10 minutes before he broke the deadlock in the 11th minute.

This goal galvanized Hendon a little and it took them just over 10 minutes to respond, Danny Dyer shooting across former Hendon favourite Dave King. But instead of consolidating on their equaliser, Hendon dozed and were punished in the 25th minute. Henry-Hayden scored his second goal with an accurate long-range effort.

The game was certainly not over at half-time, but Tooting started the period more brightly and, in the 50th minute Vines rose to head home from six yards.

This Hendon team is nothing if not dogged and determined and they gave themselves a lifeline in the 83rd minute. A ball from Brian Haule sent Lubo Guentchev alone into the penalty area. Although two defenders tried to track back, King was clearly the last man as Guentchev knocked the ball diagonally past him, but was tripped before he could make up the five yards to reach it. There is no question it was a penalty and also none that Guentchev would have had an empty goal at which to aim. The referee, however, took a different view of the meaning of the Laws of the Game's "clear goal scoring opportunity" clause, because King was cautioned, not dismissed. Brian Haule converted the penalty, to give Hendon around 10 minutes to get an equaliser.

If King had been sent off, Tooting would have had to put an outfield player in goal and manager Billy Smith admitted later that he had no one he knew could fill the role. As it was two high crosses were gathered by King when a deputy may well have fumbled it.

Then, in the last minute of stoppage time, Hendon almost snatched an equaliser when substitute Rakatahr Hudson, drilled a loose ball from a corner against the inside of a post. The rebounded inside the six-yard box but was hacked away to safety.

Hendon: Wilmot, Parker, Burgess, Leach, S. Page (Hudell, 66), Dyer (Hudson, 66). L. Guentchev, D. Haule (I. Guentchev, 70), B. Haule, Aiteouakrim, J. Page. Subs: Hyatt, Blackmore.

Tooting & Mitcham United: D. King, D. Hamlin, C. Hartburn, R. Bouadji, C. Hutchings, O. Hunt, A. McLeod (V. Francis 68), J. Pinnock, P. Vines, J. Henry-Hayden, J. Byatt. Subs: R. Gray, B. Abbey, R. Green, G. Lopez-Dacruz

Middlesex Senior Cup Final: Sam Page receives his runners up medal. (PL)

303

The London Senior Cup Final

The pre-match presentation (PL)

Above: Hendon on the attack. Below: The Hendon dug out (PL)

Although the 2007–08 season finished a bit flatly, it should not diminish the incredible job carried out by Gary McCann, his assistants Freddie Hyatt and Bontcho Guentchev, plus physio Mark Findlay and, of course, the players in providing a season of fantastic entertainment and some memorable matches. To reach the play-offs, McCann said, he needed to have the squad intact for the whole season. However, Ben Hudell missed more than six months with a knee injury, Dean Green left for AFC Hornchurch in November, Davis Haule and Belal Aiteouakrim both had injuries that sidelined them for three months and Wilmot two spells which cost him almost as long, added to which both Craig Vargas and O'Sullivan moved on in the months either side of Christmas.

Hendon played some fantastic football, full of imagination and ambition. Although there were two flat spots in the season, when the quality of football wasn't as good, there were almost 20 matches in which five goals were scored (for and against) and a total of 195 came in 56 games. Of those, Hendon scored 109, almost two per game.

The loss of O'Sullivan was probably the hardest to overcome. He had found a rich vein of form at the end of 2006–07 and continued, playing even better, in the first half of 2007–08. His move to Stevenage Borough left Hendon without their most inspirational player and it came at a time when Davis Haule and Aiteouakrim, plus Rakatahr Hudson, were all injured and Hendon didn't have the money to bring in replacements. O'Sullivan scored 18 goals in 31 appearances, a superb strike rate, especially considering he probably set up as many as he scored himself.

The Ryman League recognised Hendon's fine season. Gary McCann collected his first manager-of-the-month award, Wilmot earned the top goalkeeping award in another month, both O'Sullivan and Davis Haule were top goalscorers in different months and team's victory at Staines in April was also rewarded. It meant for the first time since these awards were handed out that Hendon collected all of them at one time or another. Missing from all this – unusually – was Brian Haule, who finished as the team's top goalscorer with 27 and won the Supporters Association's Player of the Year award.

Two players who have contributed much to the club are twins Mark and James Burgess. Mark left in the 2005–06 season, but James is still a key squad member.

Hendon heroes: Mark and James Burgess

It is not uncommon for brothers to play for the same team – Hendon had Iavor and Lubomir Guentchev, Jack and Sam Page and Davis and Brian Haule on the pitch at the same time in 2008, but it is very unusual to have identical twins playing together in senior football. Mark and James Burgess are one such pair. They were born on 8 February 1977 and look almost identical – for the uninitiated, James wears an ear stud.

It would be wrong not to mention, when discussing the Burgess twins, their parents, Herbie and Cathy, who have been regulars at Claremont Road since the twins started playing senior football. As Hendon is – after Kingsbury – the closest ground to the family, it is rare for them to miss a game at Claremont Road, although with James and Mark now playing for different clubs, they can't watch both on a Saturday afternoon. Cathy has also assisted Hendon Supporters Association when the need has arisen.

The twins have also been stalwarts of local Sunday football and took on almost pantomime villain status when Hendon's Claremont Road ground was used as the backdrop for Bravo television series on Fash FC, a club in the Hendon & District Sunday League. James and Mark played for Kings United, the League's top team and had some acrimonious battles with the made-for-television club in 2003–04.

Both twins have had relatively nomadic careers, with Hendon at the heart, with both passing the 100 games mark for the Greens. Mark has made 92+18 appearances, while James has made 170+47 to the end of 2007–08.

Amongst Mark's clubs are: Kingsbury Town, Northwood, Wingate & Finchley, Edgware Town, Aylesbury United, St Albans City, Windsor & Eton and Boreham Wood. James has stayed more local, but has also played for Kingsbury and Northwood.

Of the two, Mark is the more defensive-minded, rarely being selected in front of the back line, whereas James has played many games, especially for Hendon, in midfield. With almost identical builds, it is unsurprising that their styles and strengths are also similar. Both players are tough tacklers, solid and dependable, though neither is blessed with exceptional pace. Both are astute at reading the game, and are usually left defending when their teams have attacking corners. Even so from almost 330 Hendon matches between them, one goal – scored by Mark, the sixth in a 6–0 FA Cup rout of Biggleswade in 2005 – is a remarkably low return. The twins are expert penalty takers, using identical styles. They start on the edge of the centre circle and sprint to the ball before lashing it goalwards.

James's loyalty to Hendon has been laudable. Not always a first-choice, he has never – like his twin – given less than 100 per cent effort.

The future

Thus ended Hendon's centenary season. However, off the field events moved on, and on 6 August 2008, the Supporters Trust agreed to take over running Hendon FC and to prepare to move to ground share with Wembley FC. The Supporters Trust issued the following statement:

Hendon Football Club Supporters Trust

PRESS RELEASE

The following press release was issued by the Hendon Football Club Supporters Trust at 8am on Thursday 7 August 2008.

Hendon Football Club Supporters Trust to take control of Hendon Football Club (i.e. the football club, as opposed to Hendon Football Club Limited).

Hendon Football Club planning to Ground share with Wembley Football Club

On Wednesday 6 August, the Board of the Hendon Football Club Supporters Trust (the Trust) held a special general meeting (SGM) at Hendon Football Club's (the club's) Claremont Road ground. Trust members were asked to approve a proposal that the Trust should reach an agreement in principle with the Club's current owners, the Arbiter Group, to take ownership of the Club (i.e. the football club, as opposed to Hendon Football Club Limited) by 31 October 2008. All Trust members in attendance voted to approve the proposal and a letter setting out the agreement in principle has now been signed by both parties.

There are many details to be agreed but the two parties will now work together to execute a formal Agreement and to obtain the approval of the relevant authorities. In the meantime, the two parties will work together to ensure stability in the run-up to the coming season.

In addition, Trust members were advised that steps have now been taken to secure the permission of the relevant football authorities for the Club to enter into a ground sharing agreement with Wembley Football Club. All parties are working towards securing agreement for the Club to play its home games at Wembley Football Club's Vale Farm ground. This agreement will be effected as soon as possible.

Simon Lawrence, Chairman of the Trust, said: "The first key step towards Trust ownership was taken back in March 2006 when the Trust was formed. The agreement in principle to take ownership of the Club represents the second key step in the process and moves us closer to our goal of ensuring the long-term survival of the Club. While it is desperately disappointing to have to leave Claremont Road, we have been aware for some years that our time there will come to a close at some point and we have been in discussions with Wembley Football Club for quite a while.

We are nervous about the challenges ahead but excited at the prospect of securing our great club's long-term future."

So as this book comes to an end, a whole new era for Hendon FC will start. The club has been in limbo for some years, hopefully a new home will mean new opportunities to build support. The Supporters Trust has worked very hard to make the new set up viable, and the meeting on 6 August looked positively towards the future.

The current management team have made a huge contribution to the club over the last few seasons, supported by Graham Etchell's work as club secretary. It seems appropriate to finish the book with profiles of them.

A Hendon hero: Gary McCann

Gary McCann was born in Hammersmith on 25 July 1972. A distant relative of German international defender Torsten Frings, Gary was a trainee at Fulham from the age of 11 until he was released at 18. Because of his lack of inches, he stood only 5 feet 6 inches at 16 - he grew to reach 5 feet 11 inches - the Cottagers didn't give him a YTS place, but he played in almost half of the club's under–18 fixtures over the next two seasons.

After that, Gary joined Sutton United, where he was back up to Nicky Sullivan and he played a number of games in the GM Vauxhall Conference for Sutton when Sullivan was injured. During this time he also got married to Dawn and became the father of the first of his four boys, Sam. This was followed by a move to Enfield and, later, stops at Walton & Hersham, Chesham United, a return to Sutton and Dulwich Hamlet, where he played under Frank Murphy. His second son, Max, was born during this time.

On 31 March 1997, a few weeks after Frank had taken over as Hendon's boss, he signed Gary, whose debut – that day – was a 3–0 defeat at home to Aylesbury United. The club was battling to avoid relegation and McCann was a key figure in the fight for survival, saving a penalty with the last kick of a 1–0 victory at Hitchin that guaranteed safety with three matches to play. This penalty save wasn't down to luck, as Gary explained: "Before the game, I was reading the programme and there was a picture of a recent Hitchin game in which they scored a penalty. I saw which way it was struck and when the penalty was awarded, I knew which way I was going to dive. I didn't remember that it was the last kick of the game."

The following season, Gary's best at Hendon, was highlighted by the FA Cup victory over Leyton Orient. "I don't remember much about many games," he admitted, "but I do remember when Orient scored on the stroke of half-time, Frank absolutely slaughtered Freddie Hyatt for not picking up the player who scored from the edge of the box.

The 2008 end of season presentations

Top left: Mike Hogan presents Brian Haule with the Player of the Year award.
Top right: Gary McCann with James Burgess.
Bottom left: Graham Etchell with Richard Wilmot and his son Ben.
Bottom right: Mike Hogan presents Jacqui Cox with the Supporter of the Year award.
(Photos: Peter Lush)

Top left: Simon Lawrence, chair of the Supporters Trust.
Top right: Steve Lytton running an auction to raise funds for the Supporters Trust.
Bottom: The 2008 Supporters Association committee:
Les Vincent, Sandra Wood, Mike Hogan, Geraldine Clarke, Tony Wood.
(Photos Peter Lush)

Just before the replay, I heard their manager Tommy Taylor doing an interview and he was justifying the 2–2 draw at Claremont Road, complaining about the pitch, ground and conditions. 'We'll win four or five-nil tonight,' he said. I mentioned this to Frank and I don't think there was much more needed to be said in his pre-match team-talk.

"I don't remember making many saves in the game, but I was very busy and they forced a lot of corners. I played a part in our goal. I threw the ball out and it was passed to Freddie, who sent the ball to John-Simon White. His cross was headed home by Junior Lewis and it was enough for us to win. We celebrated in the small bar under the stand at Brisbane Road before I went home with Dawn. At training on Thursday some of the players told me that the celebrations had continued well into Wednesday morning. I had my shop to run, so I missed all of that.

Cardiff were far too professional for us in the second round and although Naseem Bashir scored the goal of the game, we were well beaten 3–1."

It wasn't the end of Gary's involvement in FA Cup first or second round ties as he played against Notts County, Bath City and Blackpool in 1998 and 1999.

"The day at Bath was horrible, but I had a really good game. It poured throughout the game and the pitch was very slippery. After the game, their manager, former Welsh international full-back Paul Bodin complimented me, saying that my handling was 'exemplary'. It's nice when a former pro says something like that.

The Blackpool game was so disappointing. Then, out of nothing, they scored and got a second one a few minutes later. Until then, they hadn't really troubled us. It was a game we really could have won. And the disappointment was even greater when we found out we would have played at Arsenal.

We didn't so well in the league, but I believe it is very hard to have great FA Cup runs and do well in the league. A trip to Carshalton is not easy to get up for after winning at Leyton Orient." For the record, Hendon's next match after Leyton Orient was at Carshalton and the Robins won 3–1 against a less-than-motivated Greens team.

Gary remembers Bontcho's arrival at Hendon: "We turned up for preseason training and we were introduced to this guy wearing Bulgarian World Cup 1994 training kit. Over the years, so many players – mainly from Africa – turn up at pre-season, saying that they had played for this country and that, but they turned out to be useless. I thought, 'Oh, no. Not another one' - until the first proper training session. His attitude and professionalism shone through. After that it was total respect. Now he is part of my coaching team and he is a joy to work with."

It all changed for Gary on a wet Tuesday night, 18 April 2000. Hendon were at Harrow Borough and midway through the first half, Gary suffered an injury that effectively ended his career. His memory of the incident is, unsurprisingly, very clear: "There was a through ball which I had to come for. Warren Kelly tried to shield their striker Damien Markman away from me but Markman was somehow bumped into me. He collided with me, striking me just below the knee. I knew it was serious because the top of my shin and knee went numb. I thought it was a break or a crack at the top of my shin. I tried to continue, but when I went for a ball I couldn't move. I was stretchered off, taken hospital and was diagnosed with a torn cruciate ligament.

I had the first of seven operations on my knee in May, but I came back too quickly." Multiple goalkeeping crises meant that Gary actually played 20 matches in the 2000–01 season. The normally recovery time for knee reconstructions is around nine months; Gary played barely six months after his procedure. In May 2001, with his knee clearly not right, Gary had further surgery, this time the extremely painful and complicated micro-fracture procedure.

"Frank had left Hendon and Dave Anderson had taken over," Gary continues the story. "His first match was a preseason friendly on 12 July against Southend United and he was desperate for a goalkeeper as none had been signed. I agreed to play to do Dave a favour, but it was only eight weeks after the surgery and it was far too soon. I lasted until half-time."

It was not quite the end for Gary, but the writing was on the wall. Apart from loan spells at Slough Town and Aylesbury, Gary played 10 more times for Hendon before deciding to retire at the end of the 2002–03 season. He was only 30. Gary's family had grown, with two more children, Sid and Joe-Oliver, the latter being almost 11 years younger than Sam and eight younger than Max. "Dawn has been a full-time mother for 16 years," he said.

"I knew it was the end, so I bought a Chelsea season ticket for me and my boys and decided to spend some quality weekend time with them and my family, something I had not done before."

It wasn't quite the end because Gary came out of retirement once more, to help out Dave in a 2–0 win at Bedford in September 2003. Although he has named himself on the bench since then, Gary has not added to his 195+1 appearances for Hendon.

In the summer of 2004, when Dave Anderson left Hendon. Gary was approached about taking over, but he felt he wasn't quite ready. Business issues were a part of it, so the Greens went with Tony Choules and Gary Farrell.

Things had gone disastrously at Hendon from mid-December 2004, but with Ivor Arbiter battling cancer and off the scene, nothing could be done about making a change until the end of January. At that point, Gary was contacted again and, this time, he said "Yes. When Ivor approached me, things were not much clearer in my business life, but I had a love for the club. I spoke with family, friends and people I trust in football about taking the job. Some said I should go for it, others not. But Ivor's passion and Graham Etchell's enthusiasm persuaded me. I got a number of reports from people about the football Hendon were playing and most of them were not very good."

He brought with him Andy Pape as his assistant and Gary Anderson as fitness consultant/trainer. "Andy has been a friend of mine for many years and he was my mentor as a goalkeeper. We were very close and spoke almost every day.

One of the reasons I took over when I did was that I knew I would have five training sessions before the first game, against Cheshunt at home. One of those was on a Saturday and after the morning training session I watched Cheshunt play and lose at home to Braintree. I saw I few things I thought we could exploit."

Two goals from Dave Sargent were enough to bring all three points for Gary and this was followed by three more wins and two draws in the next six matches: "We had to be better defensively, so I went with what was really a five at the back with Gary Meakin and James Parker as full-backs and three of Dean Coppard, René Street, Jason O'Connor and Steve McGrath in the middle. We weren't pretty, but it was effective and we moved away from the relegation zone."

It went horribly wrong the following season as Hendon finished in a relegation position. Gary admits he made mistakes: "I thought I had assembled a side that was capable of achieving a lot more than they delivered. There were many players, very honest and experienced at this level, who I knew and thought that they could do a job for me but, for one reason or another, they didn't. I learned a lot in that season, more probably than I have before or since. Unfortunately Andy had to leave in December. We were probably too similar and we thought the same way. Freddie Hyatt joined me as my assistant. Not only is he my best friend in football, we are great mates and he brought something very different to the changing room.

But the season culminated with the Margate game. We were cruising at 2–0 up and had a chance for 3–0, then it's an easy win and we're safe. Instead, it's missed and within four minutes it's 2–2, then 3–2. And we were relegated. After the season, I was told that the budget, which wasn't the biggest to start with, was going to be halved. I had to get rid of all the experienced players and bring in kids for the new season."

It probably didn't help that Gary sold his business and his house during 2006. "Football was a great escape from the other pressures," he admitted, but still it didn't stop him from resigning after the FA Trophy defeat against Ramsgate in October 2006. But within a few hours, he realised he had made a big mistake.

"We had lost nine out of 11 League games and were out of the FA Cup and Trophy. I thought the team needed something different, maybe just a different voice in the dressing room, so I offered to resign. I was asked to reconsider. But so many people rang and texted me that I knew I had to give it another go," he said. The first game after this was the opening league win of the season at Walton & Hersham, and it was the start of a magnificent climb up the table.

"I said from the start of pre-season training that our goal was to win our mini-league, of seven or eight teams who I knew would be among the strugglers. We did that, and not only did we pick up 32 points against the bottom seven, we did the double over all three relegated sides. After Christmas our form was more like a play-off team than one in relegation trouble. I think we were in the top six in the current form guide for 22 weeks. Last season, I really felt we could make the play-offs if we could keep the team together. Unfortunately by the end of the season, as I feared, our small squad is what cost us. When we played our last few matches, we had only seven or eight fit players in our squad of 16 and two of them were goalkeepers. It was disappointing to miss out on the play-offs and not to win a cup, but we proved a lot of people wrong." At the end of the 2007–08 season, Gary had been manager for 178 games, with 68 wins, 38 draws and 72 defeats, a commendable record given the resources available to him.

A Hendon hero: Freddie Hyatt

Freddie Hyatt was born in Notting Hill on 18 January 1968. He married Lisa in 1995 and the couple have had three children: Tommy (born in 1997), Molly (1998) and Oscar (2003). He is always of interest to the national media when Hendon have high-profile matches because his profession is that of a rat-catcher for the local council.

A schoolboy at Brentford FC, the Bees released him at 14 because he was too small, so he joined Hounslow, making his debut at the start of the 1982–83 season, aged just 14 and a half. He then played for Ruislip Manor, Burnham, Wokingham Town (playing against Hendon in the Greens' 2–1 victory in the 1994 Loctite Cup Final at Marlow) and Hayes, where he won an Isthmian League champions medal in 1995–96, played a season in the Conference and also was selected for an FA XI. On the opening day of the 1997–98 season, Freddie joined Hendon, making his debut as a substitute in the 4–0 defeat at Gravesend. His first goal came in a 2–1 home win over Basingstoke.

"I think I played the best football of my career at Hendon," Freddie says. "I was able to express myself under Frank Murphy. Although I was at a higher level at Hayes, the football was not as much fun to play under Terry Brown.

It was a pleasure playing with Paul Whitmarsh, the best striker I have played with. His touch and running were so good that he made my bad passes look good. I also enjoyed playing with JD (Jon Daly) and Bontcho Guentchev. He is the consummate professional and he just loves the game."

In the last game of the 1999–2000 season, Hendon travelled to play Heybridge Swifts – the Greens won 2–1 – but the game was memorable for the "Freddie Flick", an outrageous back-heel lobbed over a defender in front of him. Not only did Freddie carry it off to perfection, he controlled the ball as it came down on the other side, ran on towards goal and shot.

Even Guentchev, who has rubbed shoulders with the footballing world's elite, was astounded by the manoeuvre, saying it was the best piece of skill he had ever seen on a football pitch. Hendon manager Frank Murphy said after the game, "If Freddie had scored with that shot, I would have taken him off immediately and ordered him to retire. He could never do anything better than that."

In fact, it was not the first time Freddie had tried it and succeeded. "I was at Wokingham and we were playing Chelsea in a friendly as part of Darren Barnard's transfer. I wanted to try it with Vinnie Jones, but I did it to another player, an international, instead. Next thing I know, he has gone right through me. As I was picking myself up, he whispered in my ear, 'If you ever do that again, I will break your legs!' Maybe it was just as well I didn't try it with Vinnie!"

That moment of magic apart, many of Freddie's goals for Hendon were spectacular, often free-kicks, but his most audacious came in a 4–2 victory over Sutton United in March 1988. This was a volley from 55 yards, aimed successfully at the top far corner.

After leaving Hendon, having played 150+13 games, scoring 18 goals, Freddie joined Chelmsford City, where he helped them to promotion back to the Southern League Premier Division. But he was shipped out on loan to St Albans City and, later, Bishop's Stortford, also helping them to promotion.

In 2002–03, he became assistant manager to Steve Cook at St Albans and, the following season, returned to playing at Slough Town. Freddie retired as a player upon leaving Slough and was out of football for almost two years until, in February 2006, Gary McCann invited him to return to Hendon as assistant manager.

"Gary has been my best friend in and out of football for 25 years and I was happy to come back to the club. Hendon treated me really well and they are a lovely club. Apart from failing to make it as a professional footballer, my biggest disappointment in the game must have been that first season when we were relegated. But I knew Gary would turn it around and I think we have showed in the last two seasons what we can do."

A Hendon hero: Bontcho Guentchev

It probably is fair to say that no Hendon player has ever achieved cult status starting only 36 games, with a further 47 as a substitute. There again, there have been very few players to appear in a World Cup semi-final and, later, the Isthmian League. Bontcho Guentchev has. It is a mark of the respect he is held in the non league football community that fans and officials of opposing teams were genuinely disappointed that he didn't play against them.

Born in Bulgaria on 7 July 1964, Bontcho played for Etur, taking them to their only Bulgarian championship, before joining Sporting Lisbon. He joined compatriots Yordan Lechkov and Ivaylo Iordanov in Portugal, winning the championship there. Guentchev became recognisable to English fans at the 1994 World Cup, when Bulgaria finished fourth and Ipswich Town signed him. He made three appearances, including the semi-final, when he replaced World Footballer of the Year Hristo Stoichkov.

Bontcho and Iavor after playing together against Margate in April 2007

Bontcho moved to England with his wife Sylvia and sons Lubomir and Iavor – both Of whom played for Hendon in 2007–08, and Iavor with Bontcho in the final game of the previous season. It did not take long for Ipswich fans to fall in love with the attacking midfielder, whose penchant for scoring with overhead scissors kicks is always exciting. When Bontcho left Ipswich he joined Luton before returning home to Bulgaria where he played for the country's top club CSKA Sofia. He scored against Atletico Madrid at the Estadio Calderon in a 4–2 UEFA Cup defeat in November 1998.

As his family had remained in England – his sons were at the Chelsea FC Academy, Bontcho became homesick and returned to England. While playing for Luton, he had moved to Claremont Road, living a few hundred yards from the ground. Looking to continue playing football, his representatives approached Hendon, and as remuneration was not a major issue, he was told to attend pre-season training in July 1999.

His first appearance was in a pre-season friendly at Staines. Bontcho played only 45 minutes, but the man with the golden boots had shown enough for a football romantic such as Frank Murphy to be satisfied. His Ryman League debut came at Hitchin Town on the second Saturday of the season, with *Sky Sports News* filming the game. He nearly scored an equaliser, but put the chance over the bar. Three days later, against Canvey Island, it took eight minutes for the trademark overhead scissors kick to bring his first Hendon goal. A legend was born.

It is probably stating the obvious, but the style of Ryman League football is a million miles removed from that which had earned Bontcho his reputation and he struggled to adapt. But Bontcho simply loves playing football and he turned out for the reserves. His attitude was better than first class and the young lads in the second team were in total awe of this greying midfielder. One was Paul Johnson, who has gone on to enjoy a long career at Ashford Town (Middlesex). In one of the non-league newspapers in spring 2008, he was asked to name his dream team from players he had played with; 11 received a couple of lines, Bontcho four paragraphs.

When it really mattered, though, Bontcho delivered. In the FA Cup against Bath City, he set up Dominic Gentle for the opening goal after 88 minutes and, two minutes later, made it 2–0. Although he was still 45 yards from goal, the Bath radio commentator reported the goal a good couple of seconds before Bontcho even shot, so certain was he that the Romans' cup run was over. A year later, playing against Carshalton, he volunteered to go in goal for the second half when Richard Wilmot broke his arm.

When Murphy left Hendon, Bontcho was not retained by Dave Anderson, so he went to play at Carshalton. Continuing to play football later on, he turned out with London Bulgaria in Saturday afternoon park football. In 2006, Gary McCann invited Bontcho back to the club, ostensibly as a coach, but he was given the odd game and he scored in the Middlesex Senior Cup semi-final in March 2006, at the age of almost 42. With his two sons both regulars on the Hendon team-sheet, Bontcho nearly fulfilled the wish of every footballing father of being on the pitch with his two sons. Sadly the final whistle blew with Bontcho standing stripped on the sideline and despite a 2–1 defeat of the newly-elected League champions, Chelmsford City, Bontcho could not hide his disappointment at not getting on, even for a few seconds.

A Hendon hero: Graham Etchell

No history of Hendon Football Club would be complete without a profile of the man who has held things together at Claremont Road for more than 15 years. Graham Etchell joined the club in the summer of 1990, answering an appeal for a reserve team secretary. During his time with the second team, he watched Dave Finn's side go undefeated throughout their 1992–93 Suburban League North Division campaign. Sadly the team was disbanded before the following season.

Graham had previously been with the Chelsea Boys Club, giving him a good grounding in football administration. He had also become a London Football Association councillor, giving him a great insight into non league football. Following Victor Green's takeover of Hendon in 1991, the club parted company with Dave Stanley and Michael Cox. Graham had originally turned down the chance to become secretary, not wishing to take someone else's job. However, he was made redundant just as he was offered the Hendon post for a second time, and this time he didn't refuse. He had been in charge for the 1992–93 League Cup tie at home to Aldershot Town, but that was a one-off for the absent Cox. He took over officially before a February 1993 game at Bognor Regis Town, a match he remembers for two attractive young female season-ticket sellers who walked into the Hendon dressing room at Nyewood Lane as the players were changing and "the girls didn't bat an eyelid."

Graham recalls how well he worked with Victor Green: "I had a laugh with Victor. He worked very hard, had good ideas and was very demanding. But if you did what was asked of you, then it was fine. When I got to know him better, we got on really well."

When Victor left and the club lurched towards the 1994–95 season in turmoil, Graham was a steadying hand on the tiller. He was not involved directly in the negotiations between Green and Ivor Arbiter, but made sure that all the football matters were dealt with correctly. It is very easy for a football club to fall foul of rules and regulations, but it is a testimony to Graham that Hendon have only had a problem once, when the manager ignored his advice.

In more recent times, with the Arbiter Group withdrawing from the day-to-day management of the club, Graham has become the *de facto* chief executive, though he steadfastly refuses to take that title. The last few years have been extremely difficult as the club fights above its weight. Graham sits alone in his office at Claremont Road, a soul-destroying existence for many people, but telephone conversations are always lively, when the call of work is not too great. He has also given great support and encouragement to the authors of this book.

Like a good secretary, Graham attends as many matches as he can. For all away trips, and recently most of the home ones too, he has been accompanied by his wife Lyn. They have been married for many years, and share a love of Chelsea Football Club, the team that Graham cares most about. "I like Hendon a lot and it's great when we win, but it is not the be all and end all if they lose, although I do get very upset when we are knocked out of the FA Cup earlier than we should be."

Graham's knowledge and expertise is as unrivalled as it is priceless, and it is hoped that he will stay with the club in the future.

The future

The first 100 years have been truly fantastic, seeing the club rise from humble origins to Wembley Finals and Isthmian League championships. The world has changed dramatically for non league football since the game went open in 1974. The lure of watching Premiership football live and the huge amount of live football on television has made it more difficult for local clubs to attract supporters. This is particularly true in London, where there are so many Football League clubs. Hendon have to compete with seven Football League clubs in reasonable travelling distance of Claremont Road.

It is worth reflecting that since 1974, locally, Wingate and Finchley have merged, Edgware Town went out of business in 2008, and Kingsbury Town have merged with another club. Old foes Enfield lost their Southbury Road ground and are now two clubs, both a pale shadow of the former club. Wealdstone moved from ground to ground for years after Lower Mead was sold. Other clubs have also merged, disappeared altogether or are ground-sharing

But on the other hand, the enormous cost of watching top flight football means that football at Hendon's level can still draw in supporters, offering entertainment at a local venue at a reasonable price. Another encouraging development has been a flourishing youth structure at the club. The moves by the Supporters Trust outlined above will be decisive in the club's future. As we write, a new chapter in the club's history is starting. Let us hope for another memorable 100 years.

Appendix: Statistics and records

League results

The club was in the Athenian League from 1914–15 until 1962–63, except for World War Two. From 1963–64 to the present day, the club was in the Isthmian League. Seasons when the club won the league are in bold.

Season	P	W	D	L	F	A	P	Pos	Champions' points
1908–09	**16**	**12**	**1**	**3**	**55**	**15**	**25**	**1/9**	**(Finchley & District League D3)**
1909–10	**12**	**9**	**2**	**1**	**47**	**9**	**20**	**1/7**	**(Finchley & District League D2)**
1910–11	**12**	**8**	**2**	**2**	**40**	**9**	**18**	**1/7**	**(Finchley & District League D1)**
1911–12	11	6	0	5	23	21	12	4/7	18 (London League D2)
1912–13	**14**	**12**	**0**	**2**	**42**	**12**	**24**	**1/8**	**(Middlesex & District League)**
1912–13	14	9	1	4	34	14	19	2/8	24 (London League D1)
1913–14	**12**	**8**	**3**	**1**	**25**	**12**	**19**	**1/7**	**(London League Premier -amateur)**
1913–14	14	11	1	2	38	15	23	2/9	24 (Middlesex League)
1914-15	2	0	2	0	3	3	2		(Season abandoned due to outbreak of war)
1918–19	**14**	**10**	**1**	**3**	**38**	**21**	**21**	**1/8**	**(London United Senior League)**
1919–20	22	10	6	6	43	37	26	4/12	37
1920–21	22	12	4	6	46	41	28	3/12	33
1921–22	26	12	5	9	40	38	29	4/14	41
1922–23	24	9	2	13	48	53	20	8/13	40
1923–24	24	10	6	8	49	37	26	5/13	36
1924–25	26	10	11	5	55	34	31	5/14	41
1925–26	26	15	1	10	55	34	31	4/14	44
1926–27	26	7	2	17	59	78	16	13/14	39 (re-elected)
1927–28	26	6	4	16	44	76	16	11/14	43
1928–29	26	16	3	7	64	39	35	2/14	43
1929–30	26	9	5	12	46	51	23	11/14	41
1930–31	26	11	6	9	68	60	28	8/14	46
1931–32	26	14	4	8	72	52	32	4/14	39
1932–33	26	15	6	5	82	35	36	2/14	38
1933–34	26	16	2	8	80	37	34	3/14	41
1934–35	26	12	5	9	70	56	29	6/14	35
1935–36	26	13	5	8	73	60	31	5/14	38
1936–37	26	8	5	13	58	56	21	10/14	49
1937–38	26	11	6	9	61	56	28	5/14	42
1938–39	26	9	6	11	42	57	24	8/14	42
1939–40	2	1	1	0	6	2	3	4/14	(Season abandoned due to outbreak of war)
1939–40	18	6	3	9	40	55	15	7/10	30 (Herts & Middlesex League)
1940–41	20	6	3	11	50	69	15	8/11	35 (Herts & Middlesex League)
1941–42	24	8	4	12	59	71	20	9/13	45 (Herts & Middlesex League)
1942–43	22	9	5	8	46	54	23	5/12	33 (Herts & Middlesex League)
1943–44	26	9	4	13	47	66	22	10/14	43 (Herts & Middlesex League)
1944–45	26	10	4	12	58	59	24	8/14	44 (Herts & Middlesex League)
1945–46	26	7	3	16	56	84	17	12/14	40
1946–47	26	12	2	12	62	59	26	8/14	34
1947–48	26	14	5	7	45	30	33	2/14	38
1948–49	26	15	7	4	55	33	37	2/14	41
1949–50	26	13	2	11	54	48	28	7/14	39
1950–51	30	15	6	9	45	40	36	4/16	49
1951–52	30	20	8	2	84	32	48	2/16	50
1952–53	**26**	**18**	**6**	**2**	**68**	**21**	**42**	**1/14**	
1953–54	26	12	5	9	40	32	29	5/14	38
1954–55	26	8	11	7	51	45	27	5/14	38

Season	P	W	D	L	F	A	Pts	Pos		
1955–56	**28**	**18**	**5**	**5**	**63**	**35**	**41**	**1/15**		
1956–57	28	15	4	9	85	51	34	4/15	40	
1957–58	30	15	7	8	73	40	37	3/16	43	
1958–59	30	15	6	9	69	56	36	4/16	44	
1959–60	30	9	12	9	48	39	30	8/16	46	
1960–61	**30**	**18**	**6**	**6**	**72**	**38**	**42**	**1/16**		
1961–62	30	13	5	12	54	56	31	7/16	52	
1962–63	30	12	5	13	60	60	29	7/16	54	
1963–64	38	25	4	9	124	38	54	2/20	60	
1964–65	**38**	**28**	**7**	**3**	**123**	**49**	**63**	**1/20**		(After 4–1 play-off win vs. Enfield at Dulwich FC)
1965–66	38	27	5	6	111	55	59	2/20	61	
1966–67	38	20	9	9	64	37	49	5/20	59	
1967–68	38	23	6	9	90	36	52	3/20	64	
1968–69	38	22	5	11	69	47	49	6/20	61	
1969–70	38	19	12	7	77	44	50	5/20	62	
1970–71	38	18	11	9	81	37	47	6/20	62	
1971–72	40	23	10	7	79	35	56	4/21	65	
1972–73	**42**	**34**	**6**	**2**	**88**	**18**	**74**	**1/22**		
1973–74	42	25	13	4	63	20	88	2/22	90	Three points for a win introduced
1974–75	42	15	7	20	59	74	52	13/22	95	
1975–76	42	20	11	11	60	41	71	6/22	87	
1976–77	42	19	10	13	60	48	67	4/22	84	
1977–78	42	16	7	19	57	55	55	13/22	110	
1978–79	42	16	14	12	55	48	62	9/22	93	
1979–80	42	12	13	17	50	57	49	13/22	84	
1980–81	42	18	10	14	66	58	64	6/22	82	
1981–82	42	13	13	16	56	65	52	13/22	83	
1982–83	42	18	6	18	68	61	60	12/22	85	
1983–84	42	17	10	15	62	51	61	9/22	88	
1984–85	42	9	19	14	62	65	46	17/22	84	
1985–86	42	10	13	19	59	77	43	19/22	95	
1986–87	42	22	7	13	67	53	73	4/22	101	
1987–88	42	16	12	14	62	58	60	10/22	81	
1988–89	42	13	17	12	51	68	56	12/22	89	
1989–90	42	15	10	17	54	63	55	12/22	92	
1990–91	42	12	10	20	48	62	46	15/22	93	
1991–92	42	13	9	20	59	73	48	17/22	97	
1992–93	42	12	18	12	52	54	54	11/22	98	
1993–94	42	18	9	15	61	51	63	11/22	97	
1994–95	42	12	14	16	57	65	50	17/22	93	
1995–96	42	12	10	20	52	65	46	14/22	86	
1996–97	42	13	12	17	53	59	51	16/22	101	
1997–98	42	21	10	11	69	50	73	5/22	87	
1998–99	42	16	9	17	70	71	57	13/22	88	
1999–00	42	18	8	16	61	64	62	8/22	101	
2000–01	40	16	6	18	62	62	54	12/22	99	(2 matches not played)
2001–02	42	19	5	18	66	55	62	8/22	99	
2002–03	46	22	13	11	70	56	79	3/24	105	
2003–04	46	25	8	13	68	47	83	4/24	104	
2004–05	42	17	7	18	48	60	58	11/22	86	
2005–06	42	9	12	21	44	64	39	19/22	94	
2006–07	42	16	6	20	52	64	54	14/22	82	
2007–08	42	18	11	13	79	67	65	7/22	87	

FA Cup

Matches in the final qualifying round or competition proper. Matches against Football League teams in bold

Season	Round	Opponent		Score
1934–35	4q	Ilford	A	2–2
	4qr	Ilford	H	2–0
	1	**Southend United**	**A**	**1–10**
1948–49	4q	Barnet	A	4–5
1950–51	4q	Tonbridge	A	3–3
	4qr	Tonbridge	H	1–2
1951–52	4q	Aylesbury United	A	3–4
1952–53	4q	Dartford	A	3–0
	1	**Northampton T**	**H**	**0–0**
	1r	**Northampton T**	**A**	**0–2**
1955–56	1	Halesowen Town	A	4–2
	2	**Exeter City**	**A**	**2–6**
1958–59	4q	Wycombe Wanderers	H	1–3
1960–61	1	Oxford United	H	2–2
	1r	Oxford United	A	2–3
1962–63	4q	Andover	H	1–1
	4qr	Andover	A	4–5
1963–64	4q	Enfield	A	1–3
1964–65	4q	Slough Town	H	3–1
	1	**Port Vale**	**A**	**1–2**
1965–66	1	Grantham	A	1–4
1966–67	**1**	**Reading**	**H**	**1–3**
1967–68	4q	Romford	H	1–2
1969–70	4q	Cambridge City	H	1–0
	1	Carshalton Athletic	H	5–3
	2	Brentwood Town	H	0–2
1970–71	4q	St Albans City	H	0–0
	4qr	St Albans City	A	2–1
	1	**Aldershot**	**H**	**0–2**
1971–72	4q	Barnet	H	2–2
	4qr	Barnet	A	0–2
1972–73	**1**	**Plymouth Argyle**	**A**	**0–1**
1973–74	4q	Barnet	A	2–2
	4qr	Barnet	H	3–0
	1	Leytonstone	H	3–0
	2	Merthyr Tydfil	A	3–0
	3	**Newcastle United**	**A**	**1–1**
	3r	**Newcastle United**	**H**	**0–4**
		(At Watford FC)		
1974–75	4q	Maidstone United	H	0–2
1975–76	4q	Canterbury City	H	1–0
	1	**Reading**	**H**	**1–0**
	2	**Swindon Town**	**H**	**0–1**
1976–77	4q	Waterlooville	A	1–4
1977–78	4q	Billericay Town	H	3–2
	1	**Watford**	**A**	**0–2**
1978–79	4q	Hitchin Town	H	1–3
1981–82	4q	Harrow Borough	H	2–1
	1	Wycombe Wanderers	H	1–1
	1r	Wycombe Wanderers	A	0–2
1988–89	4q	V S Rugby	A	1–1
	4qr	V S Rugby	H	2–0
	1	**Reading**	**A**	**2–4**
1989–90	4q	Aylesbury United	A	1–4
1996–97	4q	Hastings Town	A	1–1
	4qr	Hastings Town	H	2–0
	1	**Cardiff City**	**A**	**0–2**
1997–98	4q	St Albans City	A	2–1
	1	**Leyton Orient**	**H**	**2–2**
	1r	**Leyton Orient**	**A**	**1–0**
	2	**Cardiff City**	**A**	**1–3**
1998–99	4q	Bath City	H	4–0
	1	**Notts County**	**H**	**0–0**
	1r	**Notts County**	**A**	**0–3**
1999–00	4q	Margate	H	1–0
	1	Bath City	A	2–0
	2	**Blackpool**	**A**	**0–2**
2000–01	4q	Dagenham & R	H	1–3
2004–05	4q	Stevenage A	A	0–5

FA Trophy

Matches in the competition proper third round and beyond

Season	Round	Opponent		Score
1976–77	3	Weymouth	A	1–1
	3r	Weymouth	H	1–5
1977–78	3	Bedford Town	H	1–1
	3r	Bedford Town	A	1–2
1998–99	3	Worthing	A	2–0
	4	Chesham United	A	2–0
	5	Cheltenham Town	A	0–3
1999–00	3	Forest Green Rovers	A	1–4
2000–01	3	Tiverton Town	H	1–2
2001–02	3	Cambridge City	A	1–1
	3r	Cambridge City	H	2–0
		(At St Albans City)		
	4	Gravesend & Northfleet	A	1–2
2002–03	3	Heybridge Swifts	A	0–0
	3r	Heybridge Swifts	H	2–1
	4	Wakefield & Emley	A	0–0
	4r	Wakefield & Emley	H	0–1
2004–05	3	Slough Town	A	3–4

FA Amateur Cup

Matches in the semi-finals and finals. Winning Cup Finals in bold

1950–51	SF	Pegasus	1–1	Arsenal FC
	SFr	Pegasus	2–3	Crystal Palace FC
1954–55	SF	Hounslow Town	2–1	Tottenham H FC
	F	Bishop Auckland	0–2	Wembley
1959–60	SF	Enfield	2–0	Brentford FC
	F	**Kingstonian**	**2–1**	**Wembley**
1964–65	SF	Finchley	4–1	Arsenal FC
	F	**Whitby Town**	**3–1**	**Wembley**
1965–66	SF	Whitley Bay	2–1	Sunderland FC
	F	Wealdstone	1–3	Wembley
1966–67	SF	Skelmersdale United	0–0	Derby County FC
	SFr	Skelmersdale United	2–2 (aet)	Birmingham City FC
	SF2r	Skelmersdale United	1–3	West Bromwich Albion FC
1971–72	SF	Wycombe W	2–1	Brentford FC
	F	**Enfield**	**2–0**	**Wembley**

Barassi Cup

1972–73	Unione	3–1	2 legs

Isthmian League Cup

Finals

1976–77	**Barking**	**1–0**	**Harrow Borough FC**
1986–87	Bognor Regis Town	2–3	Windsor & Eton FC

Full Members Cup

Finals

1993–94	**Wokingham Town**	**2–1**	**Marlow FC**
1997–98	**Basingstoke Town**	**4–1**	**Chesham United FC**
1998–99	**Worthing**	**1–0**	**Sutton United FC**

GMAC Premier Inter-League Cup

Final

1986–87	Kettering T	1–3	A

Herts & Middlesex League Challenge Cup

Final

1944–45	Barnet	2–3 (aet)	Finchley FC

London Senior Cup

Finals

1935–36	Walthamstow A	0–1 (aet)	Ilford FC
1950–51	Bromley	3–4 (aet)	Arsenal FC
1954–55	Walthamstow A	2–3	Arsenal FC
1958–59	Tooting & M U	2–5	Arsenal FC
1963–64	**Enfield**	**1–0**	**Wealdstone FC**
1968–69	**Dagenham**	**1–0**	**Barnet FC**
1971–72	Enfield	0–2	Wealdstone FC
2005–06	Fisher Athletic	2–3	Tooting & Mitcham United FC
2007–08	Tooting & M U	2–3	Metropolitan Police FC

Middlesex Senior Cup

Finals

1924–25	Southall	0–5	Brentford FC
1930–31	Hayes	1–4	Wealdstone FC
1933–34	**Park Royal**	**2–0**	**Finchley FC**
1938–39	**Wealdstone**	**4–0**	**Finchley FC**
1944–45	Southall	1–3	Wealdstone
1946–47	Enfield	0–1	Tottenham Hotspur FC
1955–56	**Wembley**	**2–1**	**Wealdstone FC**
1956–57	Hounslow	0–1	Wealdstone FC
1957–58	**Enfield**	**4–0**	**Finchley FC**
1959–60	**Enfield**	**2–1**	**Finchley FC**
1960–61	Hounslow	2–3	Hayes FC Replay after 0–0 draw at Wealdstone FC
1964–65	**Finchley**	**1–0**	**Enfield FC**
1966–67	**Enfield**	**3–2**	**2 legs**
1970–71	Enfield	0–3	2 legs
1971–72	**Hampton**	**5–1**	**2 legs**
1972–73	**Enfield**	**3–0**	**Finchley FC Replay – 3–3 after 2 legs**
1973–74	**Edgware**	**4–1**	**2 legs**
1974–75	Staines	0–1	Wealdstone FC replay after 1–1 draw
1983–84	Wembley	1–5	Harrow Borough FC
1985–86	**Southall**	**2–0 (aet)**	**Enfield FC**
1998–99	**Wembley**	**2–2 (aet)**	**Enfield FC Hendon won 4–2 on penalties**
2001–02	**Northwood**	**4–2 (aet)**	**Hayes FC**
2002–03	**Enfield Town**	**2–0**	**Northwood FC**
2003–04	**Uxbridge**	**3–1 (aet)**	**Yeading FC**
2007–08	Hampton	0–3	Uxbridge FC

Middlesex Charity Cup

Finals. In the Second World War the competition became the Middlesex Red Cross Cup

1912–13	Uxbridge	1–2	Staines
1920–21	Botwell Mission	1–3	Brentford FC
1921–22	**Botwell Mission**	**2–1**	**Brentford FC**
1925–26	Botwell Mission	3–4	Southall FC
1926–27	Barnet	3–3	Brentford FC (joint holders)
1928–29	Botwell Mission	0–1	Brentford FC
1929–30	Wealdstone	1–3 (aet)	Brentford FC
1930–31	Wealdstone	2–3	Finchley FC
1932–33	Hayes	2–3	Wealdstone FC
1933–34	Hayes	1–2	Brentford FC
1935–36	**London Cal**	**2–0**	**Finchley FC**
1937–38	Wealdstone	0–4	A
1939–40	Wealdstone	1–4	A
1944–45	**Tufnell Park**	**4–1**	**Wembley Stadium**
1945–46	**Southall**	**3–2**	**Brentford FC**
1946–47	**Southall**	**5–0**	**Arsenal FC**
1947–48	**Hayes**	**3–2**	**Wealdstone FC**
1952–53	Hounslow	1–2	Hayes FC
1953–54	**Southall**	**1–0**	**Hayes FC**
1956–57	**Southall**	**4–2 (aet)**	**Hayes FC**
1957–58	Finchley	1–2	H
1975–76	**Wembley**	**1–0 (aet)**	**H**
1976–77	**Uxbridge**	**2–0**	**H**

1977–78	Hillingdon Borough	0–1	A
1978–79	**Harrow Borough**	**3–1**	**A**
1981–82	Uxbridge	1–2	A
1984–85	**Feltham**	**5–1**	**H**
1987–88	**Wembley**	**2–0**	**Wembley Stadium**

London Challenge Cup

Matches against Football League opposition, who usually fielded reserve teams

1921–22	Charlton A	1–1	A*
1950–51	Millwall	4–0	A
	Charlton A	0–0	H (semi-final)
	Charlton A	0–1	A (semi-final replay)
1951–52	Arsenal	1–0	A
	West Ham U	1–0	A
	Charlton A	1–1	H (semi-final)
	Charlton A	1–2 (aet)	A (semi-final replay)
1952–53	Tottenham H	2–3	H
1955–56	Chelsea	3–6	A
1959–60	West Ham U	0–2	A
1964–65	Arsenal	4–3	A
1967–68	West Ham U	0–1	A
1969–70	Millwall	2–2	H
	Millwall	0–2	A

* The club could not field a team for the replay and withdrew from the competition.

Players

International appearances

While playing for Hendon, we cannot access records for N. Ireland, Scotland or Wales, or appearance totals for the Great Britain Olympic XI.

Great Britain Olympic XI
Qualifying or finals
D. Adams
E. Beardsley
P. Deadman
R. Haider
D. Hogwood
T. Howard
J. Quail
R. Sleap
J. Swannell
L. Topp

England
D. Adams	18
A. Bass	4
E. Beardsley	3

M. Cooper	3
P. Deadman	25
F.P. Evans	1
R. Haider	55
J. Harris	4
D. Hogwood	7
T. Howard	2
D. Hyde	6
M. Pinner	9
R. Sleap	10
R. Stroud	9
J. Swannell	61
L. Topp	32
C. Wise	2

England Non league XI
| P. Gridelet | 2 |

N. Ireland
| J. Quail | 2 |

Scotland
D. Orr
| G. O'Rourke | 3 |
J. Ward

Wales
G. Davies
J. Evans
R. Evans
A. Phillips

Season by season

Except for the last 15 years, the club does not have official records of player appearances and scorers. These records have been compiled from various sources, but it is not possible in some seasons to tell if they include friendly matches. Some seasons are missing – it was not possible to trace records for them. However, we felt it was better to provide partial information than none.

Season	Top appearances	Top scorers
1918–19		T.B. Poltock 13, Charlie Allwright 6
1919–20		George Blackburn 11, J.P. Croal 11
1920–21		Cecil Wise 14, F.L. Burrage 11
1924–25		Kenneth Seabrooke 17, Cecil Wise 11 (league only)
1930–31	Freddy Young 42	
1931–32		Freddie Evans 48, W. Bramley 13, Bill Butland 13
1932–33		Freddie Evans 44, Jimmy Spalton 35
1933–34		Herbert Knott 36, Freddie Evans 31
1935–36		Tommy Evans 25, Dave Walker 18
1937–38		Dave Walker 17, Fred Boston 16
1938–39		Bob Thomas 17, Billy Breagan 15
1941–42		Les Pulling 32, Roy Stroud 20
1942–43	Bill Fisher 36, Tony Munday 30	Roy Stroud 22, Dave Chappell 14
1946–47	Bill Reay 41, Pat Lynch 39, Roy Stroud 39	Bernard Bryant 34, Bill Reay 18
1947–48	Bill Reay 41, Pat Lynch 40	Bob Avis 22, Bill Reay 18
1948–49	Bill Reay 43, Bob Avis 42, Bill Fisher 42, Glyn Hinshelwood 42	Bob Avis 26, Ted Hornsby 22
1949–50	Mickey Lane 36, Bill Reay 36	Bob Avis 18, Bill Reay 18
1950–51	G. Hinshelwood 50, Mickey Lane 48	Roy Stroud 38, Bob Avis 31
1951–52	Bill Fisher 45, Reg Ivey 42	Roy Stroud 36, Bob Avis 30
1952–53	Bill Fisher 44, Mickey Lane 44	Roy Stroud 29, Bob Avis 19
1953–54	Bill Fisher 48, Pat Austin 42	John Core 23, Cliff Nock 16
1954–55	Bill Fisher 45, Graeme Cunningham 45	Eric Parker 24, Graeme Cunningham 18
1955–56	Bill Fisher 43, Jack Rawlings 43	Jack Rawlings 24, Miles Spector 24
1956–57	Tommy Lawrence 43, Miles Spector 40	Tommy Lawrence 39, Miles Spector 35
1957–58	Tommy Lawrence 44, Roy Thomas 42	Tommy Lawrence 32, Miles Spector 22
1958–59	Jimmy Quail 48, Tommy Lawrence 47	Tommy Lawrence 33, Roy Thomas 21
1959–60	Charlie Murphy 48, Jimmy Quail 47	Miles Spector 23, Terry Howard 20
1960–61	Charie Murphy 45, Jimmy Quail 43	Jimmy Quail 26, Albert Grainger 11, Terry Howard 11
1961–62	Miles Spector 39, Charlie Murphy 36	Ken Aldridge 17, Miles Spector 16
1962–63	Mike Stanley 41, David Hogwood 38, Maurice Williams 38	Miles Spector 15, Dave Swain 15
1963–64	John Swannell 50, Peter Slade 47, Gerry O'Rourke 47	Gerry O'Rourke 39, David Hyde 37
1964–65	David Hogwood 57, Peter Slade 55, Roy Sleap 55	David Hyde 59, Jimmy Quail 36
1965–66	David Hogwood 55, Roy Sleap 53	Laurie Churchill 39, David Hyde 22
1966–67	David Hogwood 54, David Shacklock 54	Tony Harding 30, Danny Lakey 16, David Swain 16
1967–68	Bob Wilson 46, David Hogwood 45	Tony Harding 31, Bobby Wilson 19
1968–69	David Hogwood 53, Mickey Cooper 52, Rod Haider 52	Bobby Wilson 25, Peter Anderson 17
1969–70	David Shacklock 57, John Swannell 57	Johnny Baker 26, Peter Anderson 24
1970–71	Peter Deadman 52, Micky Cannon 51	Johnny Baker 21, Peter Anderson 18, Bobby Wilson 18

1971–72	John Connell 58, Peter Deadman 58	Johnny Baker 23, John Connell 22,
1972–73	John Swannell 60, Phil Fry 60	Tony Bass 31, Rod Haider 20
1973–74	Peter Deadman 67, Rod Haider 66, Alan Phillips 66	Johnny Baker 22, Roger Connell 19
1974–75	Rod Haider 55 Eggie James 53	Eggie James 19, Bobby Southam 12
1975–76	Gary Hand 50, Rod Haider 50	Johnny Baker 21, Bobby Childs 15
1976–77	Rod Haider 57, Gary Hand 57	John Butterfield 22, George Brooks 15
1977–78	George Brooks 60, Rod Haider 59+2	George Brooks 19, Tony Field 13
1978–79	Rod Haider 50+1, Gary Hand 47, Roy Butler 47, Micky Garrini 47	Micky Garrini 19, George Brooks 18
1979–80	Peter Deadman 44, Jim Hendrick 42	Micky Garrini 13, Roy Butler 9
1980–81	Peter Deadman 53, Dermot Drummy 52, Gary Hand 52	James McGleish 16, Johnny Baker 13
1981–82	Gary Hand 65, Dermot Drummy 59+4	Bobby Gough 15, Kevin Folan 12
1982–83	Dermot Drummy 49, Andy O'Brien 47	Dermot Drummy 14, Devon Gayle 13
1983–84	Andy O'Brien 55, Clive Kemplen 54	Gary Allen 10, Steve Wilkins 10
1984–85	Andy O'Brien 48, Martin Coates 45	George Duck 20, Gary Allen 17
1985–86	Colin Tate 51, Andy O'Brien 50+1	Colin Tate 21, Danny Worley 5
1986–87	Dave Root 70, Phil Gridelet 64+2	Iain Dowie 23, Colin Tate 23
1987–88	Phil Gridelet 53, Erskine Smart 53	Iain Dowie 27, Duncan Hardy 12
1988–89	Dave Root 56, Erskine Smart 56	Iain Dowie 27, Gary Keen 13
1989–90	Dave Root 61, Greg Zacharia 54+3	Uche Egbe 17, Sean Baker 14
1990–91	Andy O'Brien 61, Dave Root 59	Colin Tate 14, Uche Egbe 12
1991–92	Dave Root 51, Mark Xavier 46+3	Mark Xavier 18, Marc Das 9
1992–93	Dave Root 54, Barry Blackman 53+2	Barry Blackman 16, Jon Daly 9, Colin Sowerby 9
1993–94	Lee Hunter 51+1, Dave Root 51	Gary Crawshaw 14, Richard Cherry 12
1994–95	Dave Hudson 55, Dave Stephenson 53	Uche Egbe 10, Phil Gallagher 10, Nick Sweetman 10
1995–96	Dave Stephenson 48+1, Simon Clarke 45+3	Michael Banton 12, Junior Haynes 11
1996–97	Paul Kelly 55+1, John-Simon White 50+3	Junior Lewis 18, John Richardson 13
1997–98	Steve Bateman 59, Gary McCann 55	Junior Lewis 22, Paul Whitmarsh 15
1998–99	Gary McCann 63, Simon Clarke 58+1	Paul Whitmarsh 42, Junior Lewis 28
1999–00	Jon Daly 55, Simon Clarke 49+1, Freddie Hyatt 49	Dominic Gentle 21, Paul Whitmarsh 13
2000–01	Simon Clarke 44, Gary Fitzgerald 40+3	Dale Binns 18, David Adekola 14
2001–02	David Hook 54, , Simon Clarke 49+5, Jon-Barrie Bates 49+2	Ricci Crace 13, Martin Randall 13
2002–03	David Hook 54, Paul Yates 53+3	Ricci Crace 21, Eugene Ofori 17
2003–04	Dave King 53, Eugene Ofori 50+4, Scott Cousins 50+1	Eugene Ofori 27, Ricci Crace 12
2004–05	Dave King 51, Rene Street 49	Mark Nicholls 24, John Frendo 16
2005–06	Dave King 38, Andy Cook 37+10, Danny Murphy 37+5	John Frendo 12, Dave Hunt 8
2006–07	Richard Wilmot 50, Rakatahr Hudson 45+3	Belal Aiteouakrim 13, Dean Green 10
2007–08	Marc Leach 52+1, James Parker 47+1	Brian Haule 27, Wayne O'Sullivan 18

Appendix: The original Hendon Football Club

The original Hendon FC was playing in the 1870s. They entered the FA Cup in 1877–78, losing at Marlow 2–0, and the next season lost 1–0 to Reading FC. In 1879–80, they received a bye in the third round, but then lost 2–0 at Clapham Rovers. Another defeat to Reading followed, but in 1882–83 they beat South Reading 11–1, won 3–0 at Marlow before losing 4–2 at home to Old Etonians.

In 1883–84, they faced the mighty Old Etonians again. They had played in the last three FA Cup Finals, winning the Cup in 1882. The match was at the Cricket Field in Brampton Grove, off Brent Street, NW4. Hendon won 3–2 in front of 400 fans. The following report is from the *Hendon and Finchley Times*:

"The most eventful game that has ever been played in this neighbourhood took place last Saturday [10 November] in the Hendon cricket field, when the Old Etonians, generally considered the first club in the country, were defeated by Hendon in the first round of the Association Cup Competition. The former had twice had the honour of holding the cup and has always held a foremost position in the Competition. On each occasion that it has been thrown out of the ties, the club defeating it has won the trophy in the same season, while the old boys have competed in the final tie oftener than any other eleven.

Hendon commenced with a rush and at once attacked the Eton goals with such vigour that the old boys seemed powerless to defend themselves and it was not long before two goals were credited to Hendon. The Etonians pressed their opponents and on two occasions achieved the downfall of the Hendon fortress.

Some even play then ensued till the Hendonians for a third time sent the ball between the Eton posts. During the remaining quarter of an hour the excitement was intense, and the game waxed fast and furious, but no further point was scored, and victory remained for Hendon by three goals to two.

The weather was fine but cold and the game was witnessed by about 400 spectators. Had it been played in the North of England, there would have been as many thousands present. We regret extremely that though on the whole, the conduct of the spectators was most orderly, yet during one part of the game in a certain part of the ground some insulting expressions were made use of with reference to the umpires, and that complaints have appeared in one of the London papers on the subject. The post of umpire is by no means pleasant, and onlookers have no right to demonstrate with decisions."

The club continued to enter the FA Cup until 1888–89, although they never got beyond the first round after 1885–86 and scratched in their last season in the competition. They had been active in the Football Association – Hart Buck from the club was elected to the committee in 1880. In 1886, when the FA organized its clubs into 10 divisions, they were in number 9, along with Old Etonians, Casuals, Clapton, Corinthians, London Caledonians and other amateur London clubs.

After the apparent demise of Hendon in 1889, a Hendon Rovers team was playing, although there does not seem to be any record of them after 1892. In 1894, a Hendon club was playing in the North Middlesex League. Whether there was any link between these clubs, and the Hendon one which entered the London League in 1900 is unclear.

Hendon finished seventh out of eight teams in the London League's second division in 1900–01. They improved the next season, fifth out of nine teams, with 14 points from

16 matches. In 1902–03, the division expanded to 11 teams, including local rivals Child Hill Imperial, and Hendon finished 10th, but with six wins and 15 points. They did not play in the league in 1903–04, but returned the next season, to finish bottom of the Second Division, with a solitary win.

This club then seems to have vanished. However, a Hendon Town club was started a few years later, maybe in 1908, and it was this club who became Hampstead Town's local rivals. They played Hampstead Town before the First World War, and after the war joined the Middlesex and District League. They won the First Division (Western Section) in 1921–22, and then the name Hendon reappears in the London League in 1922–23. Hendon Town won Division Two, with 36 points from 22 matches. But they were not promoted, and finished third in Division Two in 1923–24, with 23 points from 18 matches. Division One included Enfield and Barnet's reserve teams. In 1924–25 the League combined its lower two divisions, and Hendon Town finished sixth in Division One, with 31 points from 30 matches. They dropped to eighth the following season, but in 1926–27 finished second in Division One, with 35 points from 24 games, a point behind champions Callender Athletic. In 1927–28 they came third, but in 1929–30 sunk to seventh. In 1929–30 they withdrew from the league for a season, but returned in 1930–31, finishing fifth with 31 points from 26 matches. In 1931–32, now playing as Hendon, they finished 11th in the 14 team Premier Division, which included Park Royal and Finchley. In their final season, 1932–33, they rose a place to 10th, with 10 wins and 21 points. It is believed that problems with their ground at the Lower Welsh Harp caused them to withdraw from senior amateur football.